# Introduction to Programming using SML

# INTERNATIONAL COMPUTER SCIENCE SERIES

Consulting Editor: **A D McGettrick** *University of Strathclyde*

## SELECTED TITLES IN THE SERIES

# Introduction to Programming using SML

**Michael R. Hansen and Hans Rischel**

*Technical University of Denmark*

**ADDISON-WESLEY**

**Harlow, England ● Reading, Massachusetts ● Menlo Park, California**
**New York ● Don Mills, Ontario ● Amsterdam ● Bonn ● Sydney ● Singapore**
**Tokyo ● Madrid ● San Juan ● Milan ● Mexico City ● Seoul ● Taipei**

© Pearson Education Limited 1999

Pearson Education Limited
Edinburgh Gate
Harlow
Essex CM20 2JE
England

and Associated Companies throughout the World.

Cover designed by Designers and Partners
and printed by Riverside Printing Co. (Reading) Ltd.
Typeset in 10/12 pt Times by 56
Printed and bound in Great Britain by Biddles Ltd., Guildford and King's Lynn

First published 1999

ISBN 0-201-39820-6

**British Library Cataloguing-in-Publication Data**
A catalogue record for this book is available from the British Library

**Library of Congress Cataloging-in-Publication Data**

Hansen, Michael R.Introduction to programming using SML / Michael R. and Hans Rischel.
　　　　p.　　cm. – (International computer science series)
　Includes bibliographical references and index.
　ISBN 0-201-39820-6
　1. ML (Computer program language).　2. Computer programming. I. Rischel, Hans.　II. Title.　III. Series.
QA76.73.M6H36　　1999
005.13'3–dc21

99-10830
CIP

To

Gabriela, Alexander, Ulrike,

Elisabeth

# Contents

# Preface

......................................................................................................................

The topics of this book are programming and program design. The contents are used in the introductory programming course in the Informatics Programme at the Technical University of Denmark. This is the first course on programming that many of the students attend. The contents are furthermore used in a programming course for electrical engineers in a later semester. The emphasis is on programming and program design with a systematic use of lists, trees, sets and tables to build models and programs. The book does not cover efficient implementations using specialized representations of these data structures, as this topic is covered in other textbooks on 'algorithms and data structures'.

It is a goal of the book to bring theory to practical use. The examples and exercises in the book teach the student how to use basic, theoretically well-understood, concepts from computer science in problem solving in order to achieve succinct and elegant programs and program designs which can be communicated to other people. The book does, however, avoid formalistic explanations of the theory. Fundamental concepts such as bindings of identifiers and environments are explained in an informal but precise way such that the students get the right intuitive understanding. The presented concepts are programming language independent, and the book is therefore a general book on programming.

Throughout the book we use Standard ML (abbreviated SML) as the programming language. The reasons for this choice are:

- The language is very powerful in expressing structured data as well as computations on such data. This enables students to solve interesting problems from the very beginning of the course.

- The different SML systems have a simple interactive interface to the user. This allows us to downplay the role of I/O while solving difficult problems in a brief and elegant way.

- The language is close to common mathematical notation. This means that it is not very hard for students to learn the syntax of programs.

- There is an extensive standard library, and there are several SML systems running on a number of platforms.
- The language has a complete, formal semantics. Based on this formal semantics, we give a clear (informal) semantics of the programming language constructs, so that students can appreciate a language with a well-defined semantics.

We use the Moscow ML system in our course, which has turned out to be a fast and very reliable system with moderate resource demands. The SML-mode of the Emacs editor gives a pleasant environment where the user can easily switch between program editing, compilation and program runs. The students can get the system on their own PC so that they can use the system in their home work. The distribution of the system is easy as a complete ML system for a PC can be housed on a single floppy disk.

The chapters of the book are:

1. Getting started

2. Basic values and operators

3. Tuples and records

4. Problem solving I

5. Lists

6. Problem solving II

7. Tagged values and partial functions

8. Finite trees

9. Higher-order functions

10. Finite sets

11. Modules

12. Tables

13. Problem solving III

14. Input/output in SML

15. Interactive programs

16. Problem solving IV

17. Iteration

18. Imperative programming

The main organization of the first 12 chapters follows the data types: simple types, tuples, lists, trees, sets and tables – with the associated operators. Applications of these types, with associated operators, are illustrated through a large collection of interesting programming problems.

The chapters on 'problem solving' define a standard way of writing down the solution to a programming problem. This standard emphasizes specification of interfaces by means of signatures as described in Chapter 11 on the module system of SML.

The chapter on interactive programming introduces the concepts of I/O actions and dialogue automata for designing such programs, and this is supplemented by the notion of abstract syntax for commands in the following chapter: 'Problem solving IV'.

The chapter on iteration gives a few basic techniques, which in some cases can give more efficient implementations. The last chapter introduces various aspects of imperative programming and imperative data structures, together with the imperative operators.

The book has the following appendices:

**A.** SML systems

**B.** Overview of Standard ML

**C.** Overview of the SML module system

**D.** Selected parts of the SML basis library

**E.** Modules of sets and tables

**F.** The ASCII alphabet

**G.** Further reading

Appendix A gives pointers to where to find information about existing SML systems. Appendices B and C give an overview of the SML language. The description is based on the mathematical semantics of SML, but it is presented in an informal way. Appendix D is a reference to selected parts of the Standard ML Basis Library. Appendix E contains modules for sets and tables which are used in main text. Appendix F gives a table of the ASCII alphabet. Appendix G contains some references for further reading.

The following WWW-pages describe how we use the book in our course:

```
http://www.it.dtu.dk/introSML
```

## Acknowledgements

We have received numerous comments and suggestions from many colleagues and students. Special thanks go to Jens Thyge Kristensen for his enthusiastic support in reading through all versions of the manuscript and providing many recommendations about the overall structure of the book as well as details of each chapter. Also, Ken Larsen, Jakob Lichtenberg, Anders P. Ravn, Peter Sestoft, Simon Mørk and Torben Hoffmann have given many important suggestions. Furthermore, the final version of the book has been strongly influenced by the corrections and suggestions from the anonymous referees.

The book *The Definition of Standard ML* (Revised), by Milner, Tofte, Harper and MacQueen has been an invaluable reference for us during the writing of this book. Furthermore, we are indebted to Peter Sestoft for his great help and endless patience in explaining to us details of the SML language.

Our sincere thanks go to the late Disa la Cour for proof reading a draft version of this book and for trying to improve our English writing.

Finally, we are grateful to Dines Bjørner who in the first place taught us the use of mathematical concepts in software development.

# Getting started

The topics of this book are programming and program design. In this chapter we will introduce some of the main concepts of programming languages, in particular the concepts of value, expression, declaration, recursive function and type. Furthermore, to explain the meaning of programs we will introduce the notions of binding, environment and evaluation of expressions.

The purpose of this chapter is to acquaint the reader with the above-mentioned concepts, in order to address interesting problems from the very beginning. The reader will obtain a thorough knowledge of these concepts and skills in applying them as we elaborate on them throughout this book.

We will use Standard ML (abbreviated to SML) as our programming language. Originally, ML was invented to assist formalized reasoning in a logical language, i.e. it was used as a *Meta Language* for the logical language (ML is an acronym for Meta Language). The implementation of efficient SML systems has made it possible to use SML as a general programming language.

As programming constructs are introduced throughout this book, we give an informal explanation of the constructs which is based on the mathematical definition of the language [2]. Appendices B and C contain informal descriptions of the SML programming language and module system.

There is an extensive standard library of SML programs [3]. We will frequently use this library in order to acquaint the reader with the use of library programs and to illustrate that an SML system with this standard library is an attractive programming system in many situations. Selected parts of the standard library are described in Appendix D. We will refer to this appendix as the Library. All programs in this book can be executed on any SML system containing the standard library.

The different SML systems typically support both the compilation of programs to executable code and the execution of programs in an interactive mode. The programs in this book are illustrated by the use of an interactive mode.

The interactive interface of an SML system is very advanced since, for example, structured values such as tuples, lists, trees and functions can be communicated directly between the user and the system without any conversions. Thus, it is very easy to experiment with programs and program designs using an interactive SML system. Furthermore, it allows us to focus on the main structures and models of programs and program designs, i.e. the core of programming, as input and output of structured values are handled by the SML system.

## 1.1  Values, types, identifiers and declarations

In this section we illustrate how to use an SML system in interactive mode. The interactive interface to an SML system allows the user to enter, for example, an arithmetic expression in a line – followed by semicolon and terminated by pressing the return key, e.g.:

```
2*3 + 4;
```

The answer from the SML system contains the value and the type of the expression:

```
val it = 10 : int
```

Each specific SML system will add some leading characters in each line to make a distinction between input from the user and output from the SML system. The dialogue may look as follows:

```
- 2*3 + 4;
> val it = 10 : int
-
```

The heading string '– ' is output whenever this particular SML system is awaiting input from the user. It is called the *prompt*, as it 'prompts' for input from the user. The heading string '> ' indicates that the rest of the line contains an answer from the SML system. In the following we will omit these heading strings, and we will instead distinguish between user input and SML answer by the use of different type fonts:

```
2*3 + 4;
val it = 10 : int
```

where the input from the user is written in typewriter font while the answer from the SML system is written in *italic typewriter font*.

The above answer from SML starts with the *reserved word* val, which indicates that a value has been computed, while the special *identifier* it is a name for the computed value, i.e. 10. The *type* of the result 10 is int, denoting the subset of the integers $\{\dots, -2, -1, 0, 1, 2, \dots\}$ which can be represented using the SML system.

The user can give a name to a value by entering a *declaration*, e.g.:

```
val price = 125;
```

in which case the SML system answers:

```
val price = 125 : int
```

The *identifier* price is now a name for the integer value 125. We also say that the identifier price is *bound* to 125.

Identifiers which are bound to values can be used in expressions:

```
price * 20;
val it = 2500 : int
```

The identifier it is now bound to the integer value 2500, and this identifier can also be used in expressions:

```
it div price = 20;
val it = true : bool
```

The operator div is the division operator on integers. The last expression is a question to the SML system and the identifier it is now bound to the answer (true) of type bool, where bool is a type denoting the two-element set {true, false} of truth values. Note that the equality sign in the input is part of an expression of type bool, whereas the equality sign in the answer expresses a binding of the identifier it to a value.

## 1.2 Simple function declarations

We now consider the declaration of functions. One can name a *function*, just as one can name an integer constant. As an example, we want to compute the area of a circle with given radius $r$, using the well-known area function: circleArea$(r) = \pi r^2$ (Figure 1.1). The constant $\pi$ is found in the Library under the name Math.pi (cf. Section D.2.3):

**Figure 1.1**   Circle with radius $r$ and area $\pi r^2$.

```
Math.pi;
val it = 3.14159265359 : real
```

The type `real` denotes the subset of the real numbers, which can be represented in the SML system, and `Math.pi` is bound to a value of this type.

We choose the name `circleArea` to denote the circle area function, and the function is then declared using a `fun`-*declaration*:

```
fun circleArea r = Math.pi * r * r;
val circleArea = fn : real -> real
```

The reserved word `fun` is used in declarations where the declared value is a function, and where the argument of the function is represented by an *argument pattern* (or *formal parameter*) such as `r` in the above declaration.

The answer from SML says that the identifier `circleArea` now denotes a value, as indicated by the reserved word `val` occurring in the answer. This value is a function, as indicated by the word `fn`. The type `real -> real` contains the symbol `->` indicating a function and the argument as well as the value of the function has type `real`. Thus, the answer says that `circleArea` is bound to a value which is some function of type `real -> real`.

The function `circleArea` can be *applied* to different *arguments*. These arguments must have the type `real`, and the result has type `real` too:

```
circleArea 1.0;
val it = 3.14159265359 : real

circleArea (2.0);
val it = 12.5663706144 : real
```

Brackets around the argument '`1.0`' or '`2.0`' are optional, as indicated above.

The identifier `Math.pi` is an example of a composite identifier consisting of two parts. The first part `Math` is the name of a program library, and the second part `pi` is an identifier declared in the library `Math`. We encourage the reader to use program libraries whenever appropriate. In Chapter 11 we describe how program libraries are constructed in SML.

> **Note**
>
> The different SML systems provide different commands to get access to library functions. Please check the user's manual for your SML system.

## 1.3  Comments

A string enclosed within a matching pair (`*` and `*`) is a *comment* which is ignored by the SML system. Comments can be used to make programs more readable for a human reader by explaining the intention of the program, e.g.:

```
(* Area of circle with radius r *)
fun circleArea r = Math.pi * r * r;
val circleArea = fn : real -> real
```

Comments can be very useful, especially in large programs, but long comments should be avoided as they tend to make it more difficult for the reader to get an overview of the program.

## 1.4 Recursion

This section introduces the concept of recursion by an example.

### 1.4.1 The factorial function

The factorial function $n!$, where $n$ is a non-negative integer, is defined by:

$$0! = 1$$
$$n! = 1 \cdot 2 \cdot \ldots \cdot n \qquad \text{for } n > 0$$

The ellipses '$\cdots$' indicate that all integers from 1 to $n$ should be multiplied, so we have, e.g.:

$$4! = 1 \cdot 2 \cdot 3 \cdot 4 = 24$$

The underbraced part of the expression below for $n!$ is the expression for $(n - 1)!$:

$$n! = \underbrace{1 \cdot 2 \cdot \ldots \cdot (n - 1)}_{(n-1)!} \cdot n \qquad \text{for } n > 1$$

so we get the formula:

$$n! = n \cdot (n - 1)! \qquad \text{for } n > 1$$

This formula is actually correct also for $n = 1$ as:

$$1! = 1 \qquad \text{and} \qquad 1 \cdot (1 - 1)! = 1 \cdot 0! = 1 \cdot 1 = 1$$

so we get:

$$0! = 1 \qquad \qquad \text{(Clause 1)}$$
$$n! = n \cdot (n - 1)! \quad \text{for } n > 0 \qquad \text{(Clause 2)}$$

This formula is called a *recursion formula* for the factorial function (i.e. _!) as it expresses the value of the function for some argument $n$ in terms of the value of the function for some other argument (here: $n - 1$).

### 1.4.2   Computations

The above definition has a form which can be used in the computation of values of the function. For example:

$$
\begin{aligned}
& 4! \\
=\ & 4 \cdot (4 - 1)! \\
=\ & 4 \cdot 3! \\
=\ & 4 \cdot (3 \cdot (3 - 1)!) \\
=\ & 4 \cdot (3 \cdot 2!) \\
=\ & 4 \cdot (3 \cdot (2 \cdot (2 - 1)!)) \\
=\ & 4 \cdot (3 \cdot (2 \cdot 1!)) \\
=\ & 4 \cdot (3 \cdot (2 \cdot (1 \cdot (1 - 1)!))) \\
=\ & 4 \cdot (3 \cdot (2 \cdot (1 \cdot 0!))) \\
=\ & 4 \cdot (3 \cdot (2 \cdot (1 \cdot 1))) \\
=\ & 24
\end{aligned}
$$

The clauses of the definition of the factorial function are applied in a purely 'mechanical' way in the above computation of 4!. We will now take a closer look at this mechanical process as the SML system will compute function values in a similar manner.

### Substitution in clauses

The first step is obtained from Clause 2, by *substituting* 4 for $n$. The condition for using the second clause is satisfied as $4 > 0$. This step can be written in more detail as:

$$
\begin{aligned}
& 4! \\
=\ & 4 \cdot (4 - 1)! \qquad \text{(Clause 2, } n = 4\text{)}
\end{aligned}
$$

### Computation of arguments

The new argument $(4 - 1)$ of the factorial function in the expression $(4 - 1)!$ is computed in the next step:

$$
\begin{aligned}
& 4 \cdot (4 - 1)! \\
=\ & 4 \cdot 3! \qquad \text{(Compute argument of !)}
\end{aligned}
$$

Thus, the principles used in the first two steps of the computation of 4! are:

- Substitute a value for $n$ in Clause 2.
- Compute new argument

These are the only principles used in the above computation until we arrive at the expression:

$$
4 \cdot (3 \cdot (2 \cdot (1 \cdot 0!)))
$$

The next computation step is obtained by using Clause 1 to obtain a value of 0!:

$$4 \cdot (3 \cdot (2 \cdot (1 \cdot 0!)))$$
$$= \quad 4 \cdot (3 \cdot (2 \cdot (1 \cdot 1))) \qquad \text{(Clause 1)}$$

and the multiplications are then performed in the last step:

$$4 \cdot (3 \cdot (2 \cdot (1 \cdot 1)))$$
$$= \quad 24$$

The above recursion formula for the factorial function is an example of a general pattern which will appear over and over again throughout the book. It contains a clause for a *base case* '0!', and it contains a clause where a more general case '$n$!' is reduced to an expression '$n \cdot (n-1)$!' involving a 'smaller' instance '$(n-1)$!' of the function being characterized. For such recursion formulas, the computation process will terminate, i.e. the computation of $n$! will terminate for all $n \geq 0$.

### 1.4.3  Recursive declaration in SML

We name the factorial function `fact`, and this function is then declared as follows in SML:

```
fun fact 0 = 1
  | fact n = n * fact(n-1);
val fact = fn: int -> int
```

This declaration corresponds to the recursion formula for $n$!. It consists of two clauses `fact 0 = 1` and `fact n = n * fact(n-1)` separated by a vertical bar. The *argument pattern* of the first clause is the constant 0, while the argument pattern of the second clause is the identifier n.

The argument patterns are *matched* with integer arguments during the *evaluation* of function values as we shall see below. The only value matching the pattern 0 is 0. On the other hand, every value matches the pattern n, as an identifier can name any value.

### 1.4.4  Evaluation

The SML system uses the declaration of `fact` to evaluate function values in a way that resembles the above computation of 4!.

*Substitution in clauses*

To evaluate `fact 4`, the SML system searches for a clause in the declaration of `fact`, where 4 matches the argument pattern of the clause.

The SML system starts with the first clause of the declaration: `fact 0 = 1`. This clause is skipped as the value 4 does not match the argument pattern 0 of this clause. Then, the second clause: `fact n = n * fact(n-1)` is investigated. The value 4 matches the argument pattern of this clause, i.e. the identifier n. The value 4 is then substituted for n in the right hand side of this clause, thereby obtaining the expression: `4 * fact(4-1)`.

We say that the expression `fact 4` *evaluates to* `4 * fact(4-1)`, and this evaluation is written as:

```
    fact 4
↝   4 * fact(4-1)
```

where we use the symbol ↝ for a step in the evaluation of an SML expression. Note that the symbol ↝ is not part of any SML program, but a symbol used in explaining the evaluation of SML expressions.

### Evaluation of arguments

The next step in the evaluation is to evaluate the argument `4-1` of `fact`:

```
    4 * fact(4-1)
↝   4 * fact 3
```

The evaluation of the expression `fact 4` proceeds until a value is reached:

```
    fact 4
↝   4 * fact(4-1)                          (1)
↝   4 * fact 3                             (2)
↝   4 * (3 * fact(3-1))                    (3)
↝   4 * (3 * fact 2)                       (4)
↝   4 * (3 * (2 * fact(2-1)))              (5)
↝   4 * (3 * (2 * fact 1))                 (6)
↝   4 * (3 * (2 * (1 * fact(1-1))))        (7)
↝   4 * (3 * (2 * (1 * fact 0)))           (8)
↝   4 * (3 * (2 * (1 * 1)))                (9)
↝   4 * (3 * (2 * 1))                      (10)
↝   4 * (3 * 2)                            (11)
↝   4 * 6                                  (12)
↝   24                                     (13)
```

The argument values 4, 3, 2 and 1 do not match the argument pattern 0 in the first clause of the declaration of `fact`, but they match the second argument pattern n. Thus, the second clause is chosen for further evaluation in the evaluation steps (1), (3), (5) and (7).

The argument value 0 does, however, match the argument pattern 0, so the first clause is chosen for further evaluation in step (9). The steps (2), (4), (6) and (8) evaluate argument values to `fact`, while the last steps (10)–(13) reduce the expression that was built in the previous steps.

The evaluation of `fact` $n$ may not evaluate to a value for large $n > 0$, either because the SML system will run out of memory owing to long expressions or because the evaluation may involve bigger integers than the SML system can handle. These limitations depend on the SML system used.

**Note**

A text such as `fact` *n* is *not* part of SML. It is a *schema* where one can obtain an SML program piece by replacing the *meta symbol n* with a suitable SML entity. In the following we will often use such schemas containing meta symbols in *italic font*.

### Infinite evaluation

Applying `fact` to a negative integer leads to an *infinite evaluation*:

```
      fact ~1
  ~>  ~1 * fact(~1 - 1)
  ~>  ~1 * fact ~2
  ~>  ~1 * (~2 * fact(~2 - 1))
  ~>  ~1 * (~2 * fact ~3)
  ~>  ...
```

Note that SML uses the symbol ~ for the negative sign, so the number 'minus one' is written ~1.

### A remark on recursion formulas

The above recursive function declaration was motivated by the recursion formula:

$$0! = 1$$
$$n! = n \cdot (n - 1)! \quad \text{for } n > 0$$

which gives a unique characterization of the factorial function.

The factorial function may, however, be characterized by other recursion formulas, e.g.:

$$0! = 1$$
$$n! = \frac{(n + 1)!}{n + 1} \quad \text{for } n \geq 0$$

This formula is *not* well suited for computations of values, because the corresponding SML function declaration based on this formula (where `div` denotes integer division):

```
fun f 0 = 1
  | f n = f(n+1) div (n+1)
val f = fn : int -> int
```

gives an infinite evaluation of `f` *k* when *k* > 0. For example:

```
      f 2
  ~>  f(2+1) div (2+1)
  ~>  f 3 div 3
  ~>  f(3+1) div (3+1)
  ~>  ...
```

Thus, in finding a declaration of an SML function, one has to look for a *suitable* recursion formula expressing the computation of function values. The above declaration of f contains a base case 'f 0'. However, the second clause does not reduce the general case 'f n' to an instance which is closer to the base case, and the evaluation of $f(n)$ will not terminate when $n > 0$.

## 1.5 The power function

Consider the function:

$$x^n = x \cdot x \cdot \ldots \cdot x \qquad n \text{ occurrences of } x, \text{ where } n \geq 0$$

where $x$ is a real number and $n$ is a natural number.

The underbraced part of the expression below for $x^n$ is the expression for $x^{n-1}$:

$$x^n = x \cdot \underbrace{x \cdot \ldots \cdot x}_{x^{n-1}} \qquad n \text{ occurrences of } x, \text{ where } n > 0$$

Thus, using the convention that $x^0 = 1$, this function can be characterized by the recursion formula:

$$\begin{aligned} x^0 &= 1 \\ x^n &= x \cdot x^{n-1} \quad \text{for } n > 0 \end{aligned}$$

We give the name power to the function $x^n$. The following SML declaration for power is based on the above recursion formula, using composite argument patterns (x, 0) and (x, n):

```
fun power(x, 0) = 1.0                    (* 1 *)
  | power(x, n) = x * power(x, n-1)      (* 2 *);
val power = fn: real * int -> real
```

The type of power is real * int -> real, i.e. the arguments for power must have the type real * int, while the value of the function has type real (cf. the value '1.0').

A value of type real * int is a *pair* of the form $(u, i)$, where $u$ is a real number and $i$ is an integer. For example:

```
val a = (2.0, 3);
val a = (2.0, 3) : real * int
```

The power function can be applied to pairs with type real * int:

```
power a;
val it = 8.0 : real
```

```
power(4.0, 2);
val it = 16.0 : real
```

A function in SML has *one* argument and *one* value. In this case the argument is a pair $(u, i)$ of type `real * int`, while the value of the function is a real number.

The following evaluation shows how the SML system evaluates the expression `power(4.0, 2)`:

```
    power(4.0, 2)
~>  4.0 * power(4.0,2-1)              (Clause 2, x is 4.0, n is 2)
~>  4.0 * power(4.0,1)
~>  4.0 * (4.0 * power(4.0,1-1))      (Clause 2, x is 4.0, n is 1)
~>  4.0 * (4.0 * power(4.0,0))
~>  4.0 * (4.0 * 1.0)                 (Clause 1, x is 4.0)
~>  16.0
```

## 1.6  About types and type checking

The examples in the previous sections show that types such as `real * int -> real` or `int` form an integral part of the responses from the SML system.

In fact, the SML system will try to infer a *type* for each value, expression and declaration entered. If the SML system can infer a type for the input, then the input is accepted by the system. Otherwise the SML system will reject it with an error message.

For example, the expression `circleArea 2.0` is accepted by the SML system, because

● `circleArea` has the type `real -> real`;
● `2.0` has the type `real`; and therefore;
● `circleArea 2.0` has the type `real`.

Furthermore, the result of evaluating `circleArea 2.0`, i.e. 12.5663706144, has type `real`.

On the other hand, the SML system will reject the expression `circleArea 2` with an error message since 2 has type `int` while the argument for `circleArea` must be of type `real`:

```
circleArea 2;
! Toplevel input:
! circleArea 2;
!            ^
! Type clash: expression of type
!    int
! cannot have type
!    real
```

The above type consideration for function application is generalized in the rule: an expression $f(e)$, where the function $f$ is *applied* to an expression $e$, has type $\tau_2$, if $f$ has type $\tau_1 \to \tau_2$ and $e$ has type $\tau_1$.

Consider, for example, the function power with type `real * int -> real`. Thus in this case, $\tau_1$ is real * int and $\tau_2$ is real. Furthermore, the pair (4.0, 2) has type real * int (which is $\tau_1$). Therefore, according to the above rule, the expression power(4.0, 2) has type real (which is $\tau_2$).

## 1.7  Bindings and environments

In the previous sections we have seen that identifiers can be bound to integer values, pairs and functions. The notions of *binding* and *environment* are used to explain which entities are named by identifiers.

The *execution* of a declaration, say val $x = e$, causes the identifier $x$ to be bound to the value of the expression $e$. For example, the execution of the declaration:

```
val a = 3;
val a = 3 : int
```

causes the identifier a to be bound to 3. This binding is denoted by a $\mapsto$ 3.

Execution of more declarations gives more bindings, e.g. execution of:

```
val b = 7.0;
val b = 7.0 : real
```

gives a further binding b $\mapsto$ 7.0.

A collection of bindings is called an *environment*, and the environment $env_1$ obtained from execution of the above two declarations is denoted by:

$$env_1 = \begin{bmatrix} a & \mapsto & 3 \\ b & \mapsto & 7.0 \end{bmatrix}$$

Note that this notation is *not* part of any SML program. Bindings and environments are mathematical objects used to explain the meaning of SML programs.

The execution of an additional declaration causes an extension of $env_1$, e.g. executing:

```
val c = (2, 8);
val c = (2, 8) : int * int

fun circleArea r = Math.pi * r * r;
val circleArea = fn : real -> real
```

adds bindings of the identifiers c and circleArea to the environment $env_1$ giving the environment $env_2$:

$$env_2 = \begin{bmatrix} a & \mapsto & 3 \\ b & \mapsto & 7.0 \\ c & \mapsto & (2, 8) \\ \text{circleArea} & \mapsto & \text{'the circle area function'} \end{bmatrix}$$

The value of an expression is always evaluated in the *actual environment*, which contains the bindings of identifiers which are valid at evaluation time. When the SML system is activated, the actual environment is the *Basis Environment* which gives meanings to e.g. div, +, -, etc. When using environments we will usually not show bindings from the Basis Environment. We will usually also omit bindings of identifiers from the Library, e.g. Math.pi.

## 1.8  Summary

The main purpose of this section is to familiarize the reader with some of the main concepts of SML to an extent where she/he can start experimenting with the system. To this end, we have introduced the SML notions of values, expressions, types and declarations, including recursive function declarations.

The main mathematical concepts needed to explain the meaning of these notions are: integers and real numbers, bindings and environments, and step-by-step evaluation of expressions.

## Exercises

**1.1** Declare a function g: int -> int, where $g(n) = n + 4$.

**1.2** Declare a function h: real*real -> real, where

$$h(x, y) = \sqrt{x^2 + y^2}$$

Hint: Use the function Math.sqrt from the Library. See Section D.2.3.

**1.3** Declare a recursive function f: int -> int, where

$$f(n) = 1 + 2 + \cdots + (n - 1) + n$$

for $n \geq 0$. (Hint: use two clauses with 0 and n as argument patterns.)
State the recursion formula corresponding to the declaration.

**1.4** Declare a recursive function sum: int*int -> int, where

$$sum(m, n) = m + (m + 1) + (m + 2) + \cdots + (m + (n - 1)) + (m + n)$$

for $m \geq 0$ and $n \geq 0$. (Hint: use two clauses with (m,0) and (m,n) as argument patterns.)
State the recursion formula corresponding to the declaration.

**1.5** The sequence $F_0, F_1, F_2, \ldots$ of Fibonacci numbers is defined by:

$$
\begin{aligned}
F_0 &= 0 \\
F_1 &= 1 \\
F_n &= F_{n-1} + F_{n-2}
\end{aligned}
$$

Thus, the first members of the sequence are $0, 1, 1, 2, 3, 5, 8, 13, \ldots$.

Declare an SML function to compute $F_n$. Use a declaration with three clauses, where the argument patterns correspond to the three cases of the above definition.

**1.6** Determine a type for each of the expressions:

```
(Math.pi, fact ~1)
fact(fact 4)
power(Math.pi,fact 2)
(power, fact)
```

**1.7** Consider the declarations:

```
val a = 5;

fun f a = a + 1;

fun g b = (f b) + a;
```

Find the environment obtained from these declarations and give evaluations for the expressions f 3 and g 3.

# Chapter 2

# Basic values and operators

The purpose of this chapter is to illustrate the use of the basic types of values in SML: numbers, characters, strings and truth values, by means of some examples. After reading the chapter the reader should be able to construct simple programs using numbers, characters, strings and truth values. Lists of operators and functions on values of basic types are found in Appendix D which should be used as a reference.

## 2.1 Integers and reals

From mathematics we know the set of natural numbers as a subset of the set of integers, which again is a subset of the rational numbers, etc. In SML, however, the set of values with the type int, for integers, is considered to be disjoint from the set of values with the type `real`, for real numbers. The reason is that the encodings of integer and real values in the computer are different, and that computers have different machine instructions, e.g. for adding integer values and for adding real values.

A value of type `int` is written as a sequence of digits possibly prefixed with the SML minus sign '~'. Real numbers are written using decimal point notation or using exponent notation, or using both:

```
0;
val it = 0 : int

0.0;
val it = 0.0 : real

0123;
val it = 123 : int

~7.235;
val it = ~7.235 : real

~388890;
val it = ~388890 : int

1.23E~17;
val it = 1.23E~17 : real
```

Note that `1.23E~17` denotes $1.23 \cdot 10^{-17}$.

We will use the term *operator* as a synonym for function and the components of the argument of an operator will be called *operands*. Furthermore, a *monadic* operator is an operator with one operand, while a *dyadic* operator has two operands.

Examples of operators on numbers are monadic minus ~, and the dyadic operators addition +, subtraction −, multiplication * and division /. Furthermore, the relations: =, <> (denoting inequality $\neq$), >, >= (denoting $\geq$), < and <= (denoting $\leq$), between numbers are considered to be operators on numbers computing a truth value. A complete list of the operators is given in Section D.2.

In SML, the symbol '~' is used for two purposes. In number constants such as '~2' it denotes the sign of the constant, and in expressions such as '~ 2' and '~(2+1)' it denotes an application of the monadic minus operator. Thus, one must be careful when using spaces in connection with '~'. For example, in the expression '~ ~2' monadic minus is applied to the constant −2, while the expression '~ ~ 2' is not meaningful as it is interpreted as a double application of monadic minus '(~ ~) 2'.

> **Note**
>
> In mathematics the minus sign is used for *three* purposes: the sign in negative numbers, the *subtraction* operator and the *monadic minus* operator (sign change). This triple use of the symbol is avoided in SML by using the tilde symbol for monadic minus.

Division is *not* defined on integers, but we have instead the operators for quotient 'div' and remainder 'mod'. These operators are defined such that $|n \bmod m|$ is as small as possible while $m$ and $n \bmod m$ have the same sign, e.g.:

```
116 div 36;
val it = 3 : int

116 mod 36;
val it = 8 : int

116 div ~36;
val it = ~4 : int

116 mod ~36;
val it = ~28 : int
```

> **Note**
>
> Other programming languages may use a different definition where $n \bmod m$ is always $\geq 0$.

The reader should consult Section D.2 for further details.

## 2.2   Expressions, precedence, association

The monadic operator ˜ is written in front of the argument (like other function names), while the dyadic operators are written in *infix* notation, where the operator is placed between the operands (e.g. one writes $3+5$ instead of $+(3,5)$ for the sum function + applied to the pair $(3,5)$ of integers). Usual rules for omitting brackets in expressions apply to expressions in SML. These rules are governed by two concepts: operator *precedence* and operator *association*.

Each dyadic operator is assigned a precedence (a number between zero and nine):

**Table 2.1**   Selected infix operators.

| Operator | Precedence |
|---|---|
| * / div mod | 7 |
| + - | 6 |
| = <> > >= < <= | 4 |

Furthermore, function application has higher precedence than any dyadic operator. The idea is that higher (larger) precedence means earlier evaluation, e.g.:

$$\text{˜} \; 2 - 5 * 7 > 3 - 1 \quad \text{means} \quad ((\text{˜} \; 2) - (5*7)) > (3 - 1)$$

and

```
fact 2 - 4 means (fact 2) - 4
```

The dyadic operators for numbers *associate* to the *left*, which means that operators of the same precedence are applied starting from the left, so the evaluation of an expression will proceed as if the expression was fully bracketed. For example:

$$1 - 2 - 3 \quad \text{means} \quad (1 - 2) - 3$$

A list of infix operators with operator precedence and association is given in Section D.1.6, and lists of library functions on numbers are found in Section D.2.

## 2.3  Euclid's algorithm

This section presents the famous algorithm of Euclid for computing the greatest common divisor of two natural numbers. For a given integer $n$, an integer $d$ is called a *divisor* of $n$ (written $d|n$) if there exists an integer $q$ such that $n = q \cdot d$. Hence, the number 1 is a divisor of any integer. Any integer $n \neq 0$ has a finite number of divisors as each divisor has absolute value $\leq |n|$, while 0 has an infinite number of divisors, as any integer is a divisor of 0. Thus, integers $m, n$ have at least one common divisor (namely 1), and if either $m \neq 0$ or $n \neq 0$, then the set of common divisors of $m$ and $n$ is finite.

### 2.3.1  Euclid's greatest common divisor (gcd) theorem

The theorem of Euclid states that for any integers $m, n$ there exists an integer $\gcd(m, n)$ such that $\gcd(m, n) \geq 0$, and such that the *common divisors* of $m$ and $n$ are precisely the *divisors* of $\gcd(m, n)$.

Note that if $m \neq 0$ or $n \neq 0$ then $\gcd(m, n)$ is the *greatest* common divisor of $m$ and $n$. For $m = 0$ and $n = 0$ we have $\gcd(0, 0) = 0$, as the common divisors for 0 and 0 are precisely the divisors of 0, but 0 and 0 have no *greatest* common divisor as any number is a divisor of 0.

### 2.3.2  Euclid's algorithm

Euclid gave an algorithm to compute the gcd function. It is based on the following properties of gcd:

$$\begin{aligned}
\gcd(0, n) &= n \\
\gcd(m, n) &= \gcd(n \bmod m, m) \text{ for } m \neq 0
\end{aligned}$$

The corresponding SML formulation of the algorithm is:

```
fun gcd(0,n) = n
  | gcd(m,n) = gcd(n mod m,m);
val gcd = fn: int * int -> int
```

For example:

```
gcd(12,27);
val it = 3 : int

gcd(36, 116);
val it = 4 : int
```

### 2.3.3   Termination of Euclid's algorithm

It is not obvious that the evaluation of $\gcd(m, n)$ will terminate with a result for all integers $m$ and $n$. We will now prove that it indeed is so.

The proof is by *contradiction*: suppose the evaluation of $\gcd(m, n)$ did not terminate for some integers $m$ and $n$. Then there would be an infinite evaluation:

$$
\begin{aligned}
&\phantom{\leadsto}\ \gcd(m, n) \\
&\leadsto\ \gcd(m_1, n_1) \\
&\leadsto\ \gcd(m_2, n_2) \\
&\leadsto\ \gcd(m_3, n_3) \\
&\phantom{\leadsto}\ \vdots \\
&\leadsto\ \gcd(m_i, n_i) \\
&\leadsto\ \gcd(m_{i+1}, n_{i+1}) \\
&\phantom{\leadsto}\ \vdots
\end{aligned}
$$

and we would have

$$m \neq 0 \quad \text{and} \quad m_i \neq 0 \quad \text{for } i = 1, 2, \ldots$$

as the evaluation would otherwise use the first clause in the declaration and terminate. Each step in this evaluation is hence a use of the second clause in the declaration, so we have:

$$
\begin{aligned}
m_1 &= n \ \bmod \ m \\
m_2 &= n_1 \ \bmod \ m_1 \\
&\ \ \vdots \\
m_{i+1} &= n_i \ \bmod \ m_i \\
&\ \ \vdots
\end{aligned}
$$

As $|n \bmod m| < |m|$ when $m \neq 0$, we get:

$$|m_1| > |m_2| > \cdots > |m_i| > |m_{i+1}| > \cdots \geq 0$$

However, such an infinite, strictly decreasing sequence of natural numbers does *not* exist, so we have reached a contradiction. Thus, the evaluation of $\gcd(m, n)$ terminates for all arguments $(m, n)$.

## 2.4  Evaluations with environments

During the evaluation of expressions the SML system may create and use temporary bindings of identifiers. This is, for example, the case for function applications such as gcd(36,116), where the function gcd is applied to the argument (36,116). We will study such bindings as it gives insight into how recursive functions are evaluated. We will base the study on two examples.

### 2.4.1  Evaluation for the gcd function

The declaration:

```
fun gcd(0,n) = n
  | gcd(m,n) = gcd(n mod m,m);
val gcd = fn: int * int -> int
```

contains two clauses with patterns (0,n) and (m,n) and expressions n and gcd(n mod m,m). There are two cases in the evaluation of an expression gcd($x$, $y$) corresponding to the two patterns:

1. gcd(0, $y$): The argument (0, $y$) matches the pattern (0,n) in the first clause giving the binding n $\mapsto$ $y$, and the SML system will evaluate the corresponding right hand side expression n using this binding:

$$\mathrm{gcd}(0, y) \rightsquigarrow (\mathrm{n}, [\mathrm{n} \mapsto y]) \rightsquigarrow \ldots$$

2. gcd($x$, $y$) with $x \neq 0$: The argument ($x$, $y$) does not match the pattern (0,n) in the first clause but it matches the pattern (m,n) in the second clause giving the bindings m $\mapsto$ $x$, n $\mapsto$ $y$, and the SML system will evaluate the corresponding right hand side expression gcd(n mod m,m) using these bindings:

$$\mathrm{gcd}(x, y) \rightsquigarrow (\mathrm{gcd}(\mathrm{n\ mod\ m,\ m}), [\mathrm{m} \mapsto x, \mathrm{n} \mapsto y]) \rightsquigarrow \ldots$$

Consider, for example, the expression gcd(36,116). The value (36,116) does not match the pattern (0,n), so the first evaluation step is based on the second clause:

$$
\begin{aligned}
&\mathrm{gcd}(36,116) \\
\rightsquigarrow\ &(\mathrm{gcd}(\mathrm{n\ mod\ m,\ m}), [\mathrm{m} \mapsto 36, \mathrm{n} \mapsto 116])
\end{aligned}
$$

The expression gcd(n mod m, m) will then be further evaluated using the bindings for m and n. The next evaluation steps evaluate the argument expression (n mod m, m) using the bindings:

$$
\begin{aligned}
&(\mathrm{gcd}(\mathrm{n\ mod\ m,\ m}), [\mathrm{m} \mapsto 36, \mathrm{n} \mapsto 116]) \\
\rightsquigarrow\ &\mathrm{gcd}((\mathrm{n\ mod\ m,\ m}), [\mathrm{m} \mapsto 36, \mathrm{n} \mapsto 116]) \\
\rightsquigarrow\ &\mathrm{gcd}(116\ \mathrm{mod}\ 36,\ 36) \\
\rightsquigarrow\ &\mathrm{gcd}(8,36),
\end{aligned}
$$

The bindings for m and n are removed as the identifiers do not occur in the expression (116 mod 36, 36).

The evaluation continues evaluating the expression gcd(8,36) and this proceeds in the same way, but with different values bound to m and n:

```
    gcd(8,36)
↝   (gcd(n mod m, m),[m ↦ 8, n ↦ 36])
↝   gcd((n mod m, m),[m ↦ 8, n ↦ 36])
↝   gcd(36 mod 8, 8)
↝   gcd(4,8)
```

The evaluation will in the same way reduce the expression gcd(4,8) to gcd(0,4), but the evaluation of gcd(0,4) will use the first clause in the declaration of gcd, and the evaluation terminates with result 4:

```
    gcd(4,8)
↝   ...
↝   gcd(0,4)
↝   (n, [n ↦ 4])
↝   4
```

Note that different bindings for m and n occur in this evaluation and that all these bindings have disappeared when the result of the evaluation, i.e. 4, is reached.

## 2.4.2    Evaluations with several environments

Consider the following declaration for the factorial function where the factors n and fct(n-1) in the right hand side expression in the second clause have been taken in the opposite order (as compared with the earlier declaration of fact in Section 1.4.3):

```
fun fct 0 = 1
  | fct n = fct(n-1)*n;
val fct = fn : int -> int
```

The steps of the evaluation of the expression fct 2 starts using the second clause in the declaration of fct:

```
    fct 2
↝   (fct(n-1)*n, [n ↦ 2])
↝   fct(2-1) * (n, [n ↦ 2])
↝   fct 1 * (n, [n ↦ 2])
```

The evaluation will now continue evaluating the left operand fct 1 in the product and leave the right operand for later evaluation:

```
    fct 1 * (n, [n ↦ 2])
↝   (fct(n-1) * n, [n ↦ 1]) * (n, [n ↦ 2])
↝   (fct(1-1) * n, [n ↦ 1]) * (n, [n ↦ 2])
↝   (fct 0 * (n, [n ↦ 1])) * (n, [n ↦ 2])
↝   (1 * (n, [n ↦ 1])) * (n, [n ↦ 2])
```

where the last step used the first clause in the declaration of fct. Note that the expression contains several subexpressions with different bindings of the identifier

n. The remaining evaluation steps will gradually remove these bindings:

$$(1 \ * \ (n, [n \mapsto 1])) \ * \ (n, [n \mapsto 2])$$
$$\rightsquigarrow \quad (1 \ * \ 1) \ * \ (n, [n \mapsto 2])$$
$$\rightsquigarrow \quad 1 \ * \ (n, [n \mapsto 2])$$
$$\rightsquigarrow \quad 1 \ * \ 2$$
$$\rightsquigarrow \quad 2$$

> **Note**
>
> The above illustrations of SML evaluations have been written in a detailed (and quite long) form in order to explain all the details in the handling of bindings. Usually we will use a shorter form where the small obvious steps have been left out.

## 2.5  Characters and strings

A character is a letter, a digit or a special character (i.e. a punctuation symbol such as comma or semicolon or a control character). Characters are encoded in the computer as integer values from 0 to 127 using the *ASCII alphabet*, which is an international standard for encoding characters. The ASCII alphabet is shown in the table in Appendix F. The characters with ASCII code between 32 and 127 are *printable characters*, while the characters with ASCII code between 0 and 31 are *control characters*.

In SML a character value is written as the symbol # immediately followed by the character enclosed in quotes. Examples of values of type char are:

```
#"a";
val it = #"a" : char

#" ";
val it = #" " : char
```

where the last one denotes the space character. Note that a space is not allowed between # and ".

> **Note**
>
> Other programming languages write character values using apostrophes, e.g. 'a' for the character a. In SML the apostrophe is used in type variables like 'a and 'b, as we shall see in Section 5.4.

The new line, quote and backslash characters are written by means of *escape sequences*:

A *string* is a sequence of *characters*. In SML strings are values of the type string. A string in SML is written inside enclosing quotes which are *not* part of the string. Quote, backslash or control characters in a string are written by using the escape sequences. Comments cannot occur inside strings as comment brackets (* or *) inside a string are interpreted as parts of the string.

**Table 2.2** Selected escape sequences.

| Escape sequence | Meaning | Character |
|---|---|---|
| \n | new line | (depends on the operating system) |
| \" | quote | " |
| \\ | backslash | \ |

Examples of values of type string are:

```
"abcd---";
val it = "abcd---" : string

"\"1234\"";
val it = "\"1234\"" : string

"";
val it = "" : string
```

The first one denotes the seven-character string abcd---, the second uses escape sequences to get the six-character string "1234" including the quotes, while the last denotes the *empty string* containing no characters. Lists of functions on characters and strings are given in Section D.3. In this section we will only illustrate the use of a few of them by some examples.

The size function computes the number of characters in a string:

```
size "1234";
val it = 4 : int

size "\"1234\"";
val it = 6 : int

size ""   (* size of the empty string *);
val it = 0 : int
```

The concatenation function ^ joins two strings together, forming a new string by placing the two strings one after another. The identifier ^ is used in infix mode:

```
val text = "abcd---";
val text = "abcd---" : string

text ^ text;
val it = "abcd---abcd---" : string

text ^ " " = text;
val it = false : bool

text ^ "" = text;
val it = true : bool
```

```
"" ^ text = text;
val it = true : bool
```

The last two examples show that the empty string is the *neutral element* for concatenation of strings just like the number 0 is the neutral element for addition of integers.

There are orderings on the types `char` and `string` expressed by the infix operators `>`, `>=`, `<` and `<=`. Characters are ordered according to the ordering of the ASCII code values (cf. Appendix F) while strings are ordered in the *lexicographical* ordering, e.g. for two strings $s_1$ and $s_2$ we have that $s_1 < s_2$ if $s_1$ would occur before $s_2$ in a lexicon. For example:

```
                    (* Upper case letters precede   *)
#"A" < #"a";   (* lower case letters             *)
val it = true : bool


"automobile" < "car" ;
val it = true : bool


"automobile" < "auto" ;
val it = false : bool


"automobile" < "Automobile" ;
val it = false : bool


"" < " ";
val it = true : bool
```

Thus, the empty string is different from the string containing a space character, and the empty string precedes any other string in the lexicographical ordering.

Conversion of integer, real or Boolean values to their string representations is done by the functions `Int.toString`, `Real.toString`, or `Bool.toString` (cf. Section D.9). A simple application of a conversion function is the declaration of the function nameAge:

```
fun nameAge(name,age) =   name ^ " is "
                 ^ (Int.toString age) ^ " years old";
val nameAge = fn : string * int -> string
```

It converts the integer value of the age to the corresponding string of digits and builds a string containing the string for the name and the age, e.g.:

```
nameAge("Diana",15+4);
val it = "Diana is 19 years old" : string


nameAge("Peter Olsson",25-5);
val it = "Peter Olsson is 20 years old" : string
```

```
nameAge("Philip",1-4);
val it = "Philip is ~3 years old" : string
```

## Truth values

There are two values true and false of the type bool:

```
true;
val it = true : bool
```

```
false;
val it = false : bool
```

Functions can have truth values as results. Consider, for example, a function even determining whether an integer $n$ is even (i.e. $n \bmod 2 = 0$). This function can be declared as follows:

```
fun even n = n mod 2 = 0;
val even = fn : int -> bool
```

A truth valued function such as even is called a *predicate*.

The *negation* operator not applies to truth values, and the comparison operators = and <> are defined for truth values, e.g.:

```
not true <> false;
val it = false : bool
```

Furthermore, there are expressions $e_1$ orelse $e_2$ and $e_1$ andalso $e_2$ corresponding to the disjunction and conjunction operators of propositional logic.

Evaluations of $e_1$ orelse $e_2$ and $e_1$ andalso $e_2$ will only evaluate the expression $e_2$ when needed, i.e. the expression $e_2$ in $e_1$ orelse $e_2$ is not evaluated if $e_1$ evaluates to true, and the expression $e_2$ in $e_1$ andalso $e_2$ is not evaluated if $e_1$ evaluates to false. For example:

```
1 = 2 andalso 10.0 / 0.0 > 5.0;
val it = false : bool
```

Thus, 1 = 2 andalso 10.0 / 0.0 > 5.0 evaluates to false without attempting to evaluate 10.0 / 0.0 > 5, which would result in an error (division by zero).

When andalso and orelse occur together in expressions, andalso binds stronger than orelse. For example:

$e_1$ orelse $e_2$ andalso $e_3$    means    $e_1$ orelse ($e_2$ andalso $e_3$)

The constructs orelse and andalso are often convenient when declaring functions with results of type bool, like in the following declaration of a function isLowerCaseLetter determining whether a character is a lower case letter:

```
fun isLowerCaseLetter ch = #"a" <= ch andalso ch <= #"z";
val isLowerCaseLetter = fn : char -> bool
```

Note that Section D.3.3 describes a series of predicates Char.isAlpha, Char.isAlphaNum, etc., expressing properties of a character.

The library functions on truth values are listed in Section D.1.2.

## 2.7 The if-then-else expression

An if-then-else expression has the form:

if $e_1$ then $e_2$ else $e_3$

where $e_1$ is an expression of type bool while $e_2$ and $e_3$ are expressions of the same type. The if-then-else expression is evaluated by first evaluating $e_1$. If $e_1$ evaluates to true then the expression $e_2$ is evaluated; otherwise, $e_1$ evaluates to false and the expression $e_3$ is evaluated. Note that at most one of the expressions $e_2$ and $e_3$ will be evaluated.

An if-then-else expression is used whenever one has to express a splitting into cases which cannot be expressed conveniently by use of patterns. As an example we may declare a function on strings which adjusts a string to even size by putting a space character in front of the string if the size is odd. Using the function even in Section 2.6 and if-then-else for the splitting into cases gives the following declaration:

```
fun adjString s = if even(size s) then s else " "^s;
val adjString = fn : string -> string

adjString "123";
val it = " 123" : string

adjString "1234";
val it = "1234" : string
```

One may, of course, use an if-then-else expression instead of splitting into clauses by pattern matching. But pattern matching is to be preferred, as illustrated by the following (less readable) alternative declaration of the gcd function (cf. Section 2.3.2):

```
fun gcd(m,n) = if m=0 then n
                    else gcd(n mod m,m);
val gcd = fn: int * int -> int
```

Also one should avoid expressions of the forms:

if $e_1$ then true else $e_2$
if $e_1$ then $e_2$ else false

and instead use the shorter, equivalent forms:

$e_1$ orelse $e_2$
$e_1$ andalso $e_2$

## (2.8) Overloaded operators

Some of the built-in operators, e.g.: +, -, *, denote functions on real numbers as well as on integers. A function on real numbers is considered to be different from the corresponding function on integers, as they are implemented in SML by different machine instructions. An operator of this kind is hence *overloaded*: it denotes different functions depending on the type of the operands, and it hence depends on the context whether, for example, the operator * is denoting multiplication on integers (of type int) or multiplication on real numbers (of type real). The SML system resolves these ambiguities in the following way:

- If the type can be inferred from the context, then an overloaded operator symbol is interpreted as denoting the function on the inferred type.
- If the type cannot be inferred from the context, then an overloaded operator symbol defaults to the function on integers.

For example, the obvious declaration of a squaring function will hence yield the function on integers:

```
fun square x = x * x
val square = fn: int -> int
```

Declaring a squaring function on reals can be done either by specifying the type of the argument:

```
fun square(x:real) = x * x
val square = fn: real -> real
```

or by specifying the type of the result:

```
fun square x : real = x * x
val square = fn: real -> real
```

or by specifying the type of the expression for the function value:

```
fun square x = x * x : real
val square = fn: real -> real
```

or by choosing any mixture of the above possibilities.

A list of the overloaded identifiers is given in Section D.1.7.

## (2.9) Type inference

When an expression is entered, the SML system will try to determine a unique type using so-called *type inference*. If this does not succeed then the expression is not accepted and some error message is issued.

Reconsider the declaration of the function power (cf. Section 1.5):

```
fun power(x,0) = 1.0
  | power(x,n) = x * power(x,n-1);
```

The SML system deduces that power has the type: real * int -> real. We can follow how SML is able to infer this type of power by the following arguments:

1. The keyword fun indicates that the type of power is a function type $\tau$ -> $\tau'$, for some types $\tau$ and $\tau'$.

2. Since power is applied to a pair (x,n) in the declaration, the type $\tau$ must have the form $\tau_1$ * $\tau_2$ for some types $\tau_1$ and $\tau_2$.

3. We have $\tau_2$ = int, since the pattern of the first clause is (x,0), and 0 has type int.

4. We have that $\tau'$ = real, since the expression for the function value in the first clause: 1.0, has type real.

5. We know that power(x,n-1) has the type real since $\tau'$ = real. Thus, the multiplication x*power(x,n-1) can only be typed properly when the type of $x$ is real, i.e. when $\tau_1$ = real.

## 2.10 Summary

In this chapter we have described values and functions belonging to the basic SML types: integers, reals, characters, strings and Boolean values. Furthermore, we have discussed evaluation of infix operators with precedences, and the typing of arithmetic expressions where some operators may be overloaded. Finally, the type inference for a function declaration was illustrated by a simple example.

Appendix D contains an overview of predefined functions on values of basic types to be used when making programs.

## Exercises

**2.1** The following figure gives the first part of Pascal's triangle:

$$
\begin{array}{c}
1 \\
1\ 1 \\
1\ 2\ 1 \\
1\ 3\ 3\ 1 \\
1\ 4\ 6\ 4\ 1 \\
\cdots\cdots\cdots
\end{array}
$$

The entries of the triangle are called *binomial* coefficients. The $k$th binomial coefficient of the $n$th row is denoted $\binom{n}{k}$, for $n \geq 0$ and $0 \leq k \leq n$, e.g. $\binom{2}{1} = 2$ and $\binom{4}{2} = 6$. The first and last binomial coefficients, i.e. $\binom{n}{0}$ and $\binom{n}{n}$, of row $n$ are both 1. A binomial coefficient inside a row is the sum of the two binomial coefficients immediately above it. These properties can be expressed as follows:

$$
\binom{n}{0} = \binom{n}{n} = 1
$$

and

$$\binom{n}{k} = \binom{n-1}{k-1} + \binom{n-1}{k} \quad \text{if } n \neq 0, k \neq 0, \text{ and } n > k.$$

Declare an SML function bin: int*int -> int to compute binomial coefficients.

**2.2** Declare an SML function pow: string * int -> string, where:

$$\text{pow}(s, n) = \underbrace{s \,\hat{}\, s \,\hat{}\, \cdots \,\hat{}\, s}_{n}$$

**2.3** Declare the SML function

```
isIthChar: string * int * char -> bool
```

where isIthChar$(str, i, ch)$ = true if and only if $ch$ is the $i$th character in the string $str$ (numbering starting at zero).
Hint: use String.sub. See Section D.3.4.

**2.4** Declare the SML function

```
occFromIth: string * int * char -> int
```

where

$$\text{occFromIth}(str, i, ch) \quad = \quad \begin{aligned}&\text{the number of occurrences of character } ch\\&\text{in positions } j \text{ in the string } str \text{ with } j \geq i\end{aligned}$$

Hint: the value should be 0 for $i \geq$ size $str$. Use String.sub. See Section D.3.4.

**2.5** Declare the SML function

```
occInString: string * char -> int
```

where

$$\text{occInString}(str, ch) \quad = \quad \begin{aligned}&\text{the number of occurrences of character } ch\\&\text{in the string } str\end{aligned}$$

Hint: use String.sub and Exercise 2.4. See Section D.3.4.

**2.6** Declare the SML function

```
notDivisible: int * int -> bool
```

where notDivisible$(d, n)$ is true if and only if $d$ is not a divisor of $n$. For example notDivisible$(2, 5)$ = true and notDivisible$(3, 9)$ = false.

**2.7** (a) Declare the SML function test: int * int * int -> bool. The value of test$(a, b, c)$, for $a \leq b$, is the truth value of:

$$\begin{aligned}&\text{notDivisible}(a, c)\\\text{and}\quad&\text{notDivisible}(a + 1, c)\\&\vdots\\\text{and}\quad&\text{notDivisible}(b, c)\end{aligned}$$

(b) Declare an SML function prime: int -> bool, where prime($n$) = true, if and only if $n$ is a prime number.

(c) Declare an SML function nextPrime: int -> int, where nextPrime($n$) is the smallest prime number > $n$.

**2.8** Consider the declaration:

```
fun f(0,y) = y
  | f(x,y) = f(x-1, x*y);
```

(a) Determine the type of f.

(b) For which arguments does the evaluation of f terminate?

(c) Write the evaluation steps for f(2,3).

(d) What is the mathematical meaning of f($x$, $y$)?

**2.9** Consider the following declaration:

```
fun test(c,e) = if c then e else 0
```

(a) What is the type of test?

(b) What happens when evaluating test(false, fact ~1)?

(c) Compare this with the result of evaluating

```
if false then fact ~1 else 0
```

# Chapter 3

# Tuples and records

Tuples and records are compound values obtained by combining values of (possibly different) types. They are used in expressing 'functions of several variables' where the argument is a tuple or record, and in expressing functions where the value is a tuple or record. Tuples and records are treated as 'first class citizens' in SML: They can enter into expressions and the value of an expression can be a tuple or a record. Functions on tuples or records can be defined by use of tuple or record patterns.

## 3.1 Tuples

An ordered collection of $n$ values $(v_1, v_2, \ldots, v_n)$, where $n = 0$ or $n > 1$, is called an *n-tuple*. Examples of *n*-tuples are:

```
();
val it = () : unit

(10, true);
val it = (10, true) : int * bool
```

```
(("abc",1),~3);
val it = (("abc", 1), ~3) : (string * int) * int
```

The value () is the only 0-tuple, and it has type `unit`. A 2-tuple such as (10,true) is also called a *pair*. The last example shows that a pair, e.g. (("abc",1),~3), can have a component which is again a pair ("abc",1). In general, tuples can have arbitrary values as components. A 3-tuple is called a *triple* and a 4-tuple is called a *quadruple*. An expression such as (true) is *not* a tuple but just the expression `true` enclosed in brackets, so there is *no* concept of 1-tuple in SML.

An *n*-tuple $(v_1, v_2, \ldots, v_n)$ represents the tree in Figure 3.1. The tree emphasises the structure of the tuple.

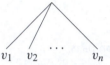

**Figure 3.1** Tree for $(v_1, v_2, \ldots, v_n)$.

Thus, the tuples (true,"abc",1,~3) and ((true,"abc"),1,~3) both contain the values `true`, "abc", 1, and ~3, but they are different because they have a different structure. This difference is easily seen from the structure of the corresponding trees, where the 4-tuple (true,"abc",1,~3) represents the tree with four branches while the 3-tuple ((true,"abc"),1,~3) represents a tree with a sub-tree (Figure 3.2)

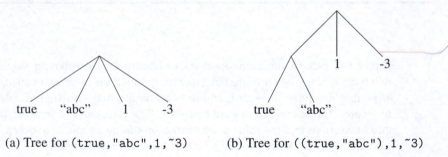

(a) Tree for (true,"abc",1,~3)      (b) Tree for ((true,"abc"),1,~3)

**Figure 3.2** Trees with different structures.

A *tuple expression* $(e_1, e_2, \ldots, e_n)$ is obtained by enclosing *n* expressions $e_1, e_2, \ldots, e_n$ in brackets. It has the type $\tau_1 * \tau_2 * \cdots * \tau_n$ when $e_1, e_2, \ldots, e_n$ have types $\tau_1, \tau_2, \ldots, \tau_n$, e.g.:

```
(1<2,"abc",1,1-4)        has type   bool * string * int * int
(true,"abc")             has type   bool * string
((2>1,"abc"),3-2,~3)     has type   (bool * string) * int * int
```

**Note**

The tuple type $\tau_1*\tau_2*\cdots*\tau_n$ corresponds to the *Cartesian Product* $A = A_1 \times A_2 \times \cdots \times A_n$ of $n$ sets $A_1, A_2, \ldots, A_n$. An element $a$ of the set $A$ is a tuple $a = (a_1, a_2, \ldots, a_n)$ of elements $a_1 \in A_1, a_2 \in A_2, \ldots, a_n \in A_n$.

A tuple expression $(e_1, e_2, \ldots, e_n)$ is *evaluated* from left to right, i.e. by first evaluating $e_1$, then $e_2$, and so on. Tuple expressions can be used in declarations whereby an identifier is bound to a tuple value, e.g.:

```
val tp1 = ((1<2, "abc"), 1, 1-4);
val tp1 = ((true, "abc"), 1, ~3)
             : (bool * string) * int * int

val tp2 = (2>1, "abc", 3-2, ~3);
val tp2 = (true, "abc", 1, ~3) : bool * string * int * int
```

Equality of $n$-tuples is defined component-wise from the equality of the components, i.e. $(v_1, v_2, \ldots, v_n)$ is equal to $(v'_1, v'_2, \ldots, v'_n)$ if $v_i$ is equal to $v'_i$ for $1 \le i \le n$. For example:

```
("abc", 2, 4, 9) = ("ABC", 2, 4, 9);
val it = false : bool

(1, (2,true)) = (2-1, (2,2>1));
val it = true : bool

(1, (2,true)) = (1, 2, 2>1);
! Toplevel input:
! (1, (2,true)) = (1, 2, 2>1);
!                  ^^^^^^^^^^^
! Type clash: expression of type
!    'a * 'b * 'c
! cannot have type
!    int * (int * bool)
! because the tuple has the wrong number of components
```

An error message occurs in the last example. The SML system recognizes that the pair (1, (2,true)) on the left hand side of the equality sign has type int * (int * bool). The tuple on the right hand side of the equality sign must have the same type. But the SML system recognizes that this tuple is a triple (indicated by 'a * 'b * 'c) and answers that it has the wrong number of components. The entities 'a, 'b and 'c are called *type variables*. We will give a thorough introduction to type variables in Chapter 5.

### 3.1.1   Selectors

The *selector* #*i* extracts the *i*th component $v_i$ of an *n*-tuple $(v_1, \ldots, v_n)$:

$$\#i(v_1, \ldots, v_i, \ldots, v_n) = v_i$$

For example:

```
#1 ((true,"abc"),1,~3);
val it = (true, "abc") : bool * string
```

The integer constant *i* in the selector #*i* cannot be replaced by an integer expression, so e.g. #(2 + 1) does not make sense.

## 3.2 Tuple patterns

It is often more convenient to use *patterns* to extract components of tuples than to use selectors. A pattern is a special kind of expression which is used on the left hand side in declarations. An example of a *tuple pattern* is (x,n). It contains identifiers x and n.

A tuple pattern represents a tree. For example, the pattern (x,n) represents the tree shown on the left in Figure 3.3 containing the identifiers x and n.

x        n                 3        2

**Figure 3.3**   Trees for pattern (x,n) and value (3,2)

The tree represented by the value (3,2) (shown to the right) *matches* the tree for the pattern in the sense that the tree for the value is obtained from the tree for the pattern by substituting suitable values for the identifiers in the pattern – in this case the value 3 for the identifier x and the value 2 for the identifier n. One says that the pattern matching gives the bindings x $\mapsto$ 3 and n $\mapsto$ 2.

Patterns can be used on the left hand side in a `val` declaration which binds the identifiers in the pattern to the values obtained by the pattern matching, e.g.:

```
val (x,n) = (3,2);
val x = 3 : int
val n = 2 : int
```

Patterns may contain constants, e.g. like the pattern (x,0) containing the constant 0. It matches any pair $(v_1, v_2)$ where $v_2 = 0$, and the binding x $\mapsto v_1$ is then obtained:

```
val (x,0) = ((3,"a"),0);
val x = (3,"a") : int * string
```

This example also illustrates that the pattern matching may bind an identifier (here: x) to a value which is a tuple.

The declaration:

```
val (x,0) = (3,2);
! Uncaught exception:
! Bind
```

generates an error message because the constant 0 in the pattern does not match the corresponding value 2 on the right hand side. The SML system does not generate any binding in this case.

There is a special pattern '_' called *wild card pattern*. Every value matches this pattern, but the matching provide no bindings. For example:

```
val ((_,x), _, z) = ((1,true), (1,2,3), false);
val x = true : bool
val z = false : bool
```

A pattern cannot contain several occurrences of the same identifier, so, for example, (x,x) is an illegal pattern:

```
val (x,x) = (1,1);
! Toplevel input:
! val (x,x) = (1,1);
!          ^
! The same variable is bound twice in a pattern
```

## 3.3  Infix functions on pairs

Expressions containing functions on pairs can often be given a more readable form by using infix notation where the function is written between the two components of the argument. Infix form is, for example used for the dyadic arithmetic operators +, −, mod, etc. where we write $x + y$, $x - y$, and $x$ mod $y$ instead of $+(x, y)$, $-(x, y)$, and $\text{mod}(x, y)$. This allows us to make arithmetic expressions more readable by use of rules for omission of brackets, e.g.: $x - y - z$ means $(x - y) - z$ and $x + y * z$ means $x + (y * z)$. These rules for omitting brackets are governed by *precedence* and *association* for the operators, cf. Section 2.2.

A function $f$ where the argument is a pair $(x, y)$ may be declared in *infix* form where the function name is written in between the two components $x$ and $y$ of the argument, i.e.:

$$x \; f \; y$$

instead of the usual prefix (or nonfix) form where the function name $f$ is written in front of the argument $(x, y)$:

$$f(x, y)$$

This is done by first giving infix status to the identifier $f$ by an `infix` or `infixr` directive:

$$\text{infix} \; d \; f \quad \text{or} \quad \text{infixr} \; d \; f$$

The `infix` directive gives left association while the `infixr` directive gives right association to the identifier $f$, and the digit $d$ is the precedence assigned to $f$. It may be omitted in which case $f$ gets precedence 0.

As an example we may declare the 'exclusive or' operator for logical values as an infix function xor where $x$ xor $y$ is true exactly when one of $x$ or $y$ is true:

```
infix xor;
infix 0 xor

fun false xor true  = true
  | true  xor false = true
  | _     xor _     = false;
val xor = fn : bool * bool -> bool

1 > 2 xor 2 + 3 < 5;
val it = false : bool
```

Note that the identifier `xor` appears in infix form in the declaration of the function as well as in the application of the function which are both in the scope of the `infix` directive. The expression `1 > 2 xor 2 + 3 < 5` is interpreted as `(1 > 2) xor ((2 + 3) < 5)` because `+` has precedence over `<`, while `>` and `<` have precedence over `xor`. Furthermore, all infix operators bind tighter than `andalso` and `orelse`, cf. Section D.1.6.

Infix status for an identifier is removed by the `nonfix` directive, e.g. continuing the above example:

```
nonfix xor;
nonfix xor

xor(1 = 2, 3 = 4);
val it = false : bool
```

The above operators do all associate to the left. In Chapter 5 we will, however, meet operators '`::`' and '`@`' associating to the right.

## Example 3.1

### Geometric vectors

A vector in the plane is a direction in the plane together with a non-negative length. The null vector is any direction together with the length 0. A vector can be *represented* by its set of Cartesian coordinates which is a pair of real numbers. Alternatively a vector might instead be represented by its set of polar coordinates, which is also a pair of real numbers for the length and the angle. These two representations are, however, different as the operators on vectors (addition of vectors, scalar product, etc.) are expressed by different functions on the representing pairs of numbers.

In the following we will consider only the Cartesian coordinate representation. In SML a vector in the plane will hence be represented by a value of type `real * real`. We will consider the following operators on vectors:

- Vector addition:

$$(x_1, y_1) + (x_2, y_2) = (x_1 + x_2, y_1 + y_2)$$

- Vector subtraction:

$$(x_1, y_1) - (x_2, y_2) = (x_1 - x_2, y_1 - y_2)$$

- Scalar multiplication:

$$x(x_1, y_1) = (xx_1, xy_1)$$

- Dot product:

$$(x_1, y_1) \cdot (x_2, y_2) = x_1 x_2 + y_1 y_2$$

- Norm (length):

$$\|(x_1, y_1)\| = \sqrt{x_1^2 + y_1^2}$$

We cannot use the identifiers +, -, *, etc. to denote the operations on vectors, as this would prevent further use of their initial meaning. Furthermore, SML does not allow the user to overload identifiers.

Using other identifiers we may, however, still define the function names in infix form with proper precedences so that expressions on vectors can be written in a way resembling usual arithmetic expressions. For the operators on two-dimensional vectors we use the names vadd2, vsub2, tim2 and dprod2 with the precedences:

```
infix 6 vadd2     (* addition of 2-dim vectors    *)
infix 6 vsub2     (* subtraction of 2-dim vectors  *)
infix 7 tim2      (* scalar multiplication         *)
infix 6 dprod2    (* dot product for 2-dim vectors *)
```

These infix operators are then declared by:

```
fun (x1,y1) vadd2 (x2,y2) = (x1+x2,y1+y2): real*real;
val vadd2 = fn
  : (real * real) * (real * real) -> real * real

fun (x1,y1) vsub2 (x2,y2) = (x1-x2,y1-y2): real*real;
val vsub2 = fn
  : (real * real) * (real * real) -> real * real

fun x tim2 (x1,y1) = (x*x1, x*y1): real*real;
val tim2 = fn : real * (real * real) -> real * real

fun (x1,y1) dprod2 (x2,y2) = x1*x2 + y1*y2: real;
val dprod2 = fn : (real * real) * (real * real) -> real
```

We might alternatively use the selector functions #1 and #2 in the declarations, e.g.:

```
fun (v1:real*real) vadd2 (v2:real*real)
          = (#1 v1 + #1 v2, #2 v1 + #2 v2);
val vadd2 = fn : (real * real) * (real * real) -> real * real
```

but the declaration using patterns is in this case shorter and more readable and hence to be preferred. The types occurring in the declarations are included in order to assist SML in resolving the overloaded arithmetic operators and the overloaded selectors #1 and #2.

The function for the norm is named norm2 and is declared using the square root function Math.sqrt (Section D.2.3) from the Library by:

```
fun norm2(x1,y1) = Math.sqrt(x1*x1+y1*y1);
val norm2 = fn : real * real -> real
```

These functions allow us to write vector expressions in a form resembling the mathematical notation for vectors, e.g.:

```
val a = (1.0,~2.0);
val a = (1.0,~2.0) : real * real

val b = (3.0,4.0);
val b = (3.0,4.0) : real * real

val c = 2.0 tim2 a vsub2 b;
val c = (~1.0,~8.0) : real * real

val d = c dprod2 a;
val d = 15.0 : real

val e = norm2 b;
val e = 5.0 : real
```

We may, of course, define similar functions for four-dimensional vectors, e.g.:

```
infix 6 dprod4  (* dot product for 4-dim vectors *)
fun (x1,x2,x3,x4) dprod4 (y1,y2,y3,y4)
        = x1*y1 + x2*y2 + x3*y3 + x4*y4: real;
val dprod4 = fn :
  (real * real * real * real) * (real * real * real * real)
  -> real

fun norm4 x = Math.sqrt(x dprod4 x);
val norm4 = fn : real * real * real * real -> real
```

Note the difference between the types of, for example, the dot product dprod2 for two-dimensional vectors and the norm norm4 of four-dimensional vectors: The arguments have different *structures*, a pair of pairs of real numbers, and a quadruple of real numbers. For example, we get an error message if we try to apply norm4 to the pair (a,b) of pairs of real numbers:

```
norm4(a,b);
! Toplevel input:
! norm4(a,b);
! ~~~~~
! Type clash: expression of type
!    real * real * real * real -> real
! cannot have type
!    'a * 'b -> real
! because the tuple has the wrong number of components
```

## 3.4  Records

A *record* is a generalized tuple where each component is identified by a *label* instead of the position in the tuple. The record below contains the string Peter with label name, and the integer 20 with label age:

```
val a = {name = "Peter", age = 20};
val a = {age=20,name="Peter"} : {age:int, name:string}
```

The record type contains the set of (mutually different) labels (age and name in the example) with associated types (int and string).

A component in a record, usually called a record *field*, is identified by its *label*. For every label *lab* there is a selector #*lab* which is used to select the component. For example:

```
#name a;
val it = "Peter" : string

#age a;
val it = 20 : int
```

The equality of two records with the same type is defined component-wise from the equality of values associated with the same labels, so the ordering of the components in the record is of no importance, but comparison is only allowed for records with the same type, i.e. with the same labels and component types:

```
{age = 20, name =  "Peter"} = {name = "Peter", age = 20};
val it = true : bool
```

```
{a = 20, b = (2,3)} = {b = (1,2,3), a = 20};
! Toplevel input:
! {a = 20, b = (2,3)} = {b = (1,2,3), a = 20};
!                       ^^^^^^^^^
! Type clash: expression of type
!    'a * 'b * 'c
! cannot have type
!    int * int
! because the tuple has the wrong number of components
```

Tuples are, in fact, records where integers are used as labels, i.e. the $n$-tuple $(v_1, v_2, \ldots, v_n)$ and the record $\{1 = v_1, 2 = v_2, \ldots n = v_n\}$ represent the same value:

```
("a",true) =  {2 = true, 1 ="a"};
val it = true : bool
```

The record $\{2 = true, 1 ="a"\}$ is actually printed as the corresponding tuple in the response from SML:

```
{2 = true, 1 = "a"};
val it = ("a", true) : string * bool
```

Note that the value $\{1 = "a"\}$ is a record, but it is *not* a tuple, as SML has no 1-tuples.

## 3.5  Record patterns

A *record pattern* is used to decompose a record into its components.    A pattern is expressed as an association of labels with identifiers, e.g. the pattern $\{name = x, age = y\}$ is a pattern that will give bindings for the identifiers x and y when it is matched with a record:

```
val a = {name = "Peter", age = 20};
val a = {age=20,name="Peter"} : {age:int, name:string}

val {name = x, age = y} = a;
val x = "Peter" : string
val y = 20 : int
```

There is a short form for patterns where labels also are used as identifiers, e.g. the pattern $\{name = name, age = age\}$ is abbreviated to $\{name, age\}$:

```
val {name, age} = a;
val name = "Peter" : string
val age = 20 : int
```

A record pattern may contain part of the labels only, and the omitted labels should then be indicated by the wild card mark '...'. This is used when only some of the components of a record should be extracted, e.g.:

```
val {name = x, ...} = a;
val x = "Peter" : string

val {age, ...} = a;
val age = 20 : int
```

Records are very useful in handling data with many components, especially when the functions use only a fraction of the components.

## 3.6 Type declarations

It is often useful to introduce abbreviations for types, e.g. when types must occur in declarations to resolve overloading or when types are used for documentation purposes. For example, the data for a person may be represented by a record type named person:

```
type person =
{age : int, birthday : int * int, name : string,
 occupation : string, sex : string};
type person =
{age : int, birthday : int * int, name : string,
 occupation : string, sex : string}
```

This *type declaration* binds the identifier person to the record type on the right hand side of the declaration. Hence, the value of john will be of type person:

```
val john = {name =  "John", age = 29, sex = "M",
               occupation = "Teacher", birthday = (2,11)};
val john =
    {age = 29, birthday = (2, 11), name = "John",
     occupation = "Teacher", sex = "M"}
    :  {age : int, birthday : int * int, name : string,
         occupation : string, sex : string}
```

The type person can be used in declaring functions on person data using selectors:

```
fun age(p: person) = #age p;
val age =
  fn :  {age : int, birthday : int * int, name : string,
          occupation : string, sex : string} -> int

age john;
val it = 29 : int
```

or using patterns:

```
fun youngLady({age,sex,...}:person) =
                    age < 25 andalso sex = "F";
val youngLady =
  fn :  {age : int, birthday : int * int, name : string,
          occupation : string, sex : string} -> bool

youngLady john;
val it = false : bool
```

The typing of the argument in the function declarations is required in order to resolve the meaning of the (potentially) overloaded record labels. For example, the following declaration is not accepted by the SML system:

```
fun age p = #age p;
! fun age p = #age p;
!            ~~~~
! Unresolved record pattern
```

The problem with this declaration is that the SML system can only infer that p is a record having age as a label. However, a unique type for p cannot be inferred, as many different record types could have age as a label. So the SML system rejects the declaration with an error message.

> **Remark**
>
> The above type declaration binds the identifier person in the *type environment* which is distinct from the value environment (cf. Section 1.7), so the identifier person may at the same time be used to denote a value.

**Example 3.2**

### Quadratic equations

In this section we consider the problem of finding solutions to quadratic equations $ax^2 + bx + c = 0$ with real coefficients $a, b, c$.

The equation has no solution in real numbers if the *discriminant* $b^2 - 4ac$ is negative; otherwise, if $b^2 - 4ac \geq 0$ and $a \neq 0$, then the equation has the solutions $x_1$ and $x_2$ where:

$$x_1 = \frac{-b + \sqrt{b^2 - 4ac}}{2a}$$

and

$$x_2 = \frac{-b - \sqrt{b^2 - 4ac}}{2a}$$

Note that $x_1 = x_2$ if $b^2 - 4ac = 0$.

We may represent the equation $ax^2+bx+c = 0$ by the triple $(a, b, c)$ of real numbers and the solutions $x_1$ and $x_2$ by the pair $(x_1, x_2)$ of real numbers. This representation is captured in the type declarations:

```
type equation = real * real * real;
type equation = real * real * real
```

```
type solution = real * real;
type solution = real * real
```

An SML function:

```
solve: equation -> solution
```

for computing the solutions of the equation should then have the indicated type. Note that type declarations such as the ones above are useful in program documentation as they communicate the intention of the program in a succinct way. The SML system does, however, treat the identifiers equation and solution as shorthand for the corresponding types.

## Exceptions

The function solve must give an error message when $b^2 - 4ac < 0$ or $a = 0$ as there is no solution in these cases. Such an error message can be signalled in SML by using an *exception*. An exception is named by an *exception declaration*. We may, for example, name an exception Solve by the declaration:

```
exception Solve;
exn Solve = Solve : exn
```

The declaration of the function solve is:

```
fun solve(a,b,c) =
      if b*b-4.0*a*c < 0.0 orelse a = 0.0 then raise Solve
      else ((~b+Math.sqrt(b*b-4.0*a*c))/(2.0*a),
            (~b-Math.sqrt(b*b-4.0*a*c))/(2.0*a));
val solve = fn : real * real * real -> real * real
```

The then branch of this declaration contains the expression: raise Solve. An evaluation of this expression terminates with an error message. For example:

```
solve(1.0, 0.0, 1.0);
! Uncaught exception:
! Solve
```

We say that the exception Solve is *raised*. Note that the use of the exception does not influence the type of solve.

Exceptions provide a convenient mechanism for handling errors and we shall give a more detailed discussion of exceptions in Chapter 7.

Other examples of the use of `solve` are:

```
solve(1.0, 1.0, ~2.0);
val it = (1.0, ~2.0) : real * real

solve(2.0, 8.0, 8.0);
val it = (~2.0, ~2.0) : real * real
```

> **Note**

The above declaration of `solve` works with Moscow ML. In most other SML systems, one has to write 'a=0.0' and 'a<>0.0' as 'Real.==(a, 0.0)' and 'Real.!=(a, 0.0)'. The point is that the type `real` is an equality type in Moscow ML, but not in most other SML systems (cf. Section D.2).

## 3.7  Locally declared identifiers

In this section we introduce two constructs supporting *locally* declared identifiers. One construct is used in expressions and the other is used in declarations.

### 3.7.1  Using `let`-expressions

A `let`-expression has the form:

    let dec in e end

with declaration *dec* and expression *e*. The bindings obtained by executing the declaration *dec* are 'local' for the evaluation of *e*. More precisely, let *env* be the actual environment. Then the expression `let` *dec* `in` *e* `end` is evaluated by SML as follows:

1. Execute the declaration *dec* in the environment *env*. This gives bindings for the identifiers declared in *dec*. The environment *env'* is obtained by adding these bindings to *env*.

2. Evaluate the expression *e* in the environment *env'*.

3. If the evaluation of *e* terminates, then restore *env* as the actual environment (i.e. the bindings obtained from *dec* are now lost).

Function declarations may sometimes be improved by use of `let`-expressions. Consider, for example, the above declaration of the function `solve`. During the evaluation of `solve(1.0,1.0,~2.0)` the expression `b*b-4.0*a*c` is evaluated three times. This is not satisfactory from an efficiency point of view. Furthermore, the readability of the declaration suffers from the repeated occurrences of subexpressions.

These problems are avoided if one uses a let-expression:

```
fun solve(a,b,c) =
   let val d = b*b-4.0*a*c
   in if d < 0.0 orelse a = 0.0 then raise Solve
       else ((~b+Math.sqrt d)/(2.0*a)
             ,(~b-Math.sqrt d)/(2.0*a))
   end;
val solve = fn : real * real * real -> real * real
```

The evaluation of solve(1.0, 1.0, ~2.0) will now lead to the evaluation of the let-expression:

```
let val d = b*b-4.0*a*c
in
   if d < 0.0 orelse a = 0.0 then raise Solve
   else ((~b+Math.sqrt d)/(2.0*a),(~b-Math.sqrt d)/(2.0*a))
end
```

with declaration and expression:

*dec*   is   val d = b*b-4.0*a*c
*e*     is   if d < 0.0 orelse a = 0.0 then ... else ...

in the environment:

$$env = [\text{a} \mapsto 1.0, \text{b} \mapsto 1.0, \text{c} \mapsto -2.0]$$

This evaluation proceeds as follows:

Step 1: Executing the declaration val d = b*b-4.0*a*c in the environment *env* gives the binding d $\mapsto$ 9.0. Adding this binding to *env* gives the environment:

$$env' = [\text{a} \mapsto 1.0, \text{b} \mapsto 1.0, \text{c} \mapsto -2.0, \text{d} \mapsto 9.0]$$

Step 2: The expression if d < 0.0 orelse a = 0.0 then ... else ... is evaluated in the environment *env'* giving the value and environment pair: ((1.0, ~2.0), *env'*).

Step 3: The 'old' environment *env* is restored, i.e. we get the value and environment pair: ((1.0, ~2.0), *env*) as a result of the evaluation of the let-expression.

Thus, this evaluation can be written as:

$$(\text{let val d} = \text{b} * \text{b} - 4.0 * \text{a} * \text{c in} \dots \text{end}, env)$$
$$\leadsto \quad (\text{if d} < 0.0 \dots \text{then} \dots \text{else} \dots, env')$$
$$\leadsto \quad (((\text{~b} + \text{Math.sqrt d})/(2.0 * \text{a}), (\text{~b} - \text{Math.sqrt d})/(2.0 * \text{a})), env')$$
$$\leadsto \quad ((1.0, \text{~}2.0), env)$$

The binding of d disappears when the evaluation of the expression terminates. We also say that the declaration of d is *local*.

The subexpressions ~b, Math.sqrt d and 2.0*a are still evaluated twice if the discriminant is positive – despite the local declaration of d – but these redundant evaluations can be eliminated by using a further let-expression:

```
fun solve(a,b,c) =
    let val d = b*b-4.0*a*c
    in if d < 0.0 orelse a = 0.0 then raise Solve
        else
            let val d' = Math.sqrt d
                val b' = ~b
                val a' = 2.0*a
            in
                ((b'+ d')/a',(b'-d')/a')
            end
    end;
```
*val solve = fn : real * real * real -> real * real*

### 3.7.2 Using `local`-declarations

A `local`-declaration has the form:

```
local dec₁ in dec₂ end
```

with declarations *dec₁* and *dec₂*.

This declaration is executed in an environment *env* as follows:

**1.** The declaration *dec₁* is executed in *env* giving bindings for the identifiers declared in *dec₁*. These bindings are added to *env*, giving a new environment *env₁*.

**2.** The declaration *dec₂* is executed in *env₁*, giving a new environment *env₂*, where bindings for the identifiers declared in *dec₂* have been added to *env₁*.

**3.** The resulting environment *env'* is obtained from *env₂* by removing the bindings obtained by the execution of *dec₁* in the first step.

We illustrate the use of a local declaration by an example:

```
local
    fun disc(a,b,c) = b*b - 4.0*a*c
in
    exception Solve;

    fun hasTwoSolutions(a,b,c) = disc(a,b,c)>0.0 andalso a<>0.0;

    fun solve(a,b,c) =
        let val d = disc(a,b,c)
        in if d < 0.0 orelse a = 0.0 then raise Solve
            else ((~b+Math.sqrt d)/(2.0*a)
                 ,(~b-Math.sqrt d)/(2.0*a))
        end
end;
```
   *exn Solve = Solve : exn*
   *val hasTwoSolutions = fn : real * real * real -> bool*
   *val solve = fn : real * real * real -> real * real*

In this example we declare two functions and one exception for quadratic equations. The predicate `hasTwoSolutions` tests whether a quadratic equation has two solutions, and the function `solve` gives the solutions. A locally declared function `disc` to compute the discriminant is used in the declaration of both `hasTwoSolutions` and `solve`. For example:

```
hasTwoSolutions(1.0, 0.0, 1.0);
val it = false : bool


solve(1.0, 2.0, 1.0);
val it = (~1.0, ~1.0) : real * real
```

but the function `disc` cannot be applied:

```
disc(1.0, 2.0, 1.0);
! Toplevel input:
!   disc(1.0, 2.0, 1.0);
!   ^^^^
! Unbound value identifier: disc
```

as it is locally declared.

## 3.8  Summary

This chapter introduces the notions of tuples and tuple types, and the notions of records and record types. Tuples and records are composite values, and we have introduced the notion of patterns which is used to decompose a composite value into its parts.

An identifier can be given infix status and precedence in SML, and this feature was exploited in writing the operators on geometric vectors in the same way as they are written in mathematical notation.

Furthermore, the notion of exceptions was introduced for handling errors and `let`-expressions and `local`-declarations were introduced for having locally declared identifiers.

## Exercises

**3.1** A time of day can be represented as a triple (*hours*, *minutes*, *f*) where *f* is either AM or PM – or as a record. Declare an SML function to test whether one time of day comes before another. For example, (`11,59,"AM"`) comes before (`1,15,"PM"`). Make solutions with triples as well as with records. Declare the functions in infix notation and use patterns to obtain readable declarations.

**3.2** The former British currency had 12 pence to a shilling and 20 shillings to a pound. Declare functions to add and subtract two amounts, represented by triples of integers (*pounds*, *shillings*, *pence*), and declare the functions when a representation by records is used. Declare the functions in infix notation with proper precedences.

**3.3** The set of *complex numbers* is the set of pairs of real numbers. Complex numbers behave almost like real numbers if addition and multiplication are defined by:

$$(a, b) + (c, d) = (a + c, b + d)$$
$$(a, b) \cdot (c, d) = (ac - bd, bc + ad)$$

(a) Declare infix SML functions ++ and ** for addition and multiplication of complex numbers.

(b) The inverse of $(a, b)$ wrt addition, i.e. $-(a, b)$, is $(-a, -b)$, and the inverse of $(a, b)$ wrt multiplication, i.e. $1/(a, b)$, is $(a/(a^2 + b^2), -b/(a^2 + b^2))$ (provided that $a$ and $b$ are not both zero). Declare infix SML functions for subtraction and division of complex numbers.

(c) Use `let`-expressions in the declaration of the division of complex numbers in order to avoid repeated evaluation of identical sub-expressions.

**3.4** A straight line $y = ax + b$ in the plane can be represented by the pair $(a, b)$ of real numbers.

(a) Declare a type `straightLine` for straight lines.

(b) Declare functions to mirror straight lines around the $x$- and $y$-axes.

(c) Declare a function to give a string representation for a straight line.

# Problem solving I

This chapter introduces the approach to program development used in this book. We identify a number of program development activities in terms of documents resulting from each activity. These documents constitute the essence of the *technical documentation* of a program.

We demonstrate the ideas on a small example, but its benefits:

● a compact, standardized and readable form of technical documentation, and

● assistance in decomposing and mastering difficult problems

first become clear in later chapters – and hopefully in later projects. Later chapters will elaborate on the ideas presented here.

We consider three activities:

1. **Problem analysis:** During this activity the necessary data and functions (including exceptions and constants) must be identified and their types must be specified. Thus, the result of this activity is an agenda for the programming activity.

2. **Programming:** The entities specified in the problem analysis are elaborated into a program.

3. **Testing:** The functions of the program are tested using selected test cases.

The problem analysis and the programming activities are often iterated, for example, because insights obtained during programming contribute to the analysis of the problem. We focus on the result of the above activities, rather than on how it was obtained. Thus, the result is typically not obtained as systematically as it is presented here.

The result of these activities is a *technical documentation* consisting of the following:

- **Interface definition:** The user's view of the program is presented in the interface. The interface contains a declaration for each type of data, which must be known to the user, and a specification of each function in the program. We show a succinct way to present the interface definition.

- **Program:** A declaration of each entity in the interface definition. Auxiliary functions, of no concern to the user, may be added.

- **Test:** Sets of test data with predicted results for program runs. We show a standard way to present the tests.

The rest of this chapter illustrates how these ideas are used on a small problem. We will elaborate on the ideas and apply them to more complex problems in later chapters.

## 4.1  Problem statement: rational numbers

A number $q$ is *rational* if $q = \frac{a}{b}$, where $a$ and $b$ are integers with $b \neq 0$. The problem is to construct a program to perform the usual arithmetic operations on rational numbers: addition, subtraction, multiplication, division and equality. The program should also contain a function for converting a rational number to a suitable textual representation.

This example is not typical since rational number arithmetic is a very well-understood notion, which does not need further (mathematical) clarification. So the problem analysis is pretty obvious, and the main point is to illustrate the approach to problem solving. This example does, however, enable us to address the question of choosing a computationally suitable representation for rational numbers. We will discuss two solutions.

## 4.2  Solution 1

### 4.2.1  Problem analysis

Ideas to express the operations on rational numbers by SML function declarations come easily from the following well-known rules of arithmetic, where $a$, $b$, $c$ and $d$ are integers such that $b \neq 0$ and $d \neq 0$:

$$\frac{a}{b} + \frac{c}{d} = \frac{ad + bc}{bd}$$

$$\frac{a}{b} - \frac{c}{d} = \frac{a}{b} + \frac{-c}{d} = \frac{ad - bc}{bd}$$

$$\frac{a}{b} \cdot \frac{c}{d} = \frac{ac}{bd}$$

$$\frac{\cancel{a}}{b} \Big/ \frac{c}{d} \;=\; \frac{a}{b} \cdot \frac{d}{c} \quad \text{where} \quad c \neq 0$$

$$\frac{a}{b} = \frac{c}{d} \quad \text{iff} \quad ad = bc$$

The problem statement mentions one kind of data, namely *rational numbers*. Hence, we give a name, say qnum, to the type representing such numbers.

Each of the functions addition, subtraction, multiplication and division operates on a pair of rational numbers computing a rational number, while the equality function operates on a pair of rational numbers computing a Boolean value. We use the identifiers ++, --, **, // and ==, since SML does not allow the programmer to overload the predefined identifiers for arithmetic operators.

Division is a partial function on rational numbers so we will need an exception QDiv to be raised when the result of a division is undefined. We include a function mkQ constructing (the representation of) the rational number $\frac{a}{b}$ from the pair $(a, b)$ of integers, and a function toString, computing a textual representation of a rational number.

This simple analysis results in an agenda for the programming activity. This agenda is documented in the *interface definition* of Table 4.1.

**Table 4.1**  Interface definition.

| Specification | Comment |
|---|---|
| type qnum = int * int | Rational numbers |
| exception QDiv | Division by zero |
| mkQ: int * int   -> qnum | Construction of rational numbers |
| ++:   qnum * qnum -> qnum | Addition of rational numbers |
| --:   qnum * qnum -> qnum | Subtraction of rational numbers |
| **:   qnum * qnum -> qnum | Multiplication of rational numbers |
| //:   qnum * qnum -> qnum | Division of rational numbers |
| ==:   qnum * qnum -> bool | Equality of rational numbers |
| toString:   qnum  -> string | String representation of rational numbers |

It contains a list of *specifications*. Each specification describes a task to be performed in later stages: We must declare a type qnum, an exception QDiv, and functions mkQ, ++, --, etc. of the indicated types.

In this chapter, the interface definition is used for *documentation* purposes only – it specifies the tasks to be done, but it is not part of the program. An interface definition like the above may be included in an SML program – it is then called a *signature*, and Chapter 11 shows how signatures are used in SML programs to declare the interface to a program module.

## 4.2.2   Programming

In the first solution we consider any pair $(a, b)$ of integers where $b \neq 0$ a legal representation of the rational number $\frac{a}{b}$. Thus, a value $(a, b)$ of type int * int represents a rational number if $b \neq 0$ and we say that the type qnum has the *invariant* $b \neq 0$:

```
type qnum = int*int;          (* (a,b) where b <> 0 *)
```

The function mkQ must form a rational number representation from a pair of integers, but it is a partial function as the fraction $\frac{a}{b}$ only makes sense when $b \neq 0$. The function must hence raise the exception QDiv for arguments which do not satisfy the invariant:

```
exception QDiv;

fun mkQ (_,0) = raise QDiv
  | mkQ pr    = pr: qnum;
```

We introduce *infix* status with suitable precedences for the identifiers ++, --,**, // and ==, in order to allow expressions of type qnum to be written like usual arithmetic expressions:

```
infix 6 ++
infix 6 --
infix 7 **
infix 7 //
infix 4 ==
```

These precedences match the precedences of the corresponding operators on integers. Using the rules from Section 4.2.1 for rational number arithmetic, we arrive at the declarations:

```
fun (a,b) ++ (c,d) = (a*d + b*c, b*d);
fun (a,b) -- (c,d) = (a*d - b*c, b*d);
fun (a,b) ** (c,d) = (a*c, b*d);
fun (a,b) // (c,d) = (a,b) ** mkQ(d,c);
fun (a,b) == (c,d) = (a*d = b*c);
```

Note the following:

- Each of these functions *respects* (or *maintains*) the invariant, i.e. it gives a legal result when applied to legal arguments (division by zero raises the exception QDiv).

- The equality function == is *not* the same as the SML equality on pairs, as e.g. (1,1) and (2,2) are two different pairs of integers representing the same rational number, so $(1, 1) == (2, 2)$ is true while $(1, 1) = (2, 2)$ is false.

Representations of rational numbers may contain large integers, e.g. (48,64) is a legal representation of $\frac{3}{4}$, but we want the function toString to convert to the textual representation of the irreducible fraction, e.g. (48,64) should be converted to "3/4" and not to "48/64". We must hence cancel common divisors before converting the numerator and the denominator to strings.

We use the gcd function from Section 2.3 to find the greatest common divisor of two non-negative integers:

```
fun toString(p,q) =
   let val sign = if p*q<0 then "~" else ""
        val ap = abs p
        val aq = abs q
        val d  = gcd(ap,aq)
   in sign ^ (Int.toString(ap div d))
            ^ "/" ^ (Int.toString(aq div d))
   end;
val toString = fn : int * int -> string
```

The technical documentation for the programming activity is:

```
Table 4.2   Program.

type qnum = int*int;          (* (a,b) where b <> 0 *)

exception QDiv;

fun mkQ (_,0) = raise QDiv
  | mkQ pr     = pr: qnum;

infix 6 ++
infix 6 --
infix 7 **
infix 7 //
infix 4 ==

fun (a,b) ++ (c,d) = (a*d + b*c, b*d);
fun (a,b) -- (c,d) = (a*d - b*c, b*d);
fun (a,b) ** (c,d) = (a*c, b*d);
fun (a,b) // (c,d) = (a,b) ** mkQ(d,c);
fun (a,b) == (c,d) = (a*d = b*c);

fun gcd(0,n) = n
  | gcd(m,n) = gcd(n mod m,m);

fun toString(p,q) =
   let val sign = if p*q<0 then "~" else ""
        val ap = abs p
        val aq = abs q
        val d  = gcd(ap,aq)
   in sign ^ (Int.toString(ap div d))
            ^ "/" ^ (Int.toString(aq div d))
   end;
```

We call gcd an *internal* or *auxiliary* function as it is not specified in the interface definition.

### 4.2.3  Testing

A test should (at least) exercise all parts of the program, i.e. all *branches* of all functions must be exercised.

There is a branch and therefore a test case for each argument pattern occurring in a function declaration. For example, the declaration of mkQ has two clauses, where the first clause has (_,0) as argument pattern and the second clause has pr as argument pattern. Thus, there are two cases to test for the mkQ function.

Furthermore, when a declaration contains an if . . . then . . . else . . . expression then there are test cases for both the then branch and the else branch. All these cases are listed in the Table 4.3.

**Table 4.3**  Test cases.

| Case | Function | Branch | Remark |
|------|----------|--------|--------|
| 1 | mkQ | (_,0) | Denominator $= 0$ |
| 2 | mkQ | pr | |
| 3 | ++ | | |
| 4 | -- | | |
| 5 | ** | | |
| 6 | // | | |
| 7 | == | | |
| 8 | toString | not p*q<0 | |
| 9 | toString | p*q<0 | Negative sign |
| 10 | gcd | (0,n) | Final value |
| 11 | gcd | (m,n) | Recursive call |

We then devise tests for the different cases and record the expected result (Table 4.4).

**Table 4.4**  Tests.

| Test | Case | Test | Expected result |
|------|------|------|-----------------|
| 1 | 1 | mkQ(3,0) | *uncaught exception QDiv* |
| 2 | 2 | val q1 = mkQ(2,~3) | *val q1 = (2,~3) :  int * int* |
| 3 | 2 | val q2 = mkQ(5,~10) | *val q2 = (5,~10) :  int * int* |
| 4 | 3 | val q3 = q1 ++ q2 | *val q3 = (~35,30) :  int * int* |
| 5 | 4 | q1 -- q2 | *val it = (~5, 30) :  int * int* |
| 6 | 5 | val q4 = q2 ** q3 | *val q4 = (~175, ~300) :  int * int* |
| 7 | 6 | val q5 = q4 // q3 | *val q5 = (~5250, 10500) :  int * int* |
| 8 | 7 | q1 == q2 | *val it = false :  bool* |
| 9 | 8, 10, 11 | toString q4 | *val it = "7/12" :  string* |
| 10 | 9 | toString q5 | *val it = "~1/2" :  string* |

Note that one test can cover more cases. For example Test 9, i.e. toString q4 (where q4 is (~175, ~300)), covers Case 8 because the condition p*q<0 is false. But it will also cover Case 10 and Case 11 as the evaluation of gcd(ap,aq), where ap is 175 and aq is 300, will exercise both clauses of the gcd function declaration.

The final step is to execute the program and check the actual results against the expected results.

## Solution 2

In the first solution, we allow several different representations for a rational number. For example, (~175, ~300) and (7, 12) are two different representations of $\frac{7}{12}$. In this section we will study a representation, where each rational number has one, and only one, representative.

### 4.3.1   Problem analysis

The problem analysis is as in solution 1. Hence, the interface definition in Table 4.1 is reused.

### 4.3.2   Programming

In this solution, we use the representation $(a, b)$, where $b > 0$ and where the fraction $\frac{a}{b}$ is irreducible, e.g. where $\gcd(a, b) = 1$. Any rational number has a unique *normal form* of this kind. This leads to the type declaration:

```
type qnum = int*int;   (* (a,b) where b > 0 and gcd(a,b) = 1 *)
```

where the invariant is again stated as a comment to the declaration.

It is convenient to declare a function `canc` which cancels common divisors and thereby reduces any fraction with non-zero denominator to the normal form satisfying the invariant:

```
fun canc(p,q) =
    let val sign = if p*q < 0 then ~1 else 1
        val ap = abs p
        val aq = abs q
        val d  = gcd(ap,aq)
    in (sign * (ap div d), aq div d)
    end;
```

In the declarations for the other functions, `canc` is applied to guarantee that the resulting values satisfy the invariant. The function `canc`, which does not appear in the interface definition, is, like `gcd` in Table 4.2, an auxiliary function of the program.

The program documentation for this solution is given below. Note that one infix directive can give infix status with the same precedence to several identifiers (e.g. ++ and --).

Note that the declaration of `toString` is simpler than in solution 1, as the pair $(p, q)$ is assumed to satisfy the invariant such that:

● No cancellation is needed.

● The integer $p$ and the rational number $\frac{p}{q}$ has the same sign (as $q > 0$).

**Table 4.5**  Program.

```
type qnum = int*int;          (* (a,b) where b > 0 and gcd(a,b) = 1 *)

fun gcd(0,n) = n
  | gcd(m,n) = gcd(n mod m,m);

fun canc(p,q) =
    let val sign = if p*q < 0 then ~1 else 1
        val ap = abs p
        val aq = abs q
        val d  = gcd(ap,aq)
    in (sign * (ap div d), aq div d) end;

exception QDiv;

fun mkQ (_,0) = raise QDiv
  | mkQ pr    = canc pr;

infix 6 ++ --   (* addition and subtraction of rational numbers    *)
infix 7 ** //   (* multiplication and division of rational numbers *)
infix 4 ==      (* equality of rational numbers                    *)

fun (a,b) ++ (c,d) = canc(a*d + b*c, b*d);
fun (a,b) -- (c,d) = canc(a*d - b*c, b*d);
fun (a,b) ** (c,d) = canc(a*c, b*d);
fun (a,b) // (c,d) = (a,b) ** mkQ(d,c);
fun (a,b) == (c,d) = (a,b) = (c,d);
fun toString(p:int,q:int) = (Int.toString p) ^ "/" ^ (Int.toString q);
```

### 4.3.3   Testing

We have a new program, so a different test must be devised (Tables 4.6 and 4.7).

## 4.4   Comparing the solutions

The characteristics of Solution 1 are:

**1.** The declarations for the arithmetic operators are simple and efficient.

**2.** There are many representations of the same rational number.

**3.** Repeated use of operators results in representations with unnecessarily large integers.

**4.** We have to define the equality function '==' ourselves, as the equality of two representations $(a, b)$ and $(a', b')$ is *not* the same as the equality of the corresponding rational numbers.

**Table 4.6**  Test Cases.

| Case | Function | Branch | Remark |
|------|----------|--------|--------|
| 1 | canc | not p*q < 0 | Non-negative number |
| 2 | canc | p*q < 0 | Negative number |
| 3 | gcd | (0,n) | |
| 4 | gcd | (m,n) | |
| 5 | mkQ | (_,0) | Denominator = 0 |
| 6 | mkQ | pr | |
| 7 | ++ | | |
| 8 | -- | | |
| 9 | ** | | |
| 10 | // | | |
| 11 | == | | |
| 12 | toString | | |

**Table 4.7**  Tests.

| Test | Case | Test | Expected result |
|------|------|------|-----------------|
| 1 | 1, 3, 4 | canc(5,10) | *val it = (1,2) : int * int* |
| 2 | 2 | canc(~5,10) | *val it = (~1,2) : int * int* |
| 3 | 5 | mkQ(3,0) | *uncaught exception QDiv* |
| 4 | 6 | val q1 = mkQ(2,~3) | *val q1 = (~2,3) : int * int* |
| 5 | 6 | val q2 = mkQ(5,10) | *val q2 = (1,2) : int * int* |
| 6 | 7 | val q3 = q1 ++ q2 | *val q3 = (~1,6) : int * int* |
| 7 | 8 | q1 -- q2 | *val it = (~7, 6) : int * int* |
| 8 | 9 | val q4 = q2 ** q3 | *val q4 = (~1, 12) : int * int* |
| 9 | 10 | val q5 = q4 // q3 | *val q5 = (1, 2) : int * int* |
| 10 | 11 | q1 == q2 | *val it = false : bool* |
| 11 | 12 | toString q3 | *val it = "~1/6" : string* |

The characteristics of Solution 2 are:

**1.** There is precisely one representation for each rational number.

**2.** Intermediate results remain as 'small' as possible.

**3.** The predefined equality in SML can be used to test equality of rational numbers.

These three properties seem advantageous compared with the characteristics of solution 1. However, there is also a drawback as evaluations may contain many applications of the cancellation function:

```
     mkQ(1,2) ** mkQ(2,1) ** mkQ(1,2)
  ↝  canc(1,2) ** canc(2,1) ** canc(1,2)
  ↝  (1,2) ** (2,1) ** (1,2)
  ↝  canc(1*2,2*1) ** (1,2)
  ↝  canc(2,2) ** (1,2)
  ↝  (1,1) ** (1,2)
  ↝  canc(1*1,1*2)
  ↝  canc(1,2)
  ↝  (1,2)
```

The conclusion is that different representations have different characteristics, and the best choice of representation may depend on the particular application of rational numbers.

## 4.5 A solution using records

We outline yet another solution which is a modification of solution 1, but with records instead of pairs in the data representation.

### 4.5.1 Problem analysis

The problem analysis is as in solution 1, except that qnum is a record type:

```
type qnum = {num: int, denom: int}    (* denom <> 0 *);
```

### 4.5.2 Programming

We just show the declaration for addition, the other functions are derived from solution 1 in a similar way:

```
infix 6 ++;
fun {num=a1,denom=b1} ++ {num=a2,denom=b2} =
                {num = a1 * b2 + a2 * b1, denom = b1*b2};
```

For this example, the tuples and tuple patterns give a shorter and more readable program than records and record patterns. This is usually the case when the tuples have a small number of components and when all components are used in the functions.

### 4.5.3 Testing

This solution can be tested along the same lines as in solution 1. The test is omitted here.

## 4.6 Summary

We have identified three program development activities – problem analysis, programming and testing – and we have presented a standard form for the technical documentation of the result of each activity.

The result of the problem analysis is an interface definition where the data and functions for the problem are specified in a succinct manner using SML types. The result of the programming activity consists of declarations for all entities specified in the interface definition, together with declarations for auxiliary functions introduced during the programming. The result of the testing activity is tables listing all branches of the program together with a test and expected result for every branch.

This approach for program development has been illustrated by solving the problem of representing rational numbers together with the operations on these numbers. We presented two detailed solutions. Each solution has the property that the type for representing rational numbers (int*int) allows values that are *not* legal representations. So only values satisfying a predicate called the *invariant* are legal representations of rational numbers. The invariant is given as a comment to the type declaration. Functions must respect the invariant in the sense that they give legal representations when applied to legal representations.

## Exercises

**4.1** Write the complete technical documentation (cf. Page 50) for the third solution of the rational number problem in this chapter.

**4.2** Write the complete technical documentation (cf. Page 50) for your solution to Exercise 3.2.

**4.3** Write the complete technical documentation (cf. Page 50) for your solution to Exercise 3.3.

**4.4** Write the complete technical documentation (cf. Page 50) for your solution to Exercise 3.4.

# Lists

In Chapter 3 we have seen examples of compound values with a fixed number of components. For example every value of type int*string has the form $(i, s)$ with just two components $i$ and $s$ of types int and string, respectively.

In this chapter we will study the notion of a *list* which is a finite sequence of an arbitrary number of values $[v_1, v_2, \ldots , v_n]$ with the same type. We introduce basic list operations and we give examples of function declarations using some typical forms of recursion with regards to lists. These functions are declared using *list patterns*.

Furthermore, we introduce the notion of *polymorphic type*, i.e. a type with many forms. The polymorphic type system of SML supports the declarations of list functions which work for lists of any kind. For example, one can declare a function to find the length of a list where the elements have type $\tau$, for any type $\tau$. Thus, the function can be applied to a list of integers, a list where the elements are pairs of strings, etc. Moreover, the notion of *equality type* is introduced in this chapter. A type is an equality type, if equality is defined on the values of the type.

Polymorphic types and equality types are not particular to lists and we shall see numerous applications of these concepts throughout this book.

Appendix D (in particular Section D.4) contains a collection of operations on lists. This appendix should be used as a reference when solving problems using lists.

## 5.1 Building lists

A *list* is a finite sequence of values with the same type, such as [2], [3,2] and [2,3,2] which are lists of integers. The values 2 and 3 are called *elements* of the lists.

Lists can be entered as values to the SML system:

```
val xs = [2,3,2];
val xs = [2,3,2] : int list
```

```
val ys = ["Big", "Mac"];
val ys = ["Big","Mac"] : string list
```

The types int list and string list, containing the *type constructor* list, indicate that the value of xs is a list of integers and that the value of ys is a list of strings. The *empty list*, denoted [], contains no elements.

We may have lists with any element type, so we can, for example, build lists of pairs:

```
[("b",2),("c",3),("e",5)];
val it = [("b",2),("c",3),("e",5)] : (string * int) list
```

lists of records:

```
[{name="Brown", age = 25}, {name = "Cook", age = 45}];
val it =
    [{age = 25, name = "Brown"}, {age = 45, name = "Cook"}]
    : {age : int, name : string} list
```

lists of functions:

```
[Math.sin, Math.cos];
val it = [fn, fn] : (real -> real) list
```

or even lists of lists:

```
[[2,3],[3],[2,3,3]];
val it = [[2,3],[3],[2,3,3]] : int list list
```

Furthermore, lists can be components of other values. We can, for example, have pairs containing lists:

```
("bce",[2,3,5]);
val it = ("bce",[2,3,5]) : string * int list
```

### 5.1.1 The type constructor `list`

The type constructor `list` has higher *precedence* than `*` and `->` in type expressions, so the type `string * int list` means `string * (int list)`. The type constructor `list` is used in postfix notation like the factorial function `_!` in `3!`, so `int list list` means `(int list) list`. (Note, that `int (list list)` would not make sense.)

All elements in a list must have the same type, so, for example:

```
["a",1];
! Toplevel input:
! ["a",1];
!      ^
! Type clash: expression of type
!    int
! cannot have type
!    string
```

is *not* a legal value in SML.

### 5.1.2 Tree for a list

A non-empty list $[x_1, x_2, \ldots, x_n]$ with $n \geq 1$ consists of two parts: the first element $x_1$ called the *head* of the list, and the remaining part $[x_2, \ldots, x_n]$ called the *tail* of the list. Thus, the head of `[2,3,2]` is 2, and the tail of `[2,3,2]` is `[3,2]`, while the head of `[3,2]` is 3, etc. The tail of a one element list like `[2]` is the empty list `[]`, while the empty list has no head or tail.

A list is in SML interpreted as a *tree*. The empty list `[]` represents the 'tag' nil. The tree represented by a non-empty list *xs* has for the *root* the tag `::`, its left subtree is the head of *xs*, and its right subtree is the tree for the tail of *xs*. Thus, the trees for `[2,3,2]` and `[2]` are given in Figure 5.1.

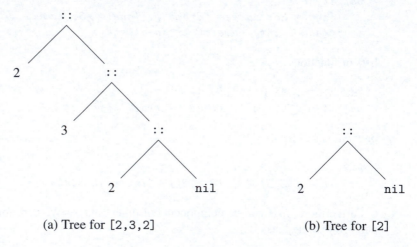

(a) Tree for `[2,3,2]`          (b) Tree for `[2]`

**Figure 5.1**   Trees for two lists.

### 5.1.3   Equality

Two lists $[a_1, a_2, \ldots, a_m]$ and $[b_1, b_2, \ldots, b_n]$ (of the same type) are *equal* when $m = n$ and $a_i = b_i$, for all $i$ such that $1 \leq i \leq m$. This corresponds to equality of the trees representing the lists. Hence, the order of the elements as well as repetitions of the same value are significant in a list.

The equality operator = of SML can be used to test equality of two lists provided that the elements of the lists are of the same type and provided that the equality operator can be used on values of the element type. For example:

```
[2,3,2] = [2,3];
val it = false : bool

[2,3,2] = [2,3,3];
val it = false : bool
```

The differences are easily recognized from the trees representing [2,3,2], [2,3] and [2,3,3].

Lists containing functions cannot be compared because SML equality is not defined for functions. For example:

```
[Math.sin, Math.cos] = [];
! Toplevel input:
! [Math.sin, Math.cos] = [];
!  ^^^^^^^^^^
! Type clash: expression of type
!   real -> real
! cannot have equality type ''a
```

## 5.2   The 'cons' operator

The infix operator :: (called 'cons') builds the tree for a list from its head and tail (Figure 5.2) so it adds an element at the front of a list:

```
val x = 2::[3,4,5];
val x = [2,3,4,5] : int list

val y = ""::[];
val y = [""] : string list
```

**Figure 5.2**   Tree for $x::xs$.

The operator *associates* to the *right*, so $x_1::x_2::xs$ means $x_1::(x_2::xs)$ where $x_1$ and $x_2$ have the same type and $xs$ is a list with elements of that same type (Figure 5.3) so we get, for example:

```
val z = 2::3::[4,5]
val z = [2,3,4,5] : int list
```

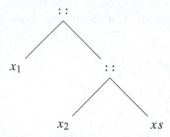

**Figure 5.3**  Tree for $x_1::x_2::xs$.

The symbols [] and nil denote the empty list, e.g.:

```
nil = [];
val it = true : bool
```

### 5.2.1  Functions generating lists

A function generating a list may be declared by the use of :: and []. Consider e.g. the function downto1 $n$ which generates the list with the elements $n, n-1, \ldots, 1$ in descending order, i.e.:

$$\text{downto1}(n) = [n,n-1,\ldots,1]$$

where we define downto1$(0)$ = []. For $n \geq 1$ we get:

$$\text{downto1}(n) = [n,n-1,\ldots,1] = n::\text{downto1}(n-1)$$

as

$$\text{downto1}(n-1) = [n-1,\ldots,1]$$

and we arrive at the declaration:

```
fun downto1 0 = []
  | downto1 n = n::downto1(n-1);
val downto1 = fn : int -> int list

downto1 4;
val it = [4, 3, 2, 1] : int list
```

This declaration resembles the declaration of the factorial function `fact`, and the evaluation of, for example, `downto1 2` proceeds according to a similar pattern, where the result `[2,1]` in this case is built from the empty list by repeated application of the cons operator:

```
      downto1 2
 ↝    2 :: downto1(2-1)
 ↝    2 :: downto1 1
 ↝    2 :: (1 :: downto1(1-1))
 ↝    2 :: (1 :: downto1 0)
 ↝    2 :: (1 :: [])
 ↝    2 :: [1]
 ↝    [2,1]
```

The idea used in the declaration of `downto1` does not work for the function `from1upto` where:

$$\texttt{from1upto}(n) = [1,2,\ldots,n]$$

We may write the value as $1::[2,\ldots,n]$ but the tail list $[2,\ldots,n]$ cannot be written as a value of the function `from1upto` for some other argument.

We can, however, obtain a recursion formula for a more general function:

$$\texttt{upto}(i,j) = \begin{cases} [] & \text{if } i > j \\ [i,i+1,\ldots,j] & \text{if } i \leq j \end{cases}$$

because we have for $i \leq j$:

$$\texttt{upto}(i,j) = [i,i+1,\ldots,j] = i::\texttt{upto}(i+1,j)$$

as

$$\texttt{upto}(i+1,j) = [i+1,\ldots,j]$$

The following declaration of `upto` in SML is based on this recursion formula:

```
fun upto(i,j) = if i>j then [] else i::upto(i+1,j);
val upto = fn : int * int -> int list

upto(~2,3);
val it = [~2, ~1, 0, 1, 2, 3] : int list

upto(3,~2);
val it = [] : int list
```

The function `from1upto` can now be expressed in terms of `upto`:

```
fun from1upto n = upto(1,n);
val from1upto = fn : int -> int list

from1upto 4;
val it = [1, 2, 3, 4] : int list
```

If we consider the function upto an auxiliary function which is only used to declare the function from1upto, then we can make it local for the declaration of from1upto using a local-declaration:

```
local
    fun upto(i,j) = if i>j then [] else i::upto(i+1,j)
in
    fun from1upto n = upto(1,n)
end;
val from1upto = fn : int -> int list
```

or using a let-expression:

```
fun from1upto n =
    let fun upto(i,j) = if i>j then [] else i::upto(i+1,j)
    in upto(1,n)
    end;
val from1upto = fn : int -> int list
```

The local declaration of upto in the let-expression above may actually be simplified, because the identifier j will be bound to $n$ only during an evaluation of from1upto($n$), for any integer $n$:

```
fun from1upto n =
    let fun uptoN i = if i>n then [] else i::uptoN(i+1)
    in uptoN 1
    end;
val from1upto = fn : int -> int list
```

## 5.3  List patterns

In this section we introduce *list patterns* and we give two typical examples illustrating the use of list patterns in declarations of recursive functions on lists.

There are list patterns, [] and nil, for the empty list. Furthermore, a pattern for a non-empty list is constructed using the cons operator, i.e. x::xs is an example of a pattern for a non-empty list.

The list patterns [] and x::xs denote the trees in Figure 5.4. The pattern [] matches the empty list only, while the pattern x::xs matches any non-empty list $[x_1, x_2, \ldots, x_n]$. The latter matching gives the bindings x $\mapsto x_1$ and xs $\mapsto [x_2, \ldots, x_n]$ of the identifiers x and xs, as the list $[x_1, x_2, \ldots, x_n]$ denotes the tree in Figure 5.5.

For example, the execution of the declarations:

```
val x::xs = [1,2,3];
val x  = 1 : int
val xs = [2,3] : int list
```

will simultaneously bind x to the value 1 and xs to the value [2,3] by matching the pattern x::xs to the value [1,2,3].

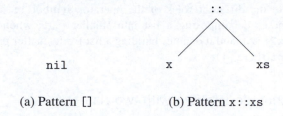

(a) Pattern []                    (b) Pattern x::xs

**Figure 5.4**   Trees for list patterns.

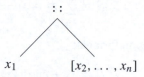

**Figure 5.5**   Tree for $[x_1, x_2, \ldots, x_n]$.

A list pattern for a list with a fixed number of elements, e.g. 3, may be written as x1::x2::x3::[] or in the shorter form [x1,x2,x3]. These patterns match any list with precisely three elements $[x_1, x_2, x_3]$, and the matching binds x1 to $x_1$, x2 to $x_2$, and x3 to $x_3$. For example:

```
val [x1,x2,x3] = [(1,true), (2,false), (3, false)];
val x1 = (1, true) : int * bool
val x2 = (2, false) : int * bool
val x3 = (3, false) : int * bool
```

This generalizes to any fixed number of elements.

List patterns may have more structure than illustrated above. For example, we can construct list patterns that match lists with two or more elements (e.g. x1::x2::xs), and list patterns matching only non-empty lists of pairs (e.g. (y1,y2)::ys), and so on. For example:

```
val x1::x2::xs = [1.1, 2.2, 3.3, 4.4, 5.5];
val x1 = 1.1 : real
val x2 = 2.2 : real
val xs = [3.3, 4.4, 5.5] : real list

val (y1, y2)::ys = [(1,[1]), (2, [2]), (3, [3]),(4,[4])];
val y1 = 1 : int
val y2 = [1] : int list
val ys = [(2, [2]), (3, [3]), (4, [4])]
         : (int * int list) list
```

We shall see examples of more involved patterns in this chapter and throughout the book.

Note the different rôles of the operator symbol :: in patterns and expressions. It denotes decomposing a list into smaller parts when used in a pattern such as x1::x2::xs, and it denotes building a list from smaller parts in an expression such as i::upto(i+1,j).

### 5.3.1    Function declarations with two clauses

Let us consider the function sum1 which computes the sum of a list of integers:

$$\text{sum1 } [x_1, x_2, \dots, x_n] = \sum_{i=1}^{n} x_i = x_1 + x_2 + \cdots + x_n = x_1 + \sum_{i=2}^{n} x_i$$

We get the recursion formula:

$$\text{sum1 } [x_1, x_2, \dots, x_n] = x_1 + \text{sum1 } [x_2, \dots, x_n]$$

If we define the value of the 'empty' sum, i.e. sum1 [], to be 0 corresponding to the convention $\Sigma_{i=1}^{0} x_i = 0$, then we arrive at a function declaration with two clauses:

```
fun sum1 []      = 0
  | sum1(x::xs) = x + sum1 xs
val sum1 = fn : int list -> int
```

The brackets around x::xs are required as SML would interpret sum1 x::xs as (sum1 x)::xs because function application has higher precedence than the infix cons operator '::'.

In evaluating a function value for sum1, SML scans the clauses and selects the first clause where the argument matches the pattern. Hence, the evaluation of sum1 [1,2] proceeds as follows:

```
      sum1 [1,2]
   ⤳  1 + sum1 [2]         (x ↦ 1 and xs ↦ [2])
   ⤳  1 + (2 + sum1 [])    (x ↦ 2 and xs ↦ [])
   ⤳  1 + (2 + 0)          (the pattern [] matches the value [])
   ⤳  1 + 2
   ⤳  3
```

The above example shows that patterns are convenient when splitting a function declaration into clauses covering different forms of the argument. In this example, one clause of the declaration gives the function value for the empty list, and the other clause reduces the computation of the function value for a non-empty list sum1$(x::xs)$ to a simple operation (addition) on the head $x$ and the value of sum1 on the tail xs, i.e. sum1 $xs$, where the length of the argument list has been reduced by one. It is easy to see that an evaluation for sum1 $[x_1, \dots, x_n]$ will terminate, as it contains precisely $n + 1$ recursive calls of sum1.

The above declaration is an example of a typical recursion schema for the declaration of functions on lists.

5.3.2    Function declarations with several clauses

One can have function declarations with any number ($\geq 1$) of clauses. Consider, for example, the alternate sum of an integer list:

$$\text{altsum } [x_1, x_2, \ldots, x_n] = x_1 - x_2 + x_3 - \cdots + (-1)^{n-1} x_n$$

In declaring this function we consider three different forms of the argument:

**1.** empty list: altsum [] = 0

**2.** list with one element: altsum [$x_1$] = $x_1$

**3.** list with two or more elements:

$$\text{altsum } [x_1, x_2, x_3, \ldots, x_n] = x_1 - x_2 + \text{altsum } [x_3, \ldots, x_n]$$

These cases are covered by the patterns in Figure 5.6.

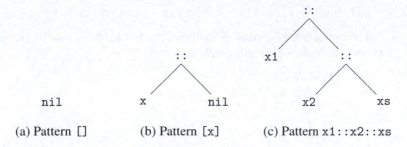

(a) Pattern []          (b) Pattern [x]          (c) Pattern x1::x2::xs

**Figure 5.6**  List patterns for altsum declaration.

Thus, the function can be declared by:

```
fun altsum []          = 0
  | altsum [x]          = x
  | altsum(x1::x2::xs) = x1 - x2 + altsum xs;
val altsum = fn : int list -> int

altsum [2, ~1, 3];
val it = 6 : int
```

It is left as an exercise to give a declaration for altsum containing only two clauses.

## 5.4  Append and reverse; polymorphic types

The infix operator @ (called 'append') joins two lists:

$$[x_1, x_2, \ldots, x_m] \,@\, [y_1, y_2, \ldots, y_n] = [x_1, x_2, \ldots, x_m, y_1, y_2, \ldots, y_n]$$

and the function `rev` (called 'reverse') reverses a list:

$$\text{rev } [x_1, x_2, \ldots, x_n] = [x_n, \ldots, x_2, x_1]$$

These functions are predefined in SML, but their declarations reveal important issues and are therefore discussed here.

### 5.4.1    Append

The declaration of `@` is based on the recursion formula:

$$
\begin{aligned}
[] \; @ \; ys &= ys \\
[x_1, x_2, \ldots, x_m] \; @ \; ys &= x_1 :: ([x_2, \ldots, x_m] \; @ \; ys)
\end{aligned}
$$

which leads to the declaration:

```
infixr 5 @
fun        [] @ ys = ys
   | (x::xs) @ ys = x::(xs @ ys);
infixr 5 @
val @ = fn : 'a list * 'a list -> 'a list
```

The evaluation of append decomposes the left hand list into its elements, which are afterwards 'cons'ed' onto the right hand list:

```
        [1,2] @ [3,4]
  ⤳     1::([2] @ [3,4])
  ⤳     1::(2::([] @ [3,4]))
  ⤳     1::(2::[3,4])
  ⤳     1::[2,3,4]
  ⤳     [1,2,3,4]
```

This evaluation comprises $m + 1$ pattern matches plus $m$ cons'es where $m$ is the length of the left hand list.

The type of `@`, i.e. `'a list * 'a list -> 'a list`, contains a *type variable* `'a`. This means that for any type $\tau$ and two lists *xs, ys* of type $\tau$ `list` the function application *xs@ys* is well defined and it gives a result of the type $\tau$ `list`.

A type containing type variables is called a *polymorphic type*, and a function (such as append) with a polymorphic type is called a *polymorphic function*. To paraphrase this, append is a function with many forms. A type containing no type variables is called a *monomorphic* type.

The notion of polymorphism is very convenient for a programmer, since one need not write a special function for appending, for example, integer lists and another function for appending lists of integer lists, as the polymorphic append function is capable of both:

```
[1,2] @ [3,4];
val it = [1,2,3,4] : int list

[[1],[2,3]] @ [[4]];
val it = [[1],[2,3],[4]] : int list list
```

The cons function :: has the type: `'a * 'a list -> 'a list`, and is therefore a polymorphic function.

The operators :: and @ have the same precedence (5) and both associate to the right. A mixture of these operators also associates to the right, so, for example, `[1]@2::[3]` is interpreted as `[1]@(2::[3])`, while `1::[2]@[3]` is interpreted as `1::([2]@[3])`:

```
[1] @ 2 :: [3];
val it = [1, 2, 3] : int list


1 :: [2] @ [3];
val it = [1, 2, 3] : int list
```

### 5.4.2   Reverse

For the function `rev` we have the recursion formula:

$$\texttt{rev } [x_1, x_2, \ldots, x_n] = [x_n, \ldots, x_2, x_1] = (\texttt{rev } [x_2, \ldots, x_n]) \texttt{ @ } [x_1]$$

as

$$\texttt{rev } [x_2, \ldots, x_n] = [x_n, \ldots, x_2]$$

which immediately leads to a naive declaration of a reverse function:

```
fun naive_rev []        = []
  | naive_rev(x::xs) = naive_rev xs @ [x];
val naive_rev = fn : 'a list -> 'a list
```

This program corresponds directly to the recursion formula for `rev`: the head element x is appended after the reversed list for the tail xs of the list – but it may be considered naive as it gives a very inefficient evaluation of the reversed list:

```
        naive_rev[1,2,3]
  ⤳   naive_rev[2,3] @ [1]
  ⤳   (naive_rev[3] @ [2]) @ [1]
  ⤳   ((naive_rev[] @ [3]) @ [2]) @ [1]
  ⤳   (([] @ [3]) @ [2]) @ [1]
  ⤳   ([3] @ [2]) @ [1]
  ⤳   (3::([] @ [2])) @ [1]
  ⤳   (3::[2]) @ [1]
  ⤳   [3,2] @ [1]
  ⤳   3::([2] @ [1])
  ⤳   3 :: (2 :: ([] @ [1]))
  ⤳   3 :: (2 :: [1])
  ⤳   3 :: [2,1]
  ⤳   [3,2,1]
```

During the evaluation, the list `[3,2]` is built from `3::[2]` and taken apart again immediately afterwards. In the library there is a more efficient function `rev` for reversing lists. In Chapter 17 we consider how to achieve more efficient evaluations.

## 5.5 Polymorphic values

The type system of SML allows *values* of polymorphic types, such as the empty list []
or the pair (5, [[]]) of the integer 5 and the list with the empty list as its only element.
They have types 'a list and int * 'a list list:

```
val z = [];
val z = [] : 'a list

(5,[[]]);
val it = (5, [[]]) : int * 'a list list
```

The above declarations have the form:

val *id* = *exp*

(with *id* being it for the second declaration) where the expressions syntactically are
*value* expressions, i.e. expressions where no further evaluation is possible. Thus, a
value expression has the same form as its value.

### Note

A list expression $a_1 :: a_2 :: \cdots :: a_k :: [a_{k+1}, \ldots, a_n]$ containing values
$a_1, a_2, \ldots, a_n$ is considered a value expression with the value $[a_1, a_2, \ldots, a_n]$.

As is apparent from these examples, the type check in SML does not put restrictions
on the use of polymorphic value expressions. It does, however, *restrict* the use of
*polymorphic expressions* which are not just values:

Expressions of polymorphic type can be used freely for intermediate results in
an evaluation, but the final (top level) result of the evaluation of an expression
(as printed in the answer from SML) cannot be of polymorphic type – unless
the expression is a value expression.

Hence, at top level SML refuses for example rev [], whereas the expressions
1::(rev []) and (rev []): int list are accepted (as they are of monomorphic
types):

```
rev [];
! Toplevel input:
! rev [];
! ^^^^^^
! Value polymorphism: Free type variable at top level: 'a

1::(rev []);
val it = [1] : int list

(rev []): int list
val it = [] : int list
```

The restrictions may be paraphrased as follows (see also Section B.4.3):

- All monomorphic expressions are OK, even non-value expressions.
- All value expressions are OK, even polymorphic ones.
- At top-level, polymorphic non-value expressions are forbidden.

The rationale for these restrictions will only become clear much later when imperative features of SML are introduced in Chapter 18 (see Section 18.3). In the meantime, we just have to accept the restrictions – and they will really not do us much harm.

## 5.6  A library of list functions

In this section we describe a set of fundamental list functions, where some are predefined in SML, while others are found in the library.

### 5.6.1  Lists, strings and characters

Conversion between strings and lists of characters is performed by means of the functions explode and implode:

```
explode "c₁···cₙ"              =   [#"c₁", ... ,#"cₙ"]
implode [#"c₁", ... ,#"cₙ"]   =   "c₁···cₙ"
```

For example:

```
explode "abcdefg";
val it = [#"a", #"b", #"c", #"d", #"e", #"f", #"g"]
        : char list

implode it;
val it = "abcdefg" : string
```

These functions are predefined in SML. See also Section D.9.2.

### 5.6.2  List attributes

The functions length and null are defined by:

```
length [a₁, ... ,aₙ]   =   n
null xs                =   length(xs) = 0
```

For example:

```
length [];
val it = 0 : int

length [1,2,3];
val it = 3 : int
```

```
null [];
val it = true : bool

null [1,2,3];
val it = false : bool
```

These functions are predefined in SML. See also Section D.4.

### 5.6.3   Selections of lists

The functions hd, tl, nth, take and drop are defined by:

$$
\begin{aligned}
\text{hd } [a_1, \ldots, a_n] &= a_1 \\
\text{tl } [a_1, a_2, \ldots, a_n] &= [a_2, \ldots, a_n] \\
\text{nth } ([a_1, \ldots, a_n], i) &= a_{i+1} \\
\text{take } ([a_1, \ldots, a_n], i) &= [a_1, \ldots, a_i] \\
\text{drop } ([a_1, \ldots, a_n], i) &= [a_{i+1}, \ldots, a_n]
\end{aligned}
$$

For example:

```
hd [[],["a"]];
val it = [] : string list

tl [[],["a"]];
val it = [["a"]] : string list list

List.nth ([1,2,3], 2);
val it = 3 : int

List.take([0,1,2,3,4,5,6], 4);
val it = [0,1,2,3] : int list

List.drop([0,1,2,3,4,5,6], 4);
val it = [4,5,6] : int list
```

These functions are all partial and may raise exceptions. For example:

```
hd([]: string list);
! Uncaught exception:
! List.Empty

tl([]: string list);
! Uncaught exception:
! List.Empty

List.nth ([1],2);
! Uncaught exception:
! Subscript
```

The explicit typing of [] is necessary in the examples with hd and tl above in order to avoid a value polymorphism error.

The functions hd and tl are predefined in SML, while the functions nth, take and drop are found as List.nth, List.take and List.drop in the Library. See also Section D.4.

## 5.6.4    Pairs of lists and lists of pairs

The functions zip and unzip convert between pairs of lists and lists of pairs:

$$\text{zip}([x_1, \ldots, x_m], [y_1, \ldots, y_n]) = [(x_1, y_1), \ldots, (x_m, y_m)] \quad \text{if } m < n$$
$$\text{zip}([x_1, \ldots, x_m], [y_1, \ldots, y_n]) = [(x_1, y_1), \ldots, (x_n, y_n)] \quad \text{if } m \geq n$$

$$\text{unzip}([(x_1, y_1), \ldots, (x_n, y_n)]) = ([x_1, \ldots, x_n], [y_1, \ldots, y_n])$$

Thus, unzip is the inverse function of zip for pairs of equal length lists. These functions are found in the library as ListPair.zip and ListPair.unzip. See also Section D.4.

The declaration for unzip reveals an interesting recursion form:

```
fun unzip []           = ([],[])
  | unzip((x,y)::rest) = let val (xs,ys) = unzip rest
                         in (x::xs,y::ys) end;
val unzip = fn : ('a * 'b) list -> 'a list * 'b list
```

Note the use of pattern matching for splitting the function value unzip rest into its components xs and ys.

Examples using these functions are:

```
zip([1,2,3], [[1],[1,2]]);
val it = [(1, [1]), (2, [1, 2])] : (int * int list) list
```

```
unzip it;
val it = ([1,2], [[1], [1,2]]) : int list * int list list
```

The following evaluation illustrates how the recursion works for unzip:

$$\text{unzip } [(1,[1]),(2,[1,2])]$$

$$\rightsquigarrow \left( \begin{array}{l} \text{let val (xs,ys) = unzip rest } \ldots, \\ [\,x \mapsto 1, y \mapsto [1], \text{rest} \mapsto [(2,[1,2])]\,] \end{array} \right)$$

$$\rightsquigarrow \left( \begin{array}{l} \text{(x::xs, y::ys),} \\ [\,x \mapsto 1, y \mapsto [1], \text{xs} \mapsto [2], \text{ys} \mapsto [[1,2]]\,] \end{array} \right)$$

$$\rightsquigarrow \ ([1,2], \ [[1], \ [1,2]])$$

In this evaluation we have omitted the evaluation:

$$(\text{unzip rest}, [\text{rest} \mapsto [(2,[1,2])]])$$
$$\rightsquigarrow \ \text{unzip } [(2,[1,2])]$$
$$\rightsquigarrow \ ([2],[[1,2]])$$

giving the above bindings for xs and ys.

## 5.7  Membership; equality types

The member function for lists determines whether a value $x$ is equal to one of the elements in a list $[y_1, y_2, \ldots, y_n]$, i.e.:

$$
\begin{aligned}
& x \text{ member } [y_1, y_2, \ldots, y_n] \\
=\ & (x = y_1) \lor (x = y_2) \lor \cdots \lor (x = y_n) \\
=\ & (x = y_1) \lor (x \text{ member } [y_2, \ldots, y_n])
\end{aligned}
$$

Since $x$ cannot be a member of the empty list, we arrive at the declaration:

```
infix member

fun x member []       = false
  | x member (y::ys) = x=y orelse x member ys;
infix 0 member
val member = fn : ''a * ''a list -> bool
```

The function member can be useful in certain cases, but is not included in the Library.

The type of member contains an *equality type variable* ''a. The equality type is inferred from the expression x=y. It means that the function only allows arguments $(x, ys)$ where the equality operator = is defined for values of the type of $x$. A type such as, for example, int * (bool * string) list * int list is an equality type, and the equality operator on values of this type is defined structurally from the equality operators defined on its constituent types.

Any type containing a function type is *not* an equality type for the following reason: values $v$ and $w$ of this type will contain components $f$ and $g$ with type $\tau_1 \rightarrow \tau_2$, for some types $\tau_1$ and $\tau_2$. The functions $f$ and $g$ must be compared in order to decide whether $v$ and $w$ are equal. Hence, one will have to find out whether

$$f(x) = g(x)$$

for all $x$ with type $\tau_1$. When $\tau_1$ is a type with infinitely many elements, for example a set of integers, the equality of $f$ and $g$ cannot, of course, be decided by testing $f(x) = g(x)$ for all possible $x$'s.

Furthermore, it is a fundamental fact of theoretical computer science that there exists no (always terminating) algorithm to determine whether two arbitrary programs f and g denote the same function. Therefore, function types cannot be parts of an equality type, as the equality operator for functions cannot be implemented in the SML system (or any other).

We now present examples illustrating more advanced use of expressions and patterns in declarations of functions on lists.

## Example 5.1

### Removing elements from a list

We first consider the function remove whose value remove$(x, ys)$ is the list obtained from $ys$ by removing all occurrences of $x$. The function is declared by:

```
fun remove(_, [])    = []
  | remove(x, y::ys) = if x=y then remove(x,ys)
                              else y::remove(x,ys);
val remove = fn : ''a * ''a list -> ''a list


remove("a", ["a", "abc", "A", "a"]);
val it = ["abc", "A"] : string list
```

Consider now the function `removeDub` whose value `removeDub(xs)` is the list obtained from *xs* by removing all elements of *xs*, which occur earlier in *xs*. The function is declared by:

```
fun removeDub []      = []
  | removeDub(x::xs) = x::removeDub(remove(x,xs));
val removeDub = fn : ''a list -> ''a list


removeDub [1,2,2,1,4,1,5];
val it = [1, 2, 4, 5] : int list
```

Note the application of the `remove` function in the recursive call of `removeDup`.

---

**Example 5.2**

---

### A register for CDs

We will now give examples where both record and list patterns are used to obtain succinct declarations of functions.

Consider a register describing CDs, where each CD is described by its title, artist, record company, year and the songs on the disc. This is modelled by the declarations:

```
type cd = {title: string,
           artist: string,
           company: string,
           year: int,
           songs: string list};


type cdRegister = cd list;
```

An example of a register is:

```
val cdreg = [{title="t1", artist="a1", company="c1",
               year=93, songs=["s1","s2","s3","s4","s5"]},
              {title="t2", artist="a2", company="c2",
               year=91, songs=["s6","s7","s8","s9"]},
              {title="t3", artist="a1", company="c2",
               year=94,  songs=["s10","s11","s12"]}
              ];
```

We declare a function:

```
titles: string * cdRegister -> string list
```

to extract from a register the titles of CDs for a given artist:

```
fun titles(_, []: cdRegister)                = []
  | titles(a, {artist, title, ...}::cdreg) =
           if a=artist then title::titles(a, cdreg)
           else titles(a, cdreg);

titles("a1", cdreg);
val it = ["t1", "t3"] : string list
```

A function:

```
findArtist: string * cdRegister -> string
```

extracting the artist of a given song in a register is a partial function, since the register may not contain a CD with the song. Therefore, we introduce the exception Cd and the function is declared by:

```
exception Cd

fun findArtist(_, []: cdRegister)                = raise Cd
  | findArtist(s, {artist, songs, ...}::cdreg) =
           if s member songs then artist
           else findArtist(s, cdreg);


findArtist("s7", cdreg);
val it = "a2" : string

findArtist("s88", cdreg);
! Uncaught exception:
! Cd
```

## 5.8  Type inference

In this section we give an example of a type inference for a polymorphic function on lists. Reconsider the declaration of the function remove:

```
fun remove(_, [])    = []
  | remove(x, y::ys) = if x=y then remove(x,ys)
                        else y::remove(x,ys);
```

The most *general type* of remove is ''a * ''a list -> ''a list. The type inference of SML can deduce that remove has this type. We can follow how SML is able to do so by the following arguments:

**1.** The keyword fun indicates that remove has function type $\tau$ -> $\tau'$, for some types $\tau$ and $\tau'$.

**2.** Since remove is applied to a pair (x, y::ys) in the second clause of the declaration, $\tau$ must be a type $\tau_1$ * $\tau_2$ list, for some types $\tau_1$ and $\tau_2$. Furthermore, x has type $\tau_1$, y has type $\tau_2$ and ys has type $\tau_2$ list in the second clause.

**3.** The expression y::remove(x,ys) occurring in the second clause has type $\tau_2$ list since y has type $\tau_2$. Hence, the type $\tau_2$ list must be equal to the type $\tau'$ of the function value.

**4.** Since the comparison x=y occurs in the second clause of the declaration, $\tau_1$ must be an equality type and it must be equal to $\tau_2$.

**5.** Since there are no further type constraints, $\tau_1$ and $\tau_2$ are some equality type variable, say ''a, and ''a * ''a list -> ''a list is the most general type for remove.

## 5.9 Summary

We have introduced the type of lists. Values of list type can be constructed from the empty list [] by (repeated) 'cons'ing an element $x$ in front of an already given list $xs$: $x::xs$. We have presented a number of fundamental functions on lists, where some are predefined in SML, while others occur in the Library: @ (append), rev (reverse), hd, tl, null, length, nth, take, drop. Conversions between strings and lists of characters are made using explode and implode, while zip and unzip convert between pairs of lists and lists of pairs.

Many of these functions are *polymorphic* in the sense that the same function, e.g. rev, can be applied to lists of different types. Polymorphic types are constructed from *type variables*, using type constructors and types. Equality type variables are used in polymorphic types where the SML equality operator is defined.

The chapter contains examples illustrating the use of list patterns in declarations of recursive functions and examples illustrating various kinds of frequently occurring recursions on lists.

## Exercises

**5.1** Give a declaration for altsum (see Page 69) containing only two clauses.

**5.2** Declare an SML function rmodd removing the odd-numbered elements from a list:

$$\text{rmodd } [x_1, x_2, x_3, x_4, \ldots] = [x_2, x_4, \ldots]$$

**5.3** Declare an SML function combine such that:

$$\text{combine } [x_1, x_2, x_3, x_4, \ldots] = [(x_1, x_2), (x_3, x_4), \ldots]$$

**5.4** Declare an SML function `pr`: `int -> int list` such that `pr` $n$ is the list of the first $n$ prime numbers. (Use solutions of Exercise 2.7.)

**5.5** Declare an SML function `pr'`: `int * int -> int list` so that `pr'`$(m, n)$ is the list of the prime numbers between $m$ and $n$. (Use solutions of Exercise 2.7.)

**5.6** Give declarations for the SML functions: `length`, `nth`, `take` and `drop` in Section 5.6.3.

**5.7** Declare an SML function to remove even numbers occurring in an integer list.

**5.8** Declare an SML function `number`$(x, ys)$ to find the number of times $x$ occurs in the list $ys$.

**5.9** Declare an SML function `split` such that:

$$\text{split } [x_1, x_2, x_3, x_4, \ldots, x_n] = ([x_1, x_3, \ldots], [x_2, x_4, \ldots])$$

**5.10** Declare an SML function

```
prefix: ''a list * ''a list -> bool
```

The value of the expression `prefix`$([x_1, x_2, \ldots, x_m], [y_1, y_2, \ldots, y_n])$ is true if $m \leq n$ and $x_i = y_i$ for $1 \leq i \leq m$, and false otherwise.

**5.11** Declare an SML function `lowerCaseOnly` : `string -> bool`, determining whether all characters in a string are small (lower-case) letters, e.g.:

```
lowerCaseOnly "abc"  =  true
lowerCaseOnly "Abc"  =  false
```

Hint: Use the functions `explode` and `Char.isLower` (cf. Section D.3.3).

**5.12** A string is called a *palindrome* if it is identical with the reversed string. For instance `"ole elo"` is a palindrome, while `"ol elo"` is not. Write a function determining whether a string is a palindrome. Make the declaration as short as possible.

**5.13** A list of integers $[x_1, x_2, \ldots, x_n]$ is *weakly ascending* if the elements satisfy:

$$x_1 \leq x_2 \leq x_3 \leq \ldots \leq x_{n-1} \leq x_n$$

or if the list is empty. The problem is now to declare functions on weakly ascending lists.

(a) Declare an SML function

```
count: int list * int -> int
```

where `count`$(xs, y)$ is the number of occurrences of the integer $y$ in the weakly ascending list $xs$.

(b) Declare an SML function

```
insert: int list * int -> int list
```

where the value of insert($xs$, $y$) is a weakly ascending list obtained by inserting the number $y$ into the weakly ascending list $xs$.

(c) Declare an SML function

```
intersect: int list * int list -> int list
```

where the value of intersect($xs$, $ys'$) is a weakly ascending list containing the common elements of the weakly ascending lists $xs$ and $ys'$. For instance:

```
intersect([1,1,1,2,2], [1,1,2,4]) = [1,1,2]
```

(d) Declare an SML function

```
plus: int list * int list -> int list
```

where the value of plus($xs$, $ys'$) is a weakly ascending list, which is the union of the weakly ascending lists $xs$ and $ys'$. For instance:

```
plus([1,1,2],[1,2,4]) = [1,1,1,2,2,4]
```

(e) Declare an SML function

```
minus: int list * int list -> int list
```

where the value of minus($xs$, $ys'$) is a weakly ascending list obtained from the weakly ascending list $xs$ by removing the elements, which are also found in the weakly ascending list $ys'$. For instance:

```
minus([1,1,1,2,2],[1,1,2,3]) = [1,2]
minus([1,1,2,3],[1,1,1,2,2]) = [3]
```

**5.14** Declare an SML function revrev working on a list of lists, which maps a list to the reversed list of the reversed elements, e.g.:

```
revrev [[1,2],[3,4,5]] = [[5,4,3],[2,1]]
```

**5.15** Declare a function sum($p$, $xs$) where $p$ is a predicate of type int -> bool and $xs$ is a list of integers. The value of sum($p$, $xs$) is the sum of the elements in $xs$ satisfying the predicate $p$. Test the function on different predicates (e.g. $p(x) = x > 0$).

**5.16** (a) Declare an SML function finding the smallest element in a non-empty integer list.

(b) Declare an SML function delete: int * int list -> int list, where the value of delete($x$, $ys$) is the list obtained by deleting one occurrence of $x$ in $ys$ (when this is possible).

(c) Declare an SML function which sorts an integer list so that the elements are placed in weakly ascending order.

**5.17** Consider the declarations:

```
fun f(x, [])    = []
  | f(x, y::ys) = (x+y)::f(x-1, ys);

fun g []         = []
  | g((x,y)::s) = (x,y)::(y,x)::g s;

fun h []        = []
  | h(x::xs) = x::(h xs)@[x];
```

Find the types for f, g and h and explain the value of the expressions:

(a) $f(x, [y_1, y_2, \ldots, y_n]), n \geq 0$

(b) $g[(x_1, y_1), (x_2, y_2), \ldots, (x_n, y_n)], n \geq 0$

(c) $h[x_1, x_2, \ldots, x_n], n \geq 0$

# Problem solving II

In this chapter we use the approach of Chapter 4 on another example where the data modelling is more complicated than in the rational number example. The new example comprises data that are sequences of other kinds of data, and we use SML `list` types to model the structure of such data.

The example is a program for a simple cash register:

An electronic cash register contains a data register associating the name of the article and its price to each valid article code. A purchase comprises a sequence of items, where each item describes the purchase of one or several pieces of a specific article.

The task is to construct a program which makes a bill of a purchase. For each item the bill must contain the name of the article, the number of pieces, and the total price, and the bill must also contain the grand total of the entire purchase.

We concentrate on describing the computations required in the example, and we do not describe the dialogue between the operator and the system. The construction of dialogue programs is addressed in Chapters 15 and 16.

## 6.1 Problem analysis: cash register

Our goal is that the main concepts of the problem formulation are found in the program we construct. To achieve this we name the important concepts of the problem and we associate types with the names.

Article code and article name are central concepts in the problem formulation. Furthermore, the problem formulation does not describe any structure for the code and name of articles, so we associate a basic type with these concepts:

```
type articleCode = string
type articleName = string
```

The choice of the `string` type is somewhat arbitrary. An alternative choice could be the `int` type.

The register associates article name and article price with each article code, and we model a register by a list of pairs. Each pair has the form:

($ac$, ($aname$, $aprice$))

where $ac$ is an article code, $aname$ is an article name and $aprice$ is an article price. We choose (non-negative) integers to represent prices (in the smallest currency unit):

```
type price = int          (* pr  where  pr >= 0 *)
```

and we get the following type for a register:

```
type register = (articleCode * (articleName*price)) list
```

The following value is an example of a register:

```
[("a1",("cheese",25)),
 ("a2",("herring",4)),
 ("a3",("soft drink",5))
]
```

A purchase comprises a *sequence* of items modelled by a list of items, where each item comprises a pair:

($np$, $ac$)

describing a number of pieces $np$ (which is a non-negative integer) purchased of an article with code $ac$:

```
type noPieces    = int         (* np  where np >= 0   *)
type item        = noPieces * articleCode
type purchase    = item list
```

The following value is an example of a purchase:

```
[(3,"a2"),(1,"a1")]
```

A bill comprises an information sequence *infos* for the individual items and the grand total *sum*, and this composite structure is modelled by a pair:

($infos$, $sum$)

where each element in the list *infos* is a triple

($np$, $aname$, $tprice$)

of the number of pieces $np$, the name $aname$, and the total price $tprice$ of a purchased article:

```
type info        = noPieces * articleName * price
type infoseq     = info list
type bill        = infoseq * price
```

The following value is an example of a bill:

```
([(3,"herring",12),(1,"cheese",25)],37)
```

The function makeBill can compute a bill given a purchase and a register, i.e. it has the type:

```
makeBill: purchase * register -> bill
```

The exception FindArticle is raised in the case where an article code of a purchase does not occur in the given register.

The result of this analysis is documented in the interface definition in Table 6.1:

**Table 6.1**   Interface definition.

```
type articleCode = string
type articleName = string
type noPieces    = int
type price       = int
type register    = (articleCode * (articleName*price)) list
type item        = noPieces * articleCode
type purchase    = item list
type info        = noPieces * articleName * price
type infoseq     = info list
type bill        = infoseq * price

exception FindArticle
makeBill: purchase * register -> bill
```

## 6.2  Programming

It is often convenient to introduce auxiliary functions in order to solve a programming problem. So the solution to our programming problem may contain declarations of functions which are not specified in the interface definition.

In our example, it is convenient to declare a function:

```
findArticle: articleCode * register -> articleName * price
```

to find the article name and price in the register for a given article code, because the declaration for the function makeBill becomes easier to comprehend using this auxiliary function.

The exception FindArticle is raised when no article with the given code occurs in the register:

```
exception FindArticle;
exn FindArticle = FindArticle : exn
```

```
fun  findArticle(ac, (ac',adesc)::reg) =
          if ac=ac' then adesc else findArticle(ac,reg)
  | findArticle _                        = raise FindArticle;
val findArticle = fn :  ''a * (''a * 'b) list -> 'b
```

Then the bill is made by the function:

```
fun makeBill([], _)                 = ([],0)
  | makeBill((np,ac)::pur, reg) =
        let val (aname,aprice) = findArticle(ac,reg)
            val tprice         = np*aprice
            val (billtl,sumtl) = makeBill(pur,reg)
        in ((np,aname,tprice)::billtl, tprice+sumtl)
        end;
val makeBill =
    fn :  (int * ''a) list * (''a * ('b * int)) list
          -> (int * 'b * int) list * int
```

The second clause of the declaration expresses how to construct a bill for a non-empty purchase (np,ac)::pur. The name and price (aname,aprice) is first found in the register for the article code ac in the 'head' item. Then we compute the total price tprice for np purchases of this article. In the third local declaration, a bill (billtl,sumtl) is (recursively) constructed for the 'tail' purchase pur. The complete bill is built in the let expression.

Note that the SML system infers a more general type for the makeBill function than the type given in the interface definition. This is, however, no problem as the specified type is an instance of the inferred type. Thus, the declared function makeBill has the specified type (among others). Example 7.1 shows how to program so that the SML system will infer exactly the specified type.

The results of these activities are collected into the program in Table 6.2:

---

**Table 6.2**  Program.

```
exception FindArticle ;

fun findArticle(ac, (ac',adesc)::reg) =
          if ac=ac' then adesc else findArticle(ac,reg)
  | findArticle _                      = raise FindArticle;

fun makeBill([], _)                = ([],0)
  | makeBill((np,ac)::pur, reg) =
        let val (aname,aprice) = findArticle(ac,reg)
            val tprice         = np*aprice
            val (billtl,sumtl) = makeBill(pur,reg)
        in ((np,aname,tprice)::billtl, tprice+sumtl)
        end;
```

## 6.3  Test

A test must exercise all branches of the functions `findArticle` and `makeBill`. The relevant cases are listed in Table 6.3.

**Table 6.3**  Test cases.

| Case | Function | Branch | Remark |
|------|----------|--------|--------|
| 1 | findArticle | _ | Empty register |
| 2 | findArticle | (ac, (ac',adesc)::reg) ac=ac' | Non-empty reg. found |
| 3 | findArticle | (ac, (ac',adesc)::reg) not ac=ac' | Non-empty reg. not found |
| 4 | makeBill | ([], _) | Empty purchase |
| 5 | makeBill | ((np,ac)::pur, reg) | Non-empty purchase |

To devise tests, we introduce the following declarations:

```
val register =
    [("a1",("cheese",25)),
     ("a2",("herring",4)),
     ("a3",("soft drink",5))
    ];
```

```
val pur = [(3,"a2"),(1,"a1")];
```

The tests for the different cases and the expected results are recorded in Table 6.4. where

$$bill = ([(3,"herring",12),(1,"cheese",25)],37)$$

**Table 6.4**  Tests.

| Test no. | Case | Test | Expected result |
|----------|------|------|-----------------|
| 1 | 1 | findArticle("a38",[]) | *uncaught exception* ... |
| 2 | 3, 2 | findArticle("a3",register) | *("soft drink",5)* |
| 3 | 4 | makeBill([],register) | *([],0)* |
| 4 | 5 | makeBill(pur,register) | *bill* |

## 6.4  Summary

We have applied the method for obtaining a program design, introduced in Chapter 4, to design a program to be embedded in a cash register.

The result of the problem analysis, i.e. the interface definition, contains a data model, which is expressed using the types introduced in the previous chapters, i.e. numbers, strings, tuples and lists. The dialogue between a user and the cash register has not been covered in this chapter. Dialogue programs are treated in Chapters 15 and 16.

**6.1** We represent the polynomial $a_0 + a_1 \cdot x + ... + a_n \cdot x^n$ with integer coefficients $a_0, a_1, ..., a_n$ by the list $[a_0, a_1, ..., a_n]$. For instance, the polynomial $x^3 + 2$ is represented by the list $[2, 0, 0, 1]$.

(a) Declare an SML function for multiplying a polynomial by a constant.

(b) Declare an SML function for multiplying a polynomial $Q(x)$ by $x$.

(c) Declare infix SML functions for addition and multiplication of polynomials in the chosen representation. The following recursion formula is useful when defining the multiplication:

$$0 \cdot Q(x) = 0$$
$$(a_0 + a_1 \cdot x + ... + a_n \cdot x^n) \cdot Q(x)$$
$$= a_0 \cdot Q(x) + x \cdot \big((a_1 + a_2 \cdot x + ... + a_n \cdot x^{n-1}) \cdot Q(x)\big)$$

(d) Declare an SML function to give a textual representation for a polynomial.

(e) Write the complete technical documentation (cf. Page 50) for the solution of this problem. (Note that all functions need not go into the interface.)

**6.2** A dating bureau has a file containing name, telephone number, sex, year of birth and themes of interest for each client. You may make a request to the bureau stating your own sex, year of birth and themes of interest and get a response listing all matching clients, i.e. clients with different sex, a deviation in age less than 10 years and with at least one common theme of interest. The problem is to construct a program for generating the responses from the dating bureau.

Write the complete technical documentation (cf. Page 50) for the solution of this problem. (Note that all functions need not go into the interface.)

**6.3** When a map is coloured, the colours should be chosen so that neighbouring countries get different colours. The problem is to construct a program computing such a colouring. A trivial solution where each country always gets its own colour is not accepted. On the other hand, the solution does not have to be an 'optimal' one.

A *country* is represented by its name which is a string, whereas the *neighbour relation* is represented by a list of pairs of names containing those pairs of countries which have a common border. For instance, the list:

```
[("a","b"), ("c","d"), ("d","a")]
```

defines a colouring problem comprising four countries a, b, c and d, where the country a has the neighbouring countries b and d, the country b has the neighbouring country a, etc.

A *colour* on a map is represented by a list of the countries having this colour, and a *colouring* is described by a list of colours. The above countries may hence be coloured by the colouring:

```
[["a","c"], ["b", "d"]]
```

where the countries a and c get one colour, e.g. red, while the countries b and d get another colour, e.g. blue.

(a) Declare SML types `country`, `neighbourRelation`, `colour` and `colouring` according to the above description.

(b) Declare an SML predicate to determine whether two countries are neighbours in a neighbour relation (it is a good idea to write down the type of the predicate first).

(c) Declare an SML predicate to determine whether a colour can be extended by a country under a given neighbour relation (e.g. the colour `["c"]` can be extended by `"a"` while the colour `["a","c"]` cannot be extended by `"b"` in the above neighbour relation).

(d) Declare an SML function which extends a partial colouring by another country under a given neighbour relation. The new country is given the first colour in the colouring which has not been used for any neighbouring country – or a new colour, if none of the colours can be used.

(e) Declare an SML function to colour a map given a neighbour relation.

(f) Write the complete technical documentation (cf. Page 50) for the solution of this problem. (Note that all functions need not go into the interface.)

(g) What happens if a country is stated to be its own neighbour in the neighbour relation?

# Chapter 7

# Tagged values and partial functions

Tagged values are used when we group together values of different kinds to form a single set of values. For example, a circle is represented by its radius $r$, a square is represented by its side length $a$, and a triangle is represented by the triple $(a, b, c)$ of its side lengths $a$, $b$ and $c$. Circles, squares and triangles can be grouped together to form a single collection of *shapes* if we put a *tag* on each representing value. The tag should be `Circle`, `Square` or `Triangle` depending on the shape. The circle with radius `1.2`, the square with side length `3.4` and the triangle with side lengths `3.0`, `4.0` and `5.0` are then represented by the tagged values shown in the Figure 7.1.

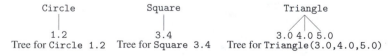

**Figure 7.1** Trees for tagged values.

## 7.1  Datatype declarations

In SML, a collection of tagged values are declared by a *datatype* declaration. For example, a type for shapes is declared by:

```
datatype shape = Circle of real | Square of real
                | Triangle of real*real*real;
datatype  shape
  con Circle = fn : real -> shape
  con Square = fn : real -> shape
  con Triangle = fn : real * real * real -> shape
```

The response from the SML system indicates that shape names a type, and that Circle, Square and Triangle are bound to *value constructors* with the indicated types. These value constructors are all functions and they give a *tagged value* when applied to an argument.

For example, Circle is a value constructor with type real -> shape. This means that Circle $r$ denotes a value of type shape, for every real number $r$. For example, Circle 1.2 denotes the leftmost tree in Figure 7.1 and Circle 1.2 is an example of a *tagged* value, where Circle is the tag.

We can observe that Circle 1.2 is a value which is not evaluated further by the SML system:

```
Circle 1.2;
val it = Circle 1.2 : shape
```

as the value in the answer is equal to the expression being evaluated, i.e. Circle 1.2. Values can be constructed using Square and Triangle in a similar way.

Since constructors are functions in SML, Circle can be applied to an expression of type real:

```
Circle(8.0 - 2.0*3.4);
val it = Circle 1.2 : shape
```

Thus, the datatype declaration of shape allows one to write tagged values like Circle 1.2, Square 3.4 and Triangle(3.0,4.0,5.0) using the constructors, and any value of type shape is of one of the forms:

- Circle $r$
- Square $a$
- Triangle$(a, b, c)$

for some real number $r$, real number $a$ or triple $(a, b, c)$ of real numbers.

Constructors can be used in patterns. For example, an area function for shapes is declared by:

```
fun area (Circle r)        = Math.pi * r * r
  | area (Square a)        = a * a
  | area (Triangle(a,b,c)) =
            let val s = (a + b + c)/2.0
            in Math.sqrt(s*(s-a)*(s-b)*(s-c))
            end;
  val area = fn : shape -> real
```

The pattern matching treats constructors differently from other identifiers: a constructor only matches itself.

For example, the value Circle 1.2 will match the pattern Circle r, but not the other patterns in the function declaration. The matching binds the identifier r to the value 1.2, and the expression Math.pi * r * r is evaluated using this binding:

```
      area (Circle 1.2)
  ↝   (Math.pi * r * r, [r ↦ 1.2])
  ↝   ...
```

The value Triangle(3.0,4.0,5.0) will in a similar way only match the pattern in the third clause in the declaration, and we get bindings of a, b and c to 3.0, 4.0 and 5.0, and the let expression is evaluated using these bindings:

```
      area (Triangle(3.0,4.0,5.0))
  ↝   (let val s = ..., [a ↦ 3.0, b ↦ 4.0, c ↦ 5.0])
  ↝   ...
```

Note that the *brackets* around 'Circle r', 'Square a' and 'Triangle(a,b,c)' are necessary in the declaration of area, because, for example, 'area Circle r' will be read as '(area Circle) r' and *not* as 'area (Circle r)'.

## 7.2   The case-expression

Some values of type shape do not represent geometric shapes. For example, Circle ~1.0 does not represent a circle, as a circle cannot have a negative radius, Square ~2.0 does not represent a square, as a square cannot have a negative side length, and Triangle(3.0, 4.0, 7.5) does not represent a triangle, as $7.5 > 3.0 + 4.0$ and one of the triangle inequalities is not satisfied.

Therefore, there is an *invariant* (cf. Section 4.2.2) for this representation of shapes: the real numbers have to be positive, and the triangle inequalities must be satisfied. This invariant can be declared as a predicate isShape in SML:

```
fun isShape (Circle r)        = r > 0.0
  | isShape (Square a)        = a > 0.0
  | isShape (Triangle(a,b,c)) =
```

```
    a > 0.0    andalso b > 0.0    andalso c > 0.0
    andalso
    a < b + c andalso b < c + a andalso c < a + b;
val isShape = fn : shape -> bool
```

We consider now the declaration of an area function for geometric shapes, which raises the exception Shape when the argument to the function does not satisfy the invariant. If we try to modify the above area function:

```
exception Shape;

fun area x = if not (isShape x) then raise Shape else ...
```

then in the else-branch we have to select the right area-expression depending on the form of x. For this purpose we introduce the SML case-expression:

```
exception Shape;
exn Shape = Shape : exn

fun area x =
    if not (isShape x) then raise Shape
    else case x of
            Circle r          => Math.pi * r * r
          | Square a          => a * a
          | Triangle(a,b,c) =>
                    let val s = (a + b + c)/2.0
                    in Math.sqrt(s*(s-a)*(s-b)*(s-c))
                    end;
val area = fn : shape -> real
```

The modified area function computes the area of legal values of the type shape and terminates the evaluation with the exception Shape for illegal values:

```
area (Triangle(3.0,4.0,5.0));
val it = 6.0 : real

area (Triangle(3.0,4.0,7.5));
! Uncaught exception:
! Shape
```

## 7.2.1    General form of case-expressions

The case-expression has the form:

case *exp* of *match*

for an expression *exp* and a match *match*. A match has the form:

$pat_1$ => $e_1$ | $pat_2$ => $e_2$ | ... | $pat_k$ => $e_k$

containing a sequence of patterns $pat_i$ with associated expressions $e_i$.

The case-expression in the above declaration for area, contains pattern Circle r with expression Math.pi*r*r, pattern Square a with expression a*a, and pattern Triangle(a,b,c) with expression let val s...end.

The evaluation of a case-expression evaluates the expression *exp* and tries to match the resulting value against the patterns $pat_1, pat_2, \ldots, pat_n$ in the match. If a matching pattern $pat_i$ is found, then the corresponding expression $e_i$ is evaluated, using the bindings obtained by the matching. Otherwise the evaluation is terminated by raising the exception Match.

> **Remark**
>
> The SML syntax does not indicate the end of a case-expression, but the extent can be marked by including the whole case-expression in brackets. This is sometimes needed to avoid a mismatch in nested case-expressions.

## 7.3 Enumeration types

Value constructors need not have any argument, so we can make special type declarations such as:

```
datatype colour = Red | Blue | Green | Yellow | Purple;
datatype   colour
  con Blue : colour
  con Green : colour
  con Purple : colour
  con Red : colour
  con Yellow : colour
```

Types such as colour are called *enumeration types*, because the declaration of colour just enumerates five constructors:

```
Red, Blue, Green, Yellow, Purple
```

where each constructor names a value of type colour, e.g.:

```
Green;
val it = Green : colour
```

Functions on enumeration types may be declared by pattern matching:

```
fun nice_colour Red  = true
  | nice_colour Blue = true
  | nice_colour _    = false;
val nice_colour = fn : colour -> bool

nice_colour Purple;
val it = false : bool
```

The predefined Boolean type is actually declared as an enumeration type:

```
datatype bool = true | false;
```

## 7.4  The order type

The predefined `order` type is an enumeration type:

```
datatype order = LESS | EQUAL | GREATER;
```

It is the result type of the 'compare' functions: `Int.compare`, `Real.compare`, `Char.compare`, `String.compare`, `Time.compare`, `Date.compare`, etc. for types with an ordering '$<$' of the values (cf. Sections D.2.2, D.3.1, D.7, D.8), e.g.:

$$
\text{String.compare}(x, y) = \begin{cases} \text{LESS} & \text{if } x \text{ precedes } y \text{ lexicographically} \\ \text{EQUAL} & \text{if } x = y \\ \text{GREATER} & \text{if } x \text{ follows } y \text{ lexicographically} \end{cases}
$$

The `compare` functions are convenient when declaring functions by using this splitting into three cases. We may, for example, declare a function:

```
countLEG: int list -> int * int * int
```

where `countLEG` $xs = (y_1, y_2, y_3)$ and $y_1$, $y_2$ and $y_3$ are the number of elements of $xs$ which are less than 0, equal to 0 and greater than 0, respectively:

```
fun countLEG []       = (0,0,0)
  | countLEG(x::rest) =
        let val (y1,y2,y3) = countLEG rest in
            case Int.compare(x,0) of
                  LESS    => (y1+1,y2  ,y3  )
                | EQUAL   => (y1  ,y2+1,y3  )
                | GREATER => (y1  ,y2  ,y3+1)
        end;
val countLEG = fn : int list -> int * int * int

countLEG [~3,0,~2,1,~3,0];
val it = (3,2,1) : int * int * int
```

## 7.5  Partial functions: the option datatype

A function $f$ is a *partial* function on a set $A$ if the domain of $f$ is a proper subset of $A$. For example, the factorial function is a partial function on the set of integers because it is undefined for the negative integers, and the head and tail functions are partial functions on lists because they are undefined for the empty list.

In declaring a partial function, SML offers the programmer three ways of handling argument values where the function is *undefined*:

**1.** The evaluation of the function value does not terminate.

**2.** The evaluation of the function value is terminated by raising an exception.

**3.** The evaluation of the function value gives a special result, indicating that the function is undefined as regards the actual argument.

The first choice was used, for instance, in the declaration of the factorial function `fact` on page 9, where, for example, the evaluation of `fact ~1` never terminates. The second choice was, for example, selected for the improved `area` function (cf. page 93). The third choice uses the predefined `option` datatype:

```
datatype 'a option = NONE | SOME of 'a;
```

where NONE is used for undefined arguments and SOME $v$ is used when the function value is $v$.

The constructor SOME is polymorphic and can be applied to values of any type:

```
SOME false;
val it = SOME false : bool option

SOME [1,2,3];
val it = SOME [1, 2, 3] : int list option

SOME [];
val it = SOME [] : 'a list option
```

The value NONE is a polymorphic value of type 'a option:

```
NONE;
val it = NONE : 'a option
```

Note that the polymorphic expression SOME [] is accepted by the SML system as it is a value expression (cf. Section 5.5).

The library function

```
valOf : 'a option -> 'a
```

'removes the SOME', i.e. valOf(SOME $n$) = $n$. It raises the exception Option when applied to NONE (cf. Table D.2). For example:

```
valOf(SOME [1,2,3]);
val it = [1, 2, 3] : int list

valOf(SOME 1);
val it = 1 : int

valOf NONE + 1;
! Uncaught exception:
! Option.Option
```

We may, for instance, declare a modified factorial function optFact(*n*) with value SOME *n*! for *n* ≥ 0 and NONE for *n* < 0:

```
fun optFact n = if n < 0 then NONE else SOME(fact n);
val optFact = fn : int -> int option
```

The function application optFact *n* always gives a result:

```
optFact 5;
val it = SOME 120 : int option
```

```
optFact ~2;
val it = NONE : int option
```

The declaration of optFact presumes that fact has already been declared. An independent declaration of optFact is achieved using the valOf function:

```
fun optFact n =
    case Int.compare(n,0) of
        GREATER => SOME(n * valOf(optFact(n-1)))
      | EQUAL   => SOME 1
      | LESS    => NONE;
val optFact = fn : int -> int option
```

Note that the expression optFact(n-1) in the above declaration cannot have the value NONE as n is greater than zero.

**Example 7.1**

### Cash register

Consider the following part of the interface definition and the program from the cash register example of Chapter 6:

```
type articleCode = string;
type articleName = string;
type price       = int;
type register    = (articleCode * (articleName*price)) list;

exception FindArticle;

fun findArticle(ac, (ac',adesc)::reg) =
            if ac=ac' then adesc else findArticle(ac,reg)
  | findArticle _                      = raise FindArticle;
val findArticle = fn : ''a * (''a * 'b) list -> 'b
```

The intended type for findArticle is:

```
findArticle: articleCode * register -> articleName * price
```

Datatype declarations and tags can be used to make the SML system infer this type. Consider the declarations:

```
datatype articleCode = AC of string;
datatype articleName = AN of string;
datatype price       = P of int;
datatype register    =
        R of (articleCode * (articleName * price)) list;

fun findArticle(ac, R((ac',adesc)::reg)) =
        if ac=ac' then adesc else findArticle(ac, R reg)
  | findArticle _                         = raise FindArticle;
val findArticle = fn
   : articleCode * register -> articleName * price
```

Note that the SML system infers the desired type for findArticle. The costs are the explicit tagging in the declarations above and in the values:

```
val reg = R [ (AC "a1", (AN "cheese", P 25)),
              (AC "a2", (AN "herring", P 4)),
              (AC "a3", (AN "soft drink", P 5)) ];

findArticle(AC "a3", reg);
val it = (AN "soft drink", P 5) : articleName * price

findArticle(AC "a38", reg);
! Uncaught exception:
! FindArticle
```

We leave it as an exercise to complete this example such that the SML system can infer the right type for makeBill also. (See Exercise 7.6.)


### 7.6  Exception handling

An *exception* is used to terminate the evaluation of an expression with an 'error' signal. Exceptions are *declared* by declarations such as:

```
exception Conflict;
exn Conflict = Conflict : exn

exception BadArgument of int;
exn BadArgument = fn : int -> exn
```

The identifiers Conflict and BadArgument are declared as *exception constructors* which are like value constructors from datatype declarations. Exception constructors can be used in patterns (and expressions) in the same way as value constructors.

An exception is *raised* by evaluating a raise expression. The exception raised will propagate through surrounding evaluations of expressions which are terminated by the raised exception – until the exception is *caught* by an *exception handler*. The top level exception handler catches any exception and prints an error message 'uncaught exception ...', containing the name of the exception.

We may use the exception BadArgument in a modified version factE of the factorial function, which raises the exception BadArgument *n* if an expression factE *n* with argument $n < 0$ is evaluated:

```
fun factE n =
    case Int.compare(n,0) of
        LESS    => raise BadArgument n
      | EQUAL   => 1
      | GREATER => n * factE(n-1);
val factE = fn : int -> int


factE 4;
val it = 24 : int


factE ~3;
! Uncaught exception:
! BadArgument
```

An *exception handler* is placed as a suffix to an expression *e*:

*e* handle *match*

The suffix consists of the word handle followed by a *match*, where the patterns should contain the exception constructors for all the exceptions to be caught by the handler. An exception handler catches a raised exception if one of the patterns matches the value of the exception, and the corresponding expression in the match is then evaluated under this binding.

As an example we may, for example, declare a function: factStr: int -> string, computing the string 'Bad argument *n*' when $n < 0$ and the string representation for *n*! when $n \geq 0$:

```
fun factStr n =
    Int.toString(factE n)
    handle BadArgument n => "Bad argument " ^ Int.toString n;
val factStr = fn : int -> string


factStr 4;
val it = "24" : string


factStr ~3;
val it = "Bad argument ~3" : string
```

Note that the handler catches the exception in the last example, as the pattern BadArgument n matches the exception BadArgument ~3 raised by factE when

evaluating the expression factE ~3. This pattern matching gives the binding
n ↦ ~3, and this is the binding being used when evaluating the expression
"Bad argument " ^ Int.toString(n). This expression must be of type string
as the value is a result value for the function factStr of type int -> string.

## 7.7  The Eight Queens problem

Exceptions can be used in programming *backtracking* algorithms in SML. We illustrate
this by the famous Eight Queens problem: place eight queens on a chessboard so that
no queen can hit another in a single move, i.e. no two queens may stand in the same
row, column or diagonal. A solution to this problem is shown in Figure 7.2.

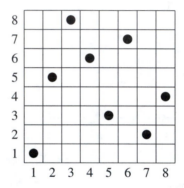

**Figure 7.2**   A solution to the Eight Queens problem.

It is obvious that no two queens can be placed in the same column, so we may look
for a solution by the following procedure:

**1.** Place a queen in the first column, say in position $(1, 1)$.

**2.** Search the rows in the second column until a safe place $(2, row2)$ is found.

**3.** Continue in the same way with the following columns.

**4.** If no row can be found for a certain column, then *backtrack* to a previous column
where we can find a row which has not yet been tried.

We represent a placement of $k$ queens in positions $(1, row1), (2, row2), \ldots, (k, rowk)$
by the list $[(1, row1), (2, row2), \ldots, (k, rowk)]$ of coordinates. The value of the
expression safe$((x, y), posl)$ tells us whether it is safe to place a queen in position
$(x, y)$, when queens have already been placed in the positions in the list *posl*:

```
fun safe ((x,y),(x1,y1)::xs) =
              x <> x1           (* not same column  *)
         andalso y <> y1        (* not same row      *)
         andalso y - x <> y1 - x1 (* not on /-diagonal *)
```

```
      andalso y + x <> y1 + x1 (* not on \-diagonal *)
      andalso safe((x,y),xs)
  | safe _                    = true;
val safe = fn : (int * int) * (int * int) list -> bool
```

The backtracking algorithm queens can now be expressed by using exceptions. The argument to queens consists of a list *posl* of positions where queens have already been placed, the column number *x* where a queen has to be placed, and a list *yl* with the remaining (not yet tried) row numbers, i.e. we arrive at the type:

```
queens : (int*int) list * int * int list -> (int*int) list
```

The value of the expression queens(*posl*, *x*, *yl*) is described as follows:

1. If the column number *x* is > 8, then we have succeeded and *posl* contains the coordinates for the eight queens.

2. Otherwise *x* is less or equal to 8 and we consider two cases:

   (a) The list *yl* is not empty, i.e. there are more rows to try. If the first row number *y* in the list *yl* gives a safe position, then we place a queen in the position $(x, y)$ (by appending $(x, y)$ to *posl*) and we try the next column $x + 1$ with all eight possibilities [1, 2, 3, 4, 5, 6, 7, 8]. If the position $(x, y)$ is unsafe, then we use the remaining rows right away.

   (b) There are no rows left to try (i.e. *yl* is empty). We then backtrack to the previous column by raising the exception Conflict. For that column the exception is handled by trying the remaining rows *yl′*:

```
exception Conflict;
exception Conflict

fun queens(posl,x,yl) =
    if x > 8 then posl else         (*    1 *)
    case yl of
       y::yl' =>                     (* 2.a *)
          if safe((x,y),posl)
          then queens(posl@[(x,y)], x+1, [1,2,3,4,5,6,7,8])
               handle Conflict => queens(posl,x,yl')
          else queens(posl,x,yl')
     | []      => raise Conflict;    (* 2.b *)
val queens = fn : (int * int) list * int * int list
                   -> (int * int) list
```

We get a solution to the problem by calling the function with an empty list of queens, starting in column 1 with $1 - 8$ as possible rows:

```
queens([],1,[1,2,3,4,5,6,7,8]);
val it = [(1,1),(2,5),(3,8),(4,6),(5,3),(6,7),(7,2),(8,4)]
         : (int * int) list
```

## 7.8 Summary

We have introduced the notion of tagged values and partial functions. In particular we have introduced the following SML notions: datatypes and constructors, case expressions, enumeration types, exceptions and exception handlers. Furthermore, we have shown by an example how exceptions can be used in programming backtracking algorithms.

## Exercises

**7.1** Make a datatype declaration for a type solution to express the three possibilities for roots in a quadratic equation: two roots, one root, no roots (cf. Example 3.2). Declare a corresponding solve function for solving the equation.

**7.2** Declare a function of type int list -> int option for finding the smallest element in an integer list.

**7.3** Declare a function partition$(x, xs)$ to split the list $xs$ of integers into three lists $(xs_1, xs_2, xs_3)$, where $xs_1, xs_2, xs_3$ are the lists of elements of $xs$ which are smaller than $x$, equal to $x$ and greater than $x$.

**7.4** At the Technical University of Denmark students are given marks for the various courses either according to the 13-scale or by a statement saying that the student has 'passed' or 'not passed' the course. The 13-scale consists of the numbers: 0, 3, 5, 6, 7, 8, 9, 10, 11, 13, and a course is passed with a mark of 6 or more.

(a) Model marks using the datatype concept of SML.

(b) Declare an invariant determining whether a given mark is legal.

(c) Declare a function to find the mean value of a collection of marks – ignoring marks 'passed' or 'not passed'.

(d) Declare a function giving the number of passed courses for a collection of marks.

**7.5** A day-care centre receives children in the day nursery, the nursery school and the recreation centre. On the basis of this we declare an SML datatype category with three values:

```
datatype category = Day_nursery
                  | Nursery_school
                  | Recreation_centre
```

A child in the day-care centre is described by its name and the category.

(a) Declare suitable types name and childDesc to model names of children and the description of a child in the day-care centre.

(b) Declare a function number of type category * childDesc list -> int, where the value of number$(c, ds)$ is the number of children described in $ds$ with place of category $c$.

(c) Parents are charged £225 per month for a child in the day nursery, £116 per month for a child in the nursery school, and £100 per month for a child in the recreation centre. However, large families are given a discount: a family with several children in the day-care centre must pay the full price for the most expensive place, and half price for the rest of the places. Declare an SML function of type `childDesc list -> real` computing the total payment for a given list of child descriptions, assuming that the children described are brothers and sisters.

**7.6** Finish the revision of the cash register program in Example 7.1 so that the SML system infers the type `purchase * register -> bill` for the `makeBill` function.

**7.7** Sets of integers e.g.  $\{1, 3, 5, 6, 7, 8, 9, 10, 11, 12, 13, 14, 15, 17\}$ may be represented using *intervals*: $\{1, 3\} \cup \text{Intv}(5, 15) \cup \{17\}$, where $\text{Intv}(a, b)$ denotes the set $\{a, a + 1, a + 2, \dots, b\}$ of integers.

We declare a representation of sets of integers using intervals by the declarations:

```
datatype e = Intg of int | Intv of (int * int);
type intset = e list;
```

We will require that the integers in the representation of a set occur in ascending order in the list, so the above set will have the representation:

```
[Intg 1, Intg 3, Intv(5,15), Intg 17]
```

(a) Declare the invariant `inv: intset -> bool` for this representation of integer sets.

(b) Declare SML functions for set operations: membership, add element, delete element, union, intersection, set difference and the subset predicate.

**7.8** Revise the program for the Eight Queens problem to find all solutions to the problem.

# Finite trees

This chapter is about trees which may contain a subcomponent of the same type. A list is an example of such a tree, e.g. the list 1::[2,3,4] contains a subcomponent [2,3,4] which is also a list. In this chapter we will introduce the concept of tree through a variety of examples.

In SML we use a *recursive* datatype declaration to represent a set of values which are trees. The constructors of the type correspond to the rules for building trees, and patterns containing constructors are used when declaring functions on trees.

We motivate the use of finite trees and recursive data types by a number of examples: Chinese boxes, symbolic differentiation, trees of ancestors, file systems, trees with different kinds of nodes and electrical circuits.

Furthermore, we introduce the notion of abstract types where representation details are hidden from the user.

## 8.1 Chinese boxes

A *Chinese box* is a coloured cube which contains a coloured cube which ... which contains a coloured cube which contains nothing. More precisely, a Chinese box is either *Nothing* or a *Cube* characterized by its *side length*, *colour* and the *contained* Chinese box. This characterization can be considered as stating rules for generating Chinese boxes, and it is used in the following definition of Chinese boxes as *trees*.

The set cbox of *Chinese boxes* can be represented as the set of trees generated by the rules:

Rule 1: The tree `Nothing` is in cbox.

Rule 2: If $r$ is a real number, if $c$ is a colour, and if $cb$ is in cbox, then the tree in Figure 8.1 is also in cbox.

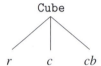

**Figure 8.1** Tree for `Cube`($r, c, cb$).

Rule 3: The set cbox contains no other values than the trees generated by repeated use of rules 1 and 2.

The following example shows how this definition can be used to generate elements of cbox.

Step a: The void tree `Nothing` is a member of cbox by rule 1.

Step b: The tree in Figure 8.2 is a member of cbox by step a and rule 2.

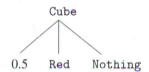

**Figure 8.2** Tree for `Cube`(0.5, Red, Nothing).

Step c: The tree in Figure 8.3 is a member of cbox by step b and rule 2.

Step d: The tree in Figure 8.4 is a member of cbox by step c and rule 2.

### 8.1.1 Datatype declaration

Using the type `colour` from Section 7.3:

```
datatype colour = Red | Blue | Green | Yellow | Purple;
```

we declare a type cbox in SML representing the set of Chinese boxes by the following `datatype` declaration:

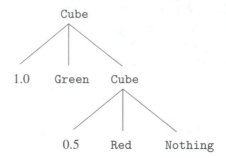

**Figure 8.3**   Tree for Chinese box in step c.

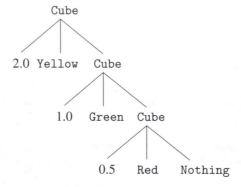

**Figure 8.4**   Tree for Chinese box in step d.

```
datatype cbox = Nothing                        (* 1. *)
              | Cube of real * colour * cbox;   (* 2. *)
datatype  cbox
  con Nothing = Nothing : cbox
  con Cube = fn : real * colour * cbox -> cbox
```

The declaration is recursive, as the declared type cbox occurs in the argument type of the constructor Cube. The constructors Nothing and Cube correspond to the above rules 1 and 2 for generating trees, so we can redo the above steps a–d with values of type cbox:

Step a′: The constructor Nothing is a value of type cbox.

Step b′: The value Cube(0.5, Red, Nothing) of type cbox represents the tree generated in step b.

Step c′: The value Cube(1.0, Green, Cube(0.5, Red, Nothing)) of type cbox represents the tree generated in step c.

Step d′: The value:

```
Cube(2.0,Yellow,Cube(1.0,Green,
                  Cube(0.5,Red,Nothing)))
```

of type cbox represents the tree generated in step d.

These examples show the relationship between trees and values of type cbox, and we note the following statements where the last one follows from rule 3 for generating trees:

- Different values of type cbox represent different trees.
- Any tree is represented by a value of type cbox.

Hence, a value of type cbox is just a way of writing a tree instead of drawing it. SML does not draw trees when printing values of type cbox – it prints the textual form of the value:

```
val cb1 = Cube(0.5, Red, Nothing);
val cb1 = Cube(0.5, Red, Nothing) : cbox

val cb2 = Cube(1.0, Green,cb1);
val cb2 = Cube(1.0, Green, Cube(0.5, Red, Nothing)) : cbox

val cb3 = Cube(2.0,Yellow,cb2);
val cb3 = Cube(2.0, Yellow, Cube(1.0, Green,
              Cube(0.5, Red, Nothing))) : cbox
```

### 8.1.2 Patterns

In the previous chapter we have seen declarations containing patterns for tagged values. Constructors for trees can occur in patterns just like constructors for tagged values. An example of a *tree pattern* is Cube(r,c,cb), containing identifiers r, c and cb for the components. This pattern denotes the tree in Figure 8.5. This pattern will, for example, match the tree corresponding to the value Cube(1.0,Green,Cube(0.5,Red,Nothing)) shown in Figure 8.6 with bindings r ↦ 1.0, c ↦ Green, and cb ↦ Cube(0.5,Red,Nothing), where the value for cb corresponds to the contained Chinese box (Figure 8.7).

The *inductive* definition of the trees implies that any tree will either match the empty tree pattern:

```
Nothing
```

corresponding to rule 1 in the definition of trees, or the tree pattern:

```
Cube(r,c,cb)
```

corresponding to rule 2 in the definition of trees.

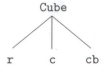

**Figure 8.5**  Pattern Cube(r,c,cb).

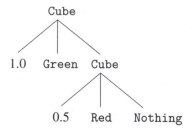

**Figure 8.6**  Tree for cb2.

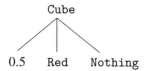

**Figure 8.7**  Tree for cb1.

## 8.1.3  Function declarations

We give a declaration of the function:

```
count: cbox -> int
```

such that the value of the expression: count (*cb*) is the number of cubes of the Chinese box *cb*:

```
fun count Nothing        = 0
  | count(Cube(r,c,cb)) = 1 + count cb;
```

The declaration has two clauses, one having Nothing as argument pattern, the other having Cube(r,c,cb) as argument pattern. Thus, the declaration follows the inductive definition of Chinese boxes.

This function can be applied to cb2:

```
count cb2;
val it = 2 : int
```

*Invariant for Chinese boxes*

A Chinese box must satisfy the invariant that the length of its sides is a positive real number, which is larger than the side length of any cube it contains. The above four Chinese boxes in steps a to d satisfy this invariant, but using the generation process for trees one can construct the tree in Figure 8.8. which does not satisfy the invariant (i.e. which does not correspond to any Chinese box).

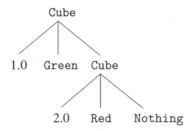

**Figure 8.8** A tree violating the invariant.

When declaring a function on Chinese boxes by the use of the type cbox we must ensure that the function respects the invariant, i.e. the function will only compute values of type cbox satisfying the invariant when applied to values satisfying the invariant.

*Insertion function*

We can declare an insertion function on Chinese boxes:

```
insert: real * colour * cbox -> cbox
```

The value of the expression insert(*r, c, cb*) is the Chinese box obtained from *cb* by inserting an extra cube with side length *r* and colour *c* at the proper place among the cubes in the box. The function insert is a partial function, which gives an exception in case the insertion would violate the invariant for Chinese boxes:

```
exception ChineseBox;
exn ChineseBox = ChineseBox : exn

fun insert(r,c,cb) =
        if r <= 0.0 then raise ChineseBox
        else case cb of
                Nothing           => Cube(r,c,Nothing)
              | Cube(r1,c1,cb1) =>
                  case Real.compare(r,r1) of
                    GREATER => Cube(r,c,cb)
                  | EQUAL   => raise ChineseBox
                  | LESS    => Cube(r1,c1,insert(r,c,cb1));
val insert = fn : real * colour * cbox -> cbox
```

```
insert(2.0,Yellow,insert(1.0,Green,Nothing));
val it = Cube(2.0, Yellow, Cube(1.0, Green, Nothing)) : cbox

insert(1.0,Green,insert(2.0,Yellow,Nothing));
val it = Cube(2.0, Yellow, Cube(1.0, Green, Nothing)) : cbox

insert(1.0,Green,Cube(2.0,Yellow,Cube(1.0,Green,Nothing)));
! Uncaught exception:
! ChineseBox

insert(0.0,Red,Nothing);
! Uncaught exception:
! ChineseBox
```

Note that any legal Chinese box can be generated from the box Nothing by repeated use of insert.

### Layered patterns

We want to declare a function:

```
difflist: cbox -> real list
```

where the elements in the list are differences between the side length of each cube and the side length of the contained cube, e.g. such that, for example:

```
difflist(Nothing)                                     =   []
difflist(Cube(1.0, Green, Nothing))                   =   []
difflist(Cube(2.0, Yellow, Cube(0.5, Green, Nothing))) =   [1.5]
```

and

```
difflist(Cube(3.0, Red, Cube(2.0, Yellow, Cube(0.5, Green, Nothing))))
= [1.0,1.5]
```

The declaration of difflist may be based on three clauses of tree patterns: a 'nothing' Chinese box, Chinese boxes with one cube, and Chinese boxes with two or more cubes (Figure 8.9). We have given the extra name cb to the subtree in the pattern for boxes with two or more cubes.

These tree patterns correspond to the following SML patterns for values of type cbox:

```
Nothing   Cube(_,_,Nothing)   Cube(r2,_,cb as Cube(r1,_,_))
```

The last pattern contains a *layered* pattern: cb as Cube(r1,_,_), where the pattern matching will bind the name cb to the component of the value matching the pattern Cube(r1,_,_).

For example, matching the pattern Cube(r2,_,cb as Cube(r1,_,_)) to the value Cube(2.0, Red, Cube(1.0, Green, Nothing)) gives the bindings r2 $\mapsto$ 2.0, r1 $\mapsto$ 1.0 and cb $\mapsto$ Cube(1.0, Green, Nothing).

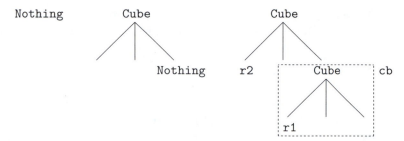

**Figure 8.9**  Trees for patterns of type cbox.

These above patterns give the required splitting into clauses, and the function difflist can be declared by:

```
fun difflist Nothing                        = []
  | difflist(Cube(_,_,Nothing))             = []
  | difflist(Cube(r2,_,cb as Cube(r1,_,_))) =
                             (r2-r1)::difflist(cb);
val difflist = fn : cbox -> real list
```

The function difflist can actually be declared using only two clauses:

```
fun difflist(Cube(r2,_,cb as Cube(r1,_,_))) =
                             (r2-r1)::difflist(cb);
  | difflist _                              = [];
val difflist = fn : cbox -> real list
```

### 8.1.4   Other SML models of Chinese boxes

One may argue that the data type cbox is unnecessarily complicated as Chinese boxes may simply be modelled using lists:

```
type cbox = (real * colour) list
```

This is, however, essentially the same as the above data type of trees, as the list type is a special case of the general concept of recursive data types (cf. Section 8.5).

One may also argue that it is strange to have a constructor Nothing denoting a non-existing Chinese box, and one might rather discard the empty box and divide the Chinese boxes into those consisting of a single cube and those consisting of multiple cubes, as expressed in the following declaration:

```
datatype cbox' = Single of real * colour
               | Multiple of real * colour * cbox';
datatype cbox'
  con Single = fn : real * colour -> cbox'
  con Multiple = fn : real * colour * cbox' -> cbox'
```

Using this type, we get the following declarations of the functions `count` and `insert` where we use a layered pattern `cb1 as Single(r2,s2)` (as used in the above declaration of `difflist`) in the declaration of `insert`:

```
exception ChineseBox;

fun count(Single _)          = 1
  | count(Multiple(_,_,cb)) =  1 + count cb;
val count = fn : cbox'  -> int

fun insert(r1,c1,cb1 as Single(r2,c2)) =
        if r1 <= 0.0 then raise ChineseBox
        else (case Real.compare(r1,r2) of
                 LESS    => Multiple(r2,c2,Single(r1,c1))
               | EQUAL   => raise ChineseBox
               | GREATER => Multiple(r1,c1,cb1)  )
  | insert(r1,c1,cb1 as Multiple(r2,c2,cb2)) =
        if r1 <= 0.0 then raise ChineseBox
        else (case Real.compare(r1,r2) of
                 LESS    => Multiple(r2,c2,insert(r1,c1,cb2))
               | EQUAL   => raise ChineseBox
               | GREATER => Multiple(r1,c1,cb1)  );
val insert = fn : real * colour * cbox' -> cbox'
```

We have now suggested several models for Chinese boxes. The preferable choice of model will in general depend on which functions we have to define. The clumsy declaration of the `insert` function above contains repeated sub-expressions and this indicates that the first model is to be preferred for Chinese boxes.

## (8.2) Symbolic differentiation

We want to construct a program for computing the derivative of a real function of one variable. The program should, for example, compute the derivative $f'(x) = 2x \cdot \cos(x^2)$ for the function $f(x) = \sin(x^2)$. The concept of *function* in SML cannot be used for this purpose, as a function declaration in SML merely gives a means of computing values of the function, e.g.:

```
fun f x = Math.sin(x * x);
val f = fn : real -> real

f 2.0;
val it = ~0.756802495308 : real
```

The differentiation is a manipulation of the *expression* denoting a function, so we need a *representation* of the *structure* of such expressions. This can be done by using expression trees.

We restrict our attention to expressions constructed from real-valued constants and the variable $x$, using the arithmetic functions addition, subtraction, multiplication and division, and the real functions sin, cos, ln and exp. We use the symbols $++$, $--$, $**$ and $//$ for the arithmetic operators, and the symbols Sin, Cos, Ln and Exp for the special functions.

For example, for expressions such as $\sin(x \cdot x)$ and $(\sin x) \cdot x$ we have the corresponding expression trees shown in Figure 8.10. The different order of the operators in these expressions is reflected in the trees: the tree for $\sin(x \cdot x)$ contains a subtree for the subexpression $x \cdot x$, which again contains two subtrees for the subexpressions $x$ and $x$, while the tree for $(\sin x) \cdot x$ contains subtrees for the subexpressions $\sin x$ and $x$, etc.

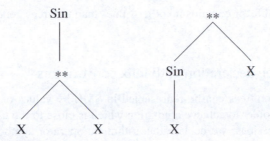

**Figure 8.10**   Trees for $\sin(x \cdot x)$ and $(\sin x) \cdot x$.

The set of finite expression trees fexpr is generated inductively by the following rules:

**1.** For every real number $r$, the tree in Figure 8.11 is a member of fexpr.

**Figure 8.11**   Tree for the constant $r$.

**2.** The tree X is in fexpr.

**3.** If $fe_1$ and $fe_2$ are in fexpr, then the trees in Figure 8.12 are members of fexpr.

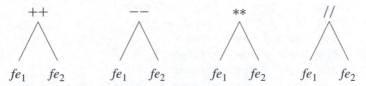

**Figure 8.12**   Trees for dyadic operators.

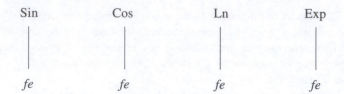

**Figure 8.13**   Trees for special functions.

**4.** If *fe* is in fexpr, then the trees in Figure 8.13 are in fexpr.

**5.** The set fexpr contains no other values than the trees generated by rules 1 to 4.

## 8.2.1   Datatype declaration with infix constructors

Expression trees can be represented in SML by values of a recursively defined data type. In order to achieve a notation which is close to the usual mathematical notation for expressions, we declare the arithmetic operator symbols to be infix constructors whose precedences are equal to the precedences of the corresponding operators on real numbers. We get the following declaration of the data type fexpr, where the comments indicate the corresponding rule above for generating expression trees:

```
infix 6 ++ --;
infix 7 ** //;

datatype fexpr =
    Const of real                                    (* 1 *)
  | X                                                (* 2 *)
  | ++ of fexpr * fexpr | -- of fexpr * fexpr        (* 3 *)
  | ** of fexpr * fexpr | // of fexpr * fexpr        (* 3 *)
  | Sin of fexpr | Cos of fexpr                       (* 4 *)
  | Ln of fexpr | Exp of fexpr ;                     (* 4 *)
```

```
datatype  fexpr
  con ** : fexpr * fexpr -> fexpr
  con ++ : fexpr * fexpr -> fexpr
  con -- : fexpr * fexpr -> fexpr
  con // : fexpr * fexpr -> fexpr
  con Cos : fexpr -> fexpr
  con Exp : fexpr -> fexpr
  con Ln  : fexpr -> fexpr
  con Sin : fexpr -> fexpr
  con X : fexpr
  con Const : real -> fexpr
```

For instance, the expression trees for $\sin(x \cdot x)$ and $(\sin x) \cdot x$ are represented by the values Sin(X ** X) and (Sin X) ** X of type fexpr.

### 8.2.2   Patterns

The following patterns correspond to values of type fexpr:

```
Const r
X
fe1 ++ fe2
fe1 -- fe2
fe1 ** fe2
fe1 // fe2
Sin fe
Cos fe
Ln fe
Exp fe
```

These patterns can be used in function declarations with a division into clauses according to the structure of expression trees. Note that the infix constructors **, ++, etc. are also written in infix form in the patterns.

### 8.2.3   Function declarations

We are now in a position to declare a function

```
D: fexpr -> fexpr
```

such that D($fe$) is a representation of the derivative of the function represented by $fe$.

We have a rule of differentiation for each building rule for expression trees. Therefore, the declaration for D has a clause for each constructor generating a value of type fexpr. This leads to the following declaration of the differentiation function D, where each clause is a direct translation of the corresponding differentiation rule from mathematics:

```
fun D(Const _)      = Const 0.0
  | D X             = Const 1.0
  | D(fe1 ++ fe2)   = (D fe1) ++ (D fe2)
  | D(fe1 -- fe2)   = (D fe1) -- (D fe2)
  | D(fe1 ** fe2)   = (D fe1) ** fe2 ++ fe1 ** (D fe2)
  | D(fe1 // fe2)   =
                ((D fe1) ** fe2 -- fe1 ** (D fe2)) // (fe2 ** fe2)
  | D(Sin fe)       = (Cos fe) ** (D fe)
  | D(Cos fe)       = ((Const ~1.0) ** (Sin fe)) ** (D fe)
  | D(Ln fe)        = (D fe) // fe
  | D(Exp fe)       = (Exp fe) ** (D fe) ;
val D = fn : fexpr -> fexpr
```

The following examples illustrate the use of the function:

```
D(Sin (X ** X));
val it = Cos (X ** X) ** (Const 1.0 ** X ++ X ** Const 1.0)
    : fexpr

D(Const 3.0 ** Exp X);
val it =
    Const 0.0 ** Exp X ++ Const 3.0 ** (Exp X ** Const 1.0)
    : fexpr
```

Note that these examples show results that can be reduced. For example, Const 3.0 ** Exp X is a simpler representation of the value of the expression D(Const 3.0 ** Exp X), where the term containing a zero factor has been removed. It is an interesting, non-trivial, task to declare a function which reduces expressions to a particular, simple form.

### Conversion to textual representation

The function toString: fexpr -> string will produce a textual representation of a function expression:

```
fun toString(Const r)    = Real.toString r
  | toString X           = "x"
  | toString(fe1 ++ fe2) =   "(" ^ (toString fe1)
                         ^ " + " ^ (toString fe2) ^ ")"
  | toString(fe1 -- fe2) =   "(" ^ (toString fe1)
                         ^ " - " ^ (toString fe2) ^ ")"
  | toString(fe1 ** fe2) =   "(" ^ (toString fe1)
                         ^ " * " ^ (toString fe2) ^ ")"
  | toString(fe1 // fe2) =   "(" ^ (toString fe1)
                         ^ " / " ^ (toString fe2) ^ ")"
  | toString(Sin fe)     = "(sin " ^ (toString fe) ^ ")"
  | toString(Cos fe)     = "(cos " ^ (toString fe) ^ ")"
  | toString(Ln fe)      = "(ln " ^ (toString fe) ^ ")"
  | toString(Exp fe)     = "(exp " ^ (toString fe) ^ ")"

toString(Cos (X ** X) ** (Const 1.0 ** X ++ X ** Const 1.0));
val it = "((cos (x * x)) * ((1.0 * x) + (x * 1.0)))" : string

toString(X ** X ** X ++ X ** X)
val it = "(((x * x) * x) + (x * x))" : string
```

The function toString will produce a pair of brackets for every operator symbol ++, --, etc. occurring in the argument. It is possible to declare a more elaborate toString function, which will take the precedences of the operators into account. In this way unnecessary brackets can be avoided.

*Computing values of expressions*

Each value of type fexpr represents a function from reals to reals. We may now declare an SML function:

```
compute: fexpr * real -> real
```

where compute(*fe*, *y*) is equal to the value obtained by applying the function corresponding to the expression tree *fe* to the argument *y*. The declaration looks as follows:

```
fun compute(Const r,_)    = r
  | compute(X,y)          = y
  | compute(fe1 ++ fe2,y) = compute(fe1,y) + compute(fe2,y)
  | compute(fe1 -- fe2,y) = compute(fe1,y) - compute(fe2,y)
  | compute(fe1 ** fe2,y) = compute(fe1,y) * compute(fe2,y)
  | compute(fe1 // fe2,y) = compute(fe1,y) / compute(fe2,y)
  | compute(Sin fe,y)     = Math.sin(compute(fe,y))
  | compute(Cos fe,y)     = Math.cos(compute(fe,y))
  | compute(Ln fe,y)      = Math.ln(compute(fe,y))
  | compute(Exp fe,y)     = Math.exp(compute(fe,y))
val compute = fn : fexpr * real -> real
```

We can, for instance, compute the value of the expression $3.0 \cdot \ln(\exp x)$ for $x = 9.0$:

```
compute(Const 3.0 ** Ln (Exp X), 9.0);
val it = 27.0 : real
```

## 8.3 Trees of ancestors; traversal of a tree

A person's tree of ancestors contains information about her/his name together with the tree of the person's mother and father – or the tree of a person may be unspecified.

### 8.3.1 Datatype declaration

Trees of ancestors can be modelled by a recursive data type as follows:

```
datatype ancTree = Unspec
                 | Info of string * ancTree * ancTree;
datatype  ancTree
  con Info : string * ancTree * ancTree -> ancTree
  con Unspec : ancTree
```

For a value Info(*n*, *mt*, *ft*) of the type ancTree, the string *n* is the name of the person, the ancestor tree *mt* is the ancestor tree of *n*'s mother, and *ft* is the ancestor tree of *n*'s father.

The ancestor tree in Figure 8.14 expresses that the name of Joachim's mother is Margrethe and the name of his father is Henrik. The name of Margrethe's mother is Ingrid and her father's name is Frederik. Both of Henrik's parents are unspecified in

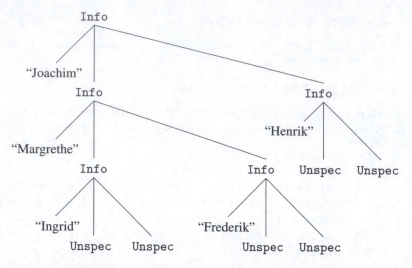

**Figure 8.14** Ancestor tree of Joachim.

this ancestor tree, and so are the parents of Ingrid and Frederik. The tree is represented by the following value of the type `ancTree`:

```
val at = Info("Joachim",
              Info("Margrethe",
                   Info("Ingrid",Unspec,Unspec),
                   Info("Frederik",Unspec,Unspec)),
              Info("Henrik",Unspec,Unspec));
```

### 8.3.2  Pre-order traversal

The following function extracts the list of names of persons occurring in an ancestor tree:

```
fun pre_listof Unspec          = []             (* 1 *)
  | pre_listof (Info(n,mt,ft)) =
          n::(pre_listof mt) @ (pre_listof ft);  (* 2 *)
val pre_listof = fn : ancTree -> string list

pre_listof at;
val it = ["Joachim","Margrethe","Ingrid","Frederik","Henrik"]
         : string list
```

From the part of the function declaration marked (* 2 *) we see that the name $n$ in the node of an ancestor tree $Info(n, mt, ft)$ (e.g. Joachim in Figure 8.14) appears before the names in the left subtree $mt$ (e.g. Margrethe, Ingrid, and Frederik), which again appear before the names (e.g. Henrik) in the right subtree *ft*. This ordering is an example of a general principle called a *pre-order traversal* of a tree, where the information in the node is 'processed' before the information in the left subtree, which is again processed before the information in the right subtree.

### 8.3.3    In-order and post-order traversal

In an *in-order traversal* of Info(*n*, *mt*, *ft*), the information in the left subtree *mt* is processed, followed by processing of the node, whereupon the right subtree is processed:

```
fun in_listof Unspec          = []
  | in_listof (Info(n,mt,ft)) =
          (in_listof mt) @ [n] @ (in_listof ft) ;
val in_listof = fn : ancTree -> string list
```

```
in_listof at;
val it = ["Ingrid","Margrethe","Frederik","Joachim","Henrik"]
        : string list
```

In a *post-order traversal* of Info(*n*, *mt*, *ft*), the information in the left subtree *mt* is processed, followed by processing of the right subtree *ft*, whereupon the node is processed:

```
fun post_listof Unspec          = []
  | post_listof (Info(n,mt,ft)) =
          (post_listof mt) @ (post_listof ft) @ [n]
val post_listof = fn : ancTree -> string list
```

```
post_listof at;
val it = ["Ingrid","Frederik","Margrethe","Henrik","Joachim"]
        : string list
```

A function extracting all male ancestors in post-order from an ancestor tree can be declared as follows:

```
fun maleanc Unspec          = []
  | maleanc (Info(_,mt,ft)) =
        (maleanc mt) @ (maleanc ft)
                   @ (case ft of
                        Unspec      => []
                      | Info(n,_,_) => [n]) ;
val maleanc = fn : ancTree -> string list
```

```
maleanc at;
val it = ["Frederik","Henrik"] : string list
```

## 8.4  Mutual recursion

A collection of declarations are called *mutual recursive* if the identifiers being declared depend on each other. SML supports the declaration of mutually recursive types and functions. We illustrate the concepts with two examples.

### 8.4.1  Mutually recursive types and functions

*File system*

The elements of a file system *fs* are named files and named catalogues, where the contents of a catalogue is a list whose elements again may be files or new catalogues, as illustrated in Figure 8.15. The catalogue $c_1$ contains two files $a_1$ and $a_4$ and two catalogues $c_2$ and $c_3$. The catalogue $c_2$ contains a file $a_2$ and a catalogue $c_3$, and so on. Note that the same name may occur in different catalogues.

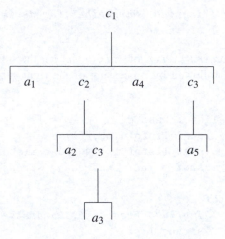

**Figure 8.15**  Structure of a file system.

We will not consider the contents of files, so we can model the elements of a file system by two declarations:

```
datatype elem = File of string
              | Catalogue of string*contents
withtype contents = elem list;
```

The first declaration refers to a type `contents` which is declared in the second declaration. This 'forward' reference to the type `contents` is allowed by the SML system because `contents` is declared in the second declaration using a `withtype` declaration. These two declarations constitute an example of mutually recursive type declarations, as the type `elem` occurs in the declaration of `contents` and the type `contents` occurs in the declaration of `elem`.

The following value represent a file with name "a1":

```
File "a1";
val it = File "a1" : elem
```

A file system is a catalogue and the file system *fs* in Figure 8.15 is represented by the value:

```
val fs =
    Catalogue("c1",
              [File "a1",
               Catalogue("c2",
                         [File "a2",
                          Catalogue("c3", [File "a3"])]),
               File "a4",
               Catalogue("c3", [File "a5"])]);
```

Functions for extracting the list of all names of files and catalogues occurring in a file system can be declared as follows:

```
fun nameElems(File s)          = [s]
  | nameElems(Catalogue(s, cnt)) = s::(nameContents cnt)

and nameContents [] = []
  | nameContents (e::es) = nameElems e @ (nameContents es);

val nameElems = fn : elem -> string list
val nameContents = fn : elem list -> string list
```

The above function declarations are mutually recursive because the identifier nameContents occurs in the declaration of nameElems and, vice versa, the identifier nameElems occurs in the declaration of nameContents. Mutually recursive functions are declared by using and for combining the individual function declarations.

The names of file and catalogues in fs may now be extracted:

```
nameElems fs;
val it = ["c1", "a1", "c2", "a2",
          "c3", "a3", "a4", "c3", "a5"] : string list
```

### 8.4.2    Mutual recursive datatype declarations

*Trees with alternating levels*

Mutual recursive datatype declarations are obtained by combining the individual datatype declarations using and. For example:

```
datatype Atr = ALeaf | ANode of Btr * Btr
and      Btr = BLeaf | BNode of Atr * Atr * Atr;
datatype Atr
datatype Btr
  con ALeaf = ALeaf : Atr
  con ANode = fn : Btr * Btr -> Atr
  con BLeaf = BLeaf : Btr
  con BNode = fn : Atr * Atr * Atr -> Btr
```

The values of type `Atr` and `Btr` are trees where the 'levels' alternate between `ALeaf`s and `ANode`s and `BLeaf`s and `BNode`s.

For example:

```
val t = ANode(BLeaf,BNode(ALeaf,ANode(BLeaf,BLeaf),ALeaf));
val t = ANode(BLeaf, BNode(ALeaf, ANode(BLeaf,BLeaf), ALeaf))
     : Atr
```

represents the tree in Figure 8.16.

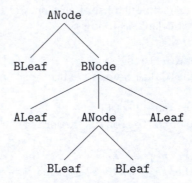

**Figure 8.16**    Tree for `ANode(BLeaf,BNode(ALeaf,ANode(BLeaf,BLeaf),ALeaf))`.

The functions extracting the number of `ALeaf`'s occurring in values of type `Atr` and `Btr` are declared as mutually recursive functions:

```
fun noALeafsInAtr ALeaf              = 1
  | noALeafsInAtr(ANode(bt1,bt2)) =
         noALeafsInBtr bt1 + noALeafsInBtr bt2

and noALeafsInBtr BLeaf              = 0
  | noALeafsInBtr (BNode(at1,at2,at3)) = noALeafsInAtr at1
                                       + noALeafsInAtr at2
                                       + noALeafsInAtr at3;
val noALeafsInAtr = fn : Atr -> int
val noALeafsInBtr = fn : Btr -> int

noALeafsInAtr t;
val it = 2 : int
```

The above examples show mutually recursive type and function declarations. One way to obtain mutually recursive type declarations is to combine a datatype declaration using a withtype declaration. This form is used when the type constructor declared in the withtype part is not an SML-datatype.

Mutually recursive datatype declarations are obtained by combining the individual declarations using and. Mutually recursive function declarations are obtained by combining the individual declarations using and.

## 8.5 Parameterized datatypes

The constructors in a datatype declaration may have polymorphic types containing type variables. These type variables are *parameters* for the type, and they are written in front of the type constructor in the declaration.

An example is the *list* type, which is in fact a parameterized type with constructors nil and :: (pronounced 'cons'):

```
infixr 5 :: ;
datatype 'a list = nil | :: of 'a * 'a list;
datatype  'a list
   con :: : 'a * 'a list -> 'a list
   con nil : 'a list
```

An *instance* of the parameterized type 'a list is obtained by replacing the type variable 'a with some type. For example, int list, (string*int) list and ('b list) list are instances of the type 'a list.

Another example of a datatype declaration with parameters is the type for *binary trees* with elements of type 'a in the leaves and elements of type 'b in the nodes.

The parameter sequence consisting of 'a and 'b is written as ('a,'b). This parameter sequence is written in front of the type constructor bintree in the declaration:

```
datatype ('a,'b) bintree =
                Leaf of 'a
            | Node of ('a,'b) bintree * 'b * ('a,'b) bintree;
```

The tree in Figure 8.17 is a value of type (int,string) bintree. The SML notation for this value is:

```
Node(Node(Leaf 1,"cd",Leaf 2),"ab",Leaf 3)
```

The type bintree is *polymorphic* and allows polymorphic values such as:

```
Node(Node(Leaf [],[],Leaf []),[],Leaf [])
```

of type ('a list,'b list) bintree.

Note that the ancestor trees in Section 8.3 could be represented by the instance:

```
(unit,string) bintree
```

of the ('a,'b) bintree type. We would then use the value Leaf () for Unspec, and the value Node($t_1$, $n$, $t_2$) for Info($n$, $mt$, $ft$) where $t_1$ and $t_2$ are the bintree values for the ancTree values *mt* and *ft*, respectively.

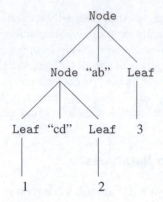

**Figure 8.17**   A binary tree.

**Electrical circuits**

We consider electrical circuits built from *components* by *serial* or *parallel* composition. We model a circuit by a value of the following type:

```
datatype 'a circuit =
    Comp of 'a
  | Ser  of 'a circuit * 'a circuit
  | Par  of 'a circuit * 'a circuit;
```

Figure 8.18 shows a circuit with three components with attached values 0.25, 1.0 and 1.5 together with the tree representing the circuit. In SML the value is written Ser(Par(Comp 0.25,Comp 1.0),Comp 1.5):

```
val cmp = Ser(Par(Comp 0.25,Comp 1.0),Comp 1.5);
val cmp = Ser(Par(Comp 0.25,Comp 1.0),Comp 1.5): real circuit
```

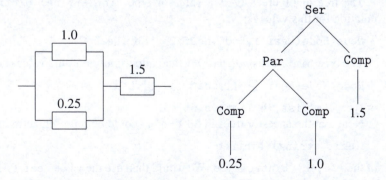

**Figure 8.18**   Circuit and corresponding tree.

Using this representation of circuits we can define a function count for computing the number of components in a circuit:

```
fun count (Comp _)      = 1
  | count (Ser(c1,c2)) = count c1 + count c2
  | count (Par(c1,c2)) = count c1 + count c2;
val count = fn : 'a circuit -> int
```

For example:

```
count cmp;
val it = 3 : int
```

We consider now circuits consisting of resistances where the attached values are the resistances of the individual components. Suppose $c_1$ and $c_2$ are two circuits with resistances $r_1$ and $r_2$, respectively. The resistance of a serial combination of $c_1$ and $c_2$ is $r_1 + r_2$, and the resistance of a parallel combination of $c_1$ and $c_2$ is given by the formula:

$$\frac{1}{1/r_1 + 1/r_2}$$

Thus, a function resistance for computing the resistance of a circuit can be declared by:

```
fun resistance (Comp r) = r
  | resistance (Ser(c1,c2)) = resistance c1 + resistance c2
  | resistance (Par(c1,c2))
              = 1.0 / (1.0/resistance c1 + 1.0/resistance c2);
val resistance = fn : real circuit -> real
```

For example:

```
resistance cmp;
val it = 1.7 : real
```

## 8.7  Abstract types

In SML there is a notion of *abstract types*, for defining a datatype with associated functions. The value constructors of the type are hidden from the user, so the user can create values of the abstract type only by use of the functions declared together with the abstract type. An abstract type can therefore be used to enforce that the invariant of a representation is not violated by the user.

We motivate and introduce the notion of abstract types by two examples.

### 8.7.1    Protecting an invariant

*Rational numbers*

Consider the rational number example from Chapter 4. In Section 4.2.2, a rational number is represented by a pair of integers $(a, b)$, where the invariant $b \neq 0$ must hold, as indicated by the type declaration:

```
type qnum = int*int;          (* (a,b) where b <> 0 *)
```

A user of this program may, however, violate the invariant without being notified about it. For example:

```
mkQ(1,1) // (1,0);
val it = (0, 1) : int * int

toString it;
val it = "0/1" : string
```

The tuple $(1,0)$ does not represent a rational number, as $\frac{1}{0}$ is undefined, and, therefore, the SML expression $mkQ(1,1)$ // $(1,0)$ does not correspond to a meaningful rational number expression.

The problem is, in this case, that the user has direct access to the representation of rational numbers and may misuse it to construct illegal values.

### An abstype-declaration

One may hide details of the data representation by means of an abstract type declaration. An abstype-declaration for rational numbers has the structure:

```
abstype qnum = MkQ of int*int
with  ...
end;
```

The first part abstype qnum = MkQ of int*int has the form of a datatype declaration, except that the reserved word abstype is used instead of datatype. In this part a type qnum is declared. Hence, the *internal* representation of values of this type has the form $MkQ(a, b)$ with a constructor MkQ and representing the tree in Figure 8.19. However, this internal representation is not visible to the user of the abstract type, as we shall see below.

**Figure 8.19**   Internal representation of $a/b$.

The with part of the declaration contains the declaration of types, exceptions, values and functions relating to the abstract type qnum. This part is adopted from the declarations in Section 4.2.2, except that:

- the internal representation for rational numbers are now trees of the form: MkQ($a$, $b$);
- infix declarations of functions are not allowed in abstype declarations;

The functions now have to operate on the internal representation, i.e. MkQ($a$, $b$), instead of ($a$, $b$). Thus, the declaration of the abstract type for rational numbers is:

```
abstype qnum = MkQ of int*int   (* MkQ(a,b) with b<>0 *)
with
    exception QDiv

    fun mkQ (_,0) = raise QDiv
      | mkQ pr    = MkQ pr

    fun ++(MkQ(a,b), MkQ(c,d)) = MkQ(a*d + b*c, b*d);
    fun --(MkQ(a,b), MkQ(c,d)) = MkQ(a*d - b*c, b*d);
    fun **(MkQ(a,b), MkQ(c,d)) = MkQ(a*c, b*d);
    fun //(MkQ(a,b), MkQ(c,d)) = **(MkQ(a,b), mkQ(d,c));
    fun ==(MkQ(a,b), MkQ(c,d)) = (a*d = b*c);

    fun gcd(0,n) = n
      | gcd(m,n) = gcd(n mod m,m);

    fun toString(MkQ(p,q)) =
      let val sign = if p*q<0 then "~" else ""
          val ap = abs p
          val aq = abs q
          val d  = gcd(ap,aq)
      in sign ^ (Int.toString(ap div d))
               ^ "/" ^ (Int.toString(aq div d))
      end;
  end;
```

and the answer from SML is:

```
abstype qnum
exn QDiv = QDiv : exn
val mkQ = fn : int * int -> qnum
val ++ = fn : qnum * qnum -> qnum
val -- = fn : qnum * qnum -> qnum
val ** = fn : qnum * qnum -> qnum
val // = fn : qnum * qnum -> qnum
val == = fn : qnum * qnum -> bool
val gcd = fn : int * int -> int
val toString = fn : qnum -> string
```

where the answer *abstype qnum* does not reveal the internal representation of values of type qnum. For example, the value constructor MkQ cannot be used by a user of the abstract type:

```
- MkQ(2,0);
! Toplevel input:
! MkQ(2,0);
! ^^^
! Unbound value identifier: MkQ
```

The operators ++, --, etc. can now be changed to infix form:

```
infix 6 ++ --
infix 7 ** //
infix 4 ==
```

and the declared functions can be applied:

```
val q1 = mkQ(2,5);
val q1 = <qnum> : qnum

val q2 = mkQ(3,7);
val q2 = <qnum> : qnum

val q3 = q1 ++ q2;
val q3 = <qnum> : qnum
```

Note that the internal representations of the values are hidden in the answers from SML. For example, in the answer *val q3 = <qnum> : qnum* we can see that q3 is some value of type qnum, but the structure of the value is hidden. The value may, however, be inspected using the toString function:

```
toString q3;
val it = "29/35" : string
```

> **Remark**
>
> All the above functions maintain the invariant. It is, therefore, impossible for the user to construct an illegal representation of a rational number, as he/she has no access to the internal representation for rational numbers.

**Example 8.1**

### Search trees

In this example we consider the representation of collections of integers by binary trees. For example, the collection of integers 2, 7, 9, 13, 21 and 25 may be represented by the

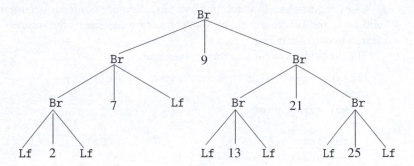

**Figure 8.20**   A binary search tree.

tree in Figure 8.20.

An SML datatype for such kinds of tree can be declared by:

```
datatype tree = Lf | Br of tree*int*tree;
  datatype tree
  con Lf = Lf : tree
  con Br = fn : tree * int * tree -> tree
```

and the above tree is denoted by:

```
Br(Br(Br(Lf,2,Lf),7,Lf),9,Br(Br(Lf,13,Lf),21,Br(Lf,25,Lf)))
```

This tree has the property that the integer 9 occurring in the root is greater than all the integers occurring in the left subtree and smaller than all integers occurring in the right subtree. In fact, every subtree $Br(t_1, i, t_2)$ of the above tree has the following property: all integers occurring in $t_1$ are smaller than $i$, and all integers occurring in $t_2$ are greater than $i$. A tree satisfying this invariant is called a *search tree*.

We will declare an abstract type $\texttt{stree}$ for search trees in order to ensure that the search tree invariant cannot be violated by a user. To this end we will declare the following identifiers in an abstype declaration:

```
empty  : stree
insert : int * stree -> stree
member : int * stree -> bool
toList : stree -> int list
```

A search tree containing $n$ integers $k_1, k_2, \ldots, k_n$ can be generated by repeated insertions of integers into the empty search tree:

$$\texttt{insert}(k_1, \texttt{insert}(k_2, \cdots, \texttt{insert}(k_n, \texttt{empty})\cdots))$$

Using the `member` function one can test whether an integer occurs in a search tree, and using the function `toList` one can obtain the list of the integers occurring in a search tree in ascending order.

The declaration of the abstract type `stree` is:

```
abstype stree = Lf | Br of stree * int * stree
with
    val empty = Lf

    fun insert(i, Lf)                = Br(Lf,i,Lf)
      | insert(i, tr as Br(t1,j,t2)) =
            case Int.compare(i,j) of
                    EQUAL   => tr
                  | LESS    => Br(insert(i,t1),j,t2)
                  | GREATER => Br(t1,j,insert(i,t2))

    fun member(i, Lf)            = false
      | member(i, Br(t1,j,t2)) =
            case Int.compare(i,j) of
                    EQUAL   => true
                  | LESS    => member(i,t1)
                  | GREATER => member(i,t2)

    fun toList Lf              = []
      | toList (Br(t1,j,t2)) = toList t1 @ [j] @ toList t2;
end;
```

Note that the `insert` function respects the invariant for search trees, as it uses the ordering of integers to insert the new value at the right place in the tree. The invariant is exploited in the declaration of the `member` function in reducing the search for the number to the relevant subtree. Furthermore, the invariant is exploited in the declaration of the `toList` function to give the list of elements in ascending order by using an in-order traversal of the search tree.

The answer from SML shows that the internal representation of values of type `stree` is hidden:

```
abstype stree
val empty = <stree> : stree
val insert = fn : int * stree -> stree
val member = fn : int * stree -> bool
val toList = fn : stree -> int list
```

and a user cannot construct a search tree violating the invariant:

```
Br(Lf, 5, Br(Lf,0,Lf));
! Toplevel input:
! Br(Lf, 5, Br(Lf,0,Lf));
! ^^
! Unbound value identifier: Br
```

Values of type stree are created and accessed using the declared functions. For example:

```
val st1 = insert(2, empty);
val st1 = <stree> : stree

val st2 = insert(~3, insert(7, st1));
val st2 = <stree> : stree

member(4, st2);
val it = false : bool

member(7, st2);
val it = true : bool

toList st2;
val it = [~3, 2, 7] : int list
```

## 8.8  Summary

The purpose of this chapter was to introduce *recursive types* which are used to represent *trees*, which are values containing subcomponents of the same type. Trees can be used to represent function expressions, and differentiation can then be expressed as an SML function on expression trees. Trees may also be used to represent trees of ancestors. Important functions on trees are defined by means of tree *traversal* which can be in pre-order, in-order or post-order.

Furthermore, we have given examples illustrating polymorphic datatypes and mutually recursive datatype and function declarations.

The notion of abstract types was introduced. The purpose of abstract types is to hide the representation details of the type from the user. Examples were given to show how abstract types can be used to protect an invariant on a representation from violation by a user.

## Exercises

**8.1** Declare a function red of type fexpr -> fexpr to reduce expressions generated from the differentiation program, e.g. subexpressions of form Const 1.0 * e can be reduced to *e*. (A solution is satisfactory if the expression becomes 'nicer'. It is difficult to design a reduce function so that all trivial sub-expressions are eliminated.)

**8.2** Postfix form is a particular representation of arithmetic expressions where each operator is preceded by its operand(s). The postfix forms of, for example, the expressions:

$$(x + 7.0) \quad \text{and} \quad (x + 7.0) * (x - 5.0)$$

are:

$$x\ 7.0\ +\quad \text{and}\quad x\ 7.0\ +\ x\ 5.0\ -\ *$$

Declare an SML function with type `fexpr -> string` which computes the textual, postfix form of expression trees.

**8.3** In this exercise we consider symbolic expressions built from real numbers and 'names' using the operators: sign change, sum, difference and product, and where a name is a character string. A set of bindings of real values $v_i$ to names $name_i$ is given by a list $[(name_1, v_1), \ldots, (name_n, v_n)]$ of pairs. Declare types for such expressions and bindings, and a function to compute the value of an expression for a given set of bindings of values to names. The function should raise an exception if a name occurring in the expression has no binding to a value.

**8.4** (a) Define a type to represent formulas in propositional logic. A proposition is either an atom given by its name which is a string, or a composite proposition built from atoms using the operators for negation ($\neg$), conjunction ($\wedge$) and disjunction ($\vee$).

(b) A proposition is in *negation normal form* if the negation operator only appears as applied directly to atoms. Write an SML function transforming a proposition into an equivalent proposition in negation normal form, using the de Morgan laws:

$$\neg(p \wedge q) \quad \Leftrightarrow \quad (\neg p) \vee (\neg q)$$
$$\neg(p \vee q) \quad \Leftrightarrow \quad (\neg p) \wedge (\neg q)$$

and the law of double negation: $\neg(\neg p) \Leftrightarrow p$.

(c) A *literal* is an atom or its negation. A proposition is in *conjunctive normal form* if it is a conjunction of propositions, where each conjunct (i.e. proposition in the conjunction) is a disjunction of literals. Write an SML function which transforms a proposition into an equivalent proposition in conjunctive normal form, using the above result and the distributive laws:

$$p \vee (q \wedge r) \quad \Leftrightarrow \quad (p \vee q) \wedge (p \vee r)$$
$$(p \wedge q) \vee r \quad \Leftrightarrow \quad (p \vee r) \wedge (q \vee r)$$

(d) A proposition is a *tautology* if it has truth value true for any assignment of truth values to the atoms. A disjunction of literals is a tautology exactly when it contains the atom as well as the negated atom for some name occurring in the disjunction. A conjunction is a tautology precisely when each conjunct is a tautology. Write a tautology checker in SML, i.e. an SML function which determines whether a proposition is a tautology or not.

**8.5** A company consists of departments with subdepartments, which again can have subdepartments, etc. The company can also be considered as a department.

(a) Assume that each department has a name and a (possibly empty) list of subdepartments. Declare an SML `datatype department`.

(b) Extend this type so that each department has its own gross income.

(c) Declare a function to extract a list of pairs (*department name*, *gross income*) for all departments.

(d) Declare a function to extract the total income for a given department by adding up its gross income, including the income of its subdepartments.

(e) Declare a function to extract a list of pairs (*department name*, *total income*) for all departments.

(f) Declare a function `format` of type `department -> string`, which can be used to get a textual form of a department such that names of subdepartments will occur suitably indented (e.g. with four spaces) on separate lines. (Use `print(format(...))` to print out the result on seperate lines. Do not use `print` in the declaration of `format`.)

**8.6** We consider a simple calculator with instructions for addition, subtraction, multiplication and division of real numbers, and the functions: sin, cos, ln and exp.

The *instruction set* of the calculator is modelled by the following SML datatype:

```
datatype instruction = +++ | --- | *** | ///
                     | SIN | COS | LN | EXP
                     | PUSH of real           ;
```

The calculator is a *stack machine*, where a *stack* is a list of real numbers.

The *execution* of an instruction maps a stack to a new stack: the execution of $+++$ with stack $\boxed{a\ b\ c\ \cdots}$ yields a new stack: $\boxed{(b+a)\ c\ \cdots}$, where the top two elements $a$ and $b$ on the stack have been replaced by the single element $(b+a)$. Similarly with regard to the instructions, $---$, $***$ and $///$, which all work on the *top* two elements of the stack.

The execution of one of the instructions SIN, COS, LN and EXP applies the corresponding function to the top element of the stack. E.g. the execution of LN with stack $\boxed{a\ b\ c\ \cdots}$ yields the new stack: $\boxed{\ln(a)\ b\ c\ \cdots}$.

The execution of PUSH $r$ with the stack $\boxed{a\ b\ c\ \cdots}$ pushes $r$ on top of the stack, i.e. the new stack is: $\boxed{r\ a\ b\ c\ \cdots}$.

(a) Declare a type `stack` for representing the stack, and declare an SML function to interpret the execution of a single instruction:

```
intpInstr: instruction * stack -> stack
```

(b) A *program* for the calculator is a list of instructions $[i_1, i_2, \ldots, i_n]$. A program is *executed* by executing the instructions $i_1, i_2, \ldots, i_n$ one after the other, in that order, starting with an empty stack. The result of the execution is the top value of the stack when all instructions have been executed.

Declare an SML function to interpret the execution of a program:

```
intpProg: instruction list -> real
```

(c) Declare an SML function

```
trans: fexpr * real -> instruction list
```

where `fexpr` is the type for expression trees declared in Section 8.2. The value of the expression $\text{trans}(fe, x)$ is a program $prg$ such that

$$\text{intpProg}(prg) = \text{compute}(fe, x)$$

Hint: The instruction list can be obtained from the postfix form of the expression. (See Exercise 8.2.)

**8.7** Give a solution to Exercise 3.4 using abstract types. Hint: add a function that generates a straight line from a pair of real numbers.

**8.8** Give a solution to Exercise 6.1 using abstract types. Hint: add a function that generates a polymonial from a list of coefficients.

**8.9** Extend the abstract type for search trees in Example 8.1 with a function for removing an integer from a search tree.

# Chapter 9

# Higher-order functions

Functions are 'first class citizens' in SML: a function is considered a *value* just like, for example, an integer, so the value of an expression can be a function, and a function may occur as an argument or value of another function. A function $f : \tau_1$ -> $\tau_2$ is of *higher order* if the argument or the value (or both) contains a component which is a function, i.e. if either of the types $\tau_1$ or $\tau_2$ (or both) contains a function type of the form $\tau$ -> $\tau'$.

A polymorphic function such as the identity function is 'higher order' in the sense that a function can be used as argument. However, in this chapter we only consider 'real' higher-order functions where the argument or the value contains a component which is treated as a function.

Higher-order functions give a very powerful notation for expressing many important abstractions in a brief way, and a systematic use of higher-order functions in programming yields a considerable reduction in the size of the programs. Furthermore, many of the programs in the Library are higher-order functions.

## 9.1 Expressions denoting functions

In this section we consider various kinds of expressions whose values are functions.

### 9.1.1 Using the op prefix

An occurrence of an infix identifier in an SML program can be given a temporary non-fix status by means of the op prefix, so, for example, op + denotes the non-fix sum function for integers:

```
op +;
val it = fn : int * int -> int

op+(2,3);
val it = 5 : int
```

We will see below that the op prefix is very useful when using higher-order functions.

### 9.1.2 Using let-expressions

An expression denoting a function can be obtained by 'packaging' a function declaration into a let-expression. For example, from the declaration of the circle area function:

```
fun circleArea r = Math.pi * r * r;
val circleArea = fn : real -> real
```

we can construct an expression having the circle area function as its value:

```
let  fun circleArea r = Math.pi * r * r in  circleArea  end;
val it = fn : real -> real
```

Note that this is an *expression*. The evaluation of this expression yields the circle area *function* as *value* and the identifier it is bound to this function. Hence, it can be applied to a real number:

```
it 2.0;
val it = 12.5663706144 : real
```

The above let-expression gives an 'anonymous' function, as the binding of the identifier circleArea is local to the expression.

Furthermore, the let expression can be used in places where expressions are used, for example as the right-hand side in a *value* declaration:

```
val f = let fun circleArea r = Math.pi * r * r
        in circleArea
        end;
val f = fn : real -> real
```

The execution of this declaration gives a binding of the identifier f to a value which is the circle area function. Hence the area of a circle with radius 2.0 may be evaluated as the value of f 2.0. Note the use of the keyword val: the declaration is a value declaration although the declared value is a function. A function declaration uses the keyword fun and it contains an argument pattern after the function name.

### 9.1.3  Using fn-expressions

Expressions denoting functions can be written using fn-expressions of the form:

$$\text{fn } pat_1 \text{ => } e_1 \mid pat_2 \text{ => } e_2 \mid \cdots \mid pat_n \text{ => } e_n$$

with patterns $pat_1, pat_2, \ldots, pat_n$ and expressions $e_1, e_2, \ldots, e_n$.

The evaluation of the fn-expression yields the value obtained by evaluation of the expression:

$$\text{let fun } f\, x = \text{case } x \text{ of } pat_1 \text{ => } e_1 \mid pat_2 \text{ => } e_2 \mid \cdots \mid pat_n \text{ => } e_n$$
$$\text{in } f \text{ end}$$

where $f$ and $x$ are 'fresh' identifiers not occurring in any of the expressions $e_i$ and where $x$ is not a constructor of a datatype or exception declaration.

The application of this function to an argument value $v$ is hence evaluated by evaluating the case-expression:

$$\text{case } v \text{ of } pat_1 \text{ => } e_1 \mid pat_2 \text{ => } e_2 \mid \cdots \mid pat_n \text{ => } e_n$$

in the environment where the fn-expression was evaluated. Identifiers in the expressions $e_i$ which do not occur in the corresponding pattern $pat_i$ are hence bound to the values found at the time when the fn-expression was evaluated.

An example of an fn-expression is:

```
fn n => 2 * n;
val it = fn : int -> int
```

It denotes the function of type int -> int which multiplies an integer by 2. For example:

```
(fn n => 2 * n) 3;
val it = 6 : int
```

The predicate of type int -> bool, which has the value false for argument 0 and the value true for other arguments, can be expressed by an fn expression with two patterns:

```
fn 0 => false | _ => true;
val it = fn : int -> bool
```

For example:

```
(fn 0 => false | _ => true) 0;
val it = false : bool
```

```
(fn 0 => false | _ => true) 7;
val it = true : bool
```

The circle area function can be expressed as:

```
fn r => Math.pi * r * r;
val it = fn : real -> real
```

```
(fn r => Math.pi * r * r)  2.0;
val it = 12.5663706144 : real
```

Any fn-expression is considered a *value expression*, cf. Section 5.5, so there are no type restrictions due to the use of polymorphic expressions on declarations of the form:

```
val g = fn ...
```

An fn-expression is called a *lambda abstraction* in theoretical computer science, and one uses the notation $\lambda x.\cdots$ instead of fn $x$ =>$\cdots$.

## 9.2  Value declarations of recursive functions

A fun-declaration of a *non-recursive* function can be written as a val-declaration with a fn-expression on the right hand side. For example, the circle area function can be declared by:

```
val circleArea = fn r => Math.pi * r * r;
val circleArea = fn : real -> real
```

A fun-declaration of a *recursive* function *cannot* be written as a val-declaration with a fn-expression in this simple way. Consider, for example, the following recursive declaration of the factorial function:

```
fun fact 0 = 1
  | fact n = n * fact(n-1);
```

This is *not* equivalent with the val-declaration:

```
val fact =  fn 0 => 1
             | n => n * fact(n-1);
!                        ~~~~
! Unbound value identifier: fact
```

The problem is that the SML system requires that there are bindings for all identifier occurring in the right hand side of a val-declaration. In this case, the actual environment does have a binding for the identifier fact under declaration.

However, there is a construct allowing recursive val-declarations. For example, the above recursive fun-declaration of fact is equivalent to the value declaration:

```
val rec fact = fn 0 => 1
               | n => n * fact(n-1);
val fact = fn : int -> int
```

where `rec` allows the name under declaration (`fact`) to occur in the expressions. The SML system is actually construing any `fun`-declaration in this way, and this becomes apparent when the system issues error messages to an erroneous `fun`-declaration. See also Section 9.4.

Note that the `fn`-expression is considered a value expression, so the type restrictions of Section 5.5 do not apply in this case. There are hence no type restrictions on `fun`-declarations.

## 9.3  The map function

This section discusses higher-order functions in SML by use of an example: the `map` function for lists. Other higher-order functions for lists are introduced in Section 9.5.

We want to declare a function `map` where the argument is some function $f$, and where the value `map` $f$ is the function which maps the list:

$$[v_1, v_2, \ldots, v_n]$$

to the list:

$$[f\ v_1, f\ v_2, \ldots, f\ v_n]$$

Hence `map` $f$ is 'the function which applies $f$ to each element in a list'. The function `map` $f$ satisfies the recursion formula:

```
(map f) []                =  []
(map f) [v₁, v₂, ... , vₙ] =  (f v₁) ::((map f) [v₂, ... , vₙ])
```

This leads to the following declaration of `map` using an `fn`-expression on the right hand side:

```
fun map f = fn []     => []
            | (x::xs) => f x :: map f xs;
val map = fn : ('a -> 'b) -> 'a list -> 'b list
```

At this point we use the `fn`-expression on the right hand side to emphasize that `map f` is a function. In declaring higher-order functions one will normally prefer the form with several argument patterns shown in the next section.

We can write the subexpression `map f xs` without brackets because function application associates to the left and `map f xs` is, hence, interpreted as `((map f) xs)`. The expression `f x :: map f xs` in the second clause is therefore interpreted as `(f x) :: ((map f) xs)` because function application has higher precedence than any infix operator (like `::`).

The function `map` has a polymorphic type:

```
('a -> 'b) -> 'a list -> 'b list
```

The first part `'a -> 'b` is the type for the argument `f`. Furthermore, when `f` has this type, then the `fn`-expression in the declaration will have the type `'a list -> 'b list`.

The type constructor '`->`' *associates* to the *right*, so the type of map:

```
('a -> 'b) -> 'a list -> 'b list
```

means:

```
('a -> 'b) -> ('a list -> 'b list)
```

saying that the *argument* to map is a function of some type `'a -> 'b`, while the *value* is a function of type `'a list -> 'b list`.

We can apply map to the function `Int.toString` of type `int -> string`:

```
val g = map Int.toString;
```

The type of map tells us that the expression `map Int.toString` has type:

```
int list -> string list
```

because the type variables `'a` and `'b` occurring in the type for map are instantiated to `int` and `string`, respectively.

The function g applies `Int.toString` to each element in a list of integers:

```
g [1,~2,3];
val it = ["1", "~2", "3"] : string list
```

A number of functions on lists can be expressed by use of map.

The function map is predefined in SML.

## Example 9.1

Consider the function posList declared by:

```
fun posList []       = []
  | posList (x::xs) = (x > 0)::posList xs;
val posList = fn : int list -> bool list
```

The function transforms a list of integers into a list of Boolean values:

```
posList [4,~5,6];
val it = [true,false,true] : bool list
```

where an element is transformed into `true` if it is positive and `false` otherwise.

Hence, the function posList applies the function:

```
fn x => x > 0
```

to each element in a list of integers, and it can be declared using map:

```
val posList = map (fn x => x > 0);
val posList = fn : int list -> bool list
```

**Example 9.2**

Consider the function addElems declared by:

```
fun addElems []            = []
  | addElems ((x,y)::zs) = (x + y)::addElems zs;
val addElems = fn : (int * int) list -> int list
```

The function transforms a list of integer pairs into a list of integers:

```
addElems [(1,2),(3,4)];
val it = [3, 7] : int list
```

where each pair of integers in the list is transformed into their sum.

Hence, the function addElems applies the sum function:

```
op+
```

to each pair of integers in a list, and it can be declared using map by:

```
val addElems = map op+
val addElems = fn : (int * int) list -> int list
```

We have to use the nonfix form op + of the sum function as a function argument to a (higher-order) function in SML always must have nonfix status.

**9.4  Declaring higher order functions**

The syntax of SML allows the above declaration of map to be written in a form where the argument patterns in the fn expression have been moved to the left hand side of the equality sign:

```
fun map f []            = []
  | map f (x::xs) = f x :: map f xs;
val map = fn : ('a -> 'b) -> 'a list -> 'b list
```

This is the most readable and most commonly used form of declaration for a function where the value is again a function. Note that only the first pattern f is a pattern for the *argument* of the function map. The other patterns [] and (x::xs) are patterns for the argument of the *value* map f for the function map.

More generally, SML allows function declarations with an arbitrary number of argument patterns:

$$
\begin{array}{ll}
\text{fun} & f\ pat_{11}\ pat_{12}\ \ldots\ pat_{1n} = e_1 \\
\mid & f\ pat_{21}\ pat_{22}\ \ldots\ pat_{2n} = e_2 \\
\mid & \ldots \\
\mid & f\ pat_{k1}\ pat_{k2}\ \ldots\ pat_{kn} = e_k
\end{array}
$$

This function declaration is interpreted as the following value declaration:

```
val rec f = fn x₁ => fn x₂ => ... fn xₙ =>
                case (x₁, x₂, ... , xₙ)  of
                    (pat₁₁, pat₁₂, ... , pat₁ₙ)  =>  e₁
                  | (pat₂₁, pat₂₂, ... , pat₂ₙ)  =>  e₂
                    ...
                  | (patₖ₁, patₖ₂, ... , patₖₙ)  =>  eₖ
```

where each $x_i$ is a 'fresh' identifier not occurring in any expression and is not a constructor of a datatype or exception declaration.

The type of the function $f$ has the form:

$$\tau_1 \rightarrow \tau_2 \rightarrow \cdots \rightarrow \tau_n \rightarrow \tau$$

where the expressions $e_i$ all have type $\tau$.

Hence, the evaluation of a value (of a value, of a value, ...) of $f$:

$$f\ a_1\ a_2\ \ldots\ a_n$$

for arguments $a_1, a_2, \ldots, a_n$ searches the patterns:

$(pat_{11}, pat_{12}, \ldots, pat_{1n})$
$(pat_{21}, pat_{22}, \ldots, pat_{2n})$
...
$(pat_{k1}, pat_{k2}, \ldots, pat_{kn})$

for a pattern matching the tuple $(a_1, a_2, \ldots, a_n)$ and evaluates the associated expression with the bindings obtained by the matching. Note that $a_1$ is the *argument* of $f$, while $a_2$ is the argument of $(f\ a_1)$, and $a_3$ is the argument of $((f\ a_1)\ a_2)$, etc.

For example, the above declaration of map is equivalent to:

```
val rec map = fn x1 => fn x2 =>
                case (x1, x2) of
                    (f, [])    => []
                  | (f, x::xs) => f x :: map f xs;
val map = fn : ('a -> 'b) -> 'a list -> 'b list
```

## 9.5  Higher-order list functions

The Library contains a number of higher-order functions on lists. They can in many cases be used to declare functions on lists in a brief and elegant way. To familiarize the reader with these functions we give declarations for some of them and examples of their use. The reader is encouraged to use library functions whenever appropriate.

### 9.5.1  Functions using a predicate on the list elements

We consider declarations for the following higher-order functions: exists, all, find, filter and partition. They are useful in cases where we have a predicate $p$ on the list elements. These functions are found in the Library under the names List.exists, List.all, List.find, List.filter and List.partition, cf. Section D.4.

*The function:* exists:   ('a -> bool) -> 'a list -> bool

The higher-order function exists is declared by:

```
fun exists p []       = false
  | exists p (x::xs) = p x orelse exists p xs;
```

The value of the expression exists *p xs* is true, if there exists an element *x* of the list *xs* such that $p(x) = $ true, and false otherwise. For example:

```
exists (fn x => x>=2) [1,3,1,4];
val it = true : bool
```

The function member (see Section 5.7) can be declared using exists:

```
infix member;
fun x member ys = exists (fn y => x=y) ys;
val member = fn : ''a * ''a list -> bool

(2,3.0) member [(2, 4.0), (3, 7.0)];
val it = false : bool

"abc" member ["", "a", "ab", "abc"];
val it = true : bool
```

The evaluation of the expression exists $p$ $[x_1,x_2,\ldots x_{i-1},x_i,\ldots,x_n]$ does not terminate, if the evaluation of the expression $p(x_i)$ does not terminate for some $i$, where $1 \leq i \leq n$ and if $p(x_j) = $ false for all $j : 1 \leq j < i$. A similar remark will apply to the other functions declared below.

*The function:* all:   ('a -> bool) -> 'a list -> bool

The higher-order function all is declared by:

```
fun all p []       = true
  | all p (x::xs) = p x andalso all p xs;
```

The value of the expression all *p xs* is true, if $p(x) = $ true for all elements *x* of the list *xs*, and false otherwise. For example:

```
all (fn x => x>=2) [1,3,1,4];
val it = false : bool
```

*The function:* find:   ('a -> bool) -> 'a list -> 'a option

The higher-order function find is declared by:

```
fun find p []       = NONE
  | find p (x::xs) = if p x then SOME x else find p xs;
```

The value of the expression find $p$ $xs$ is SOME $x$ for an element $x$ of $xs$ with $p(x) =$ true, or NONE if no such element exists. For example:

```
find Char.isDigit [#"a",#"3", #"p", #"2"];
val it = SOME #"3" : char option
```

where Char.isDigit is the predicate on characters, which is true for the characters #"0", #"1", ... #"9", and false otherwise (cf. Section D.3.3).

*The function:* filter:   ('a -> bool) -> 'a list -> 'a list

The higher-order function filter is declared by:

```
fun filter p []        = []
  | filter p (x::xs) = if p x then x :: filter p xs
                       else filter p xs;
```

The value of the expression filter $p$ $xs$ is the list of those elements $x$ of $xs$ where $p(x) =$ true. For example:

```
filter Char.isAlpha [#"1", #"p", #"F", #"-"];
val it = [#"p", #"F"] : char list
```

where Char.isAlpha is the predicate on characters, which is true for the characters: #"A",#"B",...,#"Z",#"a",#"b",...,#"z", and false otherwise (cf. Section D.3.3).

*The function:* partition

The higher-order function partition has the type:

```
('a -> bool) -> 'a list -> 'a list * 'a list
```

and it is declared by:

```
fun partition p []        = ([],[])
  | partition p (x::xs) =
          let val (ys,zs) = partition p xs
          in if p x then (x::ys,zs)
             else          (ys,x::zs)
          end;
```

The value of the expression partition $p$ $xs$ is the pair of lists $ys$ and $zs$, where $ys$ contains those elements $x$ of $xs$ where $p(x) =$ true, while $zs$ contains the remaining elements of $xs$. For example:

```
partition Char.isLower [#"P",#"a",#"3",#"%",#"b"];
val it = ([#"a", #"b"], [#"P", #"3", #"%"])
        : char list * char list
```

where Char.isLower is the predicate on characters, which is true for the characters: #"a", #"b", ... #"z", and false otherwise (cf. Section D.3.3).

## 9.5.2    The functions `foldr` and `foldl`

In this section we study two higher-order functions `foldr` and `foldl`, which are more general than the ones studied in the previous section. The functions `foldr` and `foldl` are found in the Library, cf. Section D.4.

### The function: `foldr`

The higher-order function `foldr` 'accumulates' a function $f$ from a 'start value' $b$ over the elements of a list $[x_1, x_2, \ldots, x_n]$, where the list elements are taken from the right to the left.

Let the following be given:

● Types $\tau_1$ and $\tau_2$.

● A function $f$ of type. $\tau_1 * \tau_2 \rightarrow \tau_2$.

● A value $b$ of type $\tau_2$.

● A list $[x_1, x_2, \ldots, x_{n-2}, x_{n-1}, x_n]$ with elements of type $\tau_1$.

The value `foldr` $f\ b\ [x_1, x_2, \ldots, x_{n-2}, x_{n-1}, x_n]$ is then obtained by computing the values $b$, $f(x_n, b)$, $f(x_{n-1}, f(x_n, b))$, $f(x_{n-2}, f(x_{n-1}, f(x_n, b)))$, etc., where the list elements $x_n, x_{n-1}, x_{n-2}, \ldots, x_2, x_1$ are successively used in applications of the function $f$. This is expressed in the formula:

$$\text{foldr } f\ b\ [x_1, x_2, \ldots, x_{n-1}, x_n] = f(x_1, \underbrace{f(x_2, \ldots, f(x_{n-1}, f(x_n, b))\cdots))}_{\text{foldr } f\ b\ [x_2, \ldots, x_{n-1}, x_n]}$$

We obtain a recursion formula for `foldr` by observing that the underbraced sub-expression is equal to an application of `foldr` to other arguments:

$$\text{foldr } f\ b\ [x_1, x_2, \ldots, x_{n-1}, x_n] = f(x_1, \text{foldr } f\ b\ [x_2, \ldots, x_{n-1}, x_n])$$

This leads to the SML declaration:

```
fun foldr f b []      = b
  | foldr f b (x::xs) = f(x,foldr f b xs);
val foldr = fn : ('a * 'b -> 'b) -> 'b -> 'a list -> 'b
```

Note that the argument for `foldr` is a function $f$, and that `foldr` $f$ is again a function with argument $b$ where (`foldr` $f$) $b$ is again a function where the argument is a list. For example, a summation function `sumr` of the elements in an integer list is obtained from `foldr` using the function $f(x, y) = x + y$, i.e. op+, with start value 0:

```
fun sumr xs = foldr op+ 0 xs;
val sumr = fn : int list -> int

sumr [1,2,3,4];
val it = 10 : int
```

An alternative declaration of sumr is:

```
val sumr = foldr op+ 0;
```

We will use the last form whenever it is possible, but the restriction on values of polymorphic type will sometimes require us to use a fun declaration.

The length function on lists can be obtained from foldr using the function fn (_,y) => y+1 with start value 0. However, the length function cannot be declared as follows:

```
val length = foldr (fn (_,y) => y+1) 0;
! Toplevel input:
! val length = foldr (fn (_,y) => y+1) 0;
! ^^^^^^^^^^^^^^^^^^^^^^^^^^^^^^^^^^^^^^^^^^^^^^^^^
! Value polymorphism: Free type variable at top level
```

because the expression foldr (fn (_,y) => y+1) 0 has the polymorphic type 'a list -> int and it is not a value expression, cf. Section 5.5.

Since an fn-expression is a value expression, cf. Page 138, we can declare the function by:

```
val length = fn xs => foldr (fn (_,y) => y+1) 0 xs
val length = fn : 'a list -> int
```

However, in this case we prefer the shorter fun-declaration:

```
fun length xs = foldr (fn (_,y) => y+1) 0 xs;
val length = fn : 'a list -> int

length [4,5,6];
val it = 3 : int
```

Suppose that $\oplus$ is an infix operator. Then, the expression

$$\texttt{foldr op} \oplus\ b\ [x_1, x_2, \ldots, x_n]$$

evaluates as:

$$\texttt{foldr op} \oplus\ b\ [x_1, x_2, \ldots, x_n] \rightsquigarrow x_1 \oplus (x_2 \oplus \cdots \oplus (x_n \oplus b) \cdots)$$

which is seen by a more detailed evaluation:

$$
\begin{aligned}
&\quad \texttt{foldr op} \oplus\ b\ [x_1, x_2, \ldots, x_n] \\
&\rightsquigarrow \texttt{op} \oplus (x_1, \texttt{foldr op} \oplus\ b\ [x_2, \ldots, x_n]) \\
&= x_1 \oplus (\texttt{foldr op} \oplus\ b\ [x_2, \ldots, x_n]) \\
&\vdots \\
&\rightsquigarrow x_1 \oplus (x_2 \oplus \cdots \oplus (x_n \oplus (\texttt{foldr op} \oplus\ b\ [\,])) \cdots) \\
&\rightsquigarrow x_1 \oplus (x_2 \oplus \cdots \oplus (x_n \oplus b) \cdots)
\end{aligned}
$$

Hence, the elements in the list [1,2,3,4] will be added from 'right to left' in the evaluation of the expression sumr [1,2,3,4]:

```
      sumr [1,2,3,4]
  ⤳  foldr op+ 0 [1,2,3,4]
  ⤳  1 + (2 + (3 + (4 + 0)))
```

Using the cons operator ':::' for $\oplus$ we find that the expression

$$\texttt{foldr op}::\, bs\, [x_1, x_2, \ldots, x_n]$$

evaluates to

$$x_1 :: (x_2 :: \cdots :: (x_n :: bs) \cdots)$$

This is the value of $[x_1, x_2, \ldots, x_n] \,@\, bs$, so we may hence obtain the (prefix) append function:

$$\text{append}([x_1, x_2, \ldots, x_n], bs) = x_1 :: x_2 :: \cdots :: x_n :: bs$$

using foldr:

```
    fun append(xs,bs) = foldr op:: bs xs;
    val append = fn : 'a list * 'a list -> 'a list
```

For example:

```
    append([1,2,3],[4,5]);
    val it = [1,2,3,4,5] : int list
```

### The function: foldl

The higher-order function foldl has the same type as foldr:

```
    ('a * 'b -> 'b) -> 'b -> 'a list -> 'b
```

The foldl function 'accumulates' a function $f$ from a 'start value' $b$ over the elements of a list $[x_1, x_2, \ldots, x_{n-1}, x_n]$, where the list elements are taken from the left to the right. This is expressed in the formula:

$$\texttt{foldl}\ f\ b\ [x_1, x_2, \ldots, x_{n-1}, x_n] = \underbrace{f(x_n, f(x_{n-1}, \ldots, f(x_2, \overbrace{f(x_1, b)}^{b'}) \cdots))}_{\texttt{foldl}\ f\ b'\ [x_2, \ldots, x_{n-1}, x_n]}$$

We obtain a recursion formula for foldl by using the over- and underbraced expressions:

$$\texttt{foldl}\ f\ b\ [x_1, x_2, \ldots, x_{n-1}, x_n] = \texttt{foldl}\ f\ (f(x_1, b))\ [x_2, \ldots, x_{n-1}, x_n]$$

This leads to the SML declaration:

```
    fun foldl f b []       = b
      | foldl f b (x::xs) = foldl f (f(x,b)) xs;
```

Suppose that $\oplus$ is an infix operator. Then, the expression

$$\text{foldl op}\oplus\ b\ [x_1,x_2,\ldots,x_n]$$

evaluates as:

$$\text{foldl op}\oplus\ b\ [x_1,x_2,\ldots,x_n] \rightsquigarrow (x_n \oplus \cdots \oplus (x_2 \oplus (x_1 \oplus b))\cdots)$$

which is seen by a more detailed evaluation:

$$
\begin{aligned}
&\text{foldl op}\oplus\ b\ [x_1,x_2,\ldots,x_n] \\
\rightsquigarrow\quad &\text{foldl op}\oplus\ (\text{op}\oplus\ (x_1, b))\ [x_2,\ldots,x_n] \\
=\quad &\text{foldl op}\oplus\ (x_1 \oplus b)\ [x_2,\ldots,x_n] \\
\vdots\ \ & \\
\rightsquigarrow\quad &\text{foldl op}\oplus\ (x_n \oplus \cdots \oplus (x_2 \oplus (x_1 \oplus b))\cdots)\ [\,] \\
\rightsquigarrow\quad &(x_n \oplus \cdots \oplus (x_2 \oplus (x_1 \oplus b))\cdots)
\end{aligned}
$$

Hence, a summation function `sum1` of the elements in an integer list is obtained from `foldl` using the function $f(x, y) = x + y$, i.e. op+, with start value 0:

```
val sum1 = foldl op+ 0;
val sum1 = fn : int list -> int

sum1 [1,2,3,4];
val it = 10 : int
```

The elements in the list `[1,2,3,4]` are added from 'left to right' in the evaluation of the expression `sum1 [1,2,3,4]` because:

$$
\begin{aligned}
&\text{sum1 }[1,2,3,4] \\
\rightsquigarrow\quad &\text{foldl op+ 0 }[1,2,3,4] \\
\rightsquigarrow\quad &4 + (3 + (2 + (1 + 0)))
\end{aligned}
$$

Thus, we have that `sum1` and `sumr` compute the same results, but their evaluations are different as `sum1` performs the additions from 'left to right' while `sumr` performs the additions from 'right to left'.

Consider the reverse function:

$$\text{rev}\,[x_1, x_2, \ldots, x_n] = x_n :: \cdots :: x_2 :: x_1 :: [\,]$$

Since the expression `foldl op:: [] [`$x_1,x_2,\ldots,x_n$`]` evaluates to

$$(x_n :: \cdots :: (x_2 :: (x_1 :: [\,]))\cdots)$$

according to the above evaluation form for `foldl`, we can declare the function `rev` using `foldl`:

```
fun rev xs  = foldl op:: [] xs;
val rev = fn : 'a list -> 'a list
```

For example:

```
rev [1,2,3];
val it = [3, 2, 1] : int list
```

**Example 9.3**

The difference between `foldr` and `foldl` may be illustrated by the following example using the concatenation function `^` for strings (cf. Table D.14):

```
foldr op^ "nice" ["vacation ", "is "];
val it = "vacation is nice" : string

foldl op^ "nice" ["vacation ", "is "];
val it = "is vacation nice" : string
```

The `unzip` (cf. Section 5.6.4) function for lists of pairs can be obtained using the function:

```
fn ((x,y),(xs,ys)) => (x::xs,y::ys)
```

which 'cons'es' a pair `(x,y)` of elements to the front of a pair `(xs,ys)` of lists:

```
fun unzip s = foldr (fn ((x,y),(xs,ys)) => (x::xs,y::ys))
                    ([],[]) s                                    ;
val unzip = fn : ('a * 'b) list -> 'a list * 'b list

unzip [(1,"a"),(2,"b")];
val it = ([1,2],["a","b"]) : int list * string list
```

Using `foldl` we get a function `revunzip` where the lists are reversed:

```
fun revunzip s = foldl (fn ((x,y),(xs,ys)) => (x::xs,y::ys))
                       ([],[]) s                              ;
val revunzip = fn : ('a * 'b) list -> 'a list * 'b list

revunzip [(1,"a"),(2,"b")];
val it = ([2, 1], ["b", "a"]) : int list * string list
```

## 9.6 Functional composition

There are higher-order functions for all kinds of types. Consider, for example, the infix operator o denoting functional composition. It can be declared by:

```
infix 3 o
fun f o g = fn x => f(g x);
val o = fn : ('a -> 'b) * ('c -> 'a) -> 'c -> 'b
```

Using the form with several patterns on the left hand side this declaration becomes:

```
infix 3 o
fun (f o g) x = f(g x);
val o = fn : ('a -> 'b) * ('c -> 'a) -> 'c -> 'b
```

Brackets around 'f o g' are required to ensure a correct interpretation of the left-hand side: the pattern 'f o g x' would mean 'f o (g x)', as function application has a higher precedence than the infix operator 'o'.

The infix operator o is included in the Library.

## 9.7 Tree recursion

### 9.7.1 Electrical circuits

In the chapter on finite trees, we have seen many recursive functions traversing the trees. For each kind of tree one can define a higher-order function for the tree traversals.

We illustrate the idea by means of the representation of electrical circuits from Section 8.6. The circuit is modelled by a value of the following type:

```
datatype 'a circuit =
      Comp of 'a
    | Ser  of 'a circuit * 'a circuit
    | Par  of 'a circuit * 'a circuit
```

A general function for traversing circuits must be parameterized with three functions $c$, $s$ and $p$, where

● $c$ : 'a -> 'b
The value for a single component.

● $s$ : 'b * 'b -> 'b
The combined value for two circuits connected in series.

● $p$ : 'b * 'b -> 'b
The combined value for two circuits connected in parallel.

Note that $s$ and $p$ have the type 'b * 'b -> 'b because they operate on the values for two circuits. Thus, a general higher-order recursion function for circuits will have the type:

```
circRec : ('a -> 'b) * ('b * 'b -> 'b) * ('b * 'b -> 'b)
                                  -> 'a circuit -> 'b
```

and the function is declared by:

```
fun circRec (c,s,p) (Comp x)    = c x
  | circRec (c,s,p) (Ser(c1,c2)) =
                  s(circRec (c,s,p) c1, circRec (c,s,p) c2)
  | circRec (c,s,p) (Par(c1,c2)) =
                  p(circRec (c,s,p) c1, circRec (c,s,p) c2);
val circRec = fn
   : ('a -> 'b) * ('b * 'b -> 'b) * ('b * 'b -> 'b)
                                  -> 'a circuit -> 'b
```

The function `circRec` can, for example, be used to compute the number of components in a circuit by use of the following functions $c$, $s$ and $p$:

● $c$ is fn _ => 1
Each component counts for 1.

● $s$ is op+
The count for a serial composition is the sum of the counts.

● *p* is op+
The count for a parallel composition is the sum of the counts.

```
fun count cir = circRec (fn _ => 1, op+, op+) cir;
val count = fn : 'a circuit -> int

count (Ser(Par(Comp 0.25,Comp 1.0),Comp 1.5));
val it = 3 : int
```

Suppose that the value attached to every component in a circuit is the resistance of the component. Then the function `circRec` can be used to compute the resistance of a circuit by use of the following functions *c*, *s* and *p*:

● *c* is fn r => r
The attached value is the resistance.
● *s* is op+
The resistance of a serial composition is the sum of the resistances.
● *p* is fn(r1,r2) => 1.0/(1.0/r1+1.0/r2)
The resistance of a parallel composition is computed by this formula.

Using these functions for *c*, *s* and *p* we get:

```
fun resistance cir
    = circRec (fn r => r,
               op+,
               fn (r1,r2) => 1.0/(1.0/r1 + 1.0/r2)) cir;
val resistance = fn : real circuit -> real

resistance (Ser(Par(Comp 0.25,Comp 1.0),Comp 1.5));
val it = 1.7 : real
```

## 9.8 Type inference for higher-order functions

The function declarations in this chapter show that the type inference of the SML system is capable of inferring types for higher-order functions. In this section we illustrate the type inference by an example, namely the declaration of the `foldr` function:

```
fun foldr f b []        = b
  | foldr f b (x::xs) = f(x,foldr f b xs);
```

where the SML system infers the type:

```
('a * 'b -> 'b) -> 'b -> 'a list -> 'b
```

We can follow how the SML system is able to infer this type by the following steps:

**1.** The argument patterns in the declaration shows that the type of `foldr` has form:

$$\tau_1 \;\text{->}\; \tau_2 \;\text{->}\; \tau_3 \;\text{->}\; \tau_4$$

where f has type $\tau_1$, b has type $\tau_2$, `[]` and `(x::xs)` have type $\tau_3$, and b and `f(x,foldr f b xs)` have type $\tau_4$.

**2.** As b has type $\tau_2$ as well as type $\tau_4$ it follows that:

$$\tau_4 = \tau_2$$

**3.** The pattern `(x::xs)` shows that:

$$\tau_3 = \tau_5 \;\text{list}$$

where x has type $\tau_5$.

**4.** As `f(x,foldr f b xs)` has type $\tau_2$, f has type $\tau_1$, `foldr f b xs` has type $\tau_2$, and x has type $\tau_5$ it follows that:

$$\tau_1 = \tau_5 * \tau_2 \;\text{->}\; \tau_2$$

Hence the type of `foldr` is:

$$(\tau_5 * \tau_2 \;\text{->}\; \tau_2) \;\text{->}\; \tau_2 \;\text{->}\; \tau_5 \;\text{list} \;\text{->}\; \tau_2$$

Substituting type variables `'a` and `'b` for $\tau_5$ and $\tau_2$ we get the type inferred by the SML system:

```
('a * 'b -> 'b) -> 'b -> 'a list -> 'b
```

## 9.9　Closures

In this section we take a closer look at functions and evaluations involving functions. Internally in SML a function $f$ is represented by a *closure*, which is a triple

$$(env, x, e)$$

consisting of an environment *env*, an identifier $x$ and an expression $e$. The environment *env* contains the bindings of identifiers from the environment in which the expression denoting the function was evaluated.

### 9.9.1　Creating closures

The result of evaluating an `fn`-expression:

$$\text{fn } pat_1 \;\text{=>}\; e_1 \mid \ldots \mid pat_n \;\text{=>}\; e_n$$

is the closure:

$$\left(\textit{env, } x, \text{ case } x \text{ of } pat_1 \text{ => } e_1 \mid \dots \mid pat_n \text{ => } e_n\right)$$

where $x$ is a 'fresh' identifier which does not occur in any of the expressions $e_i$, and where the environment *env* contains bindings from the actual environment of those identifiers in the expressions $e_i$ which do not occur in the corresponding patterns $pat_i$.

The execution of a `fun` declaration:

```
fun f pat₁ = e₁
  | f pat₂ = e₂
    ...
  | f patₙ = eₙ
```

is the same as executing the `val` declaration:

```
val rec f = fn x => (case x of pat₁ => e₁
                            | pat₂ => e₂
                            | ...
                            | patₙ => eₙ)
```

as described on Page 141. Hence, the declaration evaluates the value of the `fn` expression in the current environment and binds the identifier $f$ to the resulting value which is a closure. This closure's environment contains bindings of identifiers in the expressions $e_i$ which do not occur in the corresponding patterns $pat_i$.

When evaluating applications of functions we distinguish between recursive functions where the identifier for the function occurs in the expression of the closure, and non-recursive functions where this is not the case.

## 9.9.2    Application of a non-recursive function

We assume now that $f$ is not recursive. Then, the expression $f(v)$, applying $f$ to $v$, is evaluated as follows:

$$\begin{aligned} & f(v) \\ \rightsquigarrow\; & (e, \textit{env}') \end{aligned}$$

where $(env, x, e)$ is the closure for $f$ and the environment $env'$ is obtained by extending the environment *env* with the binding $x \mapsto v$.

---

**Example 9.4**

Consider the following expression:

```
fn (a,0) => a*a | (a,b) => a+b
```

The result of evaluating this expression is the closure:

$$cls_1 = ([\,], x, \text{ case } x \text{ of } (a,0) \text{ => } a*a \mid (a,b) \text{ => } a+b)$$

where the environment contains no bindings because the only identifier occurring in the expression of the first clause, i.e. a, also occurs in the first pattern, and the two identifiers occurring in the expression of the second clause, i.e. a and b, occur in the second pattern.

The application of the above fn-expression to the argument (3,4) is evaluated as follows:

$$
\begin{array}{lll}
& \text{(fn (a,0) => a*a | (a,b) => a+b) (3,4)} & \\
\rightsquigarrow & cls_1 \ \text{(3,4)} & (1) \\
\rightsquigarrow & \text{(case x of (a,0) => a*a | (a,b) => a+b, } [x \mapsto (3,4)]) & (2) \\
\rightsquigarrow & \text{(a+b, } [a \mapsto 3, b \mapsto 4]) & (3) \\
\rightsquigarrow & 7 &
\end{array}
$$

The steps of this evaluation are:

**1.** The fn-expression evaluates to $cls_1$

**2.** The expression in $cls_1$ is evaluated in the environment obtained by matching the argument (3,4) with x.

**3.** Evaluation of a case-expression is as usual, i.e. (3,4) matches (a,b) etc.

---

**Example 9.5**

We now give an example where the environment of a closure plays a rôle. Consider the following declaration:

```
val ten = 10;
```

which gives the binding: ten $\mapsto$ 10.

The evaluation of the expression:

```
fn a => a+ten
```

then gives the closure:

$cls_2 = ([\text{ten} \mapsto 10], \text{x, case x of a => a+ten})$

where the binding ten $\mapsto$ 10 occurs in the environment of the closure because the identifier ten occurs in the expression but not in the pattern.

Applying fn a = a + ten to the argument 7 gives the evaluation:

$$
\begin{array}{lll}
& \text{(fn a => a+ten) 7} & \\
\rightsquigarrow & cls_2 \ 7 & \\
\rightsquigarrow & \text{(case x of a => a+ten, } [\text{ten} \mapsto 10, x \mapsto 7]) & (*) \\
\rightsquigarrow & \text{(a+ten, } [\text{ten} \mapsto 10, a \mapsto 7]) & \\
\rightsquigarrow & 17 &
\end{array}
$$

where the closure application in step (∗) evaluates to the case-expression in the closure, which should be evaluated in the environment obtained by extending the environment in the closure with the binding for x.

### 9.9.3  Application of a recursive function

Suppose that $f$ is a recursive function with closure $cls = (env, x, e)$, i.e. we assume the binding

$$f \mapsto cls$$

occurs in the actual environment and that the identifier $f$ occurs in the expression $e$.

The evaluation rule for $f(v)$ must take into account that $f$ occurs in the expression $e$ and this is done as follows:

$$\begin{array}{l} f(v) \\ \rightsquigarrow \quad (e, env') \end{array}$$

where the environment $env'$ is obtained by extending the environment $env$ from the closure $cls = (env, x, e)$ with the binding $x \mapsto v$ and the binding $f \mapsto cls$. Thus, the binding for $f$ is copied to the environment used during the evaluation of $e$.

---

**Example 9.6**

Consider the following declaration for the factorial function:

```
fun fact 0 = 1
  | fact n = n * fact(n-1);
val fact = fn : int -> int
```

This declaration is interpreted as the following val rec-declaration:

```
val rec fact = fn x => case x of 0 => 1 | n => n*fact(n-1);
val fact = fn : int -> int
```

Execution of the declaration will add the binding:

```
fact ↦ cls₃
```
where $cls_3 = ([\,], \text{x, case x of 0} => 1 \mid \text{n} => \text{n*fact(n-1)})$

to the actual environment.

The following evaluation illustrates the application of this recursive function:

$$
\begin{array}{ll}
\text{fact 2} & \\
\rightsquigarrow \quad \left( \begin{array}{l} \text{case x of 0 => 1 | n => n*fact(n-1),} \\ [\text{x} \mapsto 2, \text{fact} \mapsto cls_3] \end{array} \right) & (1) \\[2ex]
\rightsquigarrow \quad (\text{n*fact(n-1)}, [\text{n} \mapsto 2, \text{fact} \mapsto cls_3]) & (2) \\
\rightsquigarrow \quad 2*(\text{fact 1}, [\text{fact} \mapsto cls_3]) & (3) \\
\vdots & \\
\rightsquigarrow \quad 2*(1*(\text{fact 0}, [\text{fact} \mapsto cls_3])) & (4) \\[1ex]
\rightsquigarrow \quad 2* \left( 1* \left( \begin{array}{l} \text{case x of 0 => 1 | n => n*fact(n-1),} \\ [\text{x} \mapsto 0, \text{fact} \mapsto cls_3] \end{array} \right) \right) & (5) \\[2ex]
\rightsquigarrow \quad 2*(1*1) & (6) \\
\rightsquigarrow \quad 2 & (7)
\end{array}
$$

where the steps are:

**1.** The closure $cls_3$ for `fact` is found in the actual environment, and the application is evaluated to the expression in $cls_3$. The environment contains a binding for x and one for `fact` because the declaration of `fact` is recursive.

**2.** Evaluation of the case-expression. The binding for x are removed from the environment as x does not occur in the resulting expression.

**3.** Evaluation of arguments for multiplication and `fact`. The bindings for n are removed from the environment as n does not occur in the resulting expression.

**4.** Repetition of the above steps.

**5.** Evaluate the expression in the closure with bindings for x and `fact`.

**6.** Evaluate the case-expression. Remove all local bindings as no identifiers occur in the resulting expression.

**7.** Perform multiplications.

## 9.10 Static binding

In SML it is possible to give a new declaration of an identifier, say $x$, which has already been declared. This re-declaration of $x$ gives a new binding of $x$ but it does not change the bindings of other identifiers whose declarations depend on $x$. One says that SML uses *static binding* of identifiers.

Using the notion of a closure we can explain how SML implements static binding. Consider, for example, the declarations:

```
val ten = 10;
```

```
val f = fn a => a+ten;
```

The execution of these two declarations will add the following bindings:

```
ten  ↦   10
f    ↦   ([ten ↦ 10], x, case x of a => a+ten)
```

to the actual environment. Note that the closure for f contains the binding for `ten` which was valid at the time when f was declared.

A new declaration for `ten` will change the binding for `ten` in the actual environment, but all other bindings will remain unchanged. For example, after the execution of:

```
val ten = 11;
```

the actual environment will contain the following bindings for `ten` and f:

```
ten  ↦   11
f    ↦   ([ten ↦ 10], x, case x of a => a+ten)
```

and we see that the binding for f remains unchanged. Thus the use of closures gives the static binding of functions.

The static binding in SML yields the desirable property that a re-declaration of one identifier (e.g. ten) causes a change of the binding for that identifier only, while other bindings, e.g. of f, remain unchanged.

## 9.11 Lazy evaluation

The evaluation of an SML expression is *eager*: when evaluating a function application $f(e_1, \ldots, e_n)$ with a tuple $(e_1, \ldots, e_n)$ of expressions as argument, SML first evaluates the value of $f$ (i.e. a closure) and then the values $v_1, \ldots, v_n$ of the expressions $e_1, \ldots, e_n$ to form a tuple $(v_1, \ldots, v_n)$. Afterwards, SML evaluates the function application $f(v_1, \ldots, v_n)$.

Consider, for example, the function ifthenelse declared by:

```
fun ifthenelse(x,y,z) = if x then y else z
```

An application ifthenelse$(e_1, e_2, e_3)$ is evaluated by first obtaining a closure *cls* for ifthenelse and then values $v_1$, $v_2$ and $v_3$ of $e_1$, $e_2$ and $e_3$. After that the application $cls(v_1, v_2, v_3)$ is evaluated.

This function hence does *not* work like the if-then-else- construct. A difference is that the evaluation of ifthenelse$(e_1, e_2, e_3)$ does not terminate when the evaluation of $e_3$ does not terminate, even when $e_1$ evaluates to true. Thus, the evaluation of ifthenelse$(e_1, e_2, e_3)$ eagerly evaluates all arguments $e_1$, $e_2$ and $e_3$, even when this is not necessary.

Using the fn-notation we may, however, make a construction which works exactly like if $e_1$ then $e_2$ else $e_3$:

```
(fn true => e₂ | false => e₃) e₁
```

The point is that the expressions $e_2$ and $e_3$ are packaged into the closure *without* being evaluated. The subsequent evaluation of the application of the closure to $e_1$ evaluates $e_1$ and selects one of the expressions $e_2$ or $e_3$ for evaluation while the other is left untouched.

We may, in general, 'package' any expression $e$ as the body of a function by the construct:

```
fn _ => e
```

The evaluation of this expression gives a closure containing the expression $e$ in non-evaluated form. The expression $e$ is evaluated later when the closure is applied to an argument, e.g. the dummy value ():

```
(fn _ => e ) ()
```

Using this idea we might declare an ifthenelse function:

```
fun ifthenelse(x,y,z) = if x then y() else z();
val ifthenelse = fn
  : bool * (unit -> 'a) * (unit -> 'a) -> 'a
```

The expression if $e_1$ then $e_2$ else $e_3$ is then obtained by using function expressions fn _ => $e_2$ and fn _ => $e_3$ in the argument:

ifthenelse($e_1$, fn _ => $e_2$, fn _ => $e_3$)

If $e_1$ evaluates to true then the evaluation of this expression will evaluate $e_2$, owing to the evaluation of (fn _ => $e_2$)(), and leave $e_3$ untouched. Similarly, if $e_1$ evaluates to false then the evaluation will evaluate $e_3$ and leave $e_2$ untouched. In either case *only* *one* of the expressions $e_2$ and $e_3$ will be evaluated.

Hence the idea of using fn _ => $e$ to package an expression $e$ for later evaluation gives a simulation in SML of functions with a lazy evaluation of arguments. We will, however, not pursue this idea.

## 9.12  Summary

In this chapter we introduced functions as 'first class citizens of SML', i.e. functions can be arguments of functions, and the value of a function application can be a function. The notion of *closure* was introduced to explain this meaning of functions. A function is actually represented internally in the SML system by a closure. The fn-notation was introduced as a convenient way of expressing *anonymous functions*.

The notion of higher-order functions is a powerful abstraction mechanism and can be used in declaring other functions in a succinct way. A collection of fundamental higher-order functions on lists was given: map, exists, all, find, filter, partition, foldr and foldl. The functions map, foldr and foldl are predefined in SML, whereas the others are found in the Library.

We have also shown higher-order functions for trees.

The keyword op defines a temporary conversion of an infix identifier to the corresponding (prefix) function. This is particularly convenient when higher-order functions are applied to infix identifiers.

## Exercises

**9.1** Let marks at the Technical University of Denmark (see Exercise 7.4) be modelled by

```
datatype mark = Scale of int | Passed of bool;
```

(a) Write an fn expression for an anonymous function of type mark -> bool, whose value is true for marks belonging to the 13-scale (the integers 0, 3, 5, 6, 7, 8, 9, 10, 11, 13).

(b) Declare a function remove: mark list -> mark list, where remove(*ms*) is the list of marks obtained from *ms* by removing marks not belonging to the 13-scale. Use filter and an anonymous function.

(c) Declare a function for converting a list of 13-scale marks into the corresponding list of integers. Use map and an anonymous function.

(d) Use `foldl` or `foldr` to declare a function computing the number of passed courses from a collection of marks.

(e) Declare a function for computing the mean value of a list of marks ignoring marks not belonging to the 13-scale.

**9.2** (a) Solve Exercise 5.14 using higher-order functions.

(b) Solve Exercise 5.15 using `foldr` or `foldl`.

(c) Solve Exercise 5.16(a) using higher-order functions.

(d) Solve Exercise 6.2 using higher-order functions.

**9.3** Declare a function `min` of type `(int -> int) -> int`. The value of `min(f)` is the smallest natural number $n$ where $f(n) = 0$ (if it exists).

**9.4** Declare a function `downto1` such that:

$$\begin{aligned} \texttt{downto1}\ f\ n\ e &= f(1, f(2, \ldots, f(n-1, f(n, e))\ldots)) & \text{for } n > 0 \\ \texttt{downto1}\ f\ n\ e &= e & \text{for } n \leq 0 \end{aligned}$$

Declare the factorial function by use of `downto1`.

Use `downto1` to declare a function that builds the list $[g(1), g(2), \ldots, g(n)]$ for a function $g$ and an integer $n$.

**9.5** The functions `curry` and `uncurry` of types

```
curry   : ('a * 'b -> 'c) -> 'a -> 'b -> 'c
uncurry : ('a -> 'b -> 'c) -> 'a * 'b -> 'c
```

are defined in the following way:

● curry $f$ is the function $g$ where $g\ x$ is the function $h$ where $h\ y = f(x, y)$.
● uncurry $g$ is the function $f$ where $f(x, y)$ is the value $h\ y$ for the function $h = g\ x$.

Write declarations of `curry` and `uncurry`.

**9.6** Declare a function to extract the list of components occurring in a circuit (cf. Sections 8.6 and 9.7).

**9.7** Higher-order functions can also be defined for trees. Consider for example the following fold function for ancestor trees discussed in Section 8.3:

```
fun foldAncTree f e Unspec          = e
  | foldAncTree f e (Info(s,t1,t2)) =
        f(s, foldAncTree f e t1, foldAncTree f e t2);
```

(a) Declare the SML functions `pre_listof`, `in_listof` and `post_listof` for pre-order, in-order and post-order traversal of ancestor trees using `foldAncTree`.

(b) Declare the SML function `maleanc` to extract the list of male ancestors from a ancestor tree using an expression containing `foldAncTree`.

**9.8** Consider the declaration:

```
fun p q []       = []
  | p q (x::xs) = let val ys = p q xs
                  in if q x then x::ys else ys@[x]
                  end;
```

Find the type for p and explain the value of the expression:

$$p \, q \, [x_1, x_2, x_3, \ldots, x_n]$$

**9.9** Consider the declaration:

```
fun f g []       = []
  | f g (x::xs) = g x :: f (fn y => g(g y)) xs;
```

Find the type for f and explain the value of the expression:

$$f \, g \, [x_1, x_2, x_3, \ldots, x_n]$$

## Chapter 10

# Finite sets

In solving programming problems it is often convenient to use values that are *finite sets* of form $\{a_1, a_2, \ldots, a_n\}$ with elements $a_1, \ldots, a_n$ from some set $A$. The notion of a set provides a useful abstraction in cases where we have an unordered collection of elements where repetitions among the elements are of no concern.

This chapter introduces a representation of sets and operations on sets in SML. The focus is on the principal issues so the chapter contains only declarations for a selected part of the functions on sets. The full set of declarations is found in Appendix E describing a Set module. The use of sets in programming is illustrated by an example.

## 10.1  A representation of sets

In this section we represent a set by a list of its elements, so that no element has more than one occurrence in the list. Thus, a list $[a_1, a_2, \ldots a_n]$ representing a set must satisfy the *invariant* that there are no replicated elements, i.e. $a_i \neq a_j$ for $i \neq j$.

For example [1,2,10], [1,10,2], [2,1,10], [2,10,1], [10,1,2] and [10,2,1] are the six possible representations for the integer set $\{1, 2, 10\}$. The list [1,2,10,2] is not a legal representation of an integer set as the integer 2 occurs twice in the list.

A type constructor for sets is declared by:

```
type 'a set = 'a list                    (*no replicated elements*)
```

Examples of values of type `bool set` are:

```
[] : bool set;
```

```
[true] : bool set;
```

and the following value has type `int list set`:

```
[ [1,2,3], [] , [2,7,2]] : int list set;
```

Appendix E describes a library `Set` of functions on sets using this representation. This chapter explains the declaration of some of the functions in the library and it gives some applications of sets.

## 10.2 Operations on sets

Using the above representation we can declare operations on sets.

*The value:* `empty`

The empty set is represented by the empty list:

```
val empty = [];
```

*The function:* `singleton`

The `singleton` function where $singleton(a) = \{a\}$ is declared by:

```
fun singleton a = [a];
```

*The function:* `member`

The `member` function where $member(x, ys) = x \in ys$ can be declared using the `exists` function on lists:

```
fun member(x, ys) = List.exists (fn y => x = y) ys;
```

as we have $x \in \{y_1, y_2, \dots, y_n\}$ when one of $x = y_1, x = y_2, \dots, x = y_n$ evaluates to true.

*The function:* `insert`

The `insert` function where $insert(x, ys) = \{x\} \cup ys$ adds the element $x$ to the set $ys$. It must be declared such that it preserves the invariant, i.e. the list should be unchanged if the element is already in the list:

```
fun insert(x, ys) = if member(x, ys) then ys else x::ys;
```

*The function:* `union`

The union function where $\text{union}(xs, ys) = xs \cup ys$ satisfies the identity:

$$\text{union}(\{x_1, x_2, \ldots, x_n\}, ys)$$
$$= \quad \text{insert}(x_n, \text{insert}(x_{n-1}, \cdots \text{insert}(x_2, \text{insert}(x_1, ys))\cdots))$$

so we can declare `union` by applying the `foldl` function for lists to the `insert` function:

```
fun union(xs, ys) = List.foldl insert ys xs;
```

*The function:* `inter`

The set intersection $\text{inter}(s_1, s_2) = s_1 \cap s_2$ may be expressed by using the `filter` function on lists:

```
fun inter(xs, ys) = List.filter (fn x => member(x, ys)) xs;
```

*The function:* `diff`

The set difference $\text{diff}(s_1, s_2) = s_1 \setminus s_2$ may be expressed by using the `filter` function on lists:

```
fun diff(xs, ys)  =
    List.filter (fn x => not (member(x, ys))) xs;
```

*The function:* `delete`

The `delete` function where $\text{delete}(xs, y) = xs \setminus \{y\}$ is declared by:

```
fun delete([], _)    = []
  | delete(x::xs, y) = if x=y then xs else x::delete(xs,y);
```

where we exploit the invariant, i.e. if $x :: xs$ represents a set and $x = y$, then $y$ cannot occur in $xs$ and we need not delete $y$ from $xs$ in this case.

*The function:* `subset`

The subset predicate $\subseteq$ satisfies the formula:

$$\{x_1, x_2, \ldots, x_n\} \subseteq ys \text{ if and only if } x_1 \in ys \wedge x_2 \in ys \wedge \ldots \wedge x_n \in ys$$

so the subset function where $\text{subset}(xs, ys) = xs \subseteq ys$ can be expressed using the function `all` for lists:

```
fun subset(xs, ys) = List.all (fn x => member(x, ys)) xs;
```

*The function:* `equal`

We have $s_1 = s_2$ if and only if $s_1 \subseteq s_2$ and $s_2 \subseteq s_1$, so equality of sets can be declared by:

```
fun equal(xs, ys) = subset(xs, ys) andalso subset(ys, xs);
```

*The function:* `fromList`

The function `fromList` converts from a list to a set representation. The function must remove replicated elements from the list as the resulting set representation must satisfy the invariant, i.e. there must be no replicated elements in the result. We obtain `fromList` $[x_1, \ldots , x_n]$ by gradually inserting the list elements into a set, starting with the empty set:

$$\text{fromList}\,[x_1, \ldots , x_n]$$
$$= \text{insert}(x_n, \text{insert}(x_{n-1}, (\cdots \text{insert}(x_2, \text{insert}(x_1, \text{empty}))\cdots)))$$

so `fromList` can be declared by use of the `foldl` function on lists:

```
fun fromList xs = List.foldl insert empty xs;
```

*The function:* `toList`

The function `toList` converts from a set representation to a list. The function is declared as the identity on the set representation:

```
fun toList xs = xs;
```

*The function:* `card`

Cardinality can be declared by using the `length` function on lists, since no element is repeated in a list representing a set:

```
val card = List.length;
```

*The function:* `filter`

The `filter` function is a higher-order function to denote *set comprehension*:

$$\text{filter}\,p\,s = \{x \in s \mid p(x)\}$$

i.e. `filter` $p$ $s$ is the set of elements in $s$ satisfying the predicate $p$ and it can be declared using `filter` on lists:

```
val filter = List.filter;
```

*The function:* `map`

The map function applies a function $f$ to each element of a set $s$:

$$\text{map}\,f\,\{a_1, a_2, \ldots , a_n\} \quad = \quad \{f(a_1), f(a_2), \ldots , f(a_n)\}$$

We cannot just use the `map` function for lists on the list $[a_1, \ldots , a_n]$ as the resulting list $[f(a_1), \ldots , f(a_n)]$ may contain replicated elements and may hence not satisfy the invariant. The map function can be obtained by gradually inserting the values $f(a_1)$, $f(a_2)$, $\ldots$ , $f(a_n)$ in a set, starting from the empty set. So map can be declared by using `foldl` on lists:

```
fun map f s =
   List.foldl (fn (y,ys) => insert(f y, ys)) empty s;
```

*The function:* `fold`

The higher-order function `fold` accumulates a function $f$ over the elements of a set representation:

$$\text{fold } f\ b\ \{a_1, a_2, \dots, a_n\} = f(a_1, f(a_2, f(\cdots, f(a_n, b)\cdots)))$$
$$\text{fold } f\ b\ \emptyset = b$$

It is declared using the `foldl` function on lists:

```
val fold = List.foldl;
```

*The function:* `split`

The function `split` partitions a set representation into an element and a remaining part:

```
fun split []      = NONE
  | split(x::xs) = SOME(x,xs);
```

## 10.3  An abstype for sets

It is possible for a user of the set functions declared above to violate the invariant for the set representation. For example, the following expression does not correspond to a meaningful set expression:

```
member(1, delete([1,1,2],1));
val it = true : bool
```

The problem is that the list `[1,1,2]` with two occurrences of 1 is not a legal representation of a set.

This problem can be avoided using an `abstype`-declaration, as we have seen in Section 8.7. For example, an abstract type for sets can be declared by:

```
abstype ''a absset = Set of ''a list
with
   val absempty = Set [];

   fun abssingleton a = Set [a];

   fun absmember(x, Set ys) = List.exists (fn y => x=y) ys;

   fun absinsert(x, ays as Set ys) =
           if absmember(x, ays) then ays else Set(x::ys);
```

⋮

```
      fun absdelete(Set [], _)     = Set []
        | absdelete(Set(x::xs), y) =
              if x=y then Set xs
              else let val Set xs' = absdelete(Set xs, y)
                   in Set(x::xs')
                   end;



      fun abstoList(Set xs) = xs;



  end;
```

where we have renamed the identifiers. The internal representation of a set has the form: Set $[x_1, \ldots, x_n]$, where there are no replicated elements in the list.

The answer from the SML system is:

```
abstype 'a absset
val absempty = <absset> : ''a absset
val abssingleton = fn : ''a -> ''a absset
val absmember = fn : ''a * ''a absset -> bool
val absinsert = fn : ''a * ''a absset -> ''a absset
  ⋮
val absdelete = fn : ''a absset * ''a -> ''a absset
  ⋮
val abstoList = fn : ''a absset -> ''a list
  ⋮
```

and we see that the only way to construct and manipulate abstract sets is by using the functions – the constructor Set is not visible to the user. For example:

```
val s1 = absinsert(1, abssingleton 2);
val s1 = <absset> : int absset

abstoList s1;
val it = [1, 2] : int list

Set [1, 1];
! Toplevel input:
! Set [1, 1];
! ...
! Unbound value identifier: Set
```

We will not go any further in the discussion of an abstype for sets. However, in the next chapter we show how to construct a library Set containing the declarations for set values and functions, and in Appendix E there is a documentation for the Set library.

> **Remark**
>
> The declaration: abstype ''a absset = Set of ''a list ... contains the
> equality type variable ''a. This constrains the type of the constructor Set to
> ''a list -> ''a absset, so, for example, the value absempty gets the type
> ''a absset. Note that the type constructor absset is not influenced by the
> equality type variable ''a in the declaration.

## Example 10.1

### Conference information

This section illustrates the use of the Set library (cf. Appendix E) on a simple example. The organizers of a conference keep a record of the contributions, which will be presented at the conference. Each contribution is characterized by a title and the list of contributing authors. The first mentioned author will present the work. Each author is characterized by a name and a nationality.

We model this information by the following SML types:

```
datatype country  = DK | UK | ES | SF
                  | PRC | C | D | IS | S | N
type name         = string
type title        = string
type author       = name * country
type contribution = title * author list
type conference   = contribution Set.set;
```

The set type Set.set is taken from the Set library, which contains entities Set.set, Set.empty, etc. corresponding to the specification in Appendix E.

Consider the following example of a conference with four contributions:

```
val c1 = ("Processors", [("Lu", PRC), ("Olsen",DK)]);

val c2 = ("Scheduling", [("Suonio", SF), ("Weber",D)]);

val c3 = ("RLucid", [("Plaice",C)]);

val c4 = ("Timed Observations", [("Ortega",ES)]);

val conf =  Set.fromList [c1, c2, c3, c4];
```

Questions about this conference can now be stated and answered using functions on sets and lists.

### Q1: What are the nationalities of the authors of a given contribution?

The function `nationalitiesOf: contribution -> country Set.set` answers this question:

```
fun nationalitiesOf(_,al) =
   Set.fromList (List.map (fn (_,c) => c) al);
```

where the expression

```
List.map (fn (_,c) => c) al
```

gives the list of countries for the list of authors al.

The set of countries of authors of c1 is `nationalitiesOf c1` and the corresponding list is obtained by applying the `Set.toList` function:

```
Set.toList(nationalitiesOf c1);
val it = [DK, PRC] : country list
```

### Q2: How many contributions for the conference are co-authored by Nordic authors?

The predicate `haveNordic: contribution -> bool` declared by:

```
val nordic = Set.fromList [IS, DK, S, N, SF];

fun haveNordic c
   = not ( Set.equal (Set.inter(nationalitiesOf c, nordic)
                      , Set.empty));
```

holds for contributions co-authored by Nordic authors. An answer to question Q2 can hence be given using set comprehension and cardinality:

```
Set.card (Set.filter haveNordic conf);
val it = 2 : int
```

### Q3: What is the title and the name of the first author of every conference contribution?

The title and the name of the first author of a contribution is extracted by the function:

```
fn (t,(n,_)::_) => (t,n);
```

so the set of all such pairs is obtained by applying this function to each conference contribution:

```
Set.toList(Set.map (fn (t,(n,_)::_) => (t,n)) conf);
val it = [("Processors", "Lu"),
          ("Scheduling", "Suonio"),
          ("RLucid", "Plaice"),
          ("Timed Observations", "Ortega")]
              : (title * name) list
```

The function presentations : conference -> (title * name) Set.set declared using the split function may instead be used to answer this question:

```
fun presentations cnf =
   case (Set.split cnf) of
        NONE                         => Set.empty
      | SOME((t,(n,_)::_),cnf') =>
              Set.insert((t,n), presentations cnf');
```

```
Set.toList(presentations conf);
val it = [("Timed Observations","Ortega"),
          ("RLucid","Plaice"),
          ("Scheduling","Suonio"),
          ("Processors","Lu")] : (title * name) list
```

Even though presentations can be declared by using Set.map rather than Set.split, we see that Set.split provides a kind of pattern matching for set representations and this is often useful when declaring recursive functions.

### Q4: What are the countries of the conference contributions?

The following function adds the nationalities of the contribution c to the set s:

```
fn (c,s) => Set.union(nationalitiesOf c, s);
```

We fold this function over the set of conference contributions:

```
Set.toList(
   Set.fold (fn (c,s) => Set.union(nationalitiesOf c, s))
            Set.empty conf);
val it = [PRC, DK, SF, D, C, ES] : country list
```

## 10.4  Other representations of sets

The representation discussed in Section 10.1 has a weakness when we build sets of sets using the set operations from Section 10.2. Below we analyse this weakness and give a solution.

### 10.4.1  A problem with sets of sets

We can form sets whose members are sets themselves, e.g. {{2, 3}} which is a set of sets of integers. Using the above SML representation of sets we may get two representations s1 and s2 of this set by inserting the elements 2 and 3 in different orders:

```
val e1 = insert(2, singleton 3);
val s1 = singleton e1;
val s1 = [[2,3]] : int list list
```

```
val s2 = singleton (insert(3, singleton 2));
val s2 = [[3,2]] : int list list
```

Testing for equality will, however, not recognize s1 and s2 as being equal:

```
equal(s1, s2);
val it = false : bool
```

The evaluation of equal(s1, s2) shows the problem:

```
      equal([[2,3]],[[3,2]])
  ↝   subset([[2,3]], [[3,2]]) andalso ...
  ↝   member([2,3], [[3,2]]) andalso ...
  ↝   ([2,3]=[3,2] orelse ([2,3] member [])) andalso ...
  ↝   false
```

The problem is that the function member uses the SML equality in determining membership of a set. When the elements are themselves sets, this does not give the proper result, as the plain SML equality for the representing lists does not express the equality for the elements (e.g. {2, 3} and {3, 2} are equal, while [2,3] and [3,2] are different). Hence the function equal is to be used on the representations (e.g. [2,3] and [3,2]) in deciding equality of the corresponding elements.

## 10.4.2    Representation of sets with equality function

The way to cope with the above problem is to include an explicit equality function for elements in the representation of sets instead of just using the SML equality on the elements. The representation is hence:

```
type 'a set = 'a list * ('a * 'a -> bool);
```

where the first component is a list of the elements in the set, while the second component is the equality function on elements.

The invariant of a set representation $s = ([a_1, \ldots, a_n], eq)$ is hence: $eq$ is the equality predicate, and the elements $a_1, \ldots, a_n$ are different (i.e. $eq(a_i, a_j) = \text{false}$ for $i \neq j$).

In forming the representation $([\,], eq)$ of the empty set we need to know the equality predicate $eq$, so empty becomes a function of the equality predicate:

```
fun empty eq = ([], eq): 'a set;
```

The function singleton is also a function of the equality predicate:

```
fun singleton(x, eq) = ([x],eq): 'a set;
```

The member function uses the equality predicate from the set representation instead of the equality predicate in SML:

```
fun member(x, ([],_))      = false
  | member(x, (y::l, eq)) = eq(x,y) orelse member(x, (l,eq));
```

The insertion function is obtained by modifying the declaration given in Section 10.2 taking the equality predicate into account:

```
fun insert(x, (s as (l,eq))) = if member(x, s) then s
                               else (x::l,eq);
```

Examples of the use of these functions are:

```
val s1 = insert(2, singleton(3, op=));
val s1 = ([2,3],fn) : int set

val s2 = insert(1, s1);
val s2 = ([1,2,3],fn) : int set

val s3 = insert(3, insert(2, singleton(1, op=)));
val s3 = ([3,2,1],fn) : int set
```

We give declarations for some of the remaining functions:

```
fun union(([],_),s)       = s
  | union((x::xs,eq), s) = union((xs,eq), insert(x, s));

fun inter(([],eq), _)     = ([],eq)
  | inter((x::xs,eq), s) = if member(x, s)
                           then insert(x, inter((xs,eq), s))
                           else inter((xs,eq), s);

fun subset(([],_), s)     = true
  | subset((x::xs,eq), s) = member(x, s)
                            andalso subset((xs,eq), s);

fun equal(s1, s2) = subset(s1, s2) andalso subset(s2, s1);
```

For example:

```
subset(s2, s3);
val it = true : bool

val s4 = insert(3, singleton(4, op=));
val s4 = ([3,4],fn) : int set

inter(s1, s4);
val it = ([3],fn) : int set

union(s1, s4);
val it = ([2,3,4],fn) : int set
```

```
subset(s3, s4);
val it = false : bool
```

With this representation we can handle sets of sets. For example:

```
val s5 = singleton(s1, equal);
val s5 = ([([2,3],fn)],fn) : (int set) set

val s6 = insert(3, singleton(2, op=));
val s6 = ([3,2],fn) : int set

val s7 = singleton(s6, equal);
val s7 = ([([3,2],fn)],fn) : (int set) set

equal(s5, s7);
val it = true : bool
```

The value of s5 represents the set $\{\{2, 3\}\}$ containing the single element $\{2, 3\}$, which is again a set. It has the form: $([([2, 3], eq_1)], eq_2)$, where $eq_1$ is the equality predicate on integers, and $eq_2$ is the equality predicate equal defined on sets of integers. Thus, this representation works properly also for sets where the elements themselves are sets, but we must include the equality operation on elements as part of the representation of sets.

Note that application of the above functions to a pair of set representations, e.g. union(s1,s2) is meaningful only when the set representations s1 and s2 contain the same equality function – and this condition is not checked. We shall see in Chapter 11 on the SML module system that the functor concept allows us to build a set representation where the condition on the equality predicates is checked by the SML type check.

## 10.5  Summary

The SML language does not have a predefined type for sets as it does for numbers, lists, etc. The reason is that sets are not freely generated, i.e. a given set can be generated in different ways from its elements.

We have discussed several ways to model sets in SML, and we have discussed fundamental set functions, for example, member, union, inter, diff, subset, equal, card, filter, map, fold.

## Exercises

**10.1** This exercise uses the conference example in the text, and the functions answering the below questions should (at least) be tested on the set of contributions *conf* in this example.

(a) Declare a function to compute the number of Nordic authors contributing papers to the conference.

(b) Declare a function computing the largest number of Nordic authors for any individual paper in the conference.

(c) Declare a function listing the titles of those papers where no two authors have the same nationality.

**10.2** We define a *relation* from a set $A$ to a set $B$ as a subset of $A \times B$. A relation $r'$ is said to be *smaller* than $r$, if $r'$ is a subset of $r$, i.e. if $r' \subseteq r$. A relation $r$ is called *finite* if it is a finite subset of $A \times B$. Assuming that the sets $A$ and $B$ are represented by SML equality types ''a and ''b we can represent a finite relation $r$ by a value of type (''a * ''b) set.

(a) The domain dom $r$ of a relation $r$ is the set of elements $a$ in $A$ where there exists an element $b$ in $B$ such that $(a, b) \in r$. Write an SML declaration expressing the domain function.

(b) The range rng $r$ of a relation $r$ is the set of elements $b$ in $B$ where there exists an element $a$ in $A$ such that $(a, b) \in r$. Write an SML declaration expressing the range function.

(c) If $r$ is a finite relation from $A$ to $B$ and $a$ is an element of $A$, then the application of $r$ to $a$, apply $(r, a)$, is the set of elements $b$ in $B$ such that $(a, b) \in r$. Write an SML declaration expressing the apply function.

(d) A relation $r$ from a set $A$ to the same set is said to be *symmetric* if $(a_1, a_2) \in r$ implies $(a_2, a_1) \in r$ for any elements $a_1$ and $a_2$ in $A$. The symmetric closure of a relation $r$ is the smallest symmetric relation containing $r$. Declare an SML function to compute the symmetric closure.

(e) The relation composition $r \circ\circ s$ of a relation $r$ from a set $A$ to a set $B$ and a relation $s$ from $B$ to a set $C$ is a relation from $A$ to $C$. It is defined as the set of pairs $(a, c)$ where there exist an element $b$ in $B$ such that $(a, b) \in r$ and $(b, c) \in s$. Declare an SML function to compute the relational composition.

(f) A relation $r$ from a set $A$ to the same set $A$ is said to be *transitive* if $(a_1, a_2) \in r$ and $(a_2, a_3) \in r$ implies $(a_1, a_3) \in r$ for any elements $a_1$, $a_2$ and $a_3$ in $A$. The transitive closure of a relation $r$ is the smallest transitive relation containing $r$. If $r$ contains $n$ elements, then the transitive closure can be computed as the union of the following $n$ relations:

$$r \cup (r \circ\circ r) \cup (r \circ\circ r \circ\circ r) \cup \cdots \cup (r \circ\circ r \ \circ\circ \cdots \circ\circ r)$$

Declare an SML function to compute the transitive closure.

**10.3** Use sets and the results in the previous exercise to solve Exercise 6.3.

**10.4** Declare a function subsets where subsets(n,k) is the set of all subsets of $\{1, 2, \dots, n\}$ containing exactly $k$ elements. Hint: use ideas from Exercise 2.1, e.g. $\binom{n}{k}$ is the number of subsets of $\{1, 2, \dots, n\}$ containing exactly $k$ elements.

# Chapter 11

# Modules

........................................................................................................................

Throughout the book we have used programs from the standard library, e.g. programs from `Math`, `Int`, `Real` and `List`, and we have seen that programs from the Library are reused in many different applications. In this chapter we consider how the user can make library programs. To this end we introduce new concepts:

- The notion of a *structure*, which supports the declaration of composite identifiers, like `Int.toString` and `Real.toString`. The notion of structure is very convenient as it allows a systematic naming of functions.

- The notion of a *signature*, which describes the user's interface to a program library. The notion of signature is very convenient for program documentation and we have used it informally in the chapters on 'Problem solving' to describe program interfaces.

- The notion of a *functor*, which supports parameterization of library programs.

A signature and a structure are typically combined into a form where the signature describes the user's interface and the structure contains the relevant declarations. This combination of a signature and a structure is also called a *module*. The module concept in SML supports hiding of information from the user and it complements the `abstype` and `local` declarations in that respect.

In this chapter we give an example-based description of the SML features for building modules. We refer to Appendix C for an informal description of the SML module system.

Different SML systems have different commands to compile and load modules. This information is found in the user's manual for the individual systems.

## 11.1 Structures

The notion of a structure is now introduced using the example of finite sets from Chapter 10. A *structure expression* is a sequence of declarations enclosed in struct ... end. A *structure declaration* consists of the keyword structure and the name of the structure, followed by an equality sign and a structure expression.

A structure Set for a part of our representation of finite sets (in Section 10.2) may hence be declared as follows:

```
structure Set =
struct
    type 'a set = 'a list;
    val empty = [];
    fun singleton a = [a];
    fun member(x, ys) = List.exists (fn y => x = y) ys;
    fun insert(x, ys) = if member(x, ys) then ys else x::ys;
    fun toList xs = xs;
end
```

This structure declaration binds the identifier Set to two *environments*, a type environment containing a binding for the type constructor set, and a value environment containing bindings for the value identifiers empty, singleton, etc., declared inside the structure. Thus, the execution of the declaration yields the following binding:

$$
\text{Set} \mapsto \left( [\text{set} \mapsto \ldots], \begin{bmatrix} \text{empty} & \mapsto & [] \\ \text{singleton} & \mapsto & \cdots \\ \text{member} & \mapsto & \cdots \\ \text{insert} & \mapsto & \cdots \\ \text{toList} & \mapsto & \cdots \end{bmatrix} \right)
$$

The bindings of set, empty, member, etc. are now available in the current environment through composite identifiers Set.set, Set.empty, Set.member, etc. Thus, the notion of structure supports composite identifiers so, for example, Set.member and member can name different functions.

Since bindings for type constructors and value identifiers are kept in separate environments, it is possible that the same identifier can be used to denote a type constructor as well as a value.

The entities declared in the structure Set can be used via composite identifiers:

```
Set.empty;
val it = [] : 'a list

val s1 = Set.insert(1, Set.singleton 2);
val s1 = [1, 2] : int list
```

When convenient, the identifiers declared in the structure can be made directly available by the declaration:

```
open Set
```

which declares the names set, empty, member, etc. in the current environment to denote the values given in the structure. For example:

```
insert(1, singleton 2);
val it = [1, 2] : int list
```

Execution of the declaration: open Set will override possibly existing bindings for the identifiers: empty, singleton, etc. (which may be inconvenient).

### 11.2 Specifications and signatures

A *signature* is used to specify the user's view of a structure. For example, a user of a program library for sets should express solutions to programming problems in terms of the abstract, mathematical *set* object *without* bothering about the actual representation of sets and functions on sets. This *abstraction* is captured in SML by using *specifications* such as:

**1.** type 'a set

**2.** val empty: ''a set

**3.** val member: ''a * ''a set -> bool

indicating:

**1.** a type constructor set

**2.** a value empty of type ''a set

**3.** a value member of type ''a * ''a set -> bool (which is hence a function).

Note that these specifications do not reveal the structure of the type 'a set. (The use of different kinds of type variables 'a and ''a in the specifications is explained later in this chapter.)

A *signature expression* is a sequence of specifications enclosed in sig...end. A *signature declaration* consists of the keyword signature and the name of the signature, followed by an equality sign and a signature expression. A signature should be constructed in such a way that it contains all that a user of the module needs to know — and nothing else.

A signature for sets should contain specifications of the set type constructor and the functions on sets:

```
signature Set =
sig
    type 'a set
    val empty     : ''a set
    val singleton : ''a -> ''a set
    val member    : ''a * ''a set -> bool
    val insert    : ''a * ''a set -> ''a set
    val toList    : ''a set -> ''a list
end
```

where we have selected the same identifiers as in the structure for sets in the previous section. The complete signature Set is found in Section E.3.

## 11.3  Signatures and structures

A *module* is constructed by *matching* a signature with a structure. The matching checks that each identifier *id* specified in the signature is declared in the structure. Furthermore, the type specified for *id* in the signature must be an instance of the type inferred for *id* in the structure. In this way the user's view of the structure is determined by the signature.

There are two ways to match signatures and structures in SML called *transparent signature matching* and *opaque signature matching*. Transparent signature matching gives weak support for the hiding of details of the structure, while opaque signature matching is stronger at this point. We describe each of them briefly using our set example.

### 11.3.1  Transparent signature matching

Consider the signature Set described above. A structure for sets can be matched with this signature in the following way:

```
structure Set : Set =
struct
    type 'a set = 'a list;
    val empty = [];
    fun singleton a = [a];
    fun member(x, ys) = List.exists (fn y => x = y) ys;
    fun insert(x, ys) = if member(x, ys) then ys else x::ys;
    fun toList xs = xs;
end
```

where the first line of this structure declaration gives an example of a transparent signature matching: Set : Set. The first occurrence of Set is the identifier for the structure being declared, while the second is the signature used in the matching.

The structure declaration must contain a declaration for each identifier specified in the signature. These identifiers are available for the user via composite identifiers such as Set.empty and Set.singleton. For example:

```
val s1 = Set.singleton 2;
val s1 = [2] : int Set.set

s1 = [2];
val it = true : bool

Set.member(1, Set.insert(3, s1));
val it = false : bool
```

Note that the response *val s1 = [2] : int Set.set* to the user informs about the structure of the type 'a set even though this is not specified in the signature. The type constructor Set.set is in fact just a synonym for the type constructor list, and this may be exploited by the user:

```
Set.member(1, [3,2]);
val it = false : bool
```

This is the reason why the matching is called transparent.

Consider the declaration for the function singleton. The most general type inferred from this function declaration is 'a -> 'a set, as set is a synonym for list in the structure. However, the specified type for singleton in the signature is ''a -> ''a set, and this is 'enforced' by the signature matching:

```
Set.singleton (fn x => x+1);
Error: operator and operand don't agree
       [equality type required]
  operator domain: ''Z
  operand:         int -> int
  in expression:
    Set.singleton ((fn x => <exp> <exp>))
```

## 11.3.2    Opaque signature matching

We have seen in Section 10.3 that it is important to hide the set representation from the user to prevent violations of the invariant for the representation. This can be achieved by an opaque signature matching:

```
structure Set :> Set =
struct
   type 'a set = 'a list;
   val empty = [];
   fun singleton a = [a];
   fun member(x, ys) = List.exists (fn y => x = y) ys;
   fun insert(x, ys) = if member(x, ys) then ys else x::ys;
   fun toList xs = xs;
end
```

where the first line of this structure declaration gives an example of an opaque signature matching: Set :> Set. The first occurrence of Set is the identifier for the structure being declared, while the second is the identifier for the signature used in the matching.

The representation used for sets in the structure is not visible for the user when using opaque signature matching:

```
val s1 = Set.singleton 2;
val s1 = <set> : int Set.set
```

and this is the only – but important – difference compared with using transparent signature matching.

The elements in a set can be inspected using the Set.toList function, but it is not possible to exploit the list representation for sets. For example:

```
Set.toList s1;
val it = [2] : int list

s1 = [2];
! Toplevel input:
! s1 = [2];
! ^^
! Type clash: expression of type
!    int Set.set
! cannot have equality type ''a
```

A complete structure declaration for Set is found in Section E.4. An opaque signature matching is chosen in this structure in order to prevent the user from violating the invariant for the representation of sets.

### 11.3.3 Locally declared identifiers

A structure may contain declaration of an identifier which is not specified in the signature. The signature matching (transparent or opaque) will then make the identifier invisible for the user, i.e. the identifier becomes local to the module. We illustrate this by a simple example. Consider the signature:

```
signature T =
sig
  type t = int
  val f : t -> t
end
```

and the structure:

```
structure T :> T =
struct
    type t=int

    fun aux x = x+1
    fun f(x) = aux(x+7)
end;
```

The function f specified in the signature can be accessed using the composite identifier T.f:

```
T.f (T.f 3);
val it = 19 : int
```

but there is no access to aux:

```
T.aux(3);
! Toplevel input:
! T.aux(3);
! ^^^^^
! Unbound value identifier: T.aux
```

as aux is not specified in the signature.

Note that the structure of type t (same as int) is visible to the user as the specification type t = int occurs in the signature T.

## 11.3.4    Summary

We now give a brief summary of the facilities of the module system we have introduced so far.

Using a signature in a structure declaration has the effect that the resulting bindings in the environment denoted by the structure will correspond exactly to the specifications in the signature. The use of a signature may hence restrict the 'export' from a structure in several ways:

- The user can only access the module through the identifiers specified in the signature.
- An opaque signature matching will protect a type if its structure is left unspecified in the signature. For example, a user of the above set module with opaque signature matching can use the type constructor set, but the user cannot exploit that sets are represented by lists.
- A declaration in the structure without a matching specification in the signature is considered local to the structure and is not exported. This allows a structure to contain auxiliary functions which cannot be used by the user.

In the above examples we have seen specifications of types of the forms:

type *id*          or    type *tyvarseq id*
type *id* = τ      or    type *tyvarseq id* = τ

where *tyvarseq* denotes a sequence of type variables such as 'a or ('a,'b). A specification of the first form is implemented by (satisfied by) any declaration binding the identifier to a type. An example of this is the specification type 'a set in the signature Set.

A specification of the second form is implemented by any type declaration binding the identifier *id* to a type having τ as an instance. An example of this is the specification type t = int in the structure T in Section 11.3.3.

Furthermore, we have seen specifications of values of the form:

val *id* : *τ*

A specification of this form is implemented by any declaration binding the identifier *id* to a value of a type having the type *τ* as an instance. In an importing program the value will get the type *τ* from the specification. An example of this is the `singleton` function specified in the signature Set by val singleton: ''a -> ''a set. The type inferred from the declaration is 'a -> 'a set which has the specified type ''a -> ''a set as an instance. The user can hence only apply Set.singleton to a value of some equality type.

## ( 11.4 ) Further facilities

In this section we briefly mention further facilities of the module system with regard to specifications, signatures and structures.

### 11.4.1 Specifications

*An equality type specification*

An *equality type* specification has the form:

eqtype *id*

It is implemented by any declaration binding the identifier *id* to an equality type. An equality type specification allows an importing program to use the SML equality and inequality operators ( = and <>) on values of the specified type.

*An* include *specification*

The specifications given by a signature expression *sigexp* are included as one specification as follows:

include *sigexp*

*A* datatype *specification*

A datatype specification looks just like a datatype declaration. It is implemented by a datatype declaration with the same constructors such that each type in the specification is an instance of the corresponding type in the declaration. A datatype specification allows the importing program to use the constructors in patterns and expressions.

*An* exception *specification*

An exception specification looks just like an exception declaration. It is implemented by an exception declaration with the same exception constructors such that each type in the specification is an instance of the corresponding type in the declaration. An exception specification allows the importing program to *handle* (and *raise*) the exception by use of the exception constructors in patterns and expressions.

### A type sharing specification

A type sharing specification has the form:

> *spec* sharing type
> $tycon_1$ = ... = $tycon_n$

enforcing that the type constructors $tycon_1, \dots , tycon_n$ all denote the same type, provided that this is accepted by the type check. The type check will for instance reject type sharing of, say, int and real.

A suitable adaptation of equality types is performed in a sharing. For example, the signature:

```
signature SIG1 =
sig
    eqtype t1
    type t2
        sharing type t1 = t2
end;
```

specifies two identical types t1 and t2. The following structure matches this signature:

```
structure STR1 : SIG1 =
struct
    type t1 = int
    type t2 = int
end;
```

However, the structure declaration:

```
structure STR2 : SIG1 =
struct
    type t1 = int -> bool
    type t2 = int -> bool
end;
```

will be rejected because int->bool is not an equality type as specified by eqtype t1. The types specified by:

```
signature SIGA =
sig
    eqtype    ta
    type      tb
              sharing type ta = tb
end;
```

may be implemented by datatypes, for example:

```
structure STRA : SIGA =
struct
  datatype ta = Yes | No;
  datatype tb = datatype ta
end
```

where *datatype replication* datatype tb = datatype ta is used to express that ta and tb are identical datatypes.

### 11.4.2 Signature expressions

*Type realization*

A type specified in a signature expression can be instantiated by a so-called type realization. Consider, for example, the signature declaration:

```
signature SIGI =
sig
    eqtype alpha
    type beta = alpha list
end;
```

specifying an equality type alpha, and a type beta.

The following signature expression:

```
SIGI where type alpha = int
```

denotes the signature obtained from SIGI by instantiating the type specified for alpha to int, i.e. it has the same meaning as the signature expressions:

```
sig
    type alpha = int
    type beta  = alpha list
end
```

Signature expressions such as the one above can be used in signature declarations, e.g.:

```
signature S = SIGI where type alpha = int
```

### 11.5 Fixity of identifiers

It is often convenient to give infix status to a function when the argument is a pair. The fixity status of functions is, however, not inherited through the SML module system. Hence, infix status of a function inside a structure does *not* propagate to the importing program.

Each importing program makes its own decisions about fixity by means of fixity declarations such as:

```
infix member;
infixr insert;
```

The imported functions `member`, `insert`, etc., get infix status in the importing program according to the fixity declarations. For example (assuming the above fixity declarations):

```
open Set;


1 member (2 insert 3 insert empty);
val it = false : bool
```

Imported functions always get *nonfix* status if there are no fixity declarations in the importing program – even when the functions have been declared with infix status in the structure.

The syntax of SML does not allow a fixity declaration like `infix Set.member`, so a composite name like `Set.member` *cannot* be given infix status.

## 11.6  Functors

In this section we give an example-based introduction to the *functor* concept of SML. A functor can be considered a function from structures to structures, or rather a function from environments (denoted by structures) to environments, and it is therefore an abstraction mechanism for library programs. We refer to Appendix C for more details concerning the functor concept.

### 11.6.1   Sets revisited

We will now take another look at the set example. We will express how to obtain a module of sets for every equality type of the elements. To this end we will use a functor.

Consider the following signature for sets:

```
signature SetEq =
sig
   eqtype element
   type set
   val empty : set
   val singleton : element  -> set
   val member: element * set -> bool
   val insert: element * set -> set
   val toList: set -> element list
end
```

where we have selected a few typical identifiers. In this signature we have specified the `element` type as an equality type together with a type for sets.

We want to declare a functor, which takes a structure as argument and gives a set structure as result. The argument structure must contain a declaration for the type element.

The start of the functor declaration is:

```
functor SetFct(s: sig eqtype element end)
        :> SetEq where type element = s.element =  ...
```

The functor is named SetFct, and it has a formal parameter s described by the signature: sig eqtype element end; i.e. an argument structure must declare element as some equality type.

The signature expression

```
SetEq where type element = s.element
```

describes the resulting structure. We see that the type element specified in the signature SetEq is instantiated to the type declared for element in s.

The full functor declaration is:

```
functor SetFct(s: sig eqtype element end)
        :> SetEq where type element = s.element =
struct
    type element = s.element

    type set = s.element list

    val empty = []

    fun singleton x = [x]

    fun member(x, ys) = List.exists (fn y => x = y) ys;

    fun insert(x, ys) = if member(x,ys) then ys else x::ys;

    fun toList xs = xs
end
```

A structure for integer sets can now be declared by:

```
structure intset = SetFct(type element = int);
```

Note that the declaration type element = int is accepted as a structure expression and can be used as the actual parameter of the SetFct functor.

The identifiers in the resulting structure intset can be accessed using composite identifiers, for example:

```
val is1 = intset.insert(1, intset.empty);
val is1 = - : intset.set

intset.toList is1;
val it = [1] : intset.element list
```

A structure for sets of integer lists can be declared by:

```
structure intlistset = SetFct(type element = int list);
```

but it is not possible to get a structure for sets where the elements do not have an equality type, e.g.

```
structure xxx = SetFct(type element = int -> bool);
Error: type element must be an equality type
```

### 11.6.2    Sets with equality predicate

We will now reconsider the sets with equality predicate from Section 10.3. A set is represented by a list of its elements without replication and an equality predicate on the elements:

```
type 'a set = 'a list * ('a * 'a -> bool);
```

It is actually possible for the user to misuse this representation of sets, e.g. by applying the union function to sets with different equality predicates.

Consider, for example, the case-insensitive comparison eqLetters for letters (where, for example, #"a" and #"A" are considered equal):

```
fun eqLetters(ch1, ch2) =
         Char.toUpper ch1 = Char.toUpper ch2;
val eqLetters = fn : char * char -> bool
```

A set of characters can be formed using eqLetters as equality predicate:

```
val s1 = insert(#"A", singleton(#"B", eqLetters));
val s1 = ([#"A", #"B"], fn)
       : char list * (char * char -> bool)
```

Another set of characters can be formed using the usual SML equality op= on characters:

```
val s2 = insert(#"b", singleton(#"c", op=));
val s2 = ([#"b", #"c"], fn)
       : char list * (char * char -> bool)
```

The union function of Section 10.3 allows us to form the union of these two set representations even though they do not have the same equality predicate (and hence are different kinds of sets):

```
val s3 = union(s1,s2);
val s3 = ([#"B", #"A", #"b", #"c"], fn)
       : char list * (char * char -> bool)

val s4 = union(s2,s1);
val s4 = ([#"c", #"A", #"B"], fn)
       : char list * (char * char -> bool)
```

This does not make sense and we get curious phenomena such as: the sets s3 and s4 are equal sets which do not have the same number of elements:

```
equal(s3,s4);
val it = true : bool

card s3 = card s4;
val it = false : bool
```

Functors can be used to avoid the above problem. The idea is to declare a functor having a formal parameter which is an element structure with an equality predicate. The resulting structure is then representing sets using this equality predicate and these set representations cannot be mixed with other kinds of set representations.

The following signature EQ contains a specification of a type element with an equality predicate eq:

```
signature EQ =
sig
    type element
    val eq: element * element -> bool
end
```

We consider the following signature for sets:

```
signature SetEqPr =
sig
    type element
    type set
    val empty : set
    val singleton: element -> set
    val insert: element * set -> set
    val member: element * set -> bool
    val union : set * set -> set
    val toList: set -> element list
end
```

The functor SetFctPr is then declared using the equality predicate eq from the structure s in the declaration of the member function:

```
functor SetFctPr(s: EQ)
            :> SetEqPr where type element = s.element =
struct
    type element = s.element

    type set = s.element list

    val empty = [];

    fun singleton x = [x];
```

```
        fun member(x, ys) = List.exists (fn y => s.eq(x,y)) ys

        fun insert(x, ys) = if member(x,ys) then ys else x::ys

        fun union(xs, ys) = List.foldr insert ys xs

        fun toList xs = xs
    end
```

The signature expression instantiates the type `element` to the type `s.element` in the formal parameter s.

We want to use the functor to construct sets of characters. We first declare a signature `CharSet` for sets of characters with equality predicate by instantiating the type `element` in the signature `SetEqPr` to type `char`:

```
signature CharSet = SetEqPr where type element = char;
```

We can now use the functor `SetFctPt` to get a structure for sets of characters using the SML equality of characters as equality predicate:

```
structure charEQ1 :> CharSet =
        SetFctPr(type element = char  val eq = op=);

val s1 = charEQ1.insert(#"a", charEQ1.singleton #"b");
val s1 = - : charEQ1.set

charEQ1.toList s1;
val it = [#"a",#"b"] : charEQ1.element list
```

A structure for sets of characters using the predicate `eqLetters` as equality predicate can also be obtained:

```
structure charEQ2 :> CharSet =
        SetFctPr(type element = char  val eq = eqLetters);

val s2 = charEQ2.insert(#"A", charEQ2.singleton #"B");
val s2 = - : charEQ2.set
```

but it is not possible to combine sets from these two structures:

```
charEQ2.union(s1,s2);
Error: operator and operand don't agree [tycon mismatch]
  operator domain: charEQ2.set * charEQ2.set
  operand:         charEQ1.set * charEQ2.set
  in expression:
    charEQ2.union (s1,s2)
```

although both structures match the signature `CharSet`.

**Example 11.1**

### Expression trees

Consider the expression trees introduced in Section 8.2. Several recursive functions are declared in that section, where the recursion follows the structure of the expression trees.

Consider, for example, the declarations for toString and compute. These declarations have a clause for each constructor of the datatype. For example, the clauses for the constructor ** are:

```
toString(fe1 ** fe2) =   "(" ^ (toString fe1)
                        ^ " * " ^ (toString fe2) ^ ")"


compute(fe1 ** fe2,y) = compute(fe1,y) * compute(fe2,y)
```

The clause for toString associates the function:

```
fn (s1,s2) =>   "(" ^ s1 ^ " * " ^ s2 ^ ")"
```

with the constructor ** and the clause for compute associate the multiplication function on real numbers:

```
fn (x1,x2) => x1*x2:real
```

with the constructor **.

We want to express the general recursion schema for expression trees by a functor arithEval. The argument structure for this functor must declare evaluation functions corresponding to each of the constructors for building expression trees. The following signature Arith specifies the identifiers that must be declared in the argument structure of the functor arithEval:

```
signature Arith =
sig
   type result
   val constant    : real -> result
   val add         : result * result -> result
   val minus       : result * result -> result
   val multiply    : result * result -> result
   val divide      : result * result -> result
   val sine        : result -> result
   val cosine      : result -> result
   val logarithm   : result -> result
   val exponential : result -> result
end
```

and the resulting structure of the functor `arithEval` must match the signature `Eval`:

```
signature Eval =
sig
   datatype fexpr =
      Const of real
    | X
    | ++ of fexpr * fexpr | -- of fexpr * fexpr
    | ** of fexpr * fexpr | // of fexpr * fexpr
    | Sin of fexpr | Cos of fexpr
    | Ln of fexpr  | Exp of fexpr

   type result

   val eval: fexpr -> result -> result
end
```

The declaration for the functor `arithEval` instantiates the type `result` in the signature `Eval` to the type in the argument structure `s`:

```
functor arithEval(s : Arith)
        :> Eval where type result = s.result =
struct
   datatype fexpr =
      Const of real
    | X
    | ++ of fexpr * fexpr | -- of fexpr * fexpr
    | ** of fexpr * fexpr | // of fexpr * fexpr
    | Sin of fexpr | Cos of fexpr
    | Ln of fexpr  | Exp of fexpr

   type result = s.result

   fun eval exp x =
     case exp of
         Const r      => s.constant r
       | X            => x
       | ++(fe1,fe2) => s.add(eval fe1 x, eval fe2 x)
       | --(fe1,fe2) => s.minus(eval fe1 x, eval fe2 x)
       | **(fe1,fe2) => s.multiply(eval fe1 x, eval fe2 x)
       | //(fe1,fe2) => s.divide(eval fe1 x, eval fe2 x)
       | Sin fe       => s.sine(eval fe x)
       | Cos fe       => s.cosine(eval fe x)
       | Ln fe        => s.logarithm(eval fe x)
       | Exp fe       => s.exponential(eval fe x)
end
```

Note that the `eval` function has the property: $eval\ x\ X = x$ so the argument pattern $x$ gives the value which will be used for the constructor `X`.

*Application 1 of* `arithEval`: *infix string representation*

In order to achieve infix string representations of expression trees we declare the following structure to be used in an application of the functor `arithEval`:

```
structure infixstringArith
        :> Arith where type result = string =
struct
    type result     = string
    val constant    = Real.toString
    val add         = fn(s1,s2) => "(" ^ s1 ^ " + " ^ s2 ^ ")"
    val minus       = fn(s1,s2) => "(" ^ s1 ^ " - " ^ s2 ^ ")"
    val multiply    = fn(s1,s2) => "(" ^ s1 ^ " * " ^ s2 ^ ")"
    val divide      = fn(s1,s2) => "(" ^ s1 ^ " / " ^ s2 ^ ")"
    val sine        = fn s => "(sin " ^ s ^ ")"
    val cosine      = fn s => "(cos " ^ s ^ ")"
    val logarithm   = fn s => "(ln " ^ s ^ ")"
    val exponential = fn s => "(exp " ^ s ^ ")"
end
```

The functor application `arithEval(infixstringArith)` yields a new structure containing the desired evaluation function for expression trees:

```
structure infixstringEval = arithEval(infixstringArith);

open infixstringEval;

val f = eval (++(Const 2.9, X));
val f = fn : result -> result

f "x";
val it = "(2.9 + x)" : result

eval (Sin(++(Const 2.9, X))) "y";
val it = "(sin (2.9 + y))" : result
```

*Application 2 of* `arithEval`: *computation of function values*

Similarly, we can obtain an evaluation function for computing function values using the following structure:

```
structure realArith :> Arith where type result = real =
struct
    type result     = real
    val constant    = fn x => x
    val add         = op+ : result * result -> result
    val minus       = op- : result * result -> result
    val multiply    = op* : result * result -> result
```

```
      val divide      = op/ : result * result -> result
      val sine        = Math.sin
      val cosine      = Math.cos
      val logarithm   = Math.ln
      val exponential = Math.exp
  end
```

and applying the functor arithEval:

```
  structure realEval = arithEval(realArith);

  open realEval;

  val fe = ++(Const 2.0, **(Sin (Const 2.0), X));

  val f = eval fe;
  val f = fn : result -> result

  f 7.0;
  val it = 8.36508198778 : result

  f 10.0;
  val it = 11.0929742683 : result
```

## ( 11.7 ) Summary

This chapter gives an introduction to the module system in SML. A *structure* declaration collects a sequence of declarations such that each component is available through a composite name. The components of a structure are made available under their component names by an open-declaration.

A *signature* collects a sequence of *specifications* and is used to restrict the export from a structure and can hence be used to hide information from the user of a module. Thus, a signature expresses the external interface of a module, and can hence be used for documentation purposes, as in Appendix D.

Functors provide a notion of parameterized modules. We have illustrated the use of functors by some examples.

## ( Exercises )

**11.1** Make a library module for rational numbers. See Chapter 4. Construct the module in such a way that the representation of rational numbers is hidden from the users of the module.

**11.2** Make a library module for complex numbers such that the representation of complex numbers is hidden from the users. See Exercise 3.3. Hint: add a function to generate a complex number from a pair of real numbers, and a function to give a string representation for complex numbers.

**11.3** Make a library module for straight lines such that the representation is hidden from the users. See Exercise 3.4. Hint: add a function to generate a straight line from a pair of real numbers.

**11.4** Make a library module for shapes such that the representation is hidden from the user. See Chapter 7. Hint: add functions to generate circles, squares and triangles satisfying the invariant.

**11.5** Make a library module for electrical circuits. See Section 8.6.

**11.6** Declare a structure s matching the signature Arith where a result is a set of strings representing operators, one for each function in the signature. The functor application arithEval(s) must give a structure having an evaluation function which extracts the set of operators (as strings) occurring in an expression tree.

# Chapter 12

# Tables

This chapter introduces a representation of tables and operations on tables in SML. The focus is on the principal issues so the chapter contains declarations for a selected part of the functions on tables. The full set of declarations is found in Appendix E describing a Table module.

The cash register example in Chapter 6 comprises an article register associating name and price to article codes, and this register can be viewed as a table. A key in the table is an article code and the corresponding value is the pair of the article name and price of the article.

The use of tables in programming is illustrated by examples in this and later chapters.

## 12.1 The table concept

A *table* from a set $A$ to a set $B$ is a *finite* subset $A'$ of $A$ together with a *function t* defined on $A'$:

$$t : A' \to B$$

The set $A'$ is called the *domain* of $t$ and we write $\operatorname{dom} t = A'$.

A table $t$ can be described in a tabular form as shown below. The left column contains the elements $a_1, a_2, \dots, a_n$ of the set $A'$, while the right column contains the corresponding values $t(a_1) = b_1, t(a_2) = b_2, \ldots, t(a_n) = b_n$:

| $a_1$ | $b_1$ |
|-------|-------|
| $a_2$ | $b_2$ |
| $\vdots$ | |
| $a_n$ | $b_n$ |

Each element $a_i$ in the set $A'$ is called a *key* for the table $t$. A pair $(a_i, b_i)$ is called an *entry*, and $b_i$ is called the *value* for the key $a_i$. Note that the order of the entries is of no significance, as the table only expresses an association of values to keys. Note also that any two keys $a_i$ and $a_j$ in different entries are different, as there is only one value for each key. Thus, a table may be represented as a finite set of its entries.

A particular article register is given by the following table:

$reg_1$ :

| a1 | (cheese, 25) |
|----|--------------|
| a2 | (herring, 4) |
| a3 | (soft drink, 5) |

It associates the value (cheese, 25) with the key a1, the value (herring, 4) with the key a2, and the value (soft drink, 5) with the key a3. Hence, it has the domain {a1, a2, a3}.

## 12.2  A representation of tables

A table $t$ can be represented by a list $[(a_1, b_1), \ldots, (a_n, b_n)]$ of the entries $(a_i, b_i)$ in the table. Hence, tables are represented by the polymorphic type:

```
type ('a,'b) table = ('a * 'b) list
```

The above table $reg_1$ is represented by the value:

```
[("a1",("cheese",25)),
 ("a2",("herring",4)),
 ("a3",("soft drink",5))]
```

of type (string, string*int) table. Any other list containing the same three elements (in any order) will also represent the table $reg_1$.

A list representing a table must not contain the same key twice, i.e. for any two list elements $(a_i, b_i)$ and $(a_j, b_j)$ we should have $a_i \neq a_j$. This *invariant* must be maintained by the functions on tables.

## 12.3  Operations on tables

This section explains the declarations of some of the functions in the Table module. In the types for tables and functions on tables we specify an equality type for keys, as we must be able to compare keys.

The complete signature and structure for the Table module are found in Appendix E.

*The exception:* `Table`

Some of the functions may raise the exception `Table`:

```
exception Table
```

*The value* `empty:` `(''a,'b) table`

The empty table `empty` is represented by the empty list:

```
val empty   = []
```

*The function* `singleton:` `''a * 'b -> (''a,'b) table`

The function `singleton` creates a table containing a single entry $(a, b)$:

```
fun singleton(a,b) = [(a,b)]
```

*The function* `getval:` `''a * (''a,'b) table -> 'b`

The function `getval` searches the table for an entry $(a, b)$ with given key $a$ and returns the corresponding value $b$. The exception `Table` is raised if no such entry is found in the table:

```
fun getval(a,[])          = raise Table
  | getval(a,(a1,b1)::t) = if a=a1 then b1 else getval(a,t)
```

*The function* `lookup:` `''a * (''a,'b) table -> 'b option`

The function `lookup` is similar to `getval` but it uses the `option` type instead of exceptions:

```
fun lookup(a,[])          = NONE
  | lookup(a,(a1,b1)::t) = if a=a1 then SOME b1
                           else lookup(a,t)
```

*The function* `update:` `''a * 'b * (''a,'b) table -> (''a,'b) table`

The function `update` updates the data for key $a$ to the value $b$ – or it inserts a new entry $(a, b)$ if the table has no entry with key $a$:

```
fun update(a,b,[])          = [(a,b)]
  | update(a,b,(a1,b1)::t) = if a=a1 then (a,b)::t
                             else (a1,b1)::update(a,b,t)
```

## The function `insert`

The function `insert` has the type:

```
''a * 'b * (''a,'b) table -> (''a,'b) table option
```

and it is similar to `update` but it creates a new table only when *a* is not a key in the table:

```
fun insert(a,b,[])          = SOME [(a,b)]
  | insert(a,b,(a1,b1)::t) =
                if a=a1 then NONE
                else case insert(a,b,t) of
                        NONE    => NONE
                      | SOME t1 => SOME((a1,b1)::t1)
```

## The function `fromList`: `(''a * 'b) list -> (''a,'b) table`

The function `fromList` creates the table with entries $(a_i, b_i)$ from a given list $[(a_1, b_1), \dots, (a_n, b_n)]$. It raises the exception `Table` if there are two list elements $(a_i, b_i)$ and $(a_j, b_j)$ for the same key, i.e. with $a_i = a_j$ for $i \neq j$. The function is declared by use of the `insert` function:

```
fun fromList []              = []
  | fromList ((a,b)::abs) = case insert(a,b,fromList(abs)) of
                        NONE    => raise Table
                      | SOME t => t
```

## The function `toList`: `(''a,'b) table -> (''a * 'b) list`

The function `toList` creates a list of the entries $(a_i, b_i)$ in the table:

```
fun toList t = t
```

## The function `fold`

The function `fold` has the type:

```
(''a * 'b * 'c -> 'c) -> 'c -> (''a,'b) table -> 'c
```

and it accumulates a function of type `''a * 'b * 'c -> 'c` over the entries of the table:

```
fun fold f e t = List.foldl (fn ((a,b),c) => f(a,b,c)) e t
```

## The function `split`

The function `split` has the type

```
(''a,'b) table -> (''a * 'b * (''a,'b) table) option
```

and it splits one entry from a non-empty table and returns NONE for an empty table:

```
fun split []         = NONE
  | split((a,b)::t) = SOME(a,b,t)
```

Example 12.1

### Cash register

We give a solution to the cash register problem discussed in Chapter 6 using tables. Article codes and names, number of pieces and prices are modelled as in Chapter 6:

```
type articleCode = string
type articleName = string
type noPieces    = int
type price       = int
```

The register associating article name and price with each article code can be modelled as a table:

```
type register =
        (articleCode, articleName * price) Table.table
```

A purchase was in Chapter 6 modelled as a list of items, each item consisting of a count and an article code. A list was chosen to model the sequence in which items are placed on the counter in the shop. One may, however, argue that a purchase of the three items – 3 litres of milk, one piece of cheese and 2 litres of milk – is the same as a purchase of one piece of cheese and 5 litres of milk. Furthermore, the latter form is more convenient if we have to model a discount on 5 litres of milk, as the discount applies independently of the order in which the items are placed on the counter.

Thus, it may be appropriate to model a purchase as a table:

```
type purchase = (articleCode, noPieces) Table.table
```

while the information occurring on the bill is still as in Chapter 6:

```
type info = noPieces * articleName * price
type bill = info list * price
```

The function makebill: purchase * register -> bill makes the bill for a given purchase and register using the split function on table representations to take a purchase apart:

```
fun makebill(pur,reg) =
   case Table.split pur of
       SOME (ac,np,pur') =>
               let val (aname,aprice) = Table.getval(ac,reg)
                   val tprice          = np*aprice
                   val (infs,sum)      = makebill(pur',reg)
               in ((np,aname,tprice)::infs, tprice+sum)
               end
     | NONE                   => ([],0);
```

The makebill function may instead be declared by using the fold function on tables:

```
fun makebill(pur,reg) =
  let fun f(ac,np,(infs,sum)) =
               let val (aname,aprice) = Table.getval(ac,reg)
                   val tprice          = np*aprice
               in ((np,aname,tprice)::infs, tprice+sum)
               end
  in   Table.fold f ([],0) pur
  end;
```

A register and a purchase can be constructed from a singleton table using the update function on tables:

```
val register = Table.update("a1", ("cheese",25),
               Table.update("a2", ("herring",4),
               Table.singleton("a3", ("soft drink",5))));
val register = <table> : (string, string * int) Table.table

val purchase = Table.update("a2",3, Table.singleton("a1",1));
val purchase = <table> : (string, int) Table.table

makebill(purchase,register);
val it = ([(1,"cheese",25),(3,"herring",12)],37)
  : (int * string * int) list * int
```

The register and purchase can also be constructed using the fromList function, e.g.:

```
val register = Table.fromList [("a1", ("cheese",25)),
                               ("a2", ("herring",4)),
                               ("a3", ("soft drink",5))];
val register = <table> : (string, string * int) Table.table
```

### Example 12.2

#### Symbolic differentiation

We have shown in Section 8.2 how to represent expressions as trees, and we have shown how to do symbolic differentiation of functions using expression trees. A disadvantage of the representation given in Section 8.2 is that the allowed function symbols (sin, cos, ln, exp) occur as constructors in the datatype declaration. Hence, we will need to change the datatype declaration if we want to include further function symbols (such as the tangent function tan). In the following we present a more flexible solution, using tables.

The type expr representing expressions is declared as follows:

```
infix 6 ++
infix 7 **
```

```
datatype expr = X
              | Const of real
              | ++ of expr * expr
              | ** of expr * expr
              | FC of string * expr
```

Thus, an expression is either the variable X, a real constant, a sum or a product of expressions, or it is a function applied to an expression. A function is given by its name, which is a string. We have omitted difference and quotients as they can be obtained from sum and product using the functions $-x$ and $1/x$. The sine and cosine functions $\sin(x)$ and $\cos(x)$ are hence represented by the expressions FC("sin",X) and FC("cos",X), and the functional composition $\sin(\cos(x))$, i.e. $(\sin \circ \cos)(x)$, is represented by the expression:

```
FC("sin", FC("cos", X));
val it = FC ("sin",FC ("cos",X)) : expr
```

We will use a table to associate derivatives with strings representing function names. For each entry (*key*, *value*) in this table, the key will be a string for the function name, and the value will represent the derivative of the function.

The problem is to choose the representation of the derivative such that programming the symbolic differentiation becomes a simple task. Our choice is motivated by the following observation on symbolic differentiation of composite functions:

Consider the expression:

$\sin(expr)$

for some expression *expr*. The derivative of this expression is given by the chain rule:

$$(\sin(expr))' = \sin'(expr) \cdot expr'$$

The first factor in this product is the derivative $\sin'$ *applied* to the expression *expr*, while the second factor is the derivative of the expression *expr*.

In this example an expression *expr* is substituted for the argument $x$ in the derivative $sin'(x)$. The obvious idea of representing the derivative by an expression, e.g. to represent the derivative of the sine function by the expression $\cos(x)$, is hence *not* a good idea, since arbitrary expressions must be substituted for the argument $x$.

A better idea is to use *functions* of type expr->expr to represent derivatives. Using this idea, the derivative of sine is represented by the function sin':

```
val sin' = fn x => FC("cos", x);
val sin' = fn : expr -> expr
```

and the derivative of cosine is represented by the function cos':

```
val cos' = fn x => FC("-", FC("sin", x));
val cos' = fn : expr -> expr
```

The first factor $\sin'(\cos(x))$ in the derivative $\sin'(\cos(x)) \cdot \cos'(x)$ of the composite function $\sin(\cos(x))$ can then be obtained by applying sin' to the representation of $\cos(x)$:

```
sin'(FC ("cos", X));
val it = FC ("cos",FC ("cos",X)) : expr
```

and the derivative of $\sin(\cos(x))$ is then obtained by building the product with the derivative $\cos'(x)$:

```
sin'(FC ("cos", X)) ** cos' X;
val it = (FC("cos",FC ("cos",X)))
            ** ( FC("-",FC("sin", X))) : expr
```

The same ideas will apply to other expressions of the form $f(expr)$.

We will therefore use tables of the type:

```
(string, expr->expr) Table.table
```

to associate derivatives with function symbols. The table of derivatives for the function symbols sin and cos is shown in the following figure:

| | |
|---|---|
| "sin" | fn x => FC("cos", x) |
| "cos" | fn x => FC("-", FC("sin", x)) |

It associates the above defined functions sin' and cos' to the strings "sin" and "cos". The SML value der1 for this table is obtained by the declaration:

```
val der1 = Table.fromList [("sin", sin'), ("cos", cos')];
val der1 = <table> : (string, expr -> expr) Table.table
```

The symbolic differentiation function D includes an argument t which is a table of derivatives for function symbols, and is declared by:

```
fun D X _              = Const 1.0
  | D (Const _) _      = Const 0.0
  | D (fe1 ++ fe2) t = (D fe1 t) ++ (D fe2 t)
  | D (fe1 ** fe2) t = (D fe1 t) ** fe2 ++ fe1 ** (D fe2 t)
  | D (FC(f, fe)) t  = let val f' = Table.getval(f,t)
                           in f'(fe) ** (D fe t)
                           end
val D = fn : expr -> (string, expr -> expr) Table.table
                   -> expr
```

It works well on the composite function above:

```
D (FC("sin", FC("cos", X))) der1;
val it =
  FC("cos",FC ("cos",X))
  ** (FC("-",FC("sin",X)) ** Const 1) : expr
```

But evaluating the second derivative gives an exception:

```
D it der1;
uncaught exception: Table.Table
```

The exception is raised as the table der1 has no entry for the function symbol '-' which is introduced in the first derivative of $\sin(\cos(x))$.

We might want to ensure the property that any function symbol introduced in a derivative computed using the table $t$ has a corresponding entry in the table. This property on tables $t$ is given by the formula:

$\quad$ *extTable* $t \subseteq \text{dom } t$

where *extTable* $t$ denotes the set of function symbols introduced in derivatives in the table $t$. To express the property in SML, we first declare a function that can extract the set of function symbols occurring in an expression. The last clause covers expressions of form X or Const $a$:

```
fun extExpr (FC(s,fe))   = Set.insert(s, extExpr fe)
  | extExpr (fe1 ++ fe2) = Set.union(extExpr fe1, extExpr fe2)
  | extExpr (fe1 ** fe2) = Set.union(extExpr fe1, extExpr fe2)
  | extExpr _            = Set.empty;
val extExpr = fn : expr -> string Set.set

Set.toList(extExpr (FC("-", FC("sin", X))));
val it = ["-","sin"] : string list
```

The set of function symbols introduced in a derivative $r$: expr -> expr can be obtained by extracting the function symbols from $r(e)$, where $e$ is some expression containing no function symbols, i.e. $e$ could be X:

```
fun extDerivative r = extExpr (r X);
val extDerivative = fn : (expr -> expr) -> string Set.set

Set.toList(extDerivative cos');
val it = ["-","sin"] : string list
```

The function extTable extracting the function symbols introduced in derivatives found in a table $t$ can be declared by:

```
fun extTable t =
       case Table.split t of
           NONE            => Set.empty
         | SOME(_,r,t') =>
               Set.union(extDerivative r,  extTable t');
val extTable = fn : (''a, expr -> expr) Table.table
                     -> string Set.set
```

The function extTable can alternatively be declared using the fold function on tables as it accumulates the function $f(\_, r, s) = \text{extDerivative}(r) \cup s$ over the entries of a table:

```
fun extTable t =
   Table.fold (fn (_,r,s) => Set.union(extDerivative r, s))
              Set.empty t;

Set.toList(extTable der1);
val it = ["cos","-","sin"] : string list
```

The domain function on tables can be declared as:

```
fun dom t = Table.fold (fn (a,_,c) =>  Set.insert(a,c))
                       Set.empty t;
val dom = fn : (''a, 'b) Table.table -> ''a Set.set
```

and the condition on tables for derivatives can be declared as:

```
fun cond t = Set.subset(extTable t, dom t);
val cond = fn : (string, expr -> expr) Table.table -> bool

cond der1;
val it = false : bool

val der2 = Table.update("-", fn x => Const ~1.0, der1);

cond der2;
val it = true : bool
```

The predicate $\text{isDiff}(e, t) = (\text{extExpr}(e) \subseteq \text{dom}(t)) \wedge \text{cond}(t)$ is true for expressions $e$ where derivatives of any order are defined for a given table $t$. This predicate is declared by:

```
fun isDiff(e,t) = Set.subset(extExpr e,dom t) andalso cond t;
val isDiff =
   fn : expr * (string, expr -> expr) Table.table -> bool

isDiff(FC("sin", FC("cos", X)), der1);
val it = false : bool

isDiff(FC("sin", FC("cos", X)), der2);
val it = true : bool
```

## 12.4  Summary

In this chapter we have introduced the notion of table together with some fundamental operations on tables, e.g. lookup, delete, remove, update, insert and fold.

The notion of table provides a useful abstraction in programming and many program modules for tables exist. These modules support operations on tables such as those presented in this chapter, and they provide efficient representations and operations in some cases, and must be selected according to the particular needs of the program. Efficient representation of tables and the associated algorithms are important issues in computer science. This is part of the subject 'data structures and algorithms'.

## Exercises

**12.1** Declare a function to find the union of two tables of the same type, but with disjoint domains.

**12.2** Declare an override function on tables. It takes two tables $(t_1, t_2)$ of the same type as argument. The result is obtained by updating $t_1$ with the entries of $t_2$.

**12.3** Extend the cash register example of this chapter to take discount of articles into account. For example, find a suitable representation of discounts and revise the makebill function.

**12.4** Extend the symbolic differentiation example to cover the same functions as used in the example in Section 8.2.

# Problem solving III

....................................................................................................

In this chapter we use the method introduced in Chapters 4 and 6 to design a program for handling part lists for production planning. There are several new aspects in this chapter:

● We use a signature to describe the interface to the program and the program is implemented as a structure.

● Opaque signature matching is used to hide local functions and types in order to protect invariants for data representation in the program.

● The program uses the `Table` module to get a brief solution of the problem.

The problem formulation is:

> The planning of production of machines and machine-parts uses a parts list to describe the material used in producing a part. The parts list contains identifications of the set of used parts together with the required quantity for each part. A part is either a basic part bought from another factory (which has hence an empty parts list) or a composite part produced by the factory (which has hence a non-empty parts list). A parts list may contain both basic and composite parts. Parts are associated with parts lists in a product register.
>
> The program must provide a function which gives a parts list containing all the basic parts needed to produce a given part. Furthermore, it should provide

functions to insert a new part with corresponding parts list into the register and to get the parts list for a part in the register.

## 13.1  Problem analysis

The problem formulation mentions *parts* and *parts lists*, *product register* and *functions*. We discuss each of these entities separately.

### 13.1.1  Parts and parts lists

We choose the identification of a part to be a string and a parts list is then represented by a list of pairs $(pid, qnt)$ of part identification $pid$ and corresponding positive quantity $qnt$:

```
type partId   = string
type quantity = int          (* n > 0 *)
type partsList = (partId * quantity) list
```

For example, the following parts list describes three pieces of product "prod1" and eight pieces of product "prod2":

```
[("prod1", 3), ("prod2", 8)]
```

We allow that a part identifier can occur several times with quantities in a parts list, i.e. the following list:

```
[("prod3", 4), ("prod2", 5), ("prod3", 6)]
```

is a legal parts list which conveys the same information as the parts list:

```
[("prod3", 10), ("prod2", 5)]
```

### 13.1.2  Product register

The product register should associate part identifiers with parts lists, so a table having part identifiers as keys and parts lists as values is the natural representation of a product register.

However, not all tables of this kind are meaningful representations of registers. For example, a component cannot contain itself as a subpart, so the pair:

```
("prod5", [("prod1", 3), ("prod5", 8)])
```

is not a legal entry of a table for a product register.

But there are further conditions on product registers. For example, if the pair:

```
("prod3", [("prod1", 3), ("prod2", 8)])
```

is an entry of a table for a product register, then "prod1" and "prod2" must be keys in the table. Thus, there is an invariant for product registers represented by tables. We will return to that invariant in the next section.

We want the program to ensure that the user cannot make an illegal product register and we will therefore hide the structure of the register by having the opaque type specification:

```
type prodReg
```

in the interface definition.

### 13.1.3 Functions

Since the structure of the product register is hidden from the user, the interface definition must contain specifications of values and functions that can generate all possible (legal) product registers.

To this end, we specify a value for the empty product register:

```
val newReg: prodReg
```

and a function that can add a part with associated parts list to a product register:

```
val addPart: partId * partsList * prodReg -> prodReg
```

The function addPart raises the exception specified by:

```
exception ProdReg
```

when it is applied to a illegal argument. Note that any product register can be generated from the empty register newReg by repeated application of the function addPart, without knowing the 'internal' structure of the product register.

Furthermore, we specify a function to extract a parts list for a given part from a product register:

```
val partsList: partId * prodReg -> partsList
```

and a function to extract a parts list containing all the basic parts needed for the production of a given part:

```
val partBreakDown: partId * prodReg -> partsList
```

### 13.1.4 Interface definition

The collection of the above specifications constitutes the interface definition, which is presented in Table 13.1 in the form of a signature. This signature contains the specification of a function toList which can give a list representation for a product register. This function is not mentioned in the problem formulation, but we have included it for test purposes.

**Table 13.1**   Interface definition.

```
signature PartsList =
sig

type partId = string
type quantity = int (* n>0 *)
type partsList = (partId * quantity) list

type prodReg; (* The representation is hidden. *)

exception ProdReg

val newReg:  prodReg
    (* An empty product register. *)

val addPart:  partId * partsList * prodReg -> prodReg
    (* Adds a new part with corresponding parts list to
        a product register.  May raise ProdReg. *)

val partsList:  partId * prodReg -> partsList
    (* Finds the parts list of a part in a product register.
        Raises ProdReg if the part is not found. *)

val toList:  prodReg -> (partId * partsList) list
    (* Lists a product register as a list of parts with cor-
        responding parts list.  Included for test purposes. *)

val partBreakDown:  partId * prodReg -> partsList
    (* Finds the parts list of basic parts of a
        part.  May raise ProdReg. *)

end
```

## 13.2  A sample run

The interface definition shows the user's view of the program.  The user's manual for the program should hence contain this signature together with instructions on how to use the program with examples of the use of individual functions.

We will now assume that a structure PartsList matching the signature PartsList has been declared and we give a sample run illustrating use of the individual functions. The structure declaration is found in the following section on programming.

A product register containing two basic parts "part1" and "part2" is formed by:

```
open PartsList;

val reg1 = addPart("part1", [], newReg);
val reg1 = <prodReg> : prodReg
```

```
val reg2 = addPart("part2", [], reg1);
val reg2 = <prodReg> : prodReg
```

The contents of product registers can be inspected using the `toList` function, e.g.:

```
toList reg2;
val it = [("part1", []), ("part2", [])]
          : (string * (string * int) list) list
```

A composite part "part3" is added:

```
val reg3 =  addPart("part3",[("part1",5),("part2",4)],reg2);
val reg3 = <prodReg> : prodReg
```

The parts list for a given part can be extracted using the `partsList` function, e.g.:

```
partsList("part2", reg3);
val it = [] : (string * int) list
```

A further composite part "part4" is added:

```
val reg4 =  addPart("part4",[("part2",3),("part3",4)],reg3);
val reg4 = <prodReg> : prodReg
```

and the contents of `reg4` is inspected:

```
toList reg4;
val it =
  [("part1", []),
   ("part2", []),
   ("part3", [("part1", 5), ("part2", 4)]),
   ("part4", [("part2", 3), ("part3", 4)])]
  : (string * (string * int) list) list
```

The parts list containing all the basic parts needed to produce "part4" is extracted using the partBreakDown function:

```
partBreakDown("part4", reg4);
val it = [("part2", 19), ("part1", 20)]
          : (string * int) list
```

## 13.3  Programming

The program is implemented as an SML structure `PartsList` with signature `PartsList`:

```
structure PartsList :> PartsList =
struct
type partId    = string
```

```
type quantity  = int    (* n>0 *)
type partsList = (partId * quantity) list

exception ProdReg
...
end;
```

The product register is declared as a table using the `Table` module from Chapter 12:

```
type prodReg = (partId,partsList) Table.table
```

Some tables do not represent meaningful product registers as we have seen in the previous section. We must therefore find an invariant for tables representing product registers.

### 13.3.1    Invariant for product registers

Suppose for the moment that we want to add an entry:

$$(pid, [(pid_1, c_1), \ldots, (pid_n, c_n)])$$

to a table $t$.

This addition of an entry to $t$ is called *legal* if the following two properties hold for the product identifiers:

● The identification *pid* of the part to be added is not a key of $t$.

● Each part identification $pid_i$ in the parts list of *pid* is a key of $t$.

Note that these two properties together imply that *pid* is different from $pid_i$, for all $i$. Hence, a legal addition cannot add an entry with a part containing itself as a subpart.

The invariant for a product register $t$ can be formulated as follows: the table $t$ can be generated by legal additions of entries (as described above) to the empty table. Another formulation of this invariant for a product register $t$ is by ordering: the entries $(pid_i, pl_i)$ of $t$ can be ordered in a sequence $(pid_1, pl_1), \ldots, (pid_n, pl_n)$ such that every part identification occurring in the list $pl_i$ is among the keys $pid_1, \ldots pid_{i-1}$ of the preceding entries of $t$.

*The value:* `newReg`

A new product register is an empty table:

```
val newReg = Table.empty: prodReg
```

*The function:* `addPart`

The function `addPart` must respect the invariant, i.e. it must either perform a legal addition of an entry to a product register or raise the exception `ProdReg` when applied to an illegal argument.

An auxiliary function is introduced which can check whether a parts list is legal for a given register, i.e. every quantity in the parts list is positive and every part identification in the parts list is a key (cf. the function isKey in Table E.2) of the register:

```
fun legalPartsList(pl,preg) =
    List.all
        (fn (pid,c) => c>0 andalso Table.isKey(pid,preg))
        pl
```

The function addPart is declared by:

```
fun addPart(pid,pl,preg) =
    if legalPartsList(pl,preg)
        andalso not (Table.isKey(pid,preg))
    then Table.update(pid,pl,preg)
    else raise ProdReg
```

It would be reasonable to require that every parts list:

$$[(pid_1, c_1), \ldots , (pid_n, c_n)]$$

occurring in a product register has the property that the parts in the list are mutually distinct, i.e. $i \neq j$ implies $pid_i \neq pid_j$. It is left as an exercise to revise the declaration for addPart to achieve this. See Exercise 13.1.

### The function: partsList

The function partsList is declared using the lookup function for tables:

```
fun partsList(pid,preg) = case Table.lookup(pid,preg) of
      SOME pl => pl
    | NONE    => raise ProdReg
```

### The function: toList

The function toList is declared using the toList function for tables:

```
fun toList preg = Table.toList preg
```

### The function: partBreakDown

We introduce some auxiliary functions in order to give a declaration for the partBreakDown function: the function addPartToPartsList adds a part with quantity $(pid, n)$ to a parts list $pl$. The quantity in the parts list is increased by $n$ if the part $pid$ is already present in the list, while the element $(pid, n)$ is otherwise inserted as a new element in the list:

```
fun addPartToPartsList((pid,n),[])            = [(pid,n)]
  | addPartToPartsList((pid,n),(pid',n')::pl) =
        if pid = pid' then (pid, n+n')::pl
        else (pid',n')::addPartToPartsList((pid,n),pl)
```

For example:

```
addPartToPartsList(("part2",5), [("part4",3), ("part2",8)]);
val it = [("part4",3), ("part2",13)] : (string * int) list

addPartToPartsList(("part6",5), [("part1",3), ("part2",8)]);
val it = [("part1",3), ("part2",8), ("part6",5)]
        : (string * int) list
```

The function mergePartsLists merges two parts lists *pl* and *pl'* by adding each element of *pl* to *pl'*. This is done by use of foldl for lists:

```
fun mergePartsLists(pl,pl') = foldl addPartToPartsList pl pl'
```

For example:

```
mergePartsLists([("part4",3), ("part2",8)],
               [("part2",10), ("part6",1)]);
val it = [("part4",3), ("part2",18), ("part6",1)]
        : (string * int) list
```

The function multPartsList multiplies each quantity in a parts list *pl* by the same factor *k*. This is done using the map function for lists:

```
fun multPartsList(k,pl) = map (fn (pid,n) => (pid,k*n)) pl
```

For example:

```
multPartsList(4, [("part4",3), ("part2",8)]);
val it = [("part4",12), ("part2",32)]
        : (string * int) list
```

The function partBreakDown can now be declared in mutual recursion with the function partsListBreakDown which builds the combined parts breakdown for all parts (with quantity) in a whole parts list.

The value of the expression partBreakDown(*pid*, *preg*) is [(*pid*, 1)] if the part *pid* is a basic part (i.e. when its parts list is empty), and otherwise the value of the expression partsListBreakDown(*pl*, *preg*), where *pl* is the parts list for *pid*:

```
fun partBreakDown(pid, preg) =
        case Table.getval(pid,preg) of
           [] => [(pid,1)]
         | pl => partsListBreakDown(pl,preg)

and partsListBreakDown([],_)                = []
  | partsListBreakDown((pid,n)::pl,preg) =
      let val pl' = partBreakDown(pid,preg)
          val pl1 = multPartsList(n,pl')
          val pl2 = partsListBreakDown(pl,preg)
      in
          mergePartsLists(pl1,pl2)
      end
```

The second clause for the `partsListBreakDown` function works as follows:

**1.** `pl'` is the parts list containing all the basic parts (with quantities) needed to produce one piece of the product `pid`.

**2.** `pl1` is the parts list obtained from `pl'` by multiplying all quantities with n, so `pl1` is the parts list containing all the basic parts needed to produce n pieces of product `pid`.

**3.** `pl2` is the parts list containing all the basic parts (with quantities) needed to produce the products with the quantities given in `pl`.

**4.** The resulting parts list is obtained by merging `pl1` and `pl2`.

Note that the invariant for product registers ensures that the `partBreakDown` function is well defined.

The total program is hence:

**Table 13.2** Program.

```
structure PartsList:> PartsList =
struct

type partId = string
type quantity = int (* n>0 *)
type partsList = (partId * quantity) list

type prodReg = (partId, partsList) Table.table
    (* The entries (pk,plk) can be ordered in a sequence
        (p1,pl1),...,(pn,pln) such that any part identifier
        in the list pli is one of p1,...,p(i-1) *)

exception ProdReg

val newReg = Table.empty:  prodReg

    (* local function
       legalPartsList:  partsList * prodReg -> bool *)

fun legalPartsList(pl,preg) =
    List.all
        (fn (pid,c) => c>0 andalso Table.isKey(pid,preg))
        pl

fun addPart(pid,pl,preg) =
    if legalPartsList(pl,preg)
        andalso not (Table.isKey(pid,preg))
    then Table.update(pid,pl,preg)
    else raise ProdReg
```

*Continued*

**Table 13.2**    Continued.

```
fun partsList(pid,preg) = case Table.lookup(pid,preg) of
      SOME pl => pl
   | NONE => raise ProdReg

fun toList preg = Table.toList preg

    (* local function addPartToPartsList:
       (partId * count) * partsList -> partsList *)

fun addPartToPartsList((pid,n),[])= [(pid,n)]
  | addPartToPartsList((pid,n),(pid',n')::pl) =
      if pid = pid' then (pid, n+n')::pl
      else (pid',n')::addPartToPartsList((pid,n),pl)

    (* local function
       mergePartsLists:  partsList * partsList -> partsList *)

fun mergePartsLists(pl,pl') = foldl addPartToPartsList pl pl'

    (* local function
       multPartsList:  int * partsList -> partsList *)

fun multPartsList(k,pl) = map (fn (pid,n) => (pid,k*n)) pl

fun partBreakDown(pid, preg) =
      case Table.getval(pid,preg) of
            [] => [(pid,1)]
          | pl => partsListBreakDown(pl,preg)

and partsListBreakDown([],_) = []
  | partsListBreakDown((pid,n)::pl,preg) =
      let val pl' = partBreakDown(pid,preg)
          val pl1 = multPartsList(n,pl')
          val pl2 = partsListBreakDown(pl,preg)
      in
         mergePartsLists(pl1,pl2)
      end

end;
```

## 13.4 Test

All cases are listed in Table 13.3. Some of the cases involve local functions which cannot be invoked directly by the user. One may introduce a special test signature in order to be able to invoke the local functions directly in the test, and the test signature should then contain specifications of the local functions. The tests in this example do, however, use only functions in the signature and the local functions are tested via the use of the functions in the signature.

**Table 13.3**  Test cases.

| Case | Function | Branch | Remark |
|---|---|---|---|
| 1 | legalPartsList | not c>0 | Illegal quantity |
| 2 | | not Table.isKey | Part not in table |
| 3 | | | OK |
| 4 | addPart | not legalPartsList(...) | Illegal parts list |
| 5 | | Table.isKey(pid,preg) | pid already in table |
| 6 | | | OK |
| 7 | partsList | SOME pl | OK |
| 8 | | [] | Part not found in table |
| 9 | toList | | |
| 10 | addPartsToPartsList | [] | Empty parts list |
| 11 | | pid=pid' | Non-empty list, part in list |
| 12 | | not pid=pid' | |
| 13 | mergePartsLists | | |
| 14 | multPartsLists | | |
| 15 | partBreakDown | [] | Basic part |
| 16 | | (pid,n)::pl | Composite part |
| 17 | partsListBreakDown | [] | Empty parts list |
| 18 | | (pid,n)::pl | Non-empty parts list |

The program is tested using the tests given in Table 13.4. Note that the result `[("part2",4),("part1",5)]` in test 5 and the result `[("part1",20),("part2",19)]` in test 8 would also be acceptable as the order of the elements in a parts list is of no importance.

**Table 13.4**  Tests.

| Test | Cases | Test | Expected result |
|---|---|---|---|
| | | open PartsList; | |
| 1 | 3, 6 | val reg1 = addPart("part1",[],newReg); | OK |
| 2 | 1, 4 | addPart("part2",[("part1",0)],reg1) | exception *ProdReg* |
| 3 | 2, 4 | addPart("part2",[("unknown",1)],reg1) | exception *ProdReg* |
| 4 | 3, 5 | addPart("part1",[],reg1) | exception *ProdReg* |
| | | val reg2 = addPart("part2",[],reg1); | |
| | | val reg3 = addPart("part3", | |
| | | [("part1",5),("part2",4)],reg2) | |
| | | val reg4 = addPart("part4", | |
| | | [("part2",3),("part3",4)],reg3) | |
| 5 | 7 | partsList("part3",reg4) | *[("part1",5),("part2",4)]* |
| 6 | 8 | partsList("unknown",reg4) | exception *ProdReg* |
| 7 | 9 | toList(reg1) | *[("part1",[])]* |
| 8 | 10-18 | partBreakDown("part4",reg4) | *[("part2",19),("part1",20)]* |

## 13.5 Summary

In this chapter we have illustrated how signatures and structures can be used in solving and documenting a concrete problem. The user's interface to the program is documented by a signature, while the program is implemented by a structure. Opaque signature matching is used to protect the invariant for a data representation by hiding local functions and types from the user. Test and test documentation follow the same lines as in the previous chapters on problem solving.

## Exercises

**13.1** Revise the declaration of the addPart function so that the parts lists occurring in a register do not contain several elements with the same part identifier. See also remark on Page 211.

**13.2** Extend the parts list program with a function that can delete the entry for a given part identifier in a product register. The function must respect the invariant for product registers.

**13.3** Extend the parts lists program to associate a cost to each part. The cost of a basic part is the price paid when purchasing the part while the cost associated to a composite part is the labour cost of assembling the parts in the parts list. The part breakdown function should be extended by a computation of the total costs for a part.

# Chapter 14

# Input/output in SML

This chapter introduces the basic input/output (I/O) system in SML and some examples of the use of the I/O functions, e.g. to perform input and output of text to the console and other devices, including files on the disk. More interesting applications of I/O are found in Chapter 15 on interactive programs. Further information about the I/O functions is found in Sections D.10 and D.11.

## 14.1   Input streams

The SML I/O system has a common framework for input from any kind of data *file* – such as keyboard or file on the disk – based on the concept of an *input stream*. During input from a file the stream comprises at any time the sequence of characters of the file which has not yet been input to the program. For input from a user this includes the characters that are still to be entered by the user.

The SML program accesses an input stream via a value of type `instream`. A new input stream can be created using the function:

```
TextIO.openIn: string -> instream
```

217

The evaluation of the expression TextIO.openIn(*s*) creates an input stream connected to the file named by the string *s*. Furthermore, there is a predefined input stream TextIO.stdIn for *standard input* from the user's keyboard. See also Section D.10.

In this section we give a general description of input streams. The following sections contain examples of input from disk files and from the user's keyboard.

The input of *n* characters from an input stream *is* is done by evaluating the expression TextIO.inputN(*is*, *n*). This evaluation returns the string of the first *n* characters from the stream as the result and has the *side-effect* of removing these characters from the stream, as in the following example where the three-character string 'fun' is read from the input stream '*is*' by evaluating TextIO.inputN(*is*, 3):

before TextIO.inputN(*is*, 3):          after TextIO.inputN(*is*, 3):

| f | u | n | c | ⋯ |

| c | ⋯ |

The SML I/O system transfers data from the file to the program via a *buffer* in the memory of the computer. Each transfer of data from the file to the buffer comprises a *block* of data. A disk file has fixed-sized blocks where the size is determined by the hardware characteristics of the disk, while a keyboard has variable-sized input blocks, each comprising one text line terminated by a new line character '\n'.

The I/O system transfers a new block of data from the file to the buffer when the data are needed for an input operation. The block may contain more data than requested by the input operation, and the excess data are then retained in the buffer for subsequent input operations. The I/O system is hence dividing the input stream into two parts: a leading part stored in the buffer in the memory of the computer, and a trailing part which has not yet been transferred from the file to the computer memory.

The buffering is illustrated in the following example where a program is reading a three-character string from a keyboard by evaluating the expression:

TextIO.inputN(*is*, 3)

for an input stream '*is*' connected to the keyboard:

Buffer:          Keyboard:

*empty*          | f | u | n | ⋯ |

As the buffer is empty, the SML I/O system must transfer a block of data from the keyboard into the buffer. For the keyboard a block is a complete text line, terminated by a new line character '\n'. Hence the input operation waits until the user has entered a complete line:

Buffer:          Keyboard:

*empty*          | f | u | n | c | t | i | o | n | a | l | \n | ⋯ |

The block is then transferred to the buffer:

Buffer:                                        Keyboard:

| f | u | n | c | t | i | o | n | a | l | \n |

[ ... ]

and the I/O system completes the evaluation of TextIO.inputN(*is*, 3) by returning the first three characters as the string 'fun', while leaving the rest of the line in the buffer:

Buffer:                          Keyboard:

| c | t | i | o | n | a | l | \n |

[ ... ]

In this situation extra reading from the stream can proceed without further transfer of data from the keyboard, as long as the requested number of characters is available in the buffer.

Note that a TextIO.inputN operation from a keyboard will wait until the user has entered a complete line (including the terminating 'new line'), as a complete block has to be transferred to the buffer.

## 14.2 ) Output streams

The concept of an *output stream* gives in a similar way a common framework for output to any kind of peripheral unit – like the screen on a terminal, a printer or a file on the disk. A new output stream can be created by the function:

```
TextIO.openOut: string -> outstream
```

The evaluation of the expression TextIO.openOut(*s*) gives an output stream connected to the file named by the string *s*. Furthermore, there is a predefined output stream TextIO.stdOut for *standard output* to the user's screen. See also Section D.11.

In this section we give a general description of output streams. The following sections contain examples of output to disk files and to the user's screen.

Output of a string *s* to an output stream *os* of type outstream is done by evaluating the expression TextIO.output(*os*, *s*). This gives the tuple () of type unit as result, but the evaluation has the *side-effect* of appending the string *s* to the output stream. This side-effect is illustrated below where the string "ction" is written to an output stream *os* already containing the string "fun":

before TextIO.output(*os*, "ction"):        after TextIO.output(*os*,"ction"):

| ... | f | u | n |                 | ... | f | u | n | c | t | i | o | n |

The SML I/O system transfers data from the program to the file via a *buffer* in the memory of the computer. For the above example we may, for example, have an empty buffer for the stream '*os*' before writing:

file:                        buffer:

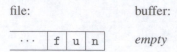

empty

and the evaluation of TextIO.output(*os*, "ction") may simply store the string in the buffer without writing any data to the file:

file:                        buffer:

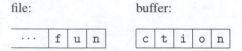

The SML program can force the transfer of the buffer to the file by evaluating the flushOut function on the output stream. In the example we may hence evaluate TextIO.flushOut(*os*) in order to get the buffer transferred to the file:

file:                                                buffer:

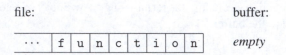

empty

## 14.3 Simple input and output

In this section we give examples of simple input and output by the introduction of some of the I/O functions from the Library. Similar functions are found in any programming language but the naming of the functions may be different.

### 14.3.1 Output

We will now introduce some of the functions from Section D.11.

*The function:* TextIO.openOut: string -> outstream

The value of the expression TextIO.openOut(*s*) is an output stream associated with the file named by the string *s*. For example:

```
val os = TextIO.openOut "myfile";
val os = <outstream> : TextIO.outstream
```

It is now possible to perform output to the file 'myfile' using the output stream denoted by os. The contents of 'myfile' is empty. Thus, when opening an already existing file, the old contents of the file is lost.

*The function:* TextIO.output: outstream * string -> unit

The evaluation of the expression TextIO.output(*os*, *str*) has the side-effect that the string *str* is added to the buffer of the output stream *os*. The evaluation may furthermore transfer a part of the buffer to the file. Hence, evaluation of the expression:

```
TextIO.output(os, "Line 1\n");
val it = () : unit
```

has the side-effect that the string `"Line 1\n"` is added to the buffer of the output stream os and perhaps transferred to the file.

### *The function:* `TextIO.flushOut: outstream -> unit`

The evaluation of the expression `TextIO.flushOut`(*os*) has the side-effect that the buffer for *os* will be emptied and the contents transferred to the file associated with the stream *os*. For example, the evaluation of:

```
TextIO.flushOut os;
val it = () : unit
```

will empty the buffer for os and the contents of the file 'myfile' is now:

> Line 1

The newline character is usually not shown if the file is inspected on the screen.

### *The function:* `TextIO.closeOut: outstream -> unit`

The evaluation of the expression `TextIO.closeOut`(*os*) has the side-effect that the buffer for *os* is emptied by writing its contents to the file associated with *os*, and this stream cannot be used to perform further output. For example (continuing the above example), evaluation of:

```
TextIO.output(os, "Line 2\n");
val it = () : unit

TextIO.closeOut os;
val it = () : unit
```

has the side-effect that a line is added to 'myfile' so that the new contents is:

> Line 1
> Line 2

where the effect of the newline character is that the file appears as two lines when inspected. Further output operations using os is rejected by the SML system:

```
TextIO.output(os, "Line 3\n");
! Uncaught exception:
! Io {cause = Fail "Stream is closed", function = "output",
        name = "myfile"}
```

*The value:* `TextIO.stdOut: outstream`

The identifier `TextIO.stdOut` denotes the predefined output stream for the user's screen. Thus, output to the screen can be performed in the following way:

```
TextIO.output(TextIO.stdOut, "This is a test");
This is a test> val it = () : unit

TextIO.output(TextIO.stdOut, "This is a test\n");
This is a test
val it = () : unit
```

where we see the effect of the newline character in the string. The output to the screen is forced by the response *val it = ...* from the SML system. The string 'This is ...' might otherwise have been stored in the buffer for later output to the screen.

### 14.3.2    Input

We will now introduce some of the functions from Section D.10.

*The function:* `TextIO.openIn: string -> instream`

The value of the expression `TextIO.openIn`(*s*) is an input stream associated with the file named by the string *s*. For example:

```
val is = TextIO.openIn "myfile";
val is = <instream> : TextIO.instream
```

It is now possible to perform input from the file 'myfile' using the input stream denoted by is. In the following we assume that the contents of 'myfile' is:

```
Line 1
Line 2
```

*The function:* `TextIO.inputLine: instream -> string`

The value of the expression `TextIO.inputLine`(*is*) is a string obtained from the file associated with the input stream *is* by transferring a line including the new line character '\n'. For example:

```
val l1 = TextIO.inputLine is;
val l1 = "Line 1\n" : string
```

*The function:* `TextIO.endOfStream: instream -> bool`

The value of the expression `TextIO.endOfStream`(*is*) is true if the whole contents of file associated with the input stream *is* have already been read; otherwise the value is false. For example:

```
TextIO.endOfStream is;
val it = false : bool
```

because the file 'myfile' still contains a line to read:

```
val l2 = TextIO.inputLine is;
val l2 = "Line 2\n" : string

TextIO.endOfStream is;
val it = true : bool
```

*The function:* `TextIO.closeIn: instream -> unit`

The evaluation of the expression `TextIO.closeIn`(*is*) is used to terminate the use of the input file. For example:

```
TextIO.closeIn is;
val it = () : unit
```

*The value:* `TextIO.stdIn: instream`

The identifier `TextIO.stdIn` denotes the predefined input stream for input from the user's keyboard. Thus, one can input a line from the keyboard as follows:

```
TextIO.inputLine(TextIO.stdIn);
abc
val it = "abc\n" : string
```

where the newline character comes from 'hitting the return key'.

## 14.4 Use of conversions

The data transferred by the `TextIO` functions are *texts*, i.e. strings of characters, which is the *external representation* of data. The program uses values of other types in the *internal representation*, so a *conversion* between different representations is often needed. This is achieved through the conversion functions described in Section D.9. The basic functions are the `fromString` functions (e.g. `Int.fromString`) for converting a string into a value of the corresponding type, and the `toString` functions (e.g. `Int.toString`) for converting a value of the corresponding type to a string.

More advanced conversions – in particular for printing numbers in a fixed format – are obtained using the formatted conversions in Section D.9.5.

Using `fromString` one may declare functions reading single values from text lines in a stream. For example, a function to read an integer from a line of an input stream can be declared as follows:

```
fun readIntLine(instrm) =
    Int.fromString(TextIO.inputLine(instrm));
val readIntLine = fn : TextIO.instream -> int option
```

The evaluation of readIntLine(TextIO.stdIn) will hence be suspended until a text line has been entered on the terminal. The result will be SOME $n$ for some integer $n$ if the first part of the line entered by the user can be interpreted as the decimal representation of an integer $n$, and otherwise NONE, as illustrated in the following dialogue where the evaluation of the expression on the right hand side of the declaration is completed when two text lines have been entered:

```
val (x,y) = (readIntLine(TextIO.stdIn),
              readIntLine(TextIO.stdIn) );
45   917
Monday
val x = SOME 45 : int option
val y = NONE : int option
```

The conversion is terminated by the exception Overflow if too large a number is entered:

```
val (x,y) = (readIntLine(TextIO.stdIn),
              readIntLine(TextIO.stdIn) );
5555555555555555555555555555555555555555555
! Uncaught exception:
! Overflow
```

This problem can be fixed by use of an exception handler:

```
fun readIntLine(instrm) =
    Int.fromString(TextIO.inputLine(instrm))
        handle Overflow => NONE ;
val readIntLine = fn : TextIO.instream -> int option

readIntLine(TextIO.stdIn);
5555555555555555555555555555555555555555555
val it = NONE : int option
```

Using the functions for date and time in Sections D.7 and D.8 and the conversion functions in Section D.9 one may, for example, declare a function to compute a string containing the actual date and time, and this string may then be output from the program:

```
fun nowStr() = Date.fmt "%c" (Date.fromTimeLocal(Time.now()));
val nowStr = fn : unit -> string

TextIO.output(TextIO.stdOut,nowStr()^"\n");
Mon Nov 30 16:50:14 1998
val it = () : unit
```

## 14.5  Sequential composition

The symbol ';' denotes the operator for *sequential composition* in SML. It combines two *expressions* $e_1$ and $e_2$ to form a new expression:

$( e_1 ; e_2 )$

This expression is evaluated as follows:

**1.** Evaluate $e_1$ and discard the result.

**2.** Evaluate $e_2$ and supply the result as resulting value of evaluating the expression $( e_1 ; e_2 )$.

Hence, if $e_2$ has type $\tau$ then $( e_1 ; e_2 )$ has also type $\tau$.

Sequential composition is useful in combining expressions where the evaluations have side-effects, e.g. where the evaluation produces output to a stream. We may for instance write a string *str* on an output stream *os* and then afterwards ensure that the buffer is emptied by evaluating the following sequential composition of expressions:

```
( TextIO.output(os,str) ; TextIO.flushOut(os) )
```

The definition of sequential composition generalizes to an arbitrary number $n$ of expressions $e_1, e_2, \ldots, e_n$:

$( e_1 ; e_2 ; \ldots ; e_n )$

This expression is worked out by evaluating the expressions from left to right and supplying the result value for the last expression $e_n$ as result of the evaluation. Hence the contribution of the expressions $e_1, \ldots, e_{n-1}$ to the evaluation is only that of the side-effects caused by evaluating their values. The type of the sequential composition will be the type of the last expression.

A sequential composition must be enclosed in brackets as shown above, but the brackets can be omitted if the sequential composition appears in a `let` construction:

```
let dec in e₁ ; e₂ ; ... ; eₙ end
```

The predefined infix operator `before` with the type `'a * 'b -> 'a` is similar to ';', but it returns the value of the first expression. Hence, the expression:

$e_1$ `before` $e_2$

is equivalent with the `let`-expression:

```
let val v = e₁
    val _ = e₂
in v end
```

For example, evaluating the expression:

`TextIO.inputLine` *is* `before TextIO.closeIn` *is*

will input a line *s* from the file connected to the input stream *is*, close the file connected to *is* and return the value *s*.

## 14.6  Input/output of composite data

When making programs that interact with the user it is often convenient to read several data items from the same input line. The following library function is then useful for splitting up a string into 'tokens':

```
String.tokens: (char -> bool) -> string -> string list
```

For example, the list of strings separated by semicolons can be extracted from a given string using the function fn x => x = #";":

```
String.tokens (fn x => x = #";") "abc;de f;;;;012";
val it = ["abc", "de f", "012"] : string list
```

and those separated by spaces can be extracted from a given string using the function Char.isSpace:

```
String.tokens Char.isSpace "123     monkey  1.24";
val it = ["123", "monkey", "1.24"] : string list
```

The functions String.tokens and Char.isSpace are found in Sections D.9.6 and D.3.3.

We can declare a function which can input an integer and a real number separated by spaces from an input stream by:

```
fun readIntAndReal instr =
  case String.tokens Char.isSpace (TextIO.inputLine instr)
  of
     [t1,t2] => (case (Int.fromString t1, Real.fromString t2)
                of
                   (SOME n, SOME r) => SOME(n,r)
                 | _               => NONE     )
   | _         =>  NONE
  handle Overflow => NONE;
val readIntAndReal =
    fn : TextIO.instream -> (int * real) option

readIntAndReal TextIO.stdIn;
34 1.2
val it = SOME(34, 1.2) : (int * real) option

readIntAndReal TextIO.stdIn;
45 ~3.7 abc
val it = NONE : (int * real) option

readIntAndReal TextIO.stdIn;
444444444444444444444444444444444444444444 2.5
val it = NONE : (int * real) option
```

## Input/output of lists

A list $[e_1, \ldots, e_n]$ of values $e_1, \ldots, e_n$ can be stored in a file on the disk containing text lines $line_1, \ldots, line_n$ where $line_k$ contains a textual representation of the value $e_k$ for $k = 1, \ldots, n$. In this way a list of integers may for example be stored in a text file where the $k$'th line contains the decimal representation of the $k$'th integer. Such a file is generated by the function outputIntList:

```
fun outputIntList(xs,fname)=
    let
        val outstr = TextIO.openOut fname
        fun outputInt x =
            TextIO.output(outstr,Int.toString(x)^"\n")
    in
        app outputInt xs ; TextIO.closeOut outstr
    end;
val outputIntList = fn : int list * string -> unit
```

The function opens a file on the disk and writes the list to the file by applying the locally declared printing function outputInt to each element in the list. The function app works like map in applying the function to each element in the list, but it does not build the list of function values (cf. Section D.4).

Input of a disk file containing a list is made by use of recursion as shown in the function inputIntList. It reads each line in the file by use of the function inputLine while the function endOfStream is used to determine when there are no more data to be read from the file:

```
fun inputIntList fname =
    let
        val instr = TextIO.openIn fname
        fun inputInt() =
            valOf(Int.fromString(TextIO.inputLine instr))
        fun inputList() =
            if TextIO.endOfStream instr then []
            else inputInt() :: inputList()
    in
        inputList() before TextIO.closeIn(instr)
    end;
val inputIntList = fn : string -> int list
```

The function raises the exception Option.Option via the function valOf if a line in the file cannot be converted to an integer value.

The following test of the functions outputs the list $[1,2,3]$ to the disk file named testFile and inputs it again from this file:

```
outputIntList([1,2,3],"testFile");
val it = () : unit
```

```
inputIntList "testFile";
val it = [1, 2, 3] : int list
```

## 14.7 Input with prompt and validation

In this section we give an example showing how to combine the input of data with a prompt and with a check of validity:

```
fun readTwoInts(prmpt,errmsg,p) =
   let fun repeat() =
       (TextIO.output(TextIO.stdOut,errmsg^"\n")
       ; readTwoInts(prmpt,errmsg,p))
   in
        TextIO.output(TextIO.stdOut,prmpt)
      ; TextIO.flushOut TextIO.stdOut
      ; case map Int.fromString
                   (String.tokens Char.isSpace
                      (TextIO.inputLine TextIO.stdIn))
          of   [SOME x, SOME y] => if p(x,y) then (x,y)
                                              else repeat()
             | _                 => repeat()
   end;
val readTwoInts = fn : string * string * (int * int -> bool)
                       -> int * int
```

The argument of the function readTwoInts is a triple (*prmpt*, *errmsg*, *p*) containing two strings *prmpt* and *errmsg*, and a predicate *p*: int*int->bool on pairs of integers. The function outputs the prompt *prmpt* on the terminal and awaits the input of a line. The evaluation of the value of the function will terminate with the result $(x, y)$ if the line contains two integers $x$ and $y$ such that $p(x, y) =$ true, while the function will otherwise output the string *errmsg* and repeat the whole operation. Note the use of ';' to sequence the input/output operations and that the use of flushOut allows the prompt and the answer from the user to be placed on the same text line.

The function can be used as shown in the following example:

```
val (x,y) = readTwoInts("Type x and y with x > y: ",
                        "Illegal input!"        ,
                        fn (x,y) => x > y          );
Type x and y with x > y: 3 4
Illegal input!
Type x and y with x > y: abcd
Illegal input!
Type x and y with x > y: 33 17
val x = 33 : int
val y = 17 : int
```

## 14.8 Summary

This chapter gives a brief introduction to the basic input/output system in SML. The TextIO functions allow a program to perform input and output of text to the console and other devices, including files on the disk. Examples show how these functions can be combined to form more flexible input/output functions.

## Exercises

**14.1** Modify the function readIntAndReal in Section 14.6 such that the function ignores characters typed at the end of the line after the real number.

**14.2** In this exercise any string is considered to be composed of *words* separated by space characters, whereas a word does not contain space characters. Write a program that reads a line from the console, reverses the characters in each word in the line and prints the reversed words separated by spaces.

**14.3** (a) Declare a function which can write a list of type (int*real*bool) list to a file. (Hint: make a suitable string representation of the list elements.)

(b) Write a corresponding function to read a file and convert it into a list of type (int*real*bool) list.

**14.4** (a) Declare a function:

```
fileFoldr: (string * 'a -> 'a) -> string -> 'a
```

such that the evaluation of the expression fileFoldr $f$ $b$ fileName will input the lines $line_1, \ldots, line_n$ of the file named '*fileName*' and compute the value of the expression:

$$f(line_1, f(line_2, \ldots, f(line_{n-1}, f(line_n, b))\cdots))$$

The function is hence working as foldr on the list of text lines in the file.

(b) Use the function fileFoldr to declare a function inputIntList which inputs a list of integers from a file where each text line contains one list element.

(c) Declare a function:

```
fileFoldl: (string * 'a -> 'a) -> string -> 'a
```

which works as foldl on the list of text lines in the file given by the argument of type string.

# Chapter 15

# Interactive programs

This chapter shows how to implement interactive programs which perform a dialogue with the user, where a dialogue is considered a sequence of *actions*. We consider two kinds of actions: *input actions*, where the user inputs data to the program, and *output actions*, where the program outputs data to the user.

The notion of *dialogue automaton* is introduced to give an abstract view of the dialogue. The data dependencies of the interactions are not considered in this automaton. An SML program for the dialogue is systematically constructed from the dialogue automaton by adding the data-dependent part. The construction is illustrated by a simple example.

## 15.1 A quiz program

As a running example we consider a quiz program guessing a natural number inside a given interval of integers by asking questions to the user. This program may, for example, perform the following dialogue guessing the natural number 8. As usual, the data entered by the user are shown in typewriter font while the data from the program is shown in *italic typewriter* font:

```
quiz(1,10);
Think of a number between 1 and 10
Is the number <= 5 ? no
Is the number <= 8 ? yes
Is the number <= 7 ? no
The number is 8
val it = () : unit
```

We find immediately that we have to construct a function:

```
quiz: int * int -> unit
```

The type of quiz accounts for the limiting interval (1 to 10 in the above sample run of the program), while the dialogue between user and program consists of side-effects which do not show up in the type of this function.

## 15.2 Actions

The above dialogue consists of a sequence of data transfers, where some parts are *output* from the program while other parts are *input* from the user. The parts that are output from the program are called *output actions* and the parts that are input from the user are called *input actions*. An *action* is either an input action or an output action.

The output actions from the above dialogue are:

- *Think of a number between 1 and 10*
- *Is the number <= 5 ?*
- *Is the number <= 8 ?*
- *Is the number <= 7 ?*
- *The number is 8*

The input actions from the above dialogue are:

- no
- yes
- no

The whole dialogue is a sequence of these actions.

## 15.3 Action schemas

The next step is to consider *action schemas*, where each action is an instance of a schema. The output action schemas are:

```
prelude:   Think of a number between  min and  max
question:  Is the number <= n ?
okmsg:     The number is n
```

where *min*, *max* and *n* can be arbitrary numbers.

We just have one input action schema:

```
answer:  ans
```

where *ans* can be either yes or no.

Note that these four action schemas cover infinitely many possible actions.

## 15.4 Functions for action schemas

We declare a function for each action schema corresponding to a single output or input of a data item.

For the output action schemas, we introduce:

```
prelude:   int * int -> unit
question:  int        -> unit
okmsg:     int        -> unit
```

where

● prelude(*min*, *max*) outputs: *Think of a number between min and max*

● question(*n*) outputs: *Is the number <=n ?*

● okmsg(*n*) outputs: *The number is n*

In general, a function for an output action schema has type:

```
τ -> unit
```

for some type $\tau$. It outputs a string which is composed of *fixed parts* such as, for example, *Think of a number between* and *and*, and *variable parts* such as the decimal representations of *min* and *max* which depend on the argument of the function.

The function for the input action schema must read input from the user and convert it to an internal representation that is convenient for the program. The internal representation for answers is given by the following type declaration:

```
datatype answer = Yes | No
```

If the user inputs a string that is not legal, then an exception is raised:

```
exception Quiz
```

We introduce the following function for the input action schema:

```
answer: unit -> answer
```

where `answer()` inputs a line from the user. The value of `answer()` is Yes, if the user inputs "yes\n", the value is No, if the user inputs "no\n", and otherwise the exception Quiz is raised.

In general, a function for an input action schema has the type:

```
unit -> τ
```

for some type $\tau$. It inputs some data from the user and returns a corresponding value of type $\tau$.

The functions for the action schemas are declared by:

```sml
open TextIO;

fun prelude(min,max) =
    (   output(stdOut,"Think of a number between ")
    ; output(stdOut,Int.toString(min))
    ; output(stdOut," and ")
    ; output(stdOut,Int.toString(max))
    ; output(stdOut,"\n")
    ; flushOut(stdOut)
    ) ;

fun question(n) =
    (   output(stdOut,"Is the number <= ")
    ; output(stdOut,Int.toString(n))
    ; output(stdOut," ? ")
    ; flushOut(stdOut)
    ) ;

fun okmsg(n) = (   output(stdOut,"The number is ")
                ; output(stdOut,Int.toString(n))
                ; output(stdOut,"\n")
                ; flushOut(stdOut)
                ) ;

datatype answer = Yes | No;

exception Quiz;

fun answer() = case inputLine(stdIn) of
                    "yes\n" => Yes
                | "no\n"  => No
                | _       => raise Quiz
```

The declaration open TextIO is included in order to avoid writing TextIO. in front of output, stdOut, flushOut and inputLine.

## 15.5  Dialogue automaton

So far we have described the actions and we have declared functions for implementing them. To describe the dialogue we must describe all possible wanted sequences of actions. To achieve this we introduce an intermediate step where we abstract from the values in the actions of the dialogue. (This means, for this example, that the natural numbers occurring in the actions, and the concrete answers from the user, are ignored.) The purpose is to extract the program structure for the dialogue program without having to deal with too many details.

For our example we have:

> The program first issues a `prelude` action. This is followed by a question/ answer cycle which is terminated by an `okmsg` action, upon which the program terminates. Each round in a question/answer cycle consists of a `question` action followed by an `answer` action.

It is convenient to describe this sequencing of occurrences of actions in a *dialogue automaton* as shown in Figure 15.1. It is a directed graph with one start node, which is marked *quiz* as this node corresponds to the function `quiz` for our quiz program. Names are introduced for *nodes* (other than the start node) for which there are outgoing edges. There are two such nodes named *A* and *B* in the graph. Nodes without outgoing edges are not named as these nodes correspond to the termination of our dialogue. Such nodes are called *stop* nodes. If a dialogue automaton has no stop node, the interaction with the user may go on forever. The *edges* are *labelled* by function names for action schemas. (We also allow *unlabelled* edges, as they are sometimes convenient in expressing the desired behaviour.)

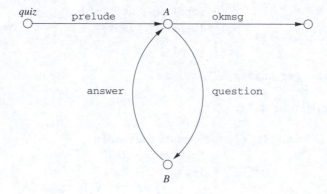

**Figure 15.1**   Dialogue automaton for quiz program.

A sequence of nodes $node_0\ node_1 \cdots node_n$, is called a *path* of a dialogue automaton if there exists an edge from $node_i$ to $node_{i+1}$, for $0 \le i < n$. Only the last node in a path may be a stop node. Furthermore, this path describes an action sequence $a_1 a_2 \cdots a_n$ if there is an edge labelled $a_i$ from $node_{i-1}$ to $node_i$, for $0 < i \le n$.

A *run* of a dialogue automaton is an action sequence for a path from the start node. We note that the dialogue automaton has been designed such that the runs of the automaton are the desired (possibly partial) sequences of actions for the program, e.g.:

```
prelude okmsg

prelude question answer okmsg

prelude question answer question answer okmsg

prelude question answer question answer question
```

Note that a sequence of actions need not end with an action leading to a stop node in the automaton. For example, a dialogue would not stop if the user at a given point did not enter an answer to a question.

We can systematically derive a *skeleton program* for the dialogue program. It consists of a set of mutual recursive declarations of skeleton functions, where the data-dependent part is still to be filled in. There is a function declaration for all nodes in the dialogue automaton, except for the stop nodes. The functions must be mutual recursive because there may be cycles in the dialogue automaton.

For the example we may get the following skeleton program:

```
fun quiz(···) = ( prelude(···) ; A(···) )

and A(···)    = if    ···
                then okmsg(···)
                else ( question(···) ; B(···) )

and B(···)    = case answer() of
                    Yes => A(···)
                  | No  => A(···)
```

Note that sequencing of output actions is expressed in the program using sequential composition ';'. The sequencing of an input action (answer in this example) is expressed using a composite expression making the input value available for the computations. The example uses a case expression to give a branch for each kind of possible input. Furthermore, since there are two edges going out from node $A$, there is an if-then-else expression to select between the two outgoing edges in the declaration for the function A. There are several ways in which branching can be expressed in SML and one should always choose the most convenient way.

## 15.6 Dialogue program

To derive a dialogue program from the above program skeleton we must have a strategy to guess a number in an interval [*min, max*] of the natural numbers $n : min \leq n \leq max$. We assume the invariant $min \leq max$, as the quiz would otherwise not be meaningful.

The strategy distinguishes between two cases:

**1.** *min* $\geq$ *max*: The number is *min*, owing to the invariant $min \leq max$, and the program has guessed the number, i.e. *min*.

**2.** *min* < *max*: Let *t* be the number (*min* + *max*) div 2 in the middle of the interval. Consider the question:

```
Is the number <=  t ?
```

If the answer to this question is yes, then the number must be in the interval [*min*, *t*], and if the answer is no, then the number must be in the interval [*t* + 1, *max*]. Thus, the number is guessed by repeatedly dividing the interval of consideration into halves.

Using this strategy the dialogue program is declared by:

```
fun quiz(min,max) = ( prelude(min,max) ; A(min,max) )

and A(min,max)    = if  min >= max
                    then okmsg(min)
                    else ( question((min+max) div 2) ;
                           B(min, (min+max) div 2, max) )

and B(min,t,max)  = case answer() of
                         Yes => A(min,t)
                       | No  => A(t+1,max)
```

The two occurrences of the expression `(min+max) div 2` in the declaration for A can be avoided using a `let`-expression.

A sample run of the quiz program was shown in Section 15.1.

## 15.7 Action refinement

A dialogue automaton may be very difficult to comprehend for complicated dialogues. The notion of *action refinement* may be helpful to avoid complication. The idea is to let actions denote dialogues.

We illustrate the idea on our example. This program terminates immediately with an exception if the user mistypes an answer. For example:

```
quiz(1,10);
Think of a number between 1 and 10
Is the number <= 5 ? nop
! Uncaught exception:
! Quiz
```

We will now refine the `answer` action so that the user gets a chance to correct the input. The `answer` action should validate the input as illustrated in Section 14.7. This refined `answer` action becomes a dialogue in itself, and it is described by the dialogue automaton in Figure 15.2.

When this dialogue ends, i.e. when the evaluation of `answer()` terminates, it gives

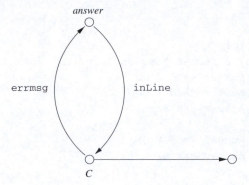

**Figure 15.2** Dialogue automaton for answers.

a legal answer, i.e. Yes or No, as result. This is not an action that is visible to the user and, therefore, there is no action on the edge leading to the stop node.

The functions for the action schemas errmsg and inLine are declared by:

```
fun errmsg() = (   output(stdOut, "Please answer yes or no\n")
                 ; flushOut(stdOut)
                 )
val errmsg = fn : unit -> unit

fun inLine() = inputLine(stdIn)
val inLine = fn : unit -> string
```

This dialogue automaton is very simple, so we give the corresponding dialogue program directly:

```
fun answer() = case inLine() of
                      "yes\n" => C(SOME Yes)
                    | "no\n"  => C(SOME No)
                    | _       => C NONE

and C (SOME Yes) = Yes
  | C (SOME No)  = No
  | C NONE       = ( errmsg() ; answer() )

val answer = fn : unit -> answer
val C = fn : answer option -> answer
```

The declaration for answer can be simplified to:

```
fun answer() = case inLine(stdIn) of
                      "yes\n" => Yes
                    | "no\n"  => No
                    | _       => ( errmsg() ; answer() );
```

Example:

```
quiz(1,10);
Think of a number between 1 and 10
Is the number <= 5 ? no
Is the number <= 8 ? yep
Please answer yes or no
no
Is the number <= 9 ? OK
Please answer yes or no
no
The number is 10
val it = () : unit
```

## 15.8  Summary

We have considered interactive programs performing a dialogue with the user, and
we have illustrated how such a dialogue program can be implemented using a simple
example. The dialogue consists of a sequence of input and output actions. Data are
transferred from the user to the program in an input action, while data are transferred
from the program to the user in an output action.

A dialogue automaton is introduced to describe all possible sequences of actions.
A skeleton program is systematically derived from the dialogue automaton. Input and
output actions are treated differently, as the program uses the input data from the user.
The final step is to add the data-dependent part to the skeleton program.

### Exercises

**15.1** Make a quiz program with the rôles interchanged, i.e. the user should guess an
integer by asking the program.

Use a dialogue as in the following example:

```
Quiz: You should guess a number between 0 and 59
Ask questions of form:  "< n",  "= n" or "> n":
> 19
no
< 19
yes
It is 17
Ask questions of form:  "< n",  "= n" or "> n":
= 17
You guessed it!
```

where a question to the program is a line with two items: a string ('>', '=', or
'<'), and an integer.

The program must fix the number between 0 and 59 to be guessed before starting the dialogue, and each run of the program should give a new number to be guessed. One may use the seconds of the current time which is obtained as the value of the expression:

```
Date.second(Date.fromTimeLocal(Time.now()))
```

15.2 Make a geography program guessing a country in Europe. The program asks questions to the user who answers yes or no. The program should use a binary tree with country names in the leaves and with a question in each node, such that the left subtree is chosen in case of answer yes and the right in case of answer no.

The program can be made to look more 'intelligent' by inserting some random questions in between the systematic questions taken from the tree. The random questions should be of two kinds: silly questions where the answer is not used by the program, and direct questions guessing a specific country where the answer is used by the program in case it gets answer yes. The seconds of the current time (cf. the previous exercise) can be used to generate random numbers for the program.

15.3 The game of Nim is played as follows. Any number of matches are arranged in heaps, the number of heaps, and the number of matches in each heap, being arbitrary. There are two players $A$ and $B$. The first player $A$ takes any number of matches from a heap; he or she may take one only, or any number up to the whole of the heap, but he or she must touch one heap only. $B$ then makes a move conditioned similarly, and the players continue to take alternately. The player who takes the last match wins the game.

The game has a precise mathematical theory: We define an operator xorb for non-negative integers by forming the *exclusive or* of each binary digit in the binary representation of the numbers, e.g.

$$
\begin{aligned}
109 &= 1101101_2 \\
70 &= 1000110_2 \\
109 \text{ xorb } 70 &= 0101011_2 &= 43
\end{aligned}
$$

The operator xorb is associative and commutative, and 0 is the unit element for the operator.

Let the non-negative integers $a_1, \ldots, a_n$ be the number of matches in the $n$ heaps, and let $m$ denote the integer:

$$m = a_1 \text{ xorb } a_2 \text{ xorb } \cdots \text{ xorb } a_n$$

The following can then be proved:

(a) If $m \neq 0$ then there exists an index $k$ such that $a_k \text{ xorb } m < a_k$. Replacing the number $a_k$ by $a_k \text{ xorb } m$ then gives a new set of $a_i$s with $m = 0$.

(b) If $m = 0$ and if one of the numbers $a_k$ is replaced by a smaller number, then the $m$-value for the new set of $a_i$s will be $\neq 0$.

This theory gives a strategy for playing Nim:

(a) If $m \neq 0$ before a move, then make a move to obtain $m = 0$ after the move (cf. the above remark 1).

(b) If $m = 0$ before a move, then remove one match from the biggest heap (hoping that the other player will make a mistake, cf. the above remark 2).

Use this strategy to make a program playing Nim with the user. Use the type Word.word for representing the number of matches in each heap, and use the function Word.xorb which implements the operator xorb on values of type Word.word. (See Section D.2.4.)

# Problem solving IV

In this chapter we use the method introduced in Chapters 4, 6 and 13 to design a program for a simple flight reservation system. There are two new aspects in this chapter:

● The program executes a dialogue with a user, where the commands given by the user have more structure than we have seen in previous examples.

● The program is divided into several modules by using the signature and structure concepts.

The problem formulation is:

> A flight reservation system must contain a register where flights are associated with the persons who have reservations and the persons who are on the waiting list for the flight.
>
> The system must provide a command for the creation of a new flight with a given number of seats, and commands for making and cancelling a reservation for a given flight. A person who makes a reservation for a fully booked flight is placed on a waiting list for the flight.

## 16.1  Problem analysis

We will construct a flight reservation system that can participate in a dialogue with the user. The dialogue will consist of command lines entered by the user and the system reacts by writing answers on the screen, as we have seen in Chapter 15.

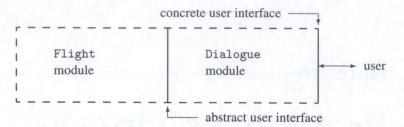

**Figure 16.1**    Modules and interfaces for flight reservation system.

However, other kinds of interaction with the user could be used instead, e.g. a window-based dialogue, and we want to anticipate a change of technology for the interaction with the user. So we will design the program as shown in Figure 16.1 with modules Flight and Dialogue, and abstract and concrete interfaces to the user:

● **Abstract user interface:** Specifies types command, register and result and a function:

        eval: register * command -> register * result

The abstract user interface is designed so that it is independent of the technology used for user interaction. Thus, the values of type command describe the possible commands to the system in an interaction-independent manner, and the eval function executes these commands.

● **Concrete user interface:** Specifies the (line-based) dialogue between the user and the program.

Using these modules a command should be executed in the following way:

**1.** The Dialogue module inputs the command from the user and converts it to a value *cmd* of type command.

**2.** The eval function in the Flight module is used to compute updated register *reg'* and result *res*:

$$(reg', res) = \text{eval}(reg, cmd)$$

**3.** The Dialogue module converts the value *res* of type result to textual form which is output to the user.

The idea is hence that the Flight module should implement a suitable abstraction of the flight system – independent of the technology used for communication with the user – while the Dialogue module should implement the dialogue with the user in the selected technology (line-oriented terminal I/O in our case). A change in the concrete user interface to another technology, e.g. data entry via a window on the terminal, may then be obtained by replacing the Dialogue module, while the Flight module is reused without changes.

In the rest of this section we specify the abstract and concrete user interfaces.

### 16.1.1   The abstract user interface

In order to specify this interface we have to model the data for the flight reservation system by SML types.

First of all, *persons* can make flight reservations. A realistic representation of a person could contain information such as name, address, nationality, smoker/non-smoker, age, sex, etc. We simply specify a person by:

```
type person = string
```

Similarly, a flight is specified by:

```
type flight = string
```

A person can only make one reservation for a given flight. Furthermore, we ignore the assignment of seats as we assume that seats are assigned to persons when they check in at the airport. Thus, there is no ordering among the persons with reservations for a flight and it is, therefore, natural to model such a collection of persons by a set:

```
type reservations  = person Set.set
```

If a person cancels a reservation on a fully booked flight, then the person whose name is first on the waiting list gets the reservation just cancelled. Thus, the sequence in which persons get on the waiting list is of importance, so we represent a waiting list as a list in the SML sense of the word. This does, however, not entirely capture the concept of a waiting list, as a person should not occur twice on a waiting list. Thus, the type for waiting lists is accompanied by an invariant, expressing the absence of replicas among the persons on the waiting list:

```
type waitingList  = person list  (* without replicas *)
```

The data for a flight consist of number of seats *seats*, the reservations *rsv* and the waiting list *wl* of the flight. These data must satisfy the invariant that *seats* is positive, that the cardinality of *rsv* does not exceed *seats*, that *wl* is empty when the cardinality of *rsv* is smaller than *seats*, and that no person occurs in both *rsv* and *wl*:

```
type numberOfSeats = int (* > 0 *)

type flightData
           = numberOfSeats * reservations * waitingList
 (* (seats, rsv, wl) with
       (card(rsv) <= seats and  wl = [])
    or ((card(rsv) = seats) and (p in rsv => p not in wl))
  *)

type flightDescr  = flight * flightData
```

### Abstract syntax

We will now declare a type command which represents commands presented to the system at the abstract user interface. At this interface we only consider the essential entities of the commands also called the *abstract syntax* for commands. This description of commands is called abstract because it does *not* consider how a user should input a command. In the dialogue part we consider the concrete syntax for how a user inputs a command.

The *abstract syntax* for commands is defined by a `datatype` declaration with a constructor for each command:

- CmdCreate(*f*, *seats*) represents the *create* command for flight *f* with *seats* seats.
- CmdReserve(*f*, *p*) represents the *reserve* command for flight *f* and person *p*.
- CmdCancel(*f*, *p*) represents the *cancel* command for flight *f* and person *p*.
- CmdListAll represents the *list* command which is added to the system for test purposes. It lists all flights in the system.

Thus, the type is declared by:

```
datatype command =
    CmdCreate  of flight * numberOfSeats
  | CmdReserve of flight * person
  | CmdCancel  of flight * person
  | CmdListAll
```

The type `result` represents the possible responses from the system, and it is called the *abstract syntax* for results:

```
datatype result =
    ResOK
  | ResIllegalNoOfSeats
  | ResFlightAlreadyExists
  | ResUnknownFlight
  | ResAlreadyReserved
  | ResOnWaitList
  | ResAlreadyOnWaitList
  | ResAllList of flightDescr list
```

The first constructor signals a successful execution of a command. The last constructor `ResAllList` is used for the result of a *list* command and it contains a list of flight descriptions. The others are simple values corresponding to results without parameters. They signal different error situations, as indicated by their names.

The flight reservation system contains a register, where number of seats, reservations and waiting lists are associated with flights. But the `eval` function for commands can be specified without revealing the internal structure of the register, Thus, the register is specified as an opaque type:

```
type register
```

The evaluation of commands is given by a function `eval` specified by:

```
val eval: register * command -> register * result
```

In order to initialize the system we need furthermore an initial value for the register. It is specified by:

```
val initialReg: register
```

The result of this part of the problem analysis is documented in the following interface definition:

**Table 16.1**   Abstract user interface.

```
signature Flight =
sig
   type person        = string
   type reservations  = person Set.set
   type waitingList   = person list   (* without replicas *)
   type numberOfSeats = int           (* > 0              *)
   type flight        = string
   type flightData    = numberOfSeats * reservations * waitingList
      (* (seats, rsv, wl) with
              ( card(rsv) <= seats and  wl = []                    )
           or ((card(rsv) = seats) and (p in rsv => p not in wl))
         *)
   type flightDescr   = flight * flightData

   datatype command =
        CmdCreate     of flight * numberOfSeats
      | CmdReserve    of flight * person
      | CmdCancel     of flight * person
      | CmdListAll

   datatype result =
        ResOK
      | ResIllegalNoOfSeats
      | ResFlightAlreadyExists
      | ResUnknownFlight
      | ResAlreadyReserved
      | ResOnWaitList
      | ResAlreadyOnWaitList
      | ResAllList of flightDescr list

   type register

   val initialReg: register

   val eval: register * command -> register * result

end;
```

### 16.1.2    Concrete user interface

We will use an interface where the key-word for a command and each parameter is entered in a separate line. A sketch of a sample run of a dialogue at the interface to the user is:

```
flightRes();
Flight reservation system
Enter command: create
Enter flight: SK234
Enter no of seats: 0
Illegal no of seats

Enter command: create
Enter flight: SK234
Enter no of seats: 1
OK

    ...

Enter command: cancel
Enter flight: SK234
Enter person: Peter
OK

Enter command: list
FLIGHT: SK234    NO OF SEATS: 1
RESERVATIONS:
Philip
WAITING LIST:

    ...

Enter command: exit
Exit
val it = () : unit
```

The key-words and parameters are given in Table 16.2. The output of a result

| Table 16.2 | Concrete user interface. | |
| --- | --- | --- |
| **Command** | **Key-word** | **Parameters** |
| create flight | create | *flight*    *numberOfSeats* |
| reserve | reserve | *flight*    *person* |
| cancel | cancel | *flight*    *person* |
| list | list | |
| exit program | exit | |

is a single text line for each of the results: ResOk, ResIllegalNoOfSeats, ...,
ResAlreadyOnWaitList, while the flight description list of ResAllList is printed
over several lines.

---

**Note**

The reader should note that we need a better notation in order to describe the
structure of the textual input and output in a brief and concise way. The formalism
(called BNF grammars) used in Section B.2 for describing the syntax of the SML
language is actually such a notation, but we will not pursue this issue further here.

## 16.2  Programming

The result of the programming activity is a pair of modules Flight and Dialogue.

### 16.2.1  The Flight module

A register is modelled by a table having flights as keys and flight data as values:

```
type register = (flight, flightData) Table.table
```

The initial register is the empty table:

```
val initialReg = Table.empty: register
```

The function *eval* is divided into cases according to the command to be executed. Note
that lists, tables and sets provide convenient abstractions in the function declaration.
This gives the declaration of the Flight structure in Table 16.3. The dots indicate that
the structure contains type declarations identical to the type specifications for the types
person, reservations, ..., result in the signature.

---

**Table 16.3**  Flight program.

```
structure Flight :> Flight = struct

    type person         = string
    ⋮
    datatype result = ...

    type register = (flight,flightData) Table.table

    val initialReg = Table.empty: register
```
                                                                    *Continued*

**Table 16.3** Continued.

```
fun eval(reg,cmd) =  case cmd of

  CmdCreate(f,seats) =>                                    (* 1  *)
    if seats <= 0
    then (reg, ResIllegalNoOfSeats)                        (* 1a *)
    else
    (case Table.insert(f,(seats,Set.empty,[]),reg) of
        NONE     => (reg , ResFlightAlreadyExists) (* 1b *)
      | SOME reg' => (reg', ResOK) )                        (* 1c *)

| CmdReserve(f,p) =>                                        (* 2  *)
    (case Table.lookup(f,reg) of
        NONE            => (reg, ResUnknownFlight)   (* 2a *)
      | SOME (seats,res,wl) =>
         if Set.member(p,res)
            then (reg, ResAlreadyReserved)                 (* 2b *)
         else if Set.card(res) < seats then               (* 2c *)
            let val res' = Set.insert(p,res) in
                (Table.update(f,(seats,res',wl),reg), ResOK)
            end
         else if List.exists (fn x => x = p) wl then   (* 2d *)
            (reg, ResAlreadyOnWaitList)
         else (Table.update(f,(seats,res,wl @ [p]),reg)
              , ResOnWaitList)  )                          (* 2e *)

| CmdCancel(f,p) =>                                         (* 3  *)
    (case Table.lookup(f,reg) of
        NONE            => (reg, ResUnknownFlight)   (* 3a *)
      | SOME (seats,res,wl) =>
         if Set.member(p,res) then
            let val res' = Set.delete(res,p)
                val (res'',wl'') =
                    case wl of
                        []          => (res',[])           (* 3b *)
                      | (p'::wl') =>
                            (Set.insert(p',res')),wl')   (* 3c *)
            in (Table.update(f,(seats,res'',wl''),reg),ResOK)
            end
         else                                              (* 3d *)
            let val wl' = List.filter (fn x => x <> p) wl
            in (Table.update(f,(seats,res,wl'),reg),ResOK)
       end )

| CmdListAll => (reg, ResAllList(Table.toList reg))  (* 4  *)
end;
```

Most of this program should be easy to read, but one should note the algorithm in the *reserve* command. If the number of reservations Set.card(res) is less than the number seats of seats (cf. note (* 2c *)) then the person is just added to the reservations (e.g. Set.insert(p,res)), otherwise she/he is added at the end of the waiting list (cf. wl @ [p] in (* 2e *)).

The *cancel* command moves the heading element p' from the waiting list wl to the reservations (cf. note (* 3c *)). The last branch of the cancel command (cf. note (* 3d *)) removes the person p from the waiting list. Note that the user will not be notified if p is not on the waiting list wl.

## 16.2.2 The Dialogue module

The dialogue uses the following actions:

- readCommand:  unit    -> command option    Reads a command
- prologue:     unit    -> unit              Writes the prologue text
- writeResult:  result  -> unit              Writes a result
- epilogue:     unit    -> unit              Writes the epilogue text

where readCommand returns NONE for the key-word exit.

The interaction with the user is very simple: The program starts with a prologue action. This is followed by a read command/write result cycle consisting of a readCommand action and a writeResult action. The dialogue is terminated with an epilogue action. This leads to the dialogue automaton given in Figure 16.2.

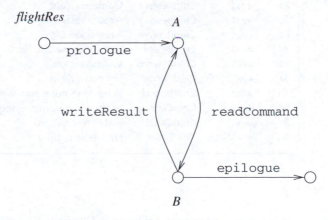

**Figure 16.2**  Dialogue automaton for flight reservation program.

Using the methods of Chapter 15 we get the program in Table 16.4 for the dialogue. The actions are not listed in the table as they are easy to program using the methods of Section 14.7.

**Table 16.4**  Dialogue program.

```
fun flightRes() = ( prologue() ; A(initialReg) )

and A(reg) = B(reg, readCommand())

and B(reg,cmd) = case cmd of
                      SOME cmd =>
                          let val (reg',res) = eval(reg,cmd)
                          in
                              writeResult(res) ; A(reg')
                          end
                    | NONE    => epilogue()
```

## 16.3  Test

We will only show the test of the eval function in the Flight module. The cases are given in Table 16.5 (cf. the numbering in the program). The test consists of the commands in Table 16.6 with expected results. This table corresponds to a long dialogue with the program – a part of this dialogue was shown on Section 16.1.2.

**Table 16.5**  Test cases.

| Case | Function | Branch | Remark |
|------|----------|--------|--------|
| 1a | eval | CmdCreate | Number of seats $\leq 0$ |
| 1b | eval | CmdCreate | Flight already exists |
| 1c | eval | CmdCreate | Creation OK |
| 2a | eval | CmdReserve | Unknown flight |
| 2b | eval | CmdReserve | Already reserved |
| 2c | eval | CmdReserve | Reservation OK |
| 2d | eval | CmdReserve | Already on waiting list |
| 2e | eval | CmdReserve | Waiting list OK |
| 3a | eval | CmdCancel | Unknown flight |
| 3b | eval | CmdCancel | In reservations, empty waiting list |
| 3c | eval | CmdCancel | In reservations, non-empty waiting list |
| 3d | eval | CmdCancel | Not in reservations |
| 4 | eval | CmdListAll | List whole register |

## 16.4  Summary

The method for program design, introduced in Chapters 4, 6 and 13, has been applied to design an interactive system which is a simple flight reservation system. The design uses a division into separate modules for performing the computations (the Flight module) and for performing the user dialogue (the Dialogue module). The key point in the problem analysis is to find suitable datatype declarations for commands and results, called the abstract syntax of the interactive system. These types form the core

**Table 16.6**   Tests.

| Test | Case | Command | Expected result |
|------|------|---------|-----------------|
| 1 | 1a | CmdCreate("SK234",0) | ResIllegalNoOfSeats |
| 2 | 1c | CmdCreate("SK234",1) | ResOk |
| 3 | 1b | CmdCreate("SK234",2) | ResFlightAlreadyExists |
| 4 | 2a | CmdReserve("SK235", "Peter") | ResUnknownFlight |
| 5 | 2c | CmdReserve("SK234", "Peter") | ResOK |
| 6 | 2b | CmdReserve("SK234", "Peter") | ResAlreadyReserved |
| 7 | 2e | CmdReserve("SK234", "Philip") | ResOnWaitList |
| 8 | 2d | CmdReserve("SK234", "Philip") | ResAlreadyOnWaitList |
| 9 | 3a | CmdCancel("SK235", "Peter") | ResUnknownFlight |
| 10 | 3c | CmdCancel("SK234", "Peter") | ResOK |
| 11 | 4 | CmdListAll | rsv = {"Philip"}, wl = [] |
| 12 | 3b | CmdCancel("SK234", "Philip") | ResOk |
| 13 | 2c | CmdReserve("SK234", "Peter") | ResOK |
| 14 | 2e | CmdReserve("SK234", "Philip") | ResOnWaitList |
| 15 | 3d | CmdCancel("SK234", "Philip") | ResOk |
| 16 | 4 | CmdListAll | rsv = {"Peter"}, wl = [] |

of the interface between the modules – called the abstract user interface. This interface is expressed as a signature (Flight in the example).

This design gives a high degree of information hiding between computations and dialogue and it allows a change in the technology for communication with the user simply by replacing the dialogue module.

The example shows that tables and sets provide convenient abstractions in the construction of the data model, and in the construction of function declarations. The corresponding library modules made the construction of a prototype very easy, and made an early validation of the program design possible.

## Exercises

**16.1** Extend the flight reservation system with commands that for a given person $p$ can extract

(a) a list of the flights for which $p$ has a reservation, and

(b) a list of the flights for which $p$ is on the waiting list.

**16.2** It is occasionally necessary to replace the aeroplane of a given flight with another one. The new aeroplane may have a different number of seats than the original one, and it is in this case necessary to adjust the set of reservations and the waiting list for the flight. Extend the flight reservation system with a command to support such a change of aeroplanes.

**16.3** The reservations and waiting list for a given flight may be represented by a single list of persons (without repetitions). A person making a reservation is added to the front of the list. Thus, a suffix of the list constitutes the reservations (the 'oldest' elements in the list) and a prefix of the list (the 'youngest' elements in the list) constitutes the waiting list for the flight.

Make a new structure `Flight` based on this idea. What is achieved with the new internal representation of `register`?

**16.4** Make an interactive interface to the cash register example in Chapter 6.

# Iteration

We have not considered efficiency of programs so far in this book. In this chapter we will present a simple technique which in some situations can improve the efficiency of programs dramatically. To improve the efficiency of a given function, the idea is to search for a more general function, whose declaration has a certain form called *iterative* or *tail recursive*. We will use the term iterative from now on. We give examples showing the usefulness of this technique. Iterative functions do not, however, always give the most efficient implementations, and we give an example where a good algorithmic trick gives much better performance than an iterative solution. For a systematic study of efficient algorithms, we refer to textbooks on 'algorithms and data structures' (e.g. [9, 10]).

The notion of iterative function is used in Chapter 18 to relate while loops and recursive function declarations.

## 17.1 Resource measures

The performance of an algorithm given by a function declaration in SML is expressed by figures for the resources used in the *evaluation* of a function value:

- *Use of computer memory:* the *maximum size* of computer memory needed to represent *expressions* and *bindings* during the evaluation.
- *Computation time:* the *number* of individual *computation steps*.

The important issue is to estimate how these figures depend on the 'size' of the argument for 'large' arguments, e.g. number of digits of integer argument, length of list argument, depth (i.e. number of levels) of tree argument. These performance figures are essentially language independent, so implementations of the same program in another programming language will show a similar behaviour.

Efficiency in performance is not the only important issue in programming. Readability is often more important as the program should be understandable to the readers (including the programmer him- or herself). The choice of function declaration should therefore be based on a trade-off between performance and readability (i.e. simplicity), using the simplest declaration for any particular function in a program – unless there is a risk that it becomes a performance bottleneck for the overall program.

## 17.2 Two problems

In this section we reconsider the declarations of the factorial function `fact` (Section 1.4.3) and the reverse function for lists `naive_rev` (Section 5.4.2). We shall see that evaluation of a function value for `fact` uses more computer memory than necessary, and that the evaluation of a function value for `naive_rev` requires more evaluation steps than necessary. More efficient implementations for these functions are given in the next section.

### 17.2.1　The factorial function

The factorial function has previously been declared by:

```
fun fact 0 = 1
  | fact n = n * fact(n-1);
val fact = fn: int -> int
```

We have seen that the evaluation of the expression $\text{fact}(N)$ proceeds through a number of evaluation steps building an expression with a size proportional to the argument $N$ upon which the expression is evaluated:

$$
\begin{aligned}
&\text{fact}(N)\\
\rightsquigarrow\quad &(\texttt{n * fact(n-1)}, [\texttt{n} \mapsto N])\\
\rightsquigarrow\quad &N * \text{fact}(N-1)\\
\rightsquigarrow\quad &N * (\texttt{n * fact(n-1)}, [\texttt{n} \mapsto N-1])\\
\rightsquigarrow\quad &N * ((N-1) * \text{fact}(N-2))\\
&\vdots\\
\rightsquigarrow\quad &N * ((N-1) * ((N-2) * (\cdots(4 * (3 * (2 * 1)))\cdots)))\\
\rightsquigarrow\quad &N * ((N-1) * ((N-2) * (\cdots(4 * (3 * 2))\cdots)))\\
&\vdots\\
\rightsquigarrow\quad &N!
\end{aligned}
$$

The maximum size of the memory needed during this evaluation is proportional to $N$, as the SML system must remember all $N$ factors of the expression: $N*((N-1)*((N-2)*(\cdots(4*(3*(2*1)))\cdots)))$ during the evaluation.

## 17.2.2   The reverse function

The naive declaration for the reverse function has previously been given as:

```
fun naive_rev [] = []
  | naive_rev (x::xs) = naive_rev xs @ [x];
val naive_rev = fn : 'a list -> 'a list
```

A part of the evaluation of the expression naive_rev $[x_1, x_2, \ldots, x_n]$ is:

$$naive\_rev\ [x_1, x_2, \ldots, x_n]$$
$$\leadsto\quad naive\_rev\ [x_2, \ldots, x_n]@[x_1]$$
$$\leadsto\quad (naive\_rev\ [x_3, \ldots, x_n]@[x_2])@[x_1]$$
$$\vdots$$
$$\leadsto\quad ((\cdots(([]@[x_n])@[x_{n-1}])@\cdots@[x_2])@[x_1])$$

There are $n + 1$ evaluation steps above and a memory piece of size proportional to $n$ is required by the SML system to represent the last expression. These figures are to be expected for reversing a list of size $n$.

However, the further evaluation

$$((\cdots(([]@[x_n])@[x_{n-1}])@\cdots@[x_2])@[x_1])\ \leadsto\ [x_n, x_{n-1}, \ldots, x_2, x_1]$$

requires a number of evaluation steps that is proportional to $n^2$.

To see this, observe first that $m + 1$ evaluation steps are needed to evaluate the expression $[y_1, \ldots, y_m]@zs$ as $y_1 :: (y_2 :: \ldots :: (y_m :: zs) \ldots)$. Thus,

| | |
|---|---|
| $[]@[x_n]\ \leadsto\ [x_n]$ | requires 1 step |
| $[x_n]@[x_{n-1}]\ \leadsto\ [x_n, x_{n-1}]$ | requires 2 steps |

$$\vdots$$

| | |
|---|---|
| $[x_n, x_{n-1}, \ldots, x_2]@[x_1]\ \leadsto\ [x_n, x_{n-1}, \ldots, x_2, x_1]$ | requires $n$ steps |

Hence, the evaluation of $((\cdots(([]@[x_n])@[x_{n-1}])@\cdots@[x_2])@[x_1])$ requires

$$1 + 2 + \cdots + n = \frac{n(n + 1)}{2}$$

steps, which is proportional to $n^2$.

## ( 17.3 )  Solutions: accumulating parameters

In this section we will show that much improved implementations for both the above functions can be obtained by considering more general functions, where the argument has been extended by an extra component ('m' and 'ys'):

$$itfact(n, m) \quad = \quad n! \cdot m, \text{ for } n \geq 0$$
$$itrev([x_1, \ldots, x_n], ys) \quad = \quad [x_n, \ldots, x_1]@ys$$

Note that $n! = $ itfact$(n, 1)$ and rev $[x_1, \ldots, x_n] = $ itrev$([x_1, \ldots, x_n], [])$. So good implementations for the above functions will provide good implementations for the factorial and the reverse functions also.

### 17.3.1     The factorial function

The function `itfact` is declared by:

```
fun itfact(0,m) = m
  | itfact(n,m) = itfact(n-1,n*m)
```

Consider the following evaluation:

$$
\begin{aligned}
&\quad\ \ \text{itfact(5,1)}\\
&\rightsquigarrow\ (\text{itfact(n,m)},\ [n \mapsto 5, m \mapsto 1])\\
&\rightsquigarrow\ (\text{itfact(n-1,n*m)},\ [n \mapsto 5, m \mapsto 1])\\
&\rightsquigarrow\ \text{itfact(4,5)}\\
&\rightsquigarrow\ (\text{itfact(n,m)},\ [n \mapsto 4, m \mapsto 5])\\
&\rightsquigarrow\ (\text{itfact(n-1,n*m)},\ [n \mapsto 4, m \mapsto 5])\\
&\rightsquigarrow\ \text{itfact(3,20)}\\
&\rightsquigarrow\ \ldots\\
&\rightsquigarrow\ \text{itfact(0,120)}\\
&\rightsquigarrow\ (\text{m},\ [m \mapsto 120])\\
&\rightsquigarrow\ 120
\end{aligned}
$$

This evaluation of `itfact(5,1)` has the properties we are looking for: it does not build large expressions and the number of evaluation steps needed for evaluating $itfact(n, m)$ is proportional to $n$.

The argument pattern m in the above declaration is called an *accumulating parameter*, since the result is gradually built in this parameter during the evaluation.

The main part of the above evaluation of `itfact(5,1)` is the gradual evaluation of arguments for the recursive calls of the function:

$$(5, 1),\ (4, 5),\ (3, 20),\ (2, 60),\ (1, 120),\ (0, 120)$$

Each of these values is obtained from the previous one by applying the function:

```
fn (n,m) => (n-1, n*m)
```

so the evaluation of the arguments can be viewed as repeated (or iterated) applications of this function.

### 17.3.2     The reverse function

The function `itrev` is declared by:

```
fun itrev([], ys)    = ys
  | itrev(x::xs, ys) = itrev(xs, x::ys)
```

Consider the following evaluation (where the bindings are omitted):

```
    itrev([1,2,3],[])
⤳   itrev([2,3],1::[])
⤳   itrev([2,3],[1])
⤳   itrev([3],2::[1])
⤳   itrev([3],[2,1])
⤳   itrev([],3::[2,1])
⤳   itrev([],[3,2,1])
⤳   [3,2,1]
```

This evaluation of `itrev([1,2,3],[])` also has the properties we are looking for: it does not build large expressions and the number of evaluation steps needed for evaluating $itrev(xs, ys)$ is proportional to the number of elements of $xs$. For large lists it makes a big difference whether the number of evaluation steps needed is proportional to $n$ or to $n^2$.

The argument pattern ys in the above declaration is the accumulating parameter in this example since the result list is gradually built in this parameter during the evaluation.

Note that each argument in the recursive calls of `itrev` is obtained from the argument in the previous call by applying the function:

```
fn (x::xs, ys) => (xs, x::ys)
```

## 17.4  Iteration

The declarations for `itfact` and `itrev` have a certain form which we will study in this section.

A declaration of a function $g : \tau \rightarrow \tau'$ is said to be an *iteration of a function* $f : \tau \rightarrow \tau$ if it is an instance of the *schema*:

```
fun g z = if p z then g(f z) else h z
```

for suitable predicate $p : \tau \rightarrow$ `bool` and function $h : \tau \rightarrow \tau'$.

A function $g$ declared according to the above schema is called an *iterative function* or a *tail recursive function*.

*The function:* `itfact`

The function `itfact` is an iterative function because it can be declared as:

```
fun itfact(n,m) = if n<>0 then itfact(n-1,n*m) else m;
```

which is an instance of the above schema with:

```
fun f(n,m) = (n-1, n*m)
```

```
fun p(n,m) = n<>0
```

```
fun h(n,m) = m
```

*The function:* `itrev`

The function `itrev` is also an iterative function:

```
fun itrev(xs,ys) =
       if not (null xs) then itrev(tl xs, (hd xs)::ys) else ys;
```

which is an instance of the above schema with:

```
fun f(xs,ys) = (tl xs, (hd xs)::ys)
```

```
fun p(xs,ys) = not (null xs)
```

```
fun h(xs,ys) = ys
```

When a declaration of a function in an obvious way can be transformed into the above form, we will call it an iterative function without further argument.

*Evaluation of iterative functions*

The evaluation for an arbitrary iterative function:

```
fun g z = if p z then g(f z) else h z
```

proceeds in the same manner as the evaluations for `itfact` and `itrev`.

We define the *n*th *iteration* $f^n x$, for $n \geq 0$, of a function $f : \tau \rightarrow \tau$ as follows:

$$
\begin{aligned}
f^0 x &= x \\
f^{n+1} x &= f(f^n x), \text{ for } n \geq 0
\end{aligned}
$$

Thus,

$$
f^0 x = x, \quad f^1 x = fx, \quad \ldots, \quad f^n x = \underbrace{f(f(\cdots f x \cdots))}_{n}
$$

Suppose that

$$
\begin{aligned}
p(f^i x) &\rightsquigarrow \text{true} \quad \text{for all } i : 0 \leq i < n, \text{ and} \\
p(f^n x) &\rightsquigarrow \text{false}
\end{aligned}
$$

Then, the evaluation of the expression $g\, x$ proceeds as follows:

$$
\begin{aligned}
& g\, x \\
\rightsquigarrow\ & (\text{if } p\, z \text{ then } g(f\, z) \text{ else } h\, z,\ [z \mapsto x]) \\
\rightsquigarrow\ & (g(f\, z),\ [z \mapsto x]) \\
\rightsquigarrow\ & g(f^1 x) \\
\rightsquigarrow\ & (\text{if } p\, z \text{ then } g(f\, z) \text{ else } h\, z,\ [z \mapsto f^1 x]) \\
\rightsquigarrow\ & (g(f\, z),\ [z \mapsto f^1 x]) \\
\rightsquigarrow\ & g(f^2 x) \\
\rightsquigarrow\ & \ldots \\
\rightsquigarrow\ & (\text{if } p\, z \text{ then } g(f\, z) \text{ else } h\, z,\ [z \mapsto f^n x]) \\
\rightsquigarrow\ & (h\, z,\ [z \mapsto f^n x]) \\
\rightsquigarrow\ & h(f^n x)
\end{aligned}
$$

This evaluation has two desirable properties: (1) there are $n$ recursive calls of $g$, and (2) at most one binding for the argument pattern $z$ is 'active' at any stage in the evaluation.

We now give an example (Fibonacci numbers) where an iterative solution gives a very efficient implementation, and another example (the power function) where a declaration based on a good algorithmic trick gives a much more efficient implementation than any iterative function could do.

Thus, the notion of iterative function is good to have in mind when dealing with efficiency questions; but there is much more to the topic 'Algorithms and Data Structures'.

### Example 17.1

#### Fibonacci numbers

The sequence of Fibonacci numbers $0, 1, 1, 2, 3, 5, 8, \ldots$ is defined recursively by

$$
\begin{aligned}
F_0 &= 0 \\
F_1 &= 1 \\
F_n &= F_{n-1} + F_{n-2} \quad \text{for } n \geq 2
\end{aligned}
$$

This gives the following function to compute the Fibonacci numbers:

```
fun fib 0 = 0
  | fib 1 = 1
  | fib n = fib(n-1) + fib(n-2);
val fib = fn : int -> int
```

This algorithm is extremely inefficient because it builds a large expression and computes the same function values repeatedly, e.g. the evaluation of fib(4):

```
      fib 4
 ↝    fib 3 + fib 2
 ↝    (fib 2 + fib 1) + fib 2
 ↝    ((fib 1 + fib 0) + fib 1) + fib 2
 ↝    ((fib 1 + fib 0) + fib 1) + (fib 1 + fib 0)
 ↝    ...
```

evaluates fib 1 three times. The two base cases fib 0 and fib 1 are evaluated repeatedly in the evaluation of fib $N$ and the number of evaluations grows rapidly with $N$. The evaluation of e.g. fib 44 requires around $10^9$ evaluations of base cases, so this algorithm is utterly inefficient. Furthermore, during the evaluation large expressions are built with many simultaneous bindings of the argument pattern n.

#### Iterative solution

The idea is to iterate the function

```
fn (n,a,b) => (n-1,a+b,a)
```

while n<>0. This gives the following declaration of an iterative function:

```
fun itfib(n,a,b) = if n <> 0 then itfib(n-1,a+b,a)
                              else a;
```

The expression $\text{itfib}(n, 0, 1)$ evaluates to $F_n$, for any $n \geq 0$, as we have:

$$\text{itfib}(0, 0, 1) \rightsquigarrow 0 \ (= F_0)$$

and, for any $n > 0$:

$$
\begin{array}{ll}
 & \text{itfib}(n, 0, 1) \\
\rightsquigarrow & \text{itfib}(n-1, \ 1, \ 0) = \text{itfib}(n-1, \ F_1, \ F_0) \\
\rightsquigarrow & \text{itfib}(n-2, \ F_1 + F_0, \ F_1) \\
\rightsquigarrow & \text{itfib}(n-2, \ F_2, \ F_1) \\
\vdots & \\
\rightsquigarrow & \text{itfib}(n-(k-1), \ F_{k-1}, \ F_{k-2}) \\
\rightsquigarrow & \text{itfib}(n-k, \ F_{k-1} + F_{k-2}, \ F_{k-1}) \\
\rightsquigarrow & \text{itfib}(n-k, \ F_k, \ F_{k-1}) \\
\vdots & \\
\rightsquigarrow & \text{itfib}(0, \ F_n, \ F_{n-1}) \\
\rightsquigarrow & F_n
\end{array}
$$

where the evaluation steps use the definition of the Fibonacci numbers:

$$
\begin{array}{lll}
F_0 & = & 0 \\
F_1 & = & 1 \\
F_n & = & F_{n-1} + F_{n-2} \quad \text{for } n \geq 2
\end{array}
$$

The number of evaluation steps needed for evaluating $\text{itfib}(n, 0, 1)$ is proportional to $n$ and, furthermore, only one set of bindings for the identifiers in the argument pattern (n,a,b) is active at any stage in the evaluation. Thus, the efficiency improvements of this iterative solution is tremendous compared with the naive solution.

### Example 17.2

#### The function: power

Using iteration does not always give the most efficient declaration of a function. Other declarations may in some cases be much more efficient. As an example we consider the power function, where:

$$\text{power}(x, n) = x^n$$

A declaration for this function was given in Section 1.5 as:

```
fun power(x, 0) = 1.0
  | power(x, n) = x * power(x,n-1);
```

Using an accumulating parameter $p$ attaining the values $1, x, x^2, \ldots, x^n$ we get the iterative declaration:

```
fun itpower(x,0,p) = p:real
  | itpower(x,n,p) = itpower(x,n-1,x*p)
```

where $power(x, n) = itpower(x, n, 1)$. The evaluation of $itpower(x, n, p)$ takes $n$ steps, as the exponent is decremented by one in each recursive call, and the evaluation builds no expressions.

Instead of using the above declaration which is based on iteration, one may base a declaration on the recursion formula:

$$
\begin{aligned}
x^0 &= 1.0 \\
x^{2n} &= (x^n)^2 \\
x^{2n+1} &= x \cdot x^{2n}
\end{aligned}
$$

where the recursive step replaces the exponent $2n$ by $n$ (which for large $n$ is a much bigger reduction than replacing $n$ by $n-1$). This yields the declaration:

```
fun power2(x,0) = 1.0
  | power2(x,n) =
              if n mod 2 = 1 then x*power2(x,n-1)
              else let
                       val z = power2(x,n div 2)
                   in
                       z * z
                   end
```

The length of an evaluation for $power2(x, n)$ will be proportional to $\log_2 n$ because n is divided by 2 in the expression $power2(x,n \ div \ 2)$ of the else-branch. The maximum number of bindings in the evaluation will also be proportional to $\log_2 n$ and so will the number of pending multiplications. This is illustrated by the evaluation of $power2(2.0,10)$:

```
      power2(2.0,10)
  ⤳  (z*z, [z ↦ power2(2.0,5)])
  ⤳  (z*z, [z ↦ 2.0 * power2(2.0,4)])
  ⤳  (z*z, [z ↦ 2.0 * (z*z, [z ↦ power2(2.0,2)])])
  ⤳  (z*z, [z ↦ 2.0 * (z*z, [z ↦ (z*z, [z ↦ power2(2.0,1)])])])
  ⤳  (z*z, [z ↦ 2.0 * (z*z, [z ↦ (z*z, [z ↦ 2.0 * power2(2.0,0)])])])
  ⤳  (z*z, [z ↦ 2.0 * (z*z, [z ↦ (z*z, [z ↦ 2.0*1.0])])])
  ⤳  (z*z, [z ↦ 2.0 * (z*z, [z ↦ (z*z, [z ↦ 2.0])])])
  ⤳  (z*z, [z ↦ 2.0 * (z*z, [z ↦ 4.0])])
  ⤳  (z*z, [z ↦ 2.0 * 16.0])
  ⤳  (z*z, [z ↦ 32.0])
  ⤳  32.0*32.0
  ⤳  1024.0
```

Note that the value of $\log_2 n$ is *much* smaller than $n$ for large $n$, e.g.:

$$2^{30} \approx 10^9 \quad \text{while} \quad \log_2(2^{30}) = 30$$

A declaration such as power2, which halves the size of the argument in each recursive step, is hence much more efficient – when used for large argument values – than a declaration like itpower, which only reduces the size of the argument by one in each recursive step.

## 17.5 Summary

In this chapter we have introduced the concept of an iterative function, and we have presented examples showing that iterative functions in some cases provide efficient implementations. In the next chapter we shall establish a relationship between while loops and iterative functions.

## Exercises

**17.1** Show that the gcd function in Section 2.3 is iterative.

**17.2** Declare an iterative solution to Exercise 1.4.

**17.3** Give iterative declarations of the list functions length and nth (List.nth), cf. Section D.4

**17.4** Give an iterative declaration of the Fibonacci number function (cf. Example 17.1) by use of the following idea: introduce an auxiliary function where the argument is a pair $(m, xs)$ of an integer $m$ and a list $xs$ of integers. The integer $m$ accumulates the sum of base cases computed so far, while the list $xs$ contains integers $n$ for which the Fibonacci number $F_n$ remains to be computed and added to $m$.

The algorithm examines the front element $n$ in $xs$. If $n = 0$ or $n = 1$, then the corresponding Fibonacci number is added to $m$, otherwise the numbers $n-1$ and $n-2$ are inserted in front of $xs$ instead of the element $n$.

This algorithm is iterative, but is it more efficient than the naive declaration of the Fibonacci function?

**17.5** Give an iterative declaration of the function pre_listof in Section 8.3 by using an auxiliary function where the argument is a pair $(xt, ys)$ of a list $xt$ of family trees and a list $ys$ of strings. (The declaration is allowed to contain the append operator @).

The algorithm examines the front element $t$ in $xt$. If $t$ contains information, then the name is added at the end of the list $ys$, and the subtrees are inserted in front of the list $xt$ instead of $t$. The element $t$ is discarded if it contains no information.

# Imperative programming

Imperative features are language constructs to express commands using and modifying the state of mutable objects. The input and output streams introduced in Chapter 14 are mutable objects where the state (the contents of the stream) is changed by executing commands like inputN or output. Furthermore, the value of, for example, inputN($is, n$) depends on the actual contents of the stream $is$.

In this chapter we introduce another component, the *store*, which consists of a set of cells containing values, together with imperative constructs to access and change the store. The while loop is introduced and we study its relationship with iterative functions. Furthermore, we introduce the SML type array for a (list-like) mutable collection of objects called elements.

The imperative features in SML are useful for the following reasons:

- Input/output is needed for making interactive programs.
- In many cases imperative data structures allow a more efficient implementation of functions on important types (such as lists, sets and tables).

We are furthermore using the imperative features of SML to give a general presentation of basic concepts in imperative programming languages.

## 18.1 The store

A *store* is a set of *cells* containing values, where each cell is identified by a *reference*. In more precise, mathematical terms, the store is a table associating values $v_1, \ldots, v_n$ with references $r_1, \ldots, r_n$:

$$
\begin{bmatrix}
r_1 & \mapsto & v_1 \\
r_2 & \mapsto & v_2 \\
& \cdots & \\
r_n & \mapsto & v_n
\end{bmatrix}
$$

We may think of the references as integers, but the precise structure is a private concern for the SML system. An SML program cannot perform any arithmetic on references, they can only be used to access the associated cells in the store.

The reference $r$ of a cell containing a value $v$ of type $\tau$ has the type $\tau$ `ref`, so `ref` is the *type constructor* for reference types.

## 18.2 Operations on the SML store

The SML language comprises operators to access and manipulate the store. They can be used in expressions just like other operators, and the operations on the store are achieved through *evaluation* of *expressions* containing imperative operators. There are three basic imperative operators on the store:

- `ref : 'a -> 'a ref`          Allocation of a new cell in the store.
- `! : 'a ref -> 'a`            Value in a cell in the store.
- `:= : 'a ref * 'a -> unit`    Assignment of a value to a cell in the store.

Note that the store is not explicitly mentioned in the types and that the first occurrence of 'ref' denotes an operator, while the others denote the type constructor of reference types.

An expression is evaluated in both an actual environment and an *actual store*, and the evaluation of an expression may cause a change of the store – one says that the *evaluation* has a *side-effect* updating the store. Executing a *declaration* does *not* change the store – unless it comprises an evaluation with side-effects. We will now describe each operator in more detail.

### 18.2.1 The allocation operator `ref`

An expression of the form `ref` $e$ is evaluated as follows:

**1.** Evaluate the expression $e$ to a result $v$.

**2.** Extend the store by a new cell, and store the value $v$ in the cell.

**3.** Return the reference $r$ to the new cell as the result of evaluating the expression `ref` $e$.

Note that if the evaluation of $e$ has a side-effect, then the side-effect of evaluating `ref` $e$ accumulates the side-effect of evaluating $e$ and the extension of the store by the new cell containing the value $v$. If $e$ has type $\tau$, then `ref` $e$ will have type $\tau$ `ref`.

New cells in the store containing values 1 and 3 are created by:

```
val x = ref 1;
val x = ref 1 : int ref
```

```
val y = ref 3;
val y = ref 3 : int ref
```

Note that SML prints a reference as 'ref' followed by the associated value in the store.

The declarations bind x and y to values $r_1$ and $r_2$ which are references to cells in the store containing the values 1 and 3, respectively, so we obtain the following (extensions to) environment and store:

Environment        Store

$$\begin{bmatrix} x & \mapsto & r_1 \\ y & \mapsto & r_2 \end{bmatrix} \quad \begin{bmatrix} r_1 & \mapsto & 1 \\ r_2 & \mapsto & 3 \end{bmatrix}$$

A new cell in the store containing the value $r_1$ of x is created by:

```
val z = ref x;
val z = ref (ref 1) : int ref ref
```

The expression x has the value $r_1$. Thus, the evaluation of `ref x` has the side-effect of adding a new cell containing the value $r_1$ to the store, and the result of the evaluation will be the reference $r_3$ to this cell. Hence z is bound to the value $r_3$:

Environment        Store

$$\begin{bmatrix} x & \mapsto & r_1 \\ y & \mapsto & r_2 \\ z & \mapsto & r_3 \end{bmatrix} \quad \begin{bmatrix} r_1 & \mapsto & 1 \\ r_2 & \mapsto & 3 \\ r_3 & \mapsto & r_1 \end{bmatrix}$$

Note the printing $ref$ $(ref\ 1)$ for the value $r_3$ of z: it is the reference of a cell containing the reference $r_1$ of a cell containing the value 1.

The store may also contain lists as illustrated by the declaration:

```
val u = ref [1,2,3];
val u = ref [1,2,3] : int list ref
```

which adds a cell containing the list $[1, 2, 3]$ to the store and binds u to the reference $r_4$ of the cell:

Environment        Store

$$\begin{bmatrix} x & \mapsto & r_1 \\ y & \mapsto & r_2 \\ z & \mapsto & r_3 \\ u & \mapsto & r_4 \end{bmatrix} \quad \begin{bmatrix} r_1 & \mapsto & 1 \\ r_2 & \mapsto & 3 \\ r_3 & \mapsto & r_1 \\ r_4 & \mapsto & [1, 2, 3] \end{bmatrix}$$

The declaration:

```
val w = x;
val w = ref 1 : int ref
```

binds the identifier w to the value $r_1$ of x, so the environment is enlarged, but the store is unchanged:

Environment$\qquad$Store

$$\begin{bmatrix} x & \mapsto & r_1 \\ y & \mapsto & r_2 \\ z & \mapsto & r_3 \\ u & \mapsto & r_4 \\ w & \mapsto & r_1 \end{bmatrix} \qquad \begin{bmatrix} r_1 & \mapsto & 1 \\ r_2 & \mapsto & 3 \\ r_3 & \mapsto & r_1 \\ r_4 & \mapsto & [1, 2, 3] \end{bmatrix}$$

### 18.2.2    The pattern ref

When used in patterns, the identifier ref works like a value constructor. The pattern ref *pat* matches the value $v$ when $v$ is a reference to a cell in the store containing a value $x$, such that the pattern *pat* matches the value $x$. Continuing the above example we have that:

```
val ref p = z;
val p = ref 1 : int ref
```

will bind p to the value $r_1$: the value $r_3$ of z is a reference of a cell containing the value $r_1$ and hence matches the pattern ref p with p bound to $r_1$.

Another example is:

```
val ref (b::bs) = u;
val b = 1 : int
val bs = [2, 3] : int list
```

### 18.2.3    The dereferencing operator !

An expression of the form !$e$ is evaluated as follows:

**1.** Evaluate the expression $e$. The result of this evaluation must be a reference, say $r$.

**2.** Return the contents of the cell with reference $r$.

This is essentially a 'lookup' in the store, but it comprises the evaluation of the expression $e$ and will therefore have a side-effect if the evaluation of $e$ has a side-effect. If $e$ has type $\tau$ ref, then !$e$ will have type $\tau$.

Continuing the example, the expression !x has value 1 since the value $r_1$ of x is the reference of a cell containing the value 1. The value of !(!z) is also 1 since the value of z is $r_3$, so the value of !z is $r_1$, and the value of !(!z) is hence 1:

```
!x = 1 andalso !(!z) = !x;
val it = true : bool
```

References may be used as elements in a list:

```
[x,y,!z,w];
val it = [ref 1,ref 3,ref 1,ref 1] : int ref list
```

Note the type: a list of references of cells containing integers – while the type of u is the reference to a cell containing a list of integers.

The dereferencing operator ! can be expressed by means of the pattern `ref`:

```
fun !(ref x) = x
```

### 18.2.4    The assignment operator :=

An expression of the form $e_1 := e_2$ is evaluated as follows:

**1.** Evaluate the expression $e_1$. The result of this evaluation must be a reference, say $r$.

**2.** Evaluate the expression $e_2$. Let $v$ be the result of this evaluation.

**3.** Modify the store by storing the value $v$ in the cell with reference $r$.

**4.** Return the value () of type `unit` as the result of evaluating $e_1 := e_2$.

The 'dummy' result () conveys no information, so the interesting part of the evaluation of $e_1 := e_2$ is the side-effect on the store. It accumulates the side-effects of evaluating $e_1$ and $e_2$, together with the assignment of the value $v$ to the cell with reference $r$. If $e_1$ and $e_2$ have types $\tau$ `ref` and $\tau$ for some type $\tau$, then $e_1 := e_2$ has type `unit`.

The store can be modified by, for example, assigning new values to x and z (still continuing the same example):

```
x := !x + 1; z := y;
val it = () : unit
```

The assignments change the value of the cell for $r_1$ to 2 and the value of the cell for $r_3$ to $r_2$:

Environment
$$\begin{bmatrix} x & \mapsto & r_1 \\ y & \mapsto & r_2 \\ z & \mapsto & r_3 \\ u & \mapsto & r_4 \\ w & \mapsto & r_1 \end{bmatrix}$$

Store
$$\begin{bmatrix} r_1 & \mapsto & 2 \\ r_2 & \mapsto & 3 \\ r_3 & \mapsto & r_2 \\ r_4 & \mapsto & [1,2,3] \end{bmatrix}$$

The *space* between := and ! is important, because if it is omitted, then the string :=! will be construed as *one* identifier and not as a sequence of two identifiers.

After the assignments we have a new value for the expression [x,y,!z,w]:

```
[x,y,!z,w];
val it = [ref 2,ref 3,ref 3,ref 2] : int ref list
```

Note that the assignment to x affects w also, as they *share* the cell with reference $r_1$.

### 18.2.5    Imperative functions

The imperative constructs can also be used in function declarations. Consider, for example, the declaration:

```
fun incr(t) = t := !t + 1;
val incr = fn : int ref -> unit
```

This function requires an argument which is the reference of a cell containing an integer. Evaluation of the application incr(*r*) yields the result (); but the integer value in the cell with reference *r* is increased as a side-effect of the evaluation, e.g.:

```
y;
val it = ref 3 : int ref

incr(y);
val it = () : unit

y;
val it = ref 4 : int ref
```

Using sequential composition we may define a modified function giving the increased value as the result:

```
fun incrval(t) = (t := !t + 1 ; !t);
val incrval = fn : int ref -> int
```

It computes an increased value each time it is applied to y:

```
incrval(y);
val it = 5 : int

incrval(y);
val it = 6 : int
```

The functions incr and incrval could also be defined using ref patterns:

```
fun incr(t as ref x) = t := x + 1;
val incr = fn : int ref -> unit

fun incrval(t as ref x) = (t := x + 1 ; !t);
val incrval = fn : int ref -> int
```

## 18.3 References and polymorphism

The restriction on polymorphic values described in Section 5.5 is made in order to ensure that the use of references is type safe: if SML would allow, for example, the declaration val a = ref [] at top level, then the type inference might run into problems, as illustrated by the following hypothetical example:

```
val a = ref [];                    (* Not allowed at top level *)
val a = ref [] : 'a list ref

fun f(x) = a := x::(!a) ;          (* What is the type of f ?? *)
val f = fn : 'a -> unit

f(1);  f("A"); a;
val it = ref ["A",1] : ?? list ref    (* Oops! Type error! *)
```

The point is that the SML system would be forced to infer the type of f immediately after the declaration has been entered, as the type is part of the answer from the SML system. This would result in the type 'a -> unit for f as values of any type can be cons'ed onto the empty list. Hence, each of the applications f(1) and f("A") would type check as int as well as string are instances of the polymorphic type 'a – and the type check would fail to discover the illegal expression "A"::[1].

The situation is different when the example program is placed inside a local scope. The SML system would then be able to use the application f(1) when inferring the type of f and would hence infer the type int -> unit for f. The application f("A") would then be rejected by the type check as the argument "A" is not of type int:

```
let
    val a    = ref [];
    fun f(x) = a := x::(!a) ;
in
    f(1);  f("A"); a
end;
! Toplevel input:
!    f(1);  f("A"); a
!            ^^^
! Type clash: expression of type
!    string
! cannot have type
!    int
```

## (18.4) Arrays

The addresses in the *physical* memory of the computer are integers. Hence, if we have a sequence of $n$ equally sized memory cells $c_0, c_1, \ldots, c_{n-1}$, as shown in Figure 18.1 then the physical address of the $k$th cell $c_k$ can be computed by the formula:

$$pa_k = pa_0 + k \cdot s$$

where $s$ denotes the size of a cell. Thus, this machine code computation requires only two arithmetic operations.

This addressing scheme is used by the SML system to implement arrays. An *array* $a$ of length $n$ consists of $n$ values $v_0, v_1, \ldots, v_{n-1}$ of the same type. The values $v_i$ are

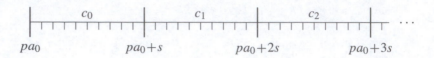

**Figure 18.1**  An array in the physical memory.

called the *elements* of the array, and the numbers $0, 1, \ldots, n-1$ are called the *indices* for the elements.

Arrays have the advantage over lists that any element can be accessed and modified in a constant (short) time, i.e. in a small number of computations which is independent of the size of the array. On the other hand, an array is a mutable object – the old value is lost when it is modified. Furthermore, an array cannot be extended by more elements in a simple way as the adjacent physical memory (after the last element in the array) might be occupied for other use.

### 18.4.1  Operations on arrays

We present a few of the basic operations on arrays from the structure `Array` from the Library. We refer to Section D.6 for further information.

*The function:* `Array.fromList:` `'a list -> 'a Array.array`

The value of the expression `Array.fromList` $[v_0, \ldots, v_{n-1}]$ is a new array of length $n$ with the elements $v_0, \ldots, v_{n-1}$. For example the declaration:

```
val a = Array.fromList [4,5,6,7];
val a = <array> : int Array.array
```

binds the identifier a to an array with four elements 4, 5, 6, 7.

*The function:* `Array.array:` `int * 'a -> 'a Array.array`

The value of the expression `Array.array`$(n, v)$ is a new array of length $n$ where each element's value is $v$. For example the declaration:

```
val b = Array.array(3,"ab");
val b = <array> : string Array.array
```

bind the identifier b to an array with three identical elements "ab", "ab", "ab".

*The function:* `Array.foldr`

The type of `Array.foldr` is:

```
('a * 'b -> 'b) -> 'b -> 'a Array.array -> 'a
```

and this function corresponds to the `foldr` function for lists.

Let $a$ be an array with elements $v_0, \ldots, v_{n-1}$. Then the value of the expression `Array.foldr` $f\ b\ a$ is $f(v_0, f(v_1, \ldots f(v_{n-1}, b) \cdots))$.

A function to extract the list of the array elements can be declared by:

```
fun toList a = Array.foldr op:: [] a;
val toList = fn : 'a Array.array -> 'a list
```

For example:

```
toList a;
val it = [4, 5, 6, 7] : int list
```

```
toList b;
val it = ["ab", "ab", "ab"] : string list
```

*The function:* `Array.length:` `'a Array.array -> int`

The value of the expression `Array.length`$(a)$ is the number of elements of array $a$. For example:

```
Array.length a;
val it = 4 : int
```

```
Array.length b;
val it = 3 : int
```

*The function:* `Array.sub:` `'a Array.array * int -> 'a`

Let $a$ be an array with elements $v_0, \ldots, v_{n-1}$. Then the value of the expression `Array.sub`$(a, i)$ is $v_i$ if $0 \leq i < n$; otherwise an exception is raised. For example:

```
Array.sub(a, 2);
val it = 6 : int
```

```
Array.sub(b,3);
! Uncaught exception:
! Subscript
```

*The function:* `Array.update:` `'a Array.array * int * 'a -> unit`

The evaluation of the expression `Array.update`$(a, i, v)$ has the side-effect that the $i$th element of $a$ is changed to $v$, if $i$ is an index of an element of $a$; otherwise an exception is raised. For example:

```
Array.update(a,5,9);
! Uncaught exception:
! Subscript
```

```
Array.update(b,1,"ccccc");
val it = () : unit


toList b;
val it = ["ab", "ccccc", "ab"] : string list
```

Consider the following declaration of a function which exchanges (swaps) two elements with indices $i$ and $j$ of an array $a$:

```
fun swap(a,i,j) = let val v = Array.sub(a,i)
                  in Array.update(a, i, Array.sub(a,j)) ;
                     Array.update(a, j, v)
                  end;
val it = fn : 'a Array.array * int * int -> unit


swap(b,0,1);
val it = () : unit


toList b;
val it = ["ccccc", "ab", "ab"] : string list
```

An evaluation of the expression swap($a$, $i$, $j$) uses a constant (small) number of evaluation steps which is independent of $i$ and $j$ and the size of the array $a$.

Example 18.1

### Binary search

We consider the problem of searching for the index of a number in an ordered collection of numbers, and we show a solution based on arrays which is more efficient than any solution based on lists.

Suppose we want to search for an integer $v$ in an ordered list of integers:

$$[a_0, a_1, \ldots a_{n-1}]$$

where $a_i < a_{i+1}$ for $0 \leq i < n - 1$. The time needed for this search would in the worst case require a number of evaluation steps proportional to the length $n$ of the list, as we would, for example, traverse the whole list in searching for a value $v$, where $v \geq a_{n-1}$. On average the number of evaluation steps needed would be proportional to $n/2$.

If the ordered collection of integers are the elements of an array, then we can exploit the idea of *bisection* to find $v$'s position in a number of evaluation steps which in the worst case is proportional to $\log_2 n$. We illustrate this idea by the array $a$ containing the eight elements $(a_0, \ldots, a_7) = (1, 3, 5, 7, 9, 11, 13, 15)$ where $a_0 < a_1 < \cdots < a_7$:

| Indices: | 0 | 1 | 2 | 3 | 4 | 5 | 6 | 7 |
|----------|---|---|---|---|---|----|----|----|
| Values:  | 1 | 3 | 5 | 7 | 9 | 11 | 13 | 15 |

We want to find the position of the value $v = 11$ in $a$. The search proceeds through a sequence of intervals $[first_k, top_k)$, $k = 1, 2, \ldots$, of indices, where $first_k$ is the *first* index while $top_k$ is the *top* index in the range of the remaining search. Each step in the search will replace the interval by an interval of half the size. At start we have $first_1 = 0$ and $top_1 = 8$.

*Step 1:* Investigate the element in the middle position:

$$mid_1 = top_1 \operatorname{div} 2 = 8 \operatorname{div} 2 = 4$$

Since $a_{mid_1} = a_4 = 9$ is less than $v$ (which is 11) and since the values in the array are ordered, the position of $v$ must be found in the upper half of $a$, so we replace our search interval by $[first_2, top_2) = [mid_1 + 1, top_1)$, i.e. $first_2 = 5$ and $top_2 = 8$, corresponding to the following part of the array:

| Indices: | 5 | 6 | 7 |
|---|---|---|---|
| Values: | 11 | 13 | 15 |

*Step 2:* Investigate the element in the middle position:

$$
\begin{aligned}
mid_2 = first_2 + ((top_2 - first_2) \operatorname{div} 2) &= (first_2 + top_2) \operatorname{div} 2 \\
&= (5 + 8) \operatorname{div} 2 = 6
\end{aligned}
$$

Since $a_{mid_2} = a_6 = 13$ is greater than $v$, we replace our search interval by $[first_3, top_3) = [first_2, mid_2)$, i.e. $first_3 = 5$ and $top_3 = 6$:

| Indices: | 5 |
|---|---|
| Values: | 11 |

*Step 3:* Investigate the element in the middle position:

$$mid_3 = (first_3 + top_3) \operatorname{div} 2 = (5 + 6) \operatorname{div} 2 = 5$$

We are now done, as $a_{mid_3} = a_5 = 11$.

This algorithm, searching for a value $v$ in an ordered array of $n$ integers by using the idea of bisection, is called *binary search*. The number of evaluations needed to find $v$ is proportional to $\log_2 n$ since the search interval of indices is halved in each step. The algorithm can be declared in SML as follows:

```
fun binSearch(v, a) =
    let fun f(first, top) = if first=top then NONE
        else let val mid = (first+top) div 2
            in case Int.compare(v, Array.sub(a,mid)) of
                    LESS    => f(first, mid)
                  | EQUAL   => SOME mid
                  | GREATER => f(mid+1, top)
            end
    in f(0, Array.length a) end;
val binSearch = fn : int * int Array.array -> int option
```

```
val a = Array.fromList [1, 3, 5, 7, 9, 11, 13, 15];
val a = <array> : int Array.array

binSearch(0,a);
val it = NONE : int option

binSearch(1, a);
val it = SOME 0 : int option

binSearch(9,a);
val it = SOME 4 : int option

binSearch(15,a);
val it = SOME 7 : int option

binSearch(16,a);
val it = NONE : int option
```

## Example 18.2

### Quicksort

In this section we consider the problem of rearranging the elements of an array of
integers so that they occur in (weakly) ascending order. This is a sorting problem.
Sorting problems occur in many applications and many good sorting algorithms have
been presented in the literature. In this example we consider the 'Quicksort' algorithm,
as an illustration of an efficient algorithm using arrays. However, most SML systems
have good sorting programs in their libraries, and we recommend using the library
programs whenever appropriate.

The main idea of the quicksort algorithm can be illustrated as follows. The array:

$$\text{To be sorted}$$

| Indices : | 0 | 1 | ...... | $n-2$ | $n-1$ |
|-----------|-----|-----|---|---------|---------|
| Values : | $v_0$ | $v_1$ | | $v_{n-2}$ | $v_{n-1}$ |

is sorted by first rearranging the elements $v_1 \ldots v_{n-2} \, v_{n-1}$ such that the resulting
elements $v_1' \ldots v_{n-2}' \, v_{n-1}'$ can be partitioned into two sections with indices $1, \ldots, k$
and $k+1, \ldots, n-1$, respectively, such that all the elements in first section are smaller
than $v_0$ and all the elements in the second section are greater than or equal to $v_0$:

| Indices : | 0 | 1 | ... | $k-1$ | $k$ | $k+1$ | ... | $n-2$ | $n-1$ |
|-----------|-----|-----|-----|---------|-----|---------|-----|---------|---------|
| Values : | $v_0$ | $v_1'$ | | $v_{k-1}'$ | $v_k'$ | $v_{k+1}'$ | | $v_{n-2}'$ | $v_{n-1}'$ |

All elements $< v_0$        All elements $\geq v_0$

The element $v_0$ can now be correctly placed in its final position by swapping it with the $k$'s element:

| | All elements $< v_0$ | | | | | | All elements $\geq v_0$ | | | |
|---|---|---|---|---|---|---|---|---|---|---|
| Indices : | $0$ | $1$ | $\ldots$ | $k-1$ | $k$ | $k+1$ | $\ldots$ | $n-2$ | $n-1$ | |
| Values : | $v'_k$ | $v'_1$ | | $v'_{k-1}$ | $v_0$ | $v'_{k+1}$ | | $v'_{n-2}$ | $v'_{n-1}$ | |
| | | To be sorted | | | | | To be sorted | | | |

This array has the property that any element in the first section is smaller than any element in the second section, as the elements in the first section are $< v_0$ while the elements in the second section are $\geq v_0$. The array can hence be sorted by sorting each of the sections separately.

*The function:* `partition`

We first declare a function `partition` with the type:

```
int Array.array * int * int * int -> int
```

to rearrange a section of an array so that the elements in the section that are smaller than a given value $v$ come before the elements that are greater than or equal to $v$.

Let $a$ be an integer array:

| Indices : | $\ldots$ | $k_1$ | $k_1+1$ | $\ldots\ldots$ | $k_2$ | $\ldots$ |
|---|---|---|---|---|---|---|
| Values : | | $v_{k_1}$ | $v_{k_1+1}$ | | $v_{k_2}$ | |

Then the evaluation of the expression $\text{partition}(a, v, k_1, k_2)$ will have the following side-effect on the section of the array $a$ with indices $k_1, k_1 + 1, \ldots, k_2$:

| Indices : | $\ldots$ | $k_1$ | $k_1+1$ | $\ldots$ | $K$ | $K+1$ | $\ldots$ | $k_2$ | $\ldots$ |
|---|---|---|---|---|---|---|---|---|---|
| Values : | | $v'_{k_1}$ | $v'_{k_1+1}$ | | $v'_K$ | $v'_{K+1}$ | | $v'_{k_2}$ | |
| | | All elements $< v$ | | | | All elements $\geq v$ | | | |

The value of the expression $\text{partition}(a, v, k_1, k_2)$ is $K$, i.e. the index of the last element in the first section containing elements smaller than $v$.

The function is declared by:

```
fun partition(a, v, k1, k2) =
    if k2=k1-1 then k2  (* empty section *)
    else if Array.sub(a,k2) >= v then partition(a, v, k1, k2-1)
        else (swap(a,k1,k2); partition(a,v,k1+1,k2))
```

where we have used the function swap declared on Page 272.

We have, for example:

```
val a1 = Array.fromList [9,5,1,~3,5,7,0];
val a1 = <array> : int Array.array
```

```
partition(a1, 2, 1, 6);
val it = 3 : int

toList a1;
val it = [9, 0, ~3, 1, 5, 7, 5] : int list
```

where the elements 0, ~3, 1 with indices 1, 2, 3 are $\leq 2$ while the elements 5, 7, 5 with indices 4, 5, 6 are $> 2$.

### The function: quicksort

The function quicksort has the type

```
int Array.array -> unit
```

The evaluation of the expression quicksort($a$) has the side-effect on the array $a$ that the elements are rearranged so that $a$ becomes sorted.

The declaration of quicksort is expressed in terms of a more general function qsort which can sort a section of an array. The function qsort has the type:

```
int Array.array * int * int -> unit
```

The evaluation of the expression qsort($a, i, j$) has the side-effect on the array $a$ that the elements with indices $i, i + 1, \ldots, j - 1$ are rearranged so that this section of $a$ is sorted. Note that if $j - i \leq 1$, then there is at most one element in the section and the section is therefore sorted already.

The function qsort is declared by:

```
fun qsort (a,i,j) =
   if j-i<=1 then ()
   else let val k = partition(a, Array.sub(a,i),i+1,j-1)
        in swap(a,i,k);
           qsort(a,i,k);
           qsort(a,k+1,j)
        end
```

For example:

```
val b1 = Array.fromList [7, 6, 5, 19, 8, 4, 10, 1];
val b1 = <array> : int Array.array

qsort(b1, 2,7);
val it = () : unit

toList b1;
val it = [7, 6, 4, 5, 8, 10, 19, 1] : int list
```

A declaration for quicksort is easily obtained using qsort:

```
fun quicksort a = qsort(a, 0, Array.length a);
```

For example:

```
val c1 = Array.fromList[1, 5, 2, ~3, 7, 0];
val c1 = <array> : int Array.array

quicksort c1;
val it = () : unit

toList c1;
val it = [~3, 0, 1, 2, 5, 7] : int list
```

On average the number of evaluation steps needed for quicksort to sort an array with $n$ elements is proportional to $n \cdot \log_2 n$. In the worst case the number of evaluation steps needed for sorting is proportional to $n^2$. So the quicksort algorithms is a good practical algorithm for many applications. There are, however, sorting algorithms where the running time in the worst case is proportional to $n \cdot \log_2 n$ to sort an array of size $n$.

## 18.5  The while loop

If $p$ denotes an expression with type bool and $e$ denotes an expression with any type, then

while $p$ do $e$

will be an expression with type unit. This expression is evaluated as follows

**1.** Evaluate the expression $p$.

**2.** If the result is true, then evaluate the expression $e$ and repeat the evaluation of while $p$ do $e$. If the result is false, then terminate the evaluation of while $p$ do $e$ and return the result () of type unit.

These rules are expressed in the following *evaluation steps* for a while loop:

| | |
|---|---|
| while $p$ do $e \rightsquigarrow$ ( $e$ ; while $p$ do $e$ ) | if $p$ evaluates to true |
| while $p$ do $e \rightsquigarrow$ () | if $p$ evaluates to false |

### 18.5.1  Loops as iterations

It follows that the expression:

while $p$ do $e$

has the same evaluation steps as the expression:

wh()

where the function wh is declared by:

fun wh() = if $p$ then wh($e$;()) else ()

and where we assume that the identifier wh does not occur in $p$ or $e$. The expressions are hence equal in the sense that they give the *same value* (namely: $()$) with the *same side-effect* on the store – or both evaluations do not terminate. The SML system does in fact use this conversion in compiling a while loop.

The declaration of the function wh can be rewritten as:

    fun wh z = if $p'$ z then wh($f$ z) else $h$ z

where:

$$
\begin{aligned}
p' &= \text{fn z => } p \\
f &= \text{fn z => } (e \; ; \; ()) \\
h &= \text{fn z => } ()
\end{aligned}
$$

This function wh is of type unit -> unit as the values of $f$ z and $h$ z both are of type unit, so $()$ is actually the only possible value for the argument z. The function declaration is an instance of the schema given in Section 17.4:

    fun $g$ z = if $p$ z then $g(f$ z) else $h$ z

and it is hence an iterative function.

Thus, any while loop can be expressed by an iteration.

## 18.5.2   Iterations as loops

It is also true that any iterative function, as the above $g$, can be expressed by a while loop. Consider the following function declaration containing a while loop but no recursive calls of the function:

    fun $g'$(z)  = let val zi = ref z
                  in while $p$(!zi) do zi := $f$(!zi)
                     ; $h$(!zi)
                  end

The point is that evaluating a function value $g'(x)$ will create a cell in the store initially containing the value $x$, and that the evaluation of the loop will subsequently assign the values

$$f^0 x = x, \quad f^1 x = f\,x, \quad \ldots, \quad f^n x = \underbrace{f(f(\cdots f\,x\cdots))}_{n}$$

to the cell, until an $n$ with $p(f^n x) = $ false is reached. The evaluation is described by triples: (*expression, environment, store*) and proceeds as follows:

$$
\begin{aligned}
&g'(x) \\
\rightsquigarrow \quad &(\text{let val zi = ref z in}\ldots, [z \mapsto x]) \\
\rightsquigarrow \quad &(\text{while } p(!zi) \text{ do zi := } f(!zi)\ldots, [z \mapsto x, zi \mapsto r], [r \mapsto x]) \\
\rightsquigarrow \quad &(\text{while } p(!zi) \text{ do zi := } f(!zi)\ldots, [z \mapsto x, zi \mapsto r], [r \mapsto fx]) \\
&\ldots \\
\rightsquigarrow \quad &(\text{while } p(!zi) \text{ do}\ldots ; h(!zi), [z \mapsto x, zi \mapsto r], [r \mapsto f^n x]) \\
\rightsquigarrow \quad &h(!zi), [z \mapsto x, zi \mapsto r], [r \mapsto f^n x]) \\
\rightsquigarrow \quad &h(f^n x)
\end{aligned}
$$

This evaluation should be compared to the evaluation of $g(x)$ in Section 17.4. It also computes the iterated applications $x, f^1x, \ldots, f^nx$ of the function $f$. However, these values occur in the evaluation of the iterative function $g$ as the argument values in the sequence of recursive calls, whereas they are successively assigned to the store cell during the evaluation of the above while loop. Hence, the declarations $g$ and $g'$ express the same function.

## Example 18.3

We will now show how to transform the iterative declaration for itfact from Section 17.3 into a while loop. The function itfact is declared as:

```
fun itfact(n,m) = if n<>0 then itfact(n-1,n*m) else m;
val itfact = fn : int * int -> int
```

In order to use the above transformation to a while loop we have to collect the argument pattern (n,m) into a single entity $z = $ (n,m). This gives a modified function declaration:

```
fun itfact z =
    if #1 z <> 0 then itfact(#1 z - 1, #1 z * #2 z)
                    else #2 z;
val itfact = fn : int * int -> int
```

where we use the functions #1 and #2 to extract the parameters n and m from (n,m).

Applying the transformation to a while loop yields the desired function declaration:

```
fun factI z =
    let val zi = ref z
    in while #1 !zi <> 0 do
                zi := (#1 !zi - 1, #1 !zi * #2 !zi)
        ; #2 !zi
    end;
val factI = fn : int * int -> int
```

The above declaration of factI is not particularly attractive – we would rather prefer a declaration of the form:

```
fun factI (n,m) =
    let val ni = ref n
        val mi = ref m
    in  while !ni <> 0 do ... end
```

where the cell zi containing a pair (n,m) of integers is replaced by a pair of cells ni and mi, containing the integers n and m, respectively.

We must be careful with the sequence of the assignments to ni and mi, which must replace the assignment to zi. For example, the following sequence of assignments cannot replace the assignment to zi:

```
(ni := !ni - 1;
 mi := !ni * !mi)
```

The problem is that the first assignment to ni replaces the value, say $n$, by $n-1$ and the second assignment to mi replaces the value, say $m$, by $(n-1) \cdot m$. The last updating is *wrong*, as the evaluation of the right hand side in the assignment uses the updated value $n-1$ for !ni instead of the old value $n$. This problem did not occur in the previous declaration of factI, which used a *multiple* assignment computing *both* values $n-1$ and $n \cdot m$ *before* doing any assignment to the store, cf. the assignment zi := (#1(!zi) - 1, #1(!zi) * #2(!zi)).

We get the desired updates of ni and mi by the sequence of assignments:

```
(mi := !ni * !mi ; ni := !ni - 1)
```

and then we arrive at the following declaration for factI using a while-loop:

```
fun factI (n,m) =
   let val ni = ref n
       val mi = ref m
   in while !ni <> 0 do (mi := !ni * !mi; ni := !ni - 1)
      ; !mi
   end;
val factI = fn : int * int -> int
```

## 18.6  Imperative data structures

In this section we illustrate by an example that the use of imperative data structures in some cases may give more efficient implementation of functions.

### 18.6.1  Cash register

We reconsider the cash register program in Chapter 6. It contains a register which relates article codes with their descriptions, where a description consists of a name and a price. In Chapter 6 this is modelled by:

```
type articleCode = string
type articleName = string
type price       = int
type register = (articleCode * (articleName * price)) list
```

The list representation is not very good for registers with many articles, because, in the worst case, one has to traverse the whole register to find an article.

If there is an upper bound on the number of articles, then we can use an array to represent a register:

```
type articleCode = int
type articleName = string
type price       = int
type register    = (articleName * price) Array.array
```

Article codes are, in this case, represented by the indices of the array. For example:

```
val register = Array.fromList [("cheese",25),
                               ("herring",4),
                               ("soft drink",5)
                              ];
val register = <array> : (string * int) Array.array
```

Thus, cheese has article code 0, herring article code 1, and soft drink article code 2 in register . For example:

```
Array.sub(register, 1);
val it = ("herring", 4) : string * int
```

One advantage of the array representation is that any article description can be found in constant time, independently of the length of the array and the value of the article code.

Furthermore, the array representation does not complicate the declarations of the makebill function:

```
fun makebill([], _)                 = ([],0)
  | makebill((np,ac)::pur, reg) =
        let val (aname,aprice) = Array.sub(reg,ac)
            val tprice          = np*aprice
            val (billtl,sumtl) = makebill(pur,reg)
        in ((np,aname,tprice)::billtl, tprice+sumtl)
        end;
```

Example:

```
val pur = [(3,1),(1,0)];
```

```
makebill(pur, register);
val it = ([(3, "herring", 12), (1, "cheese", 25)], 37)
    : (int * string * int) list * int
```

Another advantage of the array representation is that the price of any article can be changed in constant time, independently of the length of the array and the value of the article code:

```
Array.update(register, 1, ("herring",6) );
val it = () : unit
```

```
makebill(pur, register);
val it = ([(3, "herring", 18), (1, "cheese", 25)], 43)
    : (int * string * int) list * int
```

## 18.6.2    Discussion

In the above example, an array is used to represent an *imperative* table, where the article codes are keys and article descriptions are the corresponding values. The imperative aspect comes from the update of the register where the old value is lost. Significant improvement in efficiency is gained using this imperative table. The efficient implementation of imperative data structures is an important part of the topic 'algorithms and data structures', and one can, for example, find many different imperative table implementations, addressing different efficiency issues.

The program libraries distributed with the different SML systems include modules for imperative data structures and we recommend using these modules whenever it is appropriate. For example, any realistic implementation for the Flight Reservation System in Chapter 16 would use an imperative table to represent the register containing the flight information. An imperative table is certainly appropriate here as the old table is not needed after the evaluation of a user command. Furthermore, fast responses are expected/required from such a system, so efficiency is a major concern, as most flight-registers contain a lot of data.

## 18.7   Summary

We have introduced the notion of a store associating values in cells in the store with references. This notion represents the computer memory in an abstract form. The SML language contains imperative operators to access and manipulate the store: ref, to insert a new cell in the store, !, to extract the value of a cell in the store, and :=, to assign a new value to a cell in the store.

The type array was introduced together with basic array operations. An array is a list-like collection of elements with the distinguished feature that each element can be accessed and manipulated very fast, i.e. in a number of evaluation steps, which is independent of the index for the element. This property is often essential for achieving efficient algorithms, and this is illustrated by the binary search and quicksort algorithms.

The while loop was introduced and its relationship to iterative function declarations was studied.

We have given an example where an array is used as an imperative table. Imperative data structures can in many cases give significant efficiency improvements, and we recommend use of program libraries for such data structures whenever possible.

## Exercises

**18.1** Give a declaration for the gcd function using a while loop instead of a recursion. (See Section 2.3.2.)

**18.2** Declare a function for computing Fibonacci numbers using a while loop instead of a recursion (cf. Example 17.1).

**18.3** Declare a function to find the sum of all the elements in an array containing integer values. The solution should be expressed using a while loop.

**18.4** Declare a function partitionLEG: int array -> unit to rearrange an array with integer elements into three parts. The first part contains the negative elements, the second part contains the elements equal to zero, and the third part contains the positive elements.

**18.5** Make an extension to the interactive cash register program in Exercise 16.4 so that the register is represented by an array (cf. Section 18.6), and the function makebill uses a while loop rather than a recursion.

## Appendix A

# SML systems

There are a number of implementations of Standard ML and more systems are under development. A complete list can be found on the WEB-page:

```
http://www.cis.ohio-state.edu/hypertext/faq/usenet/meta-lang-faq/faq.
```

This page contains pointers to the information on SML which is available on the WEB, and the page is kept updated with new information.

The documentation of the SML basis library is found on the following WEB-page:

```
http://www.cs.bell-labs.com/~jhr/sml/basis/index.html
```

The authors of this book use the Moscow ML system. Information about this system is found on the WEB-page:

```
http://www.dina.kvl.dk/~sestoft/mosml.html
```

Note that the current implementation of Moscow ML does not support functors. The programs in Section 11.6 on 'Functors' are executed using the Standard ML of New Jersey system.

Information about the way we are using Moscow ML can be found on the WEB-page:

```
http://www.it.dtu.dk/introSML
```

# Overview of Standard ML

........................................................................................................

This appendix gives an overview of central parts of SML, excluding the module system which is described in Appendix C. It is intended to be a reference manual – not a tutorial – on SML, and it does not contain an abundance of examples. However, there will be some references to examples and definitions in the main text. The Standard ML Basis Library is described in Appendix D.

The description of a programming language like SML comprises two concepts:

● The *syntax* of the language, i.e. the *form* of programs written in the language.

● The *semantics* of the language, i.e. the *meaning* of programs written in the language.

The syntax identifies the *syntactic classes* in the language (expressions, matches, patterns, declarations, etc.) and gives *rules* for building character sequences belonging to these classes. The semantics defines the meaning of a construct of each syntactic class in terms of mathematical objects: values, environments, stores and evaluation rules for expressions. This document describes the syntax by means of so-called *BNF grammars*, whereas the semantics is described in plain English. The standard reference [2] (henceforth referred to as *The Definition*) describes semantics purely in mathematical formulas, but this appendix uses the more informal style, since reading the formulas in *The Definition* requires knowledge of the theory of programming language semantics.

## B.1  Lexical conventions

An SML program is a sequence of characters encoded in the ASCII alphabet (cf. Appendix F). The SML system interprets a program as a sequence of *items* separated by comments and formatting characters (except formatting characters inside string constants).

The process of converting a sequence of characters into the corresponding list of items is called *scanning*. An item is often called a *terminal symbol* or a *token*.

A comment is any character sequence within comment brackets (* *) where further comment brackets are properly nested. A comment (including the comment brackets) is skipped by the SML system. At each stage the longest next item is taken, so e.g. a+~b contains three items (identifiers) a, +~ and b, while a+ ~ b contains four items a, +, ~ and b.

An item is either a reserved word, a special constant, a digit, a value identifier, a record label, a type constructor, a type variable or a structure identifier.

### Note

Part of the distinction between different classes of items is purely local, e.g. an item is a string constant if the first character is a quote, while other distinctions, e.g. between a value identifier and a type constructor, depend on the context in which the item occurs.

### B.1.1  Reserved words

The following are the *reserved words* in the 'core' language:

```
abstype  and  andalso  as  case  datatype  do  else  end
exception  fn  fun  handle  if  in  infix  infixr  let
local  nonfix  of  op  open  orelse  raise  rec  then
type  val  while  with  withtype
(  )  [  ]        ,  :  ;  ...  _  |  =  =>  ->  #
```

They have special syntactical rôles and may *not* be used as identifiers. Note, however, that the word = is also used to denote the equality operator (e.g. the first = in the declaration fun f x = x = 2 is the reserved word, while the second is the equality operator).

The reserved words for the module system of SML are described in Section C.1.1.

### B.1.2  Constants

Special constants are character strings in a program denoting values:

- An *integer constant* is a non-empty sequence of digits, possibly preceded by the tilde symbol ~ denoting the negative sign, while an integer constant in hexadecimal notation is 0x followed by a non-empty sequence of hexadecimal digits 0···9a···f, possibly preceded by the tilde symbol.

● A *word constant* in decimal notation is 0w followed by a non-empty sequence of decimal digits, while a word constant in hexadecimal notation is 0wx followed by a non-empty sequence of hexadecimal digits $0 \cdots 9a \cdots f$.

● A *real constant* is an integer constant followed either by a decimal point . and one or more decimal digits – or by the exponent symbol E or e and an integer constant – or followed by decimal digits as well as an exponent.

● A *character constant* consists of the character # followed by a character or an escape sequence denoting a character enclosed in quotes. Hence #"a" denotes the letter a.

● A *string constant* is a sequence, between quotes, of zero or more printable characters (ASCII code 33–126), spaces or escape sequences. The escape sequences are described in Appendix F.

A single digit may be classified as a digit used within an infix directive, and a non-empty sequence of digits may be classified as a *numeric record label*.

## B.1.3 Identifiers

An identifier is either an *alphanumeric* identifier: any sequence of letters, digits, primes (') and underbars (_) starting with a letter, or a *type variable*: an alphanumeric identifier preceded by one or two prime characters, or a *symbolic* identifier: any non-empty sequence of the following symbols

```
   !   %   &   $   #   +   -   /   :   <   =   >   ?   @   \   ~   '   ^   |   *
```

In either case, however, reserved words are excluded. This means that, for example, # and | cannot be used as identifiers, but ## can be used as an identifier.

Depending on the context an alphanumeric identifier is interpreted as a *value identifier*, a *type constructor*, a *record label* or a *structure identifier*. Furthermore, a value identifier *id* is a *value constructor* or an *exception constructor* if it occurs within the scope of a datatype, abstype or exception declaration using *id* as a constructor.

A *long identifier* consists of several identifiers connected by periods (such as List.filter). Long identifiers are items of class value identifiers, type constructors or structure identifiers.

## B.1.4 Infixed identifiers and the op directive

An identifier *id* is given *infix status* by the infix or infixr directive, where the latter gives *association* to the right. The infix status prevails through the scope of the infix directive, so any declaration of the identifier will define an infix operator. Infix status is cancelled by the nonfix directive.

If *id* has infix status, then $exp_1$ *id* $exp_2$, resp. $pat_1$ *id* $pat_2$, may occur – in brackets if necessary – wherever the application $id(exp_1, exp_2)$, or $id\{1 = exp_1, 2 = exp_2\}$, resp. $id(pat_1, pat_2)$, would otherwise occur:

- For the infix value or exception constructor *Con*, the patterns of the form *pat*$_1$ *Con pat*$_2$ are used to match values of the form *val*$_1$ *Con val*$_2$.
- The heading in a function declaration for the infix identifier *id* uses the form

    fun *pat*$_1$ *id pat*$_2$ = ...

(or the form fun op *id* ( *pat*$_1$, *pat*$_2$) = ...).

Any occurrence of an identifier prefixed by op is treated as non-infixed:

- The form op *v* must be used when a value *v* with infix status occurs in the argument to a (higher-order) function (an argument to a function is always non-infixed).
- The pattern op *id* allows the use of an identifier *id* with infix status in the argument pattern of a function declaration. Note that the op directive is required only for an infixed identifier which is *bound* by a pattern matching – as described above, an infixed constructor *Con* may occur in the form *pat*$_1$ *Con pat*$_2$ in the argument pattern of a function.

The use of a pattern op *v* is illustrated in the following declaration of the foldr function for lists (cf. Section 9.5.2):

```
local infix $ in
fun foldr op $ b []      = b
  | foldr op $ b (x::xs) = x $ (foldr op $ b xs)
end;
val foldr = fn : ('a * 'b -> 'b) -> 'b -> 'a list -> 'b
```

The forms of the infix and infixr directives are as follows:

    infix *id*$_1$ ··· *id*$_n$
    infix *d id*$_1$ ··· *id*$_n$
    infixr *id*$_1$ ··· *id*$_n$
    infixr *d id*$_1$ ··· *id*$_n$

where *d* is an optional decimal digit denoting operator priority. The default (lowest) priority is 0. The infix directive defines left associativity while infixr defines right associativity for the identifiers.

A mix of left associative operators of the same priority associates to the left, and a mix of right associative operators of the same priority associates to the right. It is not legal to mix left and right associative operators of the same priority, so the use of brackets is mandatory in this case.

## B.2  Syntax

The *production rules* in Tables B.5–B.8 describe how to generate any syntactically legal SML program. There are production rules for declarations, expressions, patterns, types, etc. which are the *syntax classes* of SML.

## B.2.1    Example of a parse tree

Before going into technical details about production rules, we illustrate the underlying idea by an example. Figure B.1 shows the *parse tree* for the string:

```
'a -> 'b * int
```

The reader will note that the *leaves* of the tree contain the *items*:

```
'a      ->      'b      *      int
```

of the string while the *nodes* in the tree contain names for *syntax classes*: *ty* (type), *tyvar* (type variable), *tyseq* (type variable sequence) and *longtycon* (type constructor). The structure of the parse tree describes the *syntactic structure* of 'a ->'b * int:

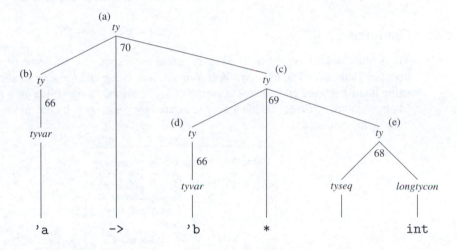

**Figure B.1**    Parse tree for the type: 'a -> 'b * int.

**(a)** The root in the parse tree describes a type consisting of three parts: a type in the left subtree (b), the reserved word -> and a type in the right subtree (c).

**(b)** This parse tree describes a type consisting of the type variable 'a.

**(c)** This parse tree describes a type consisting of three parts: a type in the left subtree (d), the reserved word *, and a type in the right subtree (e).

**(d)** This parse tree describes a type consisting of the type variable 'b.

**(e)** This parse tree describes a type consisting of two parts: the empty type variable sequence, and the type constructor int.

Each node in a parse tree is built using a *production rule* in the grammar as indicated by the numbers in Figure B.1. The production rules used in Figure B.1 are found in Table B.1 (which is a copy of Table B.8). Hence the node (a) is built using production rule 70, nodes (b) and (d) are built using production rule 66, node (c) is built using production rule 69, while node (e) is built using production rule 68.

**Table B.1**   Grammar for type expressions.

| ty | ::= | tyvar | 66 | Type variable |
|----|-----|-------|----|----|
| | | { ⟨tyrow⟩ } | 67 | Record type expression |
| | | tyseq longtycon | 68 | Type construction |
| | | $ty_1 * \cdots * ty_n$ | 69 | Tuple type, $n \geq 2$ |
| | | ty -> ty' | 70 | Function type expression |
| | | ( ty ) | 71 | |
| tyrow | ::= | lab : ty ⟨ , tyrow⟩ | 72 | Type expression row |

*Source: The Definition of Standard ML* (Revised) Robert Milner, Mads Tofte, Robert Harper, David MacQueen, MIT Press, Massachusetts, USA, 1997

## B.2.2   Grammar

The syntax describes any legal SML program as a sequence of items of the kinds listed in Table B.2. The meta-symbols *longvid*, *longtycon* and *longstrid* indicate that a value identifier, type constructor or structure identifier may appear in a *long* form (like List.exists) with several identifiers separated by periods. A long name refers to an item inside a structure.

**Table B.2**   Syntax classes of items.

| Meta symbol | Legend |
|-------------|--------|
| | Reserved word |
| scon | Special constant |
| d | Digit |
| vid, longvid | Value identifier |
| lab | Record label |
| tycon, longtycon | Type constructor |
| tyvar | Type variable |
| strid, longstrid | Structure identifier |

The main composite syntax classes are expressions, declarations and patterns as listed in Table B.3. In the syntactic description we also use the auxiliary syntax classes listed in Table B.4.

**Table B.3**   Main composite syntax classes.

| Meta symbol | Legend |
|-------------|--------|
| exp | Expression |
| dec | Declaration |
| pat | Pattern |
| ty | Type expression |

**Table B.4**  Auxiliary composite syntax classes.

| Meta symbol | Legend | Meta symbol | Legend |
|---|---|---|---|
| *atexp* | Atomic expression | *typbind* | Type binding |
| *exprow* | Expression row | *datbind* | Datatype binding |
| *appexp* | Application expression | *conbind* | Constructor binding |
| *infexp* | Infix expression | *exbind* | Exception binding |
| *match* | Match | *atpat* | Atomic pattern |
| *mrule* | Match rule | *patrow* | Pattern row |
| *valbind* | Value binding | *tyrow* | Type row |
| *fvalbind* | Value binding for function | | |

*Source: The Definition of Standard ML (Revised) Robert Milner, Mads Tofte, Robert Harper, David MacQueen, MIT Press, Massachusetts, USA, 1997*

The following conventions are used in the description of the syntax:

- Angle brackets $\langle \cdots \rangle$ enclose optional parts.
- For any syntax class with meta symbol *x* we define a syntax class of sequences with meta-symbol *xseq* as follows:

  | | | |
  |---|---|---|
  | *xseq* | ::=   *x* | (singleton sequence) |
  | | | (empty sequence) |
  | | $(x_1, \cdots, x_n)$ | (sequence, $n \geq 1$) |

  Hence, ('a,''b) is of class *tyvarseq*. (Note that the '$\cdots$' used here, meaning syntactic repetition, should not be confused with '...' which is a reserved word of the language.)
- L (resp. R) means left (resp. right) association.
- Alternative forms for each syntax class are in order of decreasing precedence, so, for example, rule 69 has higher precedence than rule 70 in Table B.1, hence * binds stronger than -> in types.

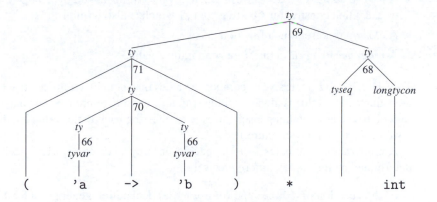

**Figure B.2**  Parse tree for the type: ('a -> 'b) * int.

- Each iterated construct (e.g. *match* in Table B.5) extends as far right as possible; thus, parentheses may be needed around an expression which terminates with a match if this occurs within a larger match.
- The syntax of types binds more strongly than that of expressions.

These conventions resolve the *ambiguity* of the grammar such that the parse tree will be unique. This is illustrated in Figure B.1 (on Page 290) where the use of rule 69 is closer to the leaves in the parse tree than the use of rule 70.

Brackets are taken care of via separate production rules such as rule 71 in Table B.1. This is illustrated by the parse tree in Figure B.2.

## B.3  Value, environment and store

### B.3.1  Values

Values in SML are of the following kinds:

- A *constant* of a basic type such as the integer 25 of type `int`.
- A non-empty *record*: $\{lab_1=val_1,\ lab_2=val_2,\ \ldots,\ lab_n=val_n\}$ for some $n \geq 1$, associating values $val_1, val_2, \ldots, val_n$ with labels $lab_1, lab_2, \ldots, lab_n$, i.e. $lab_1 \mapsto val_1, lab_2 \mapsto val_2, \ldots, lab_n \mapsto val_n$.
- The *empty record* `{}` of type `unit` (same as the *empty tuple* `()`).
- An *n-tuple:* $(val_1, val_2, \ldots, val_n)$ for some $n \geq 2$, associating values $val_1, val_2, \ldots, val_n$ with the indices $1, \ldots, n$, i.e. $1 \mapsto val_1, 2 \mapsto val_2, \ldots, n \mapsto val_n$. An *n*-tuple is actually a special case of record with labels 1, 2, ..., *n*, so the *n*-tuple $(val_1, val_2, \ldots, val_n)$ denotes the record $\{1 = val_1, 2 = val_2, \ldots, n = val_n\}$.
- A *value constructor* such as `true`, `nil` or `::` (where the last is also a function).
- An *exception constructor* such as `Match` or `Overflow`.
- A *tagged value* (or *tree*) *Con val* where a value *val* is tagged by a value constructor or exception constructor *Con* (e.g. `1::[]` which is also written `[1]`).
- A *closure* representing a function.
- A *reference* to a *cell* in the *store* containing a value.

This description is recursive as composite values may contain components which again are values, but a value is always a finite structure. (Using references one may construct 'circular' values containing a subcomponent referring back to the value itself, but such a value is still a finite structure.)

A *constructor* originates from a specific `datatype` or `exception` declaration as determined by the context, more precisely:

- Each execution of a `datatype` (or `abstype`) declaration generates a fresh type and fresh constructors.
- Each execution of an exception declaration generates a fresh exception constructor.

A *closure* is a triple $c = (env, id, exp)$ of an environment *env*, an identifier *id* (the formal argument) and an expression *exp*.

An *overloaded identifier* denotes *different* functions depending on the context in which it occurs. For instance, the overloaded addition symbol + may denote the addition function for integers: $\text{plus}_\text{Int} : \text{Int} \times \text{Int} \rightarrow \text{Int}$ or the addition function for real numbers: $\text{plus}_\text{Real} : \text{Real} \times \text{Real} \rightarrow \text{Real}$, and these two addition functions are considered to be different. Also, the selector functions #1, #2, ... on tuples are overloaded as they can be applied to tuples with an arbitrary number of components (e.g. #2 may denote the 'second component' function of a pair or of a triple). The SML system uses the type of the argument to select between the possible meanings of an overloaded identifier, while the default meaning of the identifier is used when the type of the arguments cannot be inferred. The default for arithmetic operators (such as +) is the operator on integers, while other overloaded operators such as (#2) have no defaults (so in this case the system must be able to infer the type). All overloaded identifiers are pre-defined, and the SML system does not allow the programmer to declare overloaded identifiers.

A *polymorphic value*, such as the empty list [], can be given different types depending on the context in which it occurs, but all occurrences denote the *same* value.

The equality sign = denotes *structural equality* of values. There are, however, values for which SML does not allow comparison, e.g. values having functions, values of abstract types, exceptions, input streams or output streams as components. Two tagged values $Con_1 \, val_1$ and $Con_2 \, val_2$ can be compared if the constructors $Con_1$ and $Con_2$ come from the same execution of a `datatype` (or `abstype`) declaration, and they are equal when the identifiers $Con_1$ and $Con_2$ are identical and the values $val_1$ and $val_2$ are equal. Two references are equal if they point to the same cell in the store.

## B.3.2  Environment

An *environment* is a set of *bindings* associating *meanings* with *identifiers*. The SML system maintains several environments including:

- The *value environment*, assigning values and identifier status to identifiers.
- The *type environment*, assigning types to identifiers.

The environments used by the module system are discussed in Section C.3.

The same identifier may be bound in both environments, but this does not create any ambiguity, as it can be determined from the context whether a specific occurrence of an identifier denotes a value or a type. Types and typing are described later in this appendix.

Each identifier in the value environment has an *identifier status* which is either of *value constructor*, *exception constructor* or plain *value* status. The status is of importance when the identifier is used in a pattern. In matching the pattern to a value, an identifier of constructor status (i.e. value constructor status or exception constructor status) will match only the very same constructor. An identifier of value status – or an identifier which is not bound in the current value environment – will match any value, and the match will give an overriding binding of the identifier.

New bindings are added or existing bindings are modified by *executing declarations* or by *matching patterns* to values:

- An identifier declared by a `val` or `fun` declaration gets value status in the value environment.
- Identifiers used as constructors in a `datatype` (or `abstype`) or `exception` declaration get constructor status in the value environment. The type constructor in the declaration is bound in the type environment.
- Identifiers in a pattern – apart from identifiers of constructor status – get value status in the value environment when the pattern is matched to a value.
- The type constructor in a `type` declaration is bound in the type environment.

Bindings are either *global* (at top level) or *local* for the evaluation of an expression in the program. Local bindings are deleted and the previous environments are restored when the evaluation of the expression is completed.

### B.3.3    Store

The SML *store* is a set of *cells* associating *values* with *references*. Cells in the store are *created* or *modified* by *evaluation* of suitable *expressions* (evaluating `ref e` creates a cell, and evaluating $e_1$ `:=` $e_2$ modifies a cell). Furthermore, the *value* obtained by *evaluating* an *expression* may depend on the current store (through use of the contents operator '`!`' or a pattern match with a pattern `ref` *pat*). The identifier `ref` is syntactically handled like a value constructor, e.g. with respect to pattern matching, but the evaluation of an expression `ref e` has the side-effect of allocating a new cell to the store containing the value of the expression *e*, and the result of the evaluation is the reference to this cell. Hence, repeated evaluations of the same expression `ref e` will give different results, as a fresh cell in the store will be allocated in each evaluation.

### B.3.4    Garbage collection

The execution of an SML program on a computer is managed by the SML run-time system, but this is in principle invisible to the programmer who interacts with the computer entirely according to the premises of the SML source program. Using today's SML systems one may, however, experience occasional small delays in the execution of the program, when the run-time system rearranges the use of the computer memory by performing a so-called *garbage collection*. The points in time where garbage collection takes place are not controlled by the SML program, so it can be difficult to predict the real-time behaviour of a program. (The same phenomenon may occur in the execution of programs written in other languages using a garbage collection scheme, as, for example, the Java language.)

Developing run-time systems with a predictable real-time behaviour is currently an active and promising field of research and there are already tools ('MLWorks' and 'The ML Kit') which can predict the real-time behaviour of SML programs.

## B.4 Types

Types in SML are built from the *predefined types* char, string, int, word, real, unit, bool, order, exn (for exceptions) and *type variables* (such as 'a and 'b) by means of the *predefined type constructors* such as *, ->, ref, {}, and *type constructors* defined in the program.

### B.4.1 Polymorphic types and equality types

A type is *polymorphic* if it contains type variables, and *monomorphic* if it contains no type variables. An *instance* of a polymorphic type is obtained by substituting types (which may themselves be polymorphic) for all occurrences of one or more of the type variables.

A type variable inferred by the SML system, with a double prime such as ''a denotes an *equality type* upon which the SML equality operator = must be defined, cf. Section B.3.1.

### B.4.2 Type inference and type check

The *type inference* in the SML system finds the types of expressions and identifiers with a minimum of guidance from the programmer. It proceeds by specializing the types of the involved subcomponents to instances of their types until a consistent typing is found. The type inference finds the most general type (the 'principal' type) in the sense that other legal types of the entity in question are instances of the inferred type. It terminates with an error message if the typing fails. This is the case, for example, if a function is applied to an argument of incompatible type. One says that the SML system performs a *type check*. Strictly speaking, an overloaded identifier has no 'most general type' as it denotes different functions with different types depending on the context (cf. Section B.3.1). The type inference uses the type of the function denoted by the particular occurrence of the overloaded identifier – which is the default when the meaning of the identifier cannot otherwise be determined from the context.

The programmer may specify the type by means of an explicit typing in the program. This may be needed by the SML system in the following cases.

*Resolving overloaded identifiers*

Overloaded identifiers such as + or #2 denote different functions for different types, and the SML system uses the type of the argument to find the meaning of such a symbol. Overloaded operators default to int, except the division operator '/' which default to real.

*Restricting polymorphic types at top level*

A top level declaration of polymorphic type is only allowed if the right-hand side is a value expression (cf. below). Hence one may need an explicit typing in the case of non-value expressions at top level, if the SML system would otherwise infer a polymorphic type.

B.4.3    Restrictions on polymorphic expressions

The use of *polymorphic expressions* at top level is restricted by SML:

● All monomorphic expressions are OK, even expressions that are not value expressions.

● All value expressions are OK, even polymorphic ones.

● At top-level, polymorphic expressions are forbidden if they are not value expressions.

Here an expression is called a *value expression* if it has the form of a value where no further evaluation can be made. Hence, 5 and [1,2,3] are value expressions, while 2 + 3 is not. Note that any expression of the form fn... is a value expression as it is not evaluated further, but just 'packaged' into a closure.

It follows that the right hand side expression in a *declaration* on top level must be monomorphic unless it is a value expression, so val x = [] is legal on top level while val y = rev [] is not:

```
val x = [];
val x = [] : 'a list
val y = rev [];
! Toplevel input:
! val y = rev [];
! ^^^^^^^^^^^^^^^
! Value polymorphism: Free type variable at top level: 'a
```

The restriction is made in order to ensure that the use of *references* is type safe, cf. Section 18.3.

## B.5  Semantics

The description of the semantics follows the syntax of the language, and the following subsections correspond to Tables B.5–B.8.

B.5.1    Expressions and matches

An *expression* is an entity which can be *evaluated* in a suitable *environment* and *store*. There are three possible outcomes of the evaluation:

● The evaluation terminates normally. The result is a *value* together with an (updated) *store*, whereas the *environment* is *unchanged*.

● The evaluation continues forever.

● The evaluation *raises* an *exception* and terminates abnormally. Raised exceptions propagate to a surrounding expression, unless the raised exception is *handled* by a *handler*.

The normal evaluation of an expression consists of a number of *evaluation steps* of the form:

$$(expression, environment, store) \rightsquigarrow (expression', environment', store')$$

followed by a single evaluation step of the form:

$$(expression, environment, store) \leadsto (value, store')$$

The first kind of evaluation steps leads to further evaluation, while the second kind marks the end of the evaluation. The semantics of SML defines a unique evaluation step for any legal triple $(expression, environment, store)$. The order of evaluation of sub-expressions in a composite expression is significant in describing the *side-effects* of an evaluation (i.e. the changes in the store) as the store is updated gradually during the evaluation.

It is important to distinguish between *raising* an exception and getting an exception as the *result* of an evaluation. This is illustrated by the following example where the evaluation of the expression Div terminates normally and does not use the exception handler, while the evaluation of raise Div raises the exception Div which is handled by the exception handler:

```
Div handle Div => Overflow;
val it = Div : exn
(raise Div) handle Div => Overflow;
val it = Overflow : exn
```

A *match* is an entity of the form

$$pat_1 \Rightarrow exp_1 \mid pat_2 \Rightarrow exp_2 \mid \cdots \mid pat_n \Rightarrow exp_n$$

It can be *evaluated* for a given *value* in a given *environment*. The evaluation tries to match the value to the patterns $pat_1$, $pat_2$, ..., $pat_n$ in that order. If a matching pattern $pat_i$ is found, then the corresponding expression $exp_i$ is evaluated in the given environment modified by the bindings introduced by the matching. The old environment is restored when the evaluation is completed. The exception Match is raised if none of the patterns match the value. The matching of a value to a pattern is described in Section B.5.3 below.

The expressions and matches described in rules 1–27 of Table B.5 are evaluated as follows:

**1.** A special constant evaluates to the value denoted by the constant.

**2.** A value identifier evaluates to the value in the binding of the identifier in the current environment.

**3.** A record expression $\{lab_1 = exp_1, lab_2 = exp_2, \ldots, lab_n = exp_n\}$ evaluates to the record $\{lab_1 = val_1, lab_2 = val_2, \ldots, lab_n = val_n\}$ if the expressions $exp_1$, $exp_2$, ..., $exp_n$ evaluate to the values $val_1$, $val_2$, ..., $val_n$. The expressions are evaluated from left to right.

**4.** A record selector #*lab* denotes the function fn $\{lab, \ldots\}$ => *lab* from record to component. The selectors are overloaded, and meaning must be determined by the context.

**5.** The empty tuple () denotes a value of type unit.

**Table B.5**  Grammar: Expressions and Matches.

| | | | | |
|---|---|---|---|---|
| *atexp* | ::= | *scon* | 1 | Special constant |
| | | ⟨op⟩*longvid* | 2 | Value identifier |
| | | { ⟨*exprow*⟩ } | 3 | Record |
| | | # *lab* | 4 | Record selector |
| | | ( ) | 5 | 0-tuple |
| | | ($exp_1$ , $\cdots$ , $exp_n$) | 6 | *n*-tuple, $n \geq 2$ |
| | | [$exp_1$ , $\cdots$ , $exp_n$] | 7 | List, $n \geq 0$ |
| | | ($exp_1$ ; $\cdots$ ; $exp_n$) | 8 | Sequence, $n \geq 2$ |
| | | let *dec* in $exp_1$ ; $\cdots$ ; $exp_n$ end | 9 | Local declaration, $n \geq 1$ |
| | | ( *exp* ) | 10 | |
| *exprow* | ::= | *lab* = *exp* ⟨ , *exprow*⟩ | 11 | Expression row |
| *appexp* | ::= | *atexp* | 12 | |
| | | *appexp atexp* | 13 | Application expression |
| *infexp* | ::= | *appexp* | 14 | |
| | | $infexp_1$ *vid* $infexp_2$ | 15 | Infix expression |
| *exp* | ::= | *infexp* | 16 | |
| | | *exp* : *ty* | 17 | Typed (L) |
| | | $exp_1$ andalso $exp_2$ | 18 | Conjunction |
| | | $exp_1$ orelse $exp_2$ | 19 | Disjunction |
| | | *exp* handle *match* | 20 | Handle exception |
| | | raise *exp* | 21 | Raise exception |
| | | if $exp_1$ then $exp_2$ else $exp_3$ | 22 | Conditional |
| | | while $exp_1$ do $exp_2$ | 23 | Iteration |
| | | case *exp* of *match* | 24 | Case analysis |
| | | fn *match* | 25 | Function |
| *match* | ::= | *mrule* ⟨ | *match*⟩ | 26 | |
| *mrule* | ::= | *pat* => *exp* | 27 | |

*Source: The Definition of Standard ML* (Revised) Robert Milner, Mads Tofte, Robert Harper, David MacQueen, MIT Press, Massachusetts, USA, 1997

6. A tuple expression $(exp_1, exp_2, \ldots, exp_n)$ evaluates to the tuple $(val_1, val_2, \ldots, val_n)$ if the expressions $exp_1$, $exp_2$, $\ldots$, $exp_n$ evaluate to the values $val_1, val_2, \ldots, val_n$. The expressions are evaluated from left to right.

7. A list of expressions $[exp_1, exp_2, \ldots, exp_n]$ evaluates to the list $[val_1, val_2, \ldots, val_n]$ if the expressions $exp_1$, $exp_2$, $\ldots$, $exp_n$ evaluate to the values $val_1, val_2, \ldots, val_n$. The expressions are evaluated from left to right.

8. A sequential composition of expressions is evaluated from left to right. The result of the evaluation is the result of the last expression.

9. A let expression is evaluated by modifying the current environment by the bindings

in the declaration and then evaluating the expression (the sequential composition of expressions) in this environment – after which the old environment is restored.

10. Syntax rule: brackets can be used for collecting a composite expression into a single atomic expression. The expression in brackets is evaluated as the expressions inside the brackets.

11. Syntax rule: An expression row is a syntactic part of a record expression.

12. Syntax rule.

13. An application *appexp atexp* is evaluated by evaluating the left hand expression *appexp* to a value which must be a closure $c = (env, id, exp)$, and evaluating the right hand expression *atexp* to a value $v$, upon which the expression *exp* (from the closure) is evaluated in the environment *env* (from the closure) modified by the binding $id \mapsto v$. The old environment is thereupon restored. See also Section 9.9.

14. Syntax rule.

15. An infix expression $infexp_1$ *vid* $infexp_2$ is evaluated as the (non-fix) function denoted by the identifier *vid* applied to the pair of argument expressions: op *vid* $(infexp_1, infexp_2)$.

16. Syntax rule.

17. A typing $exp : ty$ tells the system that *exp* must have type *ty*.

18. The expression $exp_1$ andalso $exp_2$ is evaluated by first evaluating $exp_1$. If this evaluation does not terminate, then the evaluation of the andalso-expression does not terminate. If false is the result of $exp_1$, then false is the result the andalso-expression; otherwise true is the result of $exp_1$ and the expression $exp_2$ is evaluated.

19. The expression $exp_1$ orelse $exp_2$ is evaluated by first evaluating $exp_1$. If this evaluation does not terminate, then the evaluation of the orelse-expression does not terminate. If true is the result of $exp_1$, then true is the result the orelse-expression; otherwise false is the result of $exp_1$ and the expression $exp_2$ is evaluated.

20. The expression *exp* handle *match* is evaluated like the expression *exp* if no exceptions are raised. If an exception *exn* is raised, and if the match contains a rule *pat* => $exp_2$ where *pat* matches *exn*, then $exp_2$ is evaluated in the environment in which the evaluation was started, modified by the bindings introduced by the matching. If *exn* is not matched by *match*, then the exception *exn* is raised again (propagating to a surrounding expression).

21. The expression raise *exp* evaluates the expression *exp* to a value *exn* and raises the exception *exn* – unless the evaluation of *exp* raises an exception.

22. The conditional expression if $exp_1$ then $exp_2$ else $exp_3$ is evaluated by first evaluating $exp_1$. If this evaluation does not terminate, then the evaluation of the if-expression does not terminate. If true is the result of $exp_1$, then $exp_2$ is evaluated; otherwise false is the result of $exp_1$ and $exp_3$ is evaluated.

**23.** The expression while $exp_1$ do $exp_2$ is evaluated by evaluating $exp_1$. If this evaluation does not terminate, then the evaluation of the while-expression does not terminate. If the result of $exp_1$ is false, then the evaluation of the while loop is terminated with the result (), otherwise the expression $exp_2$ is evaluated, upon which the evaluation of the while loop is repeated.

**24.** The expression case $exp$ of $match$ is evaluated by first evaluating the expression $exp$. If this evaluation does not terminate, then the evaluation of the case-expression does not terminate. Otherwise, some value $val$ is the result of $exp$, upon which the match is evaluated for this value (in the current environment).

**25.** The expression fn $match$ evaluates to a closure

$(env, id, $ case $id$ of $match)$

where $id$ is some identifier which does not occur in $match$.

**26.** A match can be *evaluated* for a given *value* in a given *environment* as described above.

**27.** Syntax rule.

### B.5.2    Declarations

The effect of a declaration is that one or more *identifiers* get *bound* to *values* in the current *value environment* or to *types* in the current *type environment*. Each binding in the current value environment has an *identifier status* which is either *value constructor*, *exception constructor* or plain *value* status.

The declarations described in rules 28–49 of Table B.6 have the following effect:

**28.** A val declaration val $tyvarseq$ $valbind$ adds the bindings in $valbind$ (cf. rules 42 and 43) to the environments. (The optional $tyvarseq$ can be used in controlling the scope of type variables in $valbind$ – the interested reader is referred to *The Definition* for further details.)

**29.** A fun declaration fun $tyvarseq$ $fvalbind$ adds the bindings in $fvalbind$ (cf. rule 44) to the value environment. (The optional $tyvarseq$ can be used in controlling the scope of type variables in $valbind$ – the interested reader is referred to *The Definition* for further details.)

**30.** A type declaration type $typbind$ adds the bindings in $typbind$ (cf. rule 45) to the type environment.

**31.** The declaration datatype $datbind$ ⟨withtype $typbind$⟩ adds bindings of type constructors to the type environment and bindings of value constructors to the value environment (cf. rules 45 and 46).

**32.** The declaration datatype $tycon$ = datatype $longtycon$ binds the identifier $tycon$ in the type environment to denote the same type constructor as the (possibly long) identifier $longtycon$ and binds the constructors of $longtycon$ in the value environment.

**Table B.6**   Grammar: Declarations and Bindings.

| | | | | |
|---|---|---|---|---|
| *dec* | ::= | val *tyvarseq valbind* | 28 | Value declaration |
| | | fun *tyvarseq fvalbind* | 29 | Function declaration |
| | | type *typbind* | 30 | Type declaration |
| | | datatype *datbind* ⟨withtype *typbind*⟩ | 31 | Datatype declaration |
| | | datatype *tycon* = datatype *longtycon* | 32 | Datatype replication |
| | | abstype *datbind* ⟨withtype *typbind*⟩<br>    with *dec* end | 33 | Abstype declaration |
| | | exception *exbind* | 34 | Exception declaration |
| | | local *dec*$_1$ in *dec*$_2$ end | 35 | Local declaration |
| | | open *longstrid*$_1$ ⋯ *longstrid*$_n$ | 36 | Open declaration, $n \geq 1$ |
| | | | 37 | Empty declaration |
| | | *dec*$_1$ ⟨;⟩ *dec*$_2$ | 38 | Sequential declaration |
| | | infix ⟨*d*⟩ *vid*$_1$ ⋯ *vid*$_n$ | 39 | Infix (L) directive, $n \geq 1$ |
| | | infixr ⟨*d*⟩ *vid*$_1$ ⋯ *vid*$_n$ | 40 | Infix (R) directive, $n \geq 1$ |
| | | nonfix *vid*$_1$ ⋯ *vid*$_n$ | 41 | Nonfix directive, $n \geq 1$ |
| *valbind* | ::= | *pat* = *exp* ⟨and *valbind*⟩ | 42 | |
| | | rec *valbind* | 43 | |
| *fvalbind* | ::= | ⟨op⟩*vid atpat*$_{11}$⋯*atpat*$_{1n}$⟨:*ty*⟩=*exp*$_1$ | 44 | $m, n \geq 1$ |
| | | \| ⟨op⟩*vid atpat*$_{21}$⋯*atpat*$_{2n}$⟨:*ty*⟩=*exp*$_2$ | | See also note below |
| | | \|   ⋯     ⋯ | | |
| | | \| ⟨op⟩*vid atpat*$_{m1}$⋯*atpat*$_{mn}$⟨:*ty*⟩=*exp*$_m$<br>        ⟨and *fvalbind*⟩ | | |
| *typbind* | ::= | *tyvarseq tycon* = *ty* ⟨and *typbind*⟩ | 45 | |
| *datbind* | ::= | *tyvarseq tycon* = *conbind* ⟨and *datbind*⟩ | 46 | |
| *conbind* | ::= | ⟨op⟩*vid* ⟨of *ty*⟩ ⟨ \| *conbind*⟩ | 47 | |
| *exbind* | ::= | ⟨op⟩*vid* ⟨of *ty*⟩ ⟨and *exbind*⟩ | 48 | |
| | | ⟨op⟩*vid* = ⟨op⟩*longvid* ⟨and *exbind*⟩ | 49 | |

In the *fvalbind* form, if *vid* has infix status then either op must be present, or *vid* must be infixed. Thus, at the start of any clause, ' op *vid* (*atpat*,*atpat*′) ⋯' may be written '(*atpat vid atpat*′) ⋯'; the parentheses may also be dropped if ':*ty*' or '=' follows immediately.

*Source: The Definition of Standard ML* (Revised) Robert Milner, Mads Tofte, Robert Harper, David MacQueen, MIT Press, Massachusetts, USA, 1997

**33.** Executing an abstype declaration yields bindings in the value and type environments as given by *datbind* and *decl*. The declared types are *abstract* in the sense that values of these types can only be used in connection with the values and functions declared in *decl*. The optional *typbind* allows local type bindings which can be used in *datbind* without being made available to other parts of the program.

**34.** An exception declaration exception *exbind* adds the bindings from *exbind* to the value environment.

**35.** A local declaration local *dec*$_1$ in *dec*$_2$ end is executed in an environment *env* as follows: first the declaration *dec*$_1$ is executed in the environment *env*, resulting in an environment $env'$. Next, the declaration $dec_2$ is executed in the environment $env'$, resulting in further bindings $bnd_1, \ldots, bnd_k$. Finally, the bindings $bnd_1, \ldots, bnd_k$ are inserted into the environment $env$ (while the bindings from $dec_1$ are discarded).

**36.** An open $longstrid_1 \ldots longstrid_n$ declaration is executed by adding the bindings in the structure(s) to the current environment, i.e. for each compound identifier $longstrid_i.id$ we get a binding of $id$ to the same value. An open declaration does not entail any evaluations – the declared values were evaluated when the structure declaration was executed.

**37.** The empty declaration has no effect.

**38.** A sequence of declarations is executed from left to right.

**39.** The `infix` directive is classified as a declaration. It does not bind an identifier, but it gives infix status and left associativity to identifier(s).

**40.** The `infixr` directive is classified as a declaration. It does not bind identifiers, but it gives infix status and right associativity to identifier(s).

**41.** The `nonfix` directive is classified as a declaration. It does not bind identifiers, but it gives nonfix status to identifier(s) (which may previously have been given infix status).

**42.** A value binding $pat = exp$ is executed by first evaluating the expression $exp$ and then modifying the value environment by adding the bindings obtained by matching the pattern $pat$ to the result of the evaluation. A sequence of value bindings (separated by and) is executed from left to right.

**43.** A recursive value binding `rec` *valbind* allows recursion, i.e. the right hand side expression(s) may contain identifiers from the patterns.

**44.** A nonfix function binding consists of the function name followed by an atomic pattern for the argument, followed by an expression for the value. An argument pattern sequence is used only for a higher-order function. The binding may contain several cases separated by '|', but they must all contain the same function name. A type expression can be used for restricting the type of the value of the function. A function binding may bind several identifiers where the bindings are separated by 'and'. This allows mutual recursion between the functions in the binding.

Infix function names used in nonfix form must be prefixed by op, but infix functions can also be defined in infix notation when the identifier *vid* for the function is written between the patterns (cf. the note in Table B.6).

**45.** A type binding *tyvarseq tycon* = *ty* binds the identifier *tycon* in the type environment to a (possibly parameterized) type. Several type bindings may be combined using and.

**46.** A datatype binding *tyvarseq tycon* = *conbind* binds the identifier *tycon* in the type environment and possible constructors from *conbind* in the value environment. Several (possibly recursive) type bindings may be combined using and.

**47.** A constructor binding ⟨op⟩ *vid* ⟨of *ty*⟩ (for a datatype binding, cf. rule 45) binds the identifier *vid* in the value environment to value constructor status. The constructor is a function when an argument type *ty* is present. Several constructor bindings are combined using |. The op is required when the identifier has been given infix status.

**48.** An exception binding ⟨op⟩ *vid* ⟨of *ty*⟩ binds the identifier *vid* in the value environment to exception constructor status. The exception constructor is a function when an argument type *ty* is present. Several exception constructor bindings may be combined using and. The op is required when the identifier has been given infix status.

**49.** An exception binding ⟨op⟩ *vid* = ⟨op⟩ *longvid* binds the identifier *vid* in the value environment with exception constructor status to denote the same exception constructor as the (possibly long) identifier *longvid*. Several exception constructor bindings may be combined using and. The op is required when the identifier has been given infix status.

### B.5.3    Patterns

Patterns describe the structure of (composite) values. Identifiers bound in the current environment with value constructor status or exception constructor status match the corresponding value only, while other identifiers match any value. If a pattern matches a value, then the matching is unique. A pattern matching modifies the current value environment by binding identifiers (except those with constructor status) to values which are components of the value. No pattern may bind the same identifier twice.

The patterns described in Table B.7 work as follows:

**Table B.7**    Grammar: Patterns.

| *atpat* | ::= | _ | 50 | Wildcard |
|---|---|---|---|---|
| | | *scon* | 51 | Special constant |
| | | ⟨op⟩*longvid* | 52 | Value identifier |
| | | { ⟨*patrow*⟩ } | 53 | Record |
| | | ( ) | 54 | 0-tuple |
| | | ($pat_1$ , $\cdots$ , $pat_n$) | 55 | *n*-tuple, $n \geq 2$ |
| | | [$pat_1$ , $\cdots$ , $pat_n$] | 56 | List, $n \geq 0$ |
| | | ( *pat* ) | 57 | |
| *patrow* | ::= | ... | 58 | Wildcard |
| | | *lab* = *pat* ⟨ , *patrow*⟩ | 59 | Pattern row |
| | | *vid*⟨:*ty*⟩ ⟨as *pat*⟩ ⟨, *patrow*⟩ | 60 | Label as variable |
| *pat* | ::= | *atpat* | 61 | Atomic |
| | | ⟨op⟩*longvid atpat* | 62 | Constructed value |
| | | $pat_1$ *vid* $pat_2$ | 63 | Constructed value (infix) |
| | | *pat* : *ty* | 64 | Typed |
| | | ⟨op⟩*vid*⟨: *ty*⟩ as *pat* | 65 | Layered |

*Source: The Definition of Standard ML* (Revised) Robert Milner, Mads Tofte, Robert Harper, David MacQueen, MIT Press, Massachusetts, USA, 1997

50. The *wildcard* pattern matches any value. The match does not generate any bindings.

51. A special constant matches the corresponding value only.

52. A value or exception constructor (even a long identifier) matches the corresponding value only. Other identifiers match any value (and cannot be long identifiers). A prefixing op is required for infix identifiers to get nonfix status of the pattern.

53. A record pattern matches a record if the components of the pattern row (cf. rules 58–60) match the components of the record.

54. The pattern () matches the empty tuple only.

55. A tuple pattern $(pat_1, pat_2, \dots, pat_m)$ matches a tuple $(val_1, val_2, \dots, val_n)$ if $m = n$ and each pattern $pat_i$ matches the corresponding value $val_i$.

56. A list pattern $[pat_1, pat_2, \dots, pat_m]$ matches a list $[val_1, val_2, \dots, val_n]$ if $m = n$ and if each pattern $pat_i$ matches the corresponding value $val_i$.

57. Syntax rule for enclosing a (composite) pattern in brackets.

58. The wildcard pattern row matches any remaining fields in a record (cf. rule 53).

59. The pattern *lab* = *pat* matches a record component *lab* = *val* with the same label if the pattern *pat* matches the value *val*.

60. The pattern *lab* for a non-numeric label *lab* matches a record component *lab* = *val* with the same label. The matching binds the label *lab* to the value *val* as an identifier with value status. The pattern *pat* in a layered pattern ⟨op⟩ *lab* as *pat* must also match the record component, and identifiers in this pattern become bound accordingly, so one obtains two bindings of patterns (*lab* and *pat*) for the same component in the record.

61. Syntax rule.

62. A pattern ⟨op⟩*longvid atpat* matches a tagged value *Con val* if the identifier matches the constructor *Con* (cf. rule 52) and the pattern *atpat* matches the value *val*. A prefixing op is required for infix identifiers to get nofix status of the pattern.

63. A pattern $pat_1$ *vid* $pat_2$ where the identifier *vid* has infix status matches a tagged value $Con(val_1, val_2)$ if the identifier matches the constructor *Con* (cf. rule 52), and the patterns $pat_1$ and $pat_2$ match the values $val_1$ and $val_2$.

64. A typed pattern *pat* : *ty* matches a value if the pattern *pat* matches the value. The type tells the system that the value bound to *pat* must have type *ty*.

65. A layered pattern *vid* as *pat* contains an identifier *vid* and a pattern *pat*. It matches a value *val* when the pattern *pat* matches *val* (and the identifier *vid* matches *val*, cf. rule 52). The matching bind identifiers in *pat* according to the matching of *pat* to *val*, and furthermore binds the identifier *vid* to the value *val*. Using layered patterns one may hence obtain a binding of an identifier to all of the value *val* together with bindings of other identifiers to components of the value *val*.

## B.5.4    Type expressions

Explicit typing is used in a program to guide the system in resolving overloaded operator symbols and in restricting a polymorphic type to suitable instances – as described in Section B.4. The syntax for type expressions (meta-symbol *ty*) is given in Table B.8 and the explanation below of the meaning follows the production rules in this figure.

**Table B.8**    Grammar: Type expressions.

| *ty* | ::= | *tyvar* | 66 | Type variable |
|------|-----|---------|----|----|
|  |  | { ⟨*tyrow*⟩ } | 67 | Record type expression |
|  |  | *tyseq longtycon* | 68 | Type construction |
|  |  | $ty_1 * \cdots * ty_n$ | 69 | Tuple type, $n \geq 2$ |
|  |  | *ty -> ty'* | 70 | Function type expression |
|  |  | ( *ty* ) | 71 |  |
| *tyrow* | ::= | *lab* : *ty* ⟨ , *tyrow*⟩ | 72 | Type expression row |

*Source: The Definition of Standard ML* (Revised) Robert Milner, Mads Tofte, Robert Harper, David MacQueen, MIT Press, Massachusetts, USA, 1997

**66.** Any type variable denotes a type.

**67.** A record type lists the labels together with the types of the corresponding values.

**68.** Type constructors (such as `list`) can form composite types such as `int list`.

**69.** The symbol * is used in forming tuple types.

**70.** The symbol -> is used in forming function types.

**71.** A type expression may be included in brackets.

**72.** A type expression row is part of a record type.

# Overview of the SML module system

This appendix extends the overview of the core language in Appendix B by a description of the module system, i.e. the notions of structure, signature, specification and functor. The syntax of modules is given by the production rules in Tables C.2, C.4 and C.6, and the tables of derived syntactic forms in Tables C.3, C.5 and C.7. The numbering of the production rules is a continuation of the numbering used in Appendix B.

The meaning of the constructs in the module system is described in the same manner as in Appendix B by a short, informal note for each production rule.

Tables C.1, C.2, C.4 and C.6 in this appendix have been sourced with permission from *Source: The Definition of Standard ML* (Revised) Robert Milner, Mads Tofte, Robert Harper, David MacQueen, MIT Press, Massachusetts, USA, 1997.

## C.1  Lexical conventions

### C.1.1  Reserved words

The following *reserved words* can only occur in SML modules:

```
eqtype    functor    include    sharing    sig
signature    struct    structure    where    :>
```

## C.1.2    Scope of infix directives

An infix directive in a phrase:

> let *strdec* ⋯ ent
> local *strdec* in ⋯ end
> struct *strdec* ⋯ end

does not extend beyond the scope of the phrase.

## C.2    Syntax

The extra syntax classes used for the description of the modules are given in Table C.1. They extend the syntax classes for the core language introduced in Appendix B.

**Table C.1**    Syntax classes for modules.

| Meta symbol | Legend |
|---|---|
| *strexp* | Structure expression |
| *strdec* | Structure-level declaration |
| *strbind* | Structure binding |
| | |
| *sigexp* | Signature expression |
| *sigdec* | Signature declaration |
| *sigbind* | Signature binding |
| | |
| *spec* | Specification |
| *valdesc* | Value description |
| *typdesc* | Type description |
| *datdesc* | Datatype description |
| *condesc* | Constructor description |
| *exdesc* | Exception description |
| *strdesc* | Structure description |
| | |
| *fundec* | Functor declaration |
| *funbind* | Functor binding |
| *topdec* | Top-level declaration |

The production rules in Tables C.2, C.4 and C.6 describe how to generate syntactically legal SML modules, while Tables C.3, C.5 and C.7 describe a further extension of the syntax by derived forms which are abbreviations of certain syntactic forms. Hence the form *strid* : *sigexp* = *strexp* is an abbreviation of the form *strid* = *strexp* : *sigexp* which is generated by using production rules 84 and 75. The meaning of the derived form is hence to be found by combining the meanings for production rules 84 and 75.

## C.3  Interfaces and environments

In this section we introduce notions to explain the meaning of signatures, structures and functors.

An *interface* is used to express the meaning of a signature. It consists of a set of identifiers together with restrictions on their use. The restrictions fix the kind of each identifier (value, value constructor, exception constructor, type constructor, structure). The types of values and constructors are restricted, and it is recorded for each type constructor whether the internal structure of the values should be visible. Furthermore, there is information about equality types, datatype replication and type sharing.

A *functor closure* is used to express the meaning of a functor in a declaration such as:

> functor *funid* (*strid* : *sigexp*) = *strexp*

The declaration will bind the identifier *funid* to a functor closure consisting of the (formal) structure identifier *strid*, the interface defined by the signature expression *sigexp*, the structure expression *strexp*, plus environments containing the bindings of identifiers in the structure expression which do not occur in the interface.

The SML system uses the following environments:

- *Value environment* assigning value and identifier status to identifiers.
- *Type environment* assigning types to identifiers which are used as type constructors.
- *Signature environment* assigning interfaces to identifiers.
- *Structure environment* assigning value environments to identifiers.
- *Functor environment* assigning functor closures to identifiers.

A set of such environments together with a store is called a *basis*. Declarations are evaluated in an *actual basis* and the result is a new (actual) basis.

## C.4  Semantics

In this section we give the production rules for modules together with an informal explanation of the meaning of the individual constructs.

### C.4.1  Structure and signature expressions

A structure denotes an environment and a signature denotes an interface. The syntax of structures and signatures is given in Tables C.2 and C.3.

**73.** Denotes the environment denoted by *strdec*.

**74.** Denotes the environment *longstrid* is bound to in the structure environment.

**75.** The environment denoted by *strdec* is restricted by the interface obtained from *sigexp*. The 'internal representation' for an identifier in the interface is visible, even when this representation is not specified in the signature. Thus, the internal representation is transparent.

**Table C.2**  Grammar: Structure and Signature Expressions.

| | | | | |
|---|---|---|---|---|
| *strexp* | ::= | struct *strdec* end | 73 | Basic |
| | | *longstrid* | 74 | Structure identifier |
| | | *strexp* : *sigexp* | 75 | Transparent constraint |
| | | *strexp* :> *sigexp* | 76 | Opaque constraint |
| | | *funid* ( *strexp* ) | 77 | Functor application |
| | | let *strdec* in *strexp* end | 78 | Local declaration |
| *strdec* | ::= | *dec* | 79 | Declaration |
| | | structure *strbind* | 80 | Structure |
| | | local *strdec*$_1$ in *strdec*$_2$ end | 81 | Local |
| | | | 82 | Empty |
| | | *strdec*$_1$ ⟨;⟩ *strdec*$_2$ | 83 | Sequential |
| *strbind* | ::= | *strid* = *strexp* ⟨and *strbind*⟩ | 84 | |
| *sigexp* | ::= | sig *spec* end | 85 | Basic |
| | | *sigid* | 86 | Signature identifier |
| | | *sigexp* where type | | |
| | |     *tyvarseq longtycon* = *ty* | 87 | Type realization |
| *sigdec* | ::= | signature *sigbind* | 88 | |
| *sigbind* | ::= | *sigid* = *sigexp* ⟨and *sigbind*⟩ | 89 | |

**Table C.3**  Derived forms: structure and signature expressions.

| Derived form | Equivalent form | Produced by rules |
|---|---|---|
| *strid* : *sigexp* = *strexp* | *strid* = *strexp* : *sigexp* | 84 and 75 |
| *strid* :> *sigexp* = *strexp* | *strid* = *strexp* :> *sigexp* | 84 and 76 |

**76.** The environment denoted by *strdec* is restricted by the interface obtained from *sigexp*. The 'internal representation' for an identifier in the interface is only visible when this representation is specified in the signature. Otherwise, its internal structure is hidden, i.e. it is opaque, as it is not visible outside the scope of *strdec*.

**77.** The environment denoted by *funid*(*strexp*) is obtained as follows: let *env* be the environment denoted by *strexp* and let *strid'*, *I*, *strexp'* and *B* be the structure identifier, interface, structure expression and basis, respectively, from the functor closure associated with the *funid*. Furthermore, let *B'* be the basis obtained from *B* by adding the binding of *strid'* to the environment *env* with the restrictions imposed by the interface *I*. Then, the environment denoted by the functor application is the environment denoted by *strexp'* in the basis *B'*.

**78.** Denotes the environment obtained by evaluation of the structure expression *strexp* in the actual basis extended with the bindings from the structure declarations *strdec*.

**79.** Denotes the environment given by the declarations.

**80.** Denotes the structure environment obtained from *strbind*.

**81.** The bindings obtained from *strbind*$_1$ are added to the actual basis. The environment denoted by the local construct is the environment obtained from *strbind*$_2$.

**82.** Denotes the empty environment.

**83.** A sequence of structure declarations is executed from left to right.

**84.** Denotes the structure environment where *strid* is bound to the environment denoted by *strexp*. And so on.

**85.** Denotes the interface obtained from *spec*.

**86.** Denotes the interface associated with *sigid* in the signature environment.

**87.** Denotes the interface obtained from *sigexp* by instantiation of *tyvarseq longtycon* to *ty*.

**88.** Denotes the signature environment obtained from *sigbind*.

**89.** Denotes the signature environment where *sigid* is bound to the interface for *sigexp*. And so on.

## C.4.2    Specifications

A specification denotes an interface. The syntax is given in Tables C.4 and C.5.

---

**Table C.4**    Grammar: specification.

| *spec* | ::= | `val` *valdesc* | 90 | Value |
|--------|-----|------------------|-----|-------|
| | | `type` *typdesc* | 91 | Type |
| | | `eqtype` *typdesc* | 92 | Eqtype |
| | | `datatype` *datdesc* | 93 | Datatype |
| | | `datatype` *tycon* = `datatype` *longtycon* | 94 | Replication |
| | | `exception` *exdesc* | 95 | Exception |
| | | `structure` *strdesc* | 96 | Structure |
| | | `include` *sigexp* | 97 | Include |
| | | | 98 | Empty |
| | | *spec*$_1$ ⟨;⟩ *spec*$_2$ | 99 | Sequential |
| | | *spec* `sharing type` | 100 | Sharing |
| | | *longtycon*$_1$ = $\cdots$ = *longtycon*$_n$ | | ($n \geq 2$) |
| *valdesc* | ::= | *vid* : *ty* ⟨`and` *valdesc*⟩ | 101 | |
| *typdesc* | ::= | *tyvarseq tycon* ⟨`and` *typdesc*⟩ | 102 | |
| *datdesc* | ::= | *tyvarseq tycon* = *condesc* ⟨`and` *datdesc*⟩ | 103 | |
| *condesc* | ::= | *vid* ⟨`of` *ty*⟩ ⟨ \| *condesc*⟩ | 104 | |
| *exdesc* | ::= | *vid* ⟨`of` *ty*⟩ ⟨`and` *exdesc*⟩ | 105 | |
| *strdesc* | ::= | *strid* : *sigexp* ⟨`and` *strdesc*⟩ | 106 | |

**Table C.5**  Derived forms: specification.

| Derived form | Equivalent form | Produced by rules |
|---|---|---|
| type *tyvarseq tycon* = *ty* | include<br><br>  sig type *tyvarseq tycon*<br>  end where<br>  type *tyvarseq tycon* = *ty* | 97 and 87 |
| type *tyvarseq*$_1$ *tycon*$_1$ = *ty*$_1$<br>and $\cdots$<br>$\cdots$<br>and *tyvarseq*$_n$ *tycon*$_n$ = *ty*$_n$ | type *tyvarseq*$_1$ *tycon*$_1$ = *ty*$_1$<br>type $\cdots$<br>$\cdots$<br>type *tyvarseq*$_n$ *tycon*$_n$ = *ty*$_n$ | 99 plus previous<br>derived form |
| include *sigid*$_1$ $\cdots$ *sigid*$_n$ | include *sigid*$_1$<br>; $\cdots$ ; include *sigid*$_n$ | 97 and 99 |

**90.** Denotes the interface obtained from *valdesc*.

**91.** Denotes the interface obtained from *typdesc*.

**92.** Denotes the interface obtained from *typdesc*.

**93.** Denotes the interface obtained from *datdesc*.

**94.** Denotes the interface describing *longtycon* and *tycon* as type constructors. It is furthermore recorded that the original datatype *longtycon* and the replicated datatype *tycon* share datatypes.

**95.** Denotes the interface obtained from *exdesc*.

**96.** Denotes the interface obtained from *strdesc*.

**97.** Denotes the interface obtained from *sigexp*.

**98.** Denotes the empty interface.

**99.** A sequence of specifications is evaluated from left to right.

**100.** Denotes the interface obtained from *spec* where all the type constructors denote the same type name – provided that the phrase is accepted by the type checker. The type checker will, for example, reject type sharing of, say int and real. A suitable adaptation of equality types is performed.

**101.** Denotes the interface where *vid* has value status. And so on.

**102.** Denotes the interface where *tycon* is a type constructor. And so on.

**103.** Denotes the interface obtained from *condesc* by recording *tycon* as a type constructor. And so on.

**104.** Denotes the interface where *vid* has constructor status. And so on.

**105.** Denotes the interface where *vid* has exception status. And so on.

**106.** Denotes the interface where where *strid* bound to the interface obtained from *sigexp*. And so on.

C.4.3    Functor and top-level declarations

A functor declaration modifies the functor environment in the actual basis by bindings of functor closures to identifiers. A top-level declaration modifies one or more of the environments in the actual basis (Tables C.6 and C.7).

---

**Table C.6**    Grammar: functors and top-level declarations.

| | | | | |
|---|---|---|---|---|
| *fundec* | ::= | functor *funbind* | 107 | |
| *funbind* | ::= | *funid* ( *strid* : *sigexp* ) = *strexp* | 108 | Functor binding |
| | | ⟨and *funbind*⟩ | | |
| *topdec* | ::= | *strdec* ⟨*topdec*⟩ | 109 | Structure declaration |
| | | *sigdec* ⟨*topdec*⟩ | 110 | Signature declaration |
| | | *fundec* ⟨*topdec*⟩ | 111 | Functor declaration |

*Restriction:* No *topdec* may contain, as an initial segment, a *strdec* followed by a semicolon.

---

**Table C.7**    Derived forms: functors and top-level declarations.

| Derived form | Equivalent form | Produced by |
|---|---|---|
| *funid* ⟨*strid* : *sigexp*⟩ : *sigexp'* <br> = *strexp* | *funid* ⟨*strid* : *sigexp*⟩ <br> = *strexp* : *sigexp'* | Rules 108 and 75 |
| *funid* ⟨*strid* :> *sigexp*⟩ : *sigexp'* <br> = *strexp* | *funid* ⟨*strid* :> *sigexp*⟩ <br> = *strexp* : *sigexp'* | Rules 108 and 76 |
| *funid* ⟨ *spec* ⟩ ⟨: *sigexp*⟩ <br> = *strexp* | *funid* ⟨*strid₁* : sig *spec* end ⟩ <br> = let open *strid₁* <br> in *strexp* ⟨: *sigexp*⟩ end | Above derived <br> form plus rules <br> 85, 78, 36, 75 |
| *funid* ⟨ *spec* ⟩ ⟨:> *sigexp*⟩ <br> = *strexp* | *funid* ⟨*strid₁* : sig *spec* end ⟩ <br> = let open *strid₁* <br> in *strexp* ⟨:> *sigexp*⟩ end | Above derived <br> form plus rules <br> 85, 78, 36, 76 |

*strid₁* is a new structure identifier.

---

**107.** Denotes the functor environment obtained from *funbind*.

**108.** Denotes the functor environment where *funid* is bound to the functor closure consisting of *strid*, the interface for *sigexp*, the structure expression *strexp*, and the actual basis. And so on.

**109.** The actual basis is modified with the environment obtained from *strdec*. And so on.

**110.** The actual basis is modified with the signature environment obtained from *sigdec*. And so on.

**111.** The actual basis is modified with the functor environment obtained from *fundec*. And so on.

# Selected parts of the SML basis library

This appendix describes a selection of useful types, functions, and values from the Standard ML Basis Library. It includes only some of the functions for interacting with the operating system. The interested reader should consult the *Standard ML Basis Library Manual* [3] – or the manual for the specific SML system.

In describing overloaded identifiers we will use the following abbreviations:

- `realint` for int or real
- `wordint` for int, word or word8
- `num` for int, real, word or word8
- `numtext` for int, real, word, word8, char or string

## D.1    General

### D.1.1    Predefined exceptions

Bind, Chr, Div, Domain, Empty, Fail of string, Interrupt, Match, Option, Overflow, Size, Subscript.

### D.1.2    Logical values

```
datatype bool = false | true
```

Infix operators of type bool * bool -> bool are defined by the reserved words andalso and orelse. They are sequential, short circuit operators in the sense that the second operand of andalso is not evaluated when the first operand evaluates to false, and the second operand of orelse is not evaluated when the first operand evaluates to true. The functions Bool.toString, Bool.fromString and Bool.scan are described in the section on conversions.

**Table D.1**    Logical operators.

| id | Type | Value |
|---|---|---|
| andalso | bool * bool -> bool | Reserved word for (lazy) logical and |
| orelse | bool * bool -> bool | Reserved word for (lazy) logical or |
| not | bool -> bool | Logical negation |

### D.1.3    Option

```
datatype 'a option = NONE | SOME of 'a
```

A division into cases for values of option type is usually made by pattern matching, e.g. in a case expression:

```
case opt of
      SOME v => ...
    | NONE   => ...
```

A partial function may be given the type:

$\tau_1$ -> $\tau_2$ option

returning SOME $v$ when successful and NONE otherwise. See also Table D.2.

### D.1.4    Ordering

```
datatype order     = LESS | EQUAL | GREATER
```

There is a compare function for types with an ordering, e.g. Int.compare, Real.compare, String.compare. It is often convenient to use a compare function to make division into cases by means of a CASE expression, such as:

**Table D.2**  Functions for the option type.

| id | Type | Value |
|---|---|---|
| getOpt | 'a option * 'a -> 'a | getOpt(SOME $v$,$a$) = $v$ |
|  |  | getOpt(NONE,$a$) = $a$ |
| isSome | 'a option -> bool | isSome(SOME $v$) = true |
|  |  | isSome(NONE) = false |
| valOf | 'a option -> 'a | valOf(SOME $v$) = $v$ |
|  |  | may raise Option |
| Option.filter | ('a -> bool) -> | filter $p$ $x$ = SOME $x$ if $p$ $x$ = true |
|  | 'a -> 'a option | filter $p$ $x$ = NONE otherwise |
| Option.map | ('a -> 'b) -> | map $f$ (SOME $x$) = SOME($f$ $x$) |
|  | 'a option -> | map $f$ NONE = NONE |
|  | 'b option |  |
| Option.app | ('a -> unit) -> | app $f$ (SOME $x$) evaluates $f$ $x$ |
|  | 'a option -> unit | app $f$ NONE has no side-effects |
| Option.join | 'a option option | join (SOME $x$ ) = $x$ |
|  | -> 'a option | join NONE = NONE |
| Option.compose | ('a -> 'b) | compose($f$,$g$) = SOME  ($f$ $y$) |
|  | * ('c -> 'a option) |   if $g$ $x$ = SOME $y$ |
|  | -> ('c -> 'b option) | compose($f$,$g$) = NONE otherwise |
| Option.mapPartial | ('a -> 'b option) -> | mapPartial $f$ (SOME $x$) = $f$ $x$ |
|  | ('a option | mapPartial $f$ NONE = NONE |
|  | -> 'b option) |  |
| Option.composePartial | ('a -> 'b option) | composePartial($f$,$g$) $x$ = $f$ $y$ |
|  | * ('c -> 'a option) |   if $g$ $x$ = SOME $y$ , otherwise |
|  | -> ('c -> 'b option) | composePartial($f$,$g$) $x$ = NONE |

```
case Int.compare(m, n) of
    | LESS    => ...
    | EQUAL   => ...
    | GREATER => ...
```

## D.1.5    Imperative features

A reference points to a mutable storage cell. The function `ref` works almost like a constructor in a `datatype` declaration:

```
datatype 'a ref = ref of 'a
```

but evaluating `ref` *expr* has the side-effect of creating a cell in memory containing the value of the expression *expr*. A reference matches the pattern `ref` *pat* if the pattern *pat* matches the current value in the corresponding cell, and the matching will bind identifiers in the pattern according to this matching. It is often more convenient to use pattern matching than to use the dereferencing function '!'.

## D.1.6    Precedence of predefined infix identifiers

Functional application binds more strongly than any infix identifier (cf. the sequencing of the rules in Table B.5), while infix identifiers bind more strongly than andalso and

**Table D.3**  Operators on the store.

| id | Type | Value |
|---|---|---|
| ref | 'a -> 'a ref | Create cell in store and give reference as the result |
| ! | 'a ref -> 'a | Contents in store for reference |
| := | 'a ref * 'a -> unit | Assign value to cell in store |
| ignore | 'a -> unit | Evaluate expression for side-effects and give () as the result |
| before | 'a * 'b -> 'a | a before b will first evaluate a and then b, and give the value of a as the result. |

orelse (cf. Table B.5). The precedence of the predefined infix identifiers is given in Table D.4 (where the abbreviations wordint, num, etc. are explained above). Note that the list operators :: and @ associate to the right, while the other operators associate to the left.

Details about div and mod are in the section about numbers. Note that real is an equality type in Moscow ML but *not* in most other SML systems.

**Table D.4**  Predefined infix indentifiers.

| id | Type | Value |
|---|---|---|
| **Infix precedence 7** | | |
| / | real * real -> real | Floating-point quotient |
| div | wordint * wordint -> wordint | Quotient in integer division |
| mod | wordint * wordint -> wordint | Remainder (of div) |
| * | num * num -> num | Product |
| **Infix precedence 6** | | |
| + | num * num -> num | Sum |
| − | num * num -> num | Difference |
| ^ | string * string -> string | Concatenation |
| **Infix precedence 5** | | |
| :: | 'a * 'a list -> 'a list | cons onto list (assoc. right) |
| @ | 'a list * 'a list -> 'a list | Append lists (assoc. right) |
| **Infix precedence 4** | | |
| = | ''a * ''a -> bool | Equal to |
| <> | ''a * ''a -> bool | Not equal to |
| < | numtxt * numtxt -> bool | Less than |
| <= | numtxt * numtxt -> bool | Less than or equal to |
| > | numtxt * numtxt -> bool | Greater than |
| >= | numtxt * numtxt -> bool | Greater than or equal to |
| **Infix precedence 3** | | |
| := | 'a ref * 'a -> unit | Assignment |
| o | ('b->'c) * ('a->'b) -> ('a->'c) | Function composition |
| **Infix precedence 0** | | |
| before | 'a * 'b -> 'a | Return first argument |

### D.1.7 Predefined overloaded identifiers

**Table D.5** Predefined overloaded operators.

| id | Type | Value |
|----|------|-------|
| + | num * num -> num | Sum |
| - | num * num -> num | Difference |
| * | num * num -> num | Product |
| div | wordint * wordint -> wordint | Quotient in integer division |
| mod | wordint * wordint -> wordint | Remainder of (div) |
| / | real * real -> real | Floating-point quotient |
| ~ | realint -> realint | Sign change |
| abs | realint -> realint | Absolute value |
| < | numtext * numtext -> bool | Less than |
| <= | numtext * numtext -> bool | Less than or equal to |
| > | numtext * numtext -> bool | Greater than |
| >= | numtext * numtext -> bool | Greater than or equal to |

## D.2 Numbers

Numbers are of the type int, real, word or word8. The representation of integers depends on the hardware architecture. Most implementations have a limited range for integers as they are represented by fixed size binary words with $n$ significant bits. Other implementations may use a representation where the size depends on the value. The representation of real numbers also depends on the hardware architecture. It is recommended *not* to open the structures Int, Real, etc., as this will destroy the overloading of the arithmetic and relational operators. Conversion functions, e.g. Int.toReal, are described in Section D.9 about conversions.

The type real is an equality type in the library of Moscow ML, but it is *not* an equality type in the library of most other SML systems where equality and inequality of real numbers are given by the functions Real.== and Real.!=. We follow the conventions of the Moscow ML library in this appendix (further information can be found in the chapter on real numbers in [3]).

**Table D.6** Parameters for integers.

| id | Type | Value |
|----|------|-------|
| Int.precision | int option | SOME $n$ where $n$ is the number of significant bits, or NONE for arbitrary precision |
| Int.minInt | int option | SOME $n$ if there is a minimum integer value $n$ |
| Int.maxInt | int option | SOME $n$ if there is a maximum integer value $n$ |
| Word.wordSize | int | Number of bits in a word |

D.2.1    Arithmetics

**Table D.7**    Arithmetic operators.

| id | Type | Value | Exception |
|---|---|---|---|
| ~ | realint -> realint | Sign change | |
| + | num * num -> num | Sum | Overflow |
| - | num * num -> num | Difference | Overflow |
| * | num * num -> num | Product | Overflow |
| div | wordint * wordint -> wordint | Quotient in integer division | Div, Overflow |
| mod | wordint * wordint -> wordint | Remainder (of div) | Div, Overflow |
| / | real * real -> real | Quotient of reals | Div, Overflow |
| Int.quot | int * int -> int | Quotient with remainder $\geq 0$ | Div, Overflow |
| Int.rem | int * int -> int | Remainder (of quot) | Div, Overflow |

The pairs of functions div, mod and Int.rem, Int.quot are defined for $m \neq 0$ such that:

$$n = (n \text{ div } m) \cdot m + (n \text{ mod } m),$$
$$0 \leq |n \text{ mod } m| < |m|, \text{ and } n \text{ mod } m \text{ and } m \text{ have same sign}$$

$$n = \text{Int.quot}(n, m) \cdot m + \text{Int.rem}(n, m),$$
$$0 \leq |\text{Int.rem}(n, m)| < |m|, \text{ and } \text{Int.rem}(n, m) \text{ and } n \text{ have same sign}$$

For example:

```
1 div ~2       =   ~1   and   1 mod ~2      =   ~1
Int.quot(1,~2) =    0   and   Int.rem(1,~2) =    1
```

and

```
~1 div 2       =   ~1   and   ~1 mod 2      =    1
Int.quot(~1,2) =    0   and   Int.rem(~1,2) =   ~1
```

D.2.2    **Ordering**

In Table D.8 num means int, real, word or word8 and realint means real or int. The functions Real.== and Real.!= are not defined in Moscow ML where real is an equality type.

**Table D.8**  Ordering of numbers.

| id | Type | value |
|---|---|---|
| = | num * num -> bool | Equal to |
| <> | num * num -> bool | Not equal to |
| < | num * num -> bool | Less than |
| <= | num * num -> bool | Less than or equal to |
| > | num * num -> bool | Greater than |
| >= | num * num -> bool | Greater than or equal to |
| abs | realint -> realint | Absolute value may raise `Overflow` |
| Real.== | real * real -> bool | Equal for reals |
| Real.!= | real * real -> bool | Not equal for reals |
| Int.min | int * int -> int | The smaller of two integers |
| Int.max | int * int -> int | The larger of two integers |
| Int.sign | int -> int | 1, 0 or ~1 |
| Int.sameSign | int * int -> bool | Equivalent to sign $m$ = sign $n$ |
| Int.compare | int * int -> order | LESS, EQUAL or GREATER |
| Real.min | real * real -> real | The smaller of two reals |
| Real.max | real * real -> real | The larger of two reals |
| Real.sign | real -> int | 1, 0 or ~1 |
| Real.sameSign | real * real -> bool | Equivalent to sign $m$ = sign $n$ |
| Real.compare | real * real -> order | LESS, EQUAL or GREATER |

## D.2.3    Mathematical constants and functions

**Table D.9**  Mathematical functions.

| id | Type | Value |
|---|---|---|
| Math.pi | real | Area of circle with radius 1 |
| Math.e | real | Base of natural logarithm |
| Math.sqrt | real -> real | Square root function |
| Math.sin | real -> real | Sine function |
| Math.cos | real -> real | Cosine function |
| Math.tan | real -> real | Tangent function |
| Math.atan | real -> real | Arcus tangent function |
| Math.asin | real -> real | Arcus sine function |
| Math.acos | real -> real | Arcus cosine function |
| Math.atan2 | real * real -> real | $\text{atan2}(y, x) = \text{atan}(y/x)$ for $x \neq 0$ $\text{atan2}(y, 0) = \pi/2$ for $y > 0$ $\text{atan2}(y, 0) = -\pi/2$ for $y < 0$ |
| Math.exp | real -> real | Exponential function |
| Math.pow | real * real -> real | $\text{pow}(x, y)$ is $x^y$ |
| Math.ln | real -> real | Natural logarithm |
| Math.log10 | real -> real | Decimal logarithm (base 10) |
| Math.sinh | real -> real | Hyperbolic sine function |
| Math.cosh | real -> real | Hyperbolic cosine function |
| Math.tanh | real -> real | Hyperbolic tangent function |

### D.2.4    Bit-wise operations

A value of type word is a *bit mask* of bits, each having value 0 or 1, and numbered
$0, 1, \ldots$ from right to left. Each bit denotes a logical value (0 = false, 1 = true).

**Table D.10**   Bit-wise operations.

| id | Type | Value |
|---|---|---|
| Word.orb | word * word -> word | Bit-wise logical or |
| Word.andb | word * word -> word | Bit-wise logical and |
| Word.xorb | word * word -> word | Bit-wise logical exclusive or |
| Word.notb | word -> word | Bit-wise complement |
| Word.<< | word * word -> word | Shift word $i$ to the left by $n$ positions, filling rightmost bit with 0. |
| Word.>> | word * word -> word | Shift word $i$ to the right by $n$ positions |
| Word.~>> | word * word -> word | Shift word $i$ to the right by $n$ positions, copying the leftmost bit |

Example:

| $x$ | Word.<<$(x, 2)$ | Word.>>$(x, 2)$ | Word.~>>$(x, 2)$ |
|---|---|---|---|
| $1110 \cdots 1011$ | $10 \cdots 101100$ | $001110 \cdots 10$ | $111110 \cdots 10$ |
| $0110 \cdots 1011$ | $10 \cdots 101100$ | $000110 \cdots 10$ | $000110 \cdots 10$ |

## D.3    Characters and strings

### D.3.1    Ordering

**Table D.11**   Lexicographical ordering.

| id | Type | Value |
|---|---|---|
| < | char * char -> bool | Before in character code |
| <= | char * char -> bool | Before or same character code |
| > | char * char -> bool | After in character code |
| >= | char * char -> bool | After or same in character code |
| < | string * string -> bool | Lexicographic before |
| <= | string * string -> bool | Lexicographic before or same |
| > | string * string -> bool | Lexicographic after |
| >= | string * string -> bool | Lexicographic after or same |
| Char.compare | char * char -> order | Compare character codes |
| String.compare | string * string -> order | Lexicographic compare |
| Char.minChar | char | Character with smallest code |
| Char.maxChar | char | Character with greatest code |
| Char.maxOrd | int | Max character code |
| Char.succ | char -> char | Next character in ASCII alphabet may raise Chr |
| Char.pred | char -> char | Previous char in ASCII alphabet may raise Chr |

D.3.2    Operations on characters

**Table D.12**    Functions on characters.

| id | Type | value |
|---|---|---|
| ord | char -> int | ASCII code for char |
| chr | int -> char | Char for ASCII code |
| str | char -> string | One character string |
| Char.toLower | char -> char | Corresponding lower case letter |
| Char.toUpper | char -> char | Corresponding upper case letter |
| Char.fromString | string -> char option | Char for one-char string or ML escape sequence |
| Char.toString | char -> string | One-char string or ML escape sequence for char |
| Char.fromCString | string -> char option | Char for one-char string or C escape sequence |
| Char.toCString | char -> string | One-char string or C escape sequence for char |
| Char.contains | string -> char -> bool | String contains character |
| Char.notContains | string -> char -> bool | String does not contain character |

D.3.3    Classes of characters

**Table D.13**    Classes of characters.

| id | Type | Value |
|---|---|---|
| Char.isLower | char -> bool | Is one of abcdefghijklmnopqrstuvwxyz |
| Char.isUpper | char -> bool | Is one of ABCDEFGHIJKLMNOPQRSTUVWXYZ |
| Char.isDigit | char -> bool | Is one of 0123456789 |
| Char.isAlpha | char -> bool | isUpper or isLower |
| Char.isHexDigit | char -> bool | isDigit or one of abcdefABCDEF |
| Char.isAlphaNum | char -> bool | isAlpha or isDigit |
| Char.isPrint | char -> bool | Is printable character (incl. space) |
| Char.isSpace | char -> bool | Is space or one of \t\r\n\v\f |
| Char.isPunct | char -> bool | isPrint and not isSpace and not isAlphaNum |
| Char.isGraph | char -> bool | isPrint and not isSpace |
| Char.isAscii | char -> bool | ASCII code < 128 |
| Char.isCntrl | char -> bool | Is control character |

### D.3.4    Operations on strings

**Table D.14**  Functions on strings.

| id | Type | Value |
|---|---|---|
| ^ | string * string -> string | Concatenate strings may raise Size |
| concat | string list -> string | Concatenate list of strings may raise Size |
| implode | char list -> string | List of chars to string |
| explode | string -> char list | String to list of chars |
| size | string -> int | No. of chars in string |
| str | char -> string | One character string |
| String.sub | string * int -> char | $i$th $(0, 1, \dots)$ char in string may raise Subscript |
| String.substring | string * int * int -> string | From $i$th to $j$th char may raise Subscript |
| String.isPrefix | string -> string -> bool | Is first part of string |
| String.collate | (char * char -> order) -> string * string -> order | Lexicographic compare of strings using ordering of chars. May raise Size |
| Char.contains | string -> char -> bool | String contains character |
| Char.notContains | string -> char -> bool | String does not contain char |
| String.maxSize | int | Max. size for any string |
| String.fromString | string -> string option | Converts each ML escape sequence to corresponding char |
| String.toString | string -> string | Converts each non-printable char to ML escape sequence |
| String.fromCString | string -> string option | Converts each C escape sequence to corresponding char |
| String.toCString | string -> string | Converts each non-printable char to C escape sequence |
| String.translate | (char -> string) -> string -> string | Apply function to each char in string |

Examples:

```
String.sub("abcd",1)          =  #"b"
String.substring("abcd",1,2)  =  "bc"
String.isPrefix "ab" "abc"    =  true
```

### D.3.5    Substrings

The Substring functions are useful when implementing manipulations on strings. This may give an efficient program, as string copying can be reduced to a minimum.

A value of type substring is a representation of a piece of a string. Let $s = c_0 c_1 \cdots c_{m-1}$ be a string of size $m$. The substring of $s$ starting at index $i$ and of size $n$ is then the string $s' = c_i c_{i+1} \cdots c_{i+(n-1)}$. It is well defined when $0 \leq i \leq i + n \leq m$.

**Table D.15** Functions on substrings.

| id | Type | Value |
|---|---|---|
| Substring.substring | string * int * int -> substring | Substring of string<br>May raise Subscript |
| Substring.extract | string * int * int option -> substring | Substring of string<br>NONE means tail substring<br>May raise Subscript |
| Substring.all | string -> substring | Entire string as substring |
| Substring.string | substring -> string | String for substring |
| Substring.base | substring -> (string * int * int) | Underlying string for substring |
| Substring.isEmpty | substring -> bool | Substring has size 0 |
| Substring.getc | substring -> (char * substring) option | First character and rest of string. NONE for empty |
| Substring.first | substring -> char option | First character or NONE |
| Substring.triml | int -> substring -> substring | Substring with first $k$ characters dropped |
| Substring.trimr | int -> substring -> substring | Substring with last $k$ characters dropped |
| Substring.sub | substring * int -> char | The $k$th (0,1,...) character of substring may raise Subscript |
| Substring.size | substring -> int | No. of chars in substring |
| Substring.slice | substring*int* int option -> substring | Substring with $k$ first chars dropped and with size $n$ may raise Subscript |
| Substring.concat | substring list -> string | String of concatenated substrings |
| Substring.explode | substring -> char list | List of chars in substring |
| Substring.isPrefix | string->substring->bool | String is prefix of substring |
| Substring.compare | substring * substring -> order | Lexicographic (alphabetic) comparison of substrings |
| Substring.collate | (char * char -> order) -> substring * substring -> order | Lexicographic comparison corresponding to given ordering of chars |
| Substring.dropl | (char -> bool) -> substring -> substring | Drop prefix of chars satisfying predicate |
| Substring.dropr | (char -> bool) -> substring -> substring | Drop suffix of chars satisfying predicate |
| Substring.takel | (char -> bool) -> substring -> substring | Prefix of chars satisfying predicate |
| Substring.taker | (char -> bool) -> substring -> substring | Prefix of chars satisfying predicate |
| Substring.splitl | (char->bool) -> substring -> substring * substring | Prefix satisfying predicate, and rest |
| Substring.splitr | (char->bool) -> substring -> substring * substring | First part and suffix satisfying predicate |
| Substring.splitAt | substring * int -> substring * substring | First $k$ chars and rest of substring. May raise Subscript |
| Substring.position | string -> substring -> substring * substring | First part and suffix with first occurrence of str |

*Continued*

**Table D.15**   Continued.

| id | Type | Value |
|---|---|---|
| Substring.span | substring * substring -> substring | Substring spanning from start of first to end of second. May raise Span. |
| Substring.translate | (char -> string) -> substring -> string | String of function values for chars May raise Size |
| Substring.foldl | (char * 'a -> 'a) -> 'a -> substring -> 'a | Accumulate function from left to right |
| Substring.foldr | (char * 'a -> 'a) -> 'a -> substring -> 'a | Accumulate function from right to left |
| Substring.app | (char -> unit) -> substring -> unit | Apply function to all chars for side-effects |

Let $p$ be a predicate and $xxxxfyyyyfzzzz$ a string where all characters in $xxxx$ and $zzzz$ satisfy $p$, and $f$ a character not satisfying $p$, then:

**Table D.16**   Selections in substrings.

| substr | $x\,x\,x\,x\ f\ y\,y\,y\,y\ f\ z\,z\,z\,z$ |
|---|---|
| Substring.dropl  p *substr* | $f\ y\,y\,y\,y\ f\ z\,z\,z\,z$ |
| Substring.dropr  p *substr* | $x\,x\,x\,x\ f\ y\,y\,y\,y\ f$ |
| Substring.takel  p *substr* | $x\,x\,x\,x$ |
| Substring.taker  p *substr* | $z\,z\,z\,z$ |
| Substring.splitl p *substr* | $(x\,x\,x\,x,\ f\ y\,y\,y\,y\ f\ z\,z\,z\,z)$ |
| Substring.splitr p *substr* | $(x\,x\,x\,x\ f\ y\,y\,y\,y\ f, z\,z\,z\,z)$ |

If *mask* is a string and *xxxx* is a string not containing *mask* as a substring, then:

$$\text{Substring.position } mask\ xxxxmaskyyyy = (xxxx\ ,\ maskyyyy)$$

The functions Substring.tokens and Substring.fields are described in Section D.9 on conversion of strings containing several values.

## D.4  Lists

Division into cases according to the structure of a list is conveniently done by use of list patterns like [], [x], x::xs, x1::x2::xs, etc. This is better than using null, hd and tl.

**Table D.17**  Functions on lists.

| id | Type | Value |
|---|---|---|
| @ | `'a list * 'a list`<br>`-> 'a list` | Append lists |
| rev | `'a list -> 'a list` | Reverse list |
| length | `'a list -> int` | No. of elements in list |
| foldr | `('a * 'b -> 'b) ->`<br>`'b -> 'a list -> 'b` | $\text{foldr } f\ b\ [a_1,\ldots,a_n] =$<br>$f(a_1, f(a_2,\ldots f(a_n,b)\ldots))$ |
| foldl | `('a * 'b -> 'b) ->`<br>`'b -> 'a list -> 'b` | $\text{foldl } f\ b\ [a_1,\ldots,a_n] =$<br>$f(a_n,\ldots,f(a_2,f(a_1,b))\cdots)$ |
| app | `('a -> unit) ->`<br>`'a list -> unit` | Apply a function to each<br>element for side-effects |
| map | `('a -> 'b) ->`<br>`'a list -> 'b list` | $\text{map } f\ [a_1, a_2,\ldots,a_n] =$<br>$[f(a_1), f(a_2),\ldots,f(a_n)]$ |
| null | `'a list -> bool` | Is the list empty? |
| hd | `'a list -> 'a` | Head element of list<br>May raise `Empty` |
| tl | `'a list -> 'a list` | Tail list of list<br>May raise `Empty` |
| List.nth | `'a list * int -> 'a` | $n$th element (start at 0)<br>May raise `Subscript` |
| List.last | `'a list -> 'a` | Last element of list<br>May raise `Empty` |
| List.take | `'a list * int`<br>`-> 'a list` | First $n$ elements<br>May raise `Subscript` |
| List.drop | `'a list * int`<br>`-> 'a list` | Omit first $n$ elements<br>May raise `Subscript` |
| List.concat | `'a list list`<br>`-> 'a list` | Concatenate list of lists |
| List.revAppend | `'a list * 'a list`<br>`-> 'a list` | Append reversed list<br>to other |
| List.mapPartial | `('a -> 'b option)`<br>`-> 'a list -> 'b list` | List of $b$'s where<br>$f(a) = \text{SOME } b$ |
| List.find | `('a -> bool) ->`<br>`'a list -> 'a option` | Find first element in list<br>satisfying predicate |
| List.filter | `('a -> bool) ->`<br>`'a list -> 'a list` | Form list of elements<br>satisfying predicate |
| List.partition | `('a -> bool)->'a list`<br>`->('a list * 'a list)` | Partition into two lists<br>by predicate |
| List.exists | `('a -> bool) ->`<br>`'a list -> bool` | Any element in list<br>satisfying predicate? |
| List.all | `('a -> bool) ->`<br>`'a list -> bool` | List of all elements<br>satisfying predicate. |
| List.tabulate | `int * (int -> 'a)`<br>`-> 'a list` | $\text{tabulate}(n,f) =$<br>$[f(0), f(1),\ldots,f(n-1)]$<br>May raise `Size` |
| List.getItem | `'a list ->`<br>`('a * 'a list) option` | $\text{getItem}(x::xs)$<br>$= \text{SOME}(x,xs)$<br>$\text{getItem } [] = \text{NONE}$ |
| ListPair.zip | `'a list * 'b list`<br>`-> ('a * 'b) list` | $([x_1,\ldots,x_m], [y_1,\ldots,y_n])$<br>gives $[(x_1,y_1),\ldots,(x_k,y_k)]$<br>where $k = \min(m,n)$ |

*Continued*

**Table D.17**    Continued.

| id | Type | Value |
|---|---|---|
| ListPair.unzip | (’a * ’b) list -><br>’a list * ’b list | $([(x_1, y_1), \ldots, (x_n, y_n)])$ gives<br>$([x_1, \ldots, x_n], [y_1, \ldots, y_n])$ |
| ListPair.map | (’a*’b -> ’c)-><br>’a list * ’b list<br>-> ’c list | Maps a function $f$ over a pair<br>of lists |
| ListPair.app | (’a * ’b -> unit)<br>-> ’a list * ’b list<br>-> unit | Maps a function $f$ over a pair<br>of lists for side effects |
| ListPair.all | (’a * ’b -> bool)<br>-> ’a list * ’b list<br>-> bool | Do all pairs of corresponding<br>elements satisfy predicate ? |
| ListPair.exists | (’a * ’b -> bool)<br>-> ’a list * ’b list<br>-> bool | Does any pair of corresponding<br>elements satisfy predicate? |
| ListPair.foldr | (’a * ’b * ’c -> ’c)<br>-> ’c<br>-> ’a list * ’b list<br>-> ’c | Fold function over pair of lists<br>from right to left |
| ListPair.foldl | (’a * ’b * ’c -> ’c)<br>-> ’c<br>-> ’a list * ’b list<br>-> ’c | Fold function over pair of lists<br>from left to right |

## D.5    Vectors

A value of $v$ type $\tau$ vector contains values $v_0$, $v_1$, $\ldots$, $v_{n-1}$ of type $\tau$ which can be accessed in constant time (via the function Vector.sub). The type $\tau$ vector admits equality if $\tau$ does, and two vectors are equal if they have the same length and if their elements are equal. The slice $v, i$, SOME $j$ defines the subvector $v_i, v_{i+1}, \ldots, v_{i+j-1}$ of length $j$, while the slice $v, i$, NONE defines the subvector $v_i, v_{i+1}, \ldots, v_{n-1}$ extending to the end of the vector (Table D.18).

**Table D.18**    Vector slices.

| Slice | Meaning | |
|---|---|---|
| v, 0, NONE | The whole vector | v[0..len-1] |
| v, 0, SOME n | A left subvector (prefix) | v[0..n-1] |
| v, i, NONE | A right subvector (suffix) | v[i..len-1] |
| v, i, SOME n | A general slice | v[i..i+n-1] |

We describe the following functions on vectors (Table D.19).

**Table D.19**    Functions on vectors.

| id | Type | Value |
|---|---|---|
| Vector.maxLen | int | Max. length of a vector |
| Vector.fromList | 'a list<br>-> 'a vector | Create vector containing the<br>list elements. May raise Size |
| Vector.tabulate | int * (int -> 'a)<br>-> 'a vector | Create vector of length $n$<br>with elements $f(0) \ldots f(n-1)$<br>May raise Size |
| Vector.length | 'a vector -> int | Length of vector |
| Vector.sub | 'a vector * int -> 'a | Get $i$th element of vector (index<br>$0 \ldots n-1$). May raise Subscript |
| Vector.extract | 'a vector * int * int option<br>-> 'a vector | Subvector for slice<br>May raise Subscript |
| Vector.concat | 'a vector list<br>-> 'a vector | Vector of concatenated<br>vectors |
| Vector.app | ('a -> unit) -><br>'a vector -> unit | Apply function to elements<br>left-to-right for side-effects |
| Vector.foldl | ('a * 'b -> 'b)<br>-> 'b -><br>'a vector -> 'b | Fold function over<br>vector from left to right |
| Vector.foldr | ('a * 'b -> 'b)<br>-> 'b -><br>'a vector -> 'b | Fold function over<br>vector from right to left |
| Vector.appi | (int * 'a -> unit) -><br>'a vector * int * int option<br>-> unit | Apply function for each index<br>to (index,element) for side-<br>effects. May raise Subscript |
| Vector.foldli | (int * 'a * 'b -> 'b)<br>-> 'b -><br>'a vector * int * int option<br>-> 'b | Fold function over slice from left<br>to right using index in function<br>argument |
| Vector.foldri | (int * 'a * 'b -> 'b)<br>-> 'b -><br>'a vector * int * int option<br>-> 'b | Fold function over slice from right<br>to left using index in function<br>argument |

## D.6  Arrays

An array of type $\tau$ array is a piece of the physical memory containing a sequence of cells with values of type $\tau$. The cells are numbered by indices $0, 1, \ldots n-1$ where $n$ is the length of the array. Some functions work on a *slice* of an array (Table D.20).

**Table D.20**    Array slices.

| Slice | Meaning | |
|---|---|---|
| a, 0, NONE | The whole array | a[0..len-1] |
| a, 0, SOME n | A left subarray (prefix) | a[0..n-1] |
| a, i, NONE | A right subarray (suffix) | a[i..len-1] |
| a, i, SOME n | A general slice | a[i..i+n-1] |

We describe the following functions on arrays (Table D.21).

**Table D.21**  Functions on arrays.

| id | Type | Value |
|----|------|-------|
| Array.maxLen | int | Max. length of array |
| Array.array | int * 'a<br>-> 'a array | Create array of length $n$ whose<br>elements are all $= x$<br>May raise Size |
| Array.tabulate | int * (int -> 'a)<br>-> 'a array | Create array of length $n$ with<br>elements $f(0) \ldots f(n-1)$<br>May raise Size |
| Array.fromList | 'a list<br>-> 'a array | Create array containing the list<br>elements. May raise Size |
| Array.length | 'a array -> int | Length of array |
| Array.sub | 'a array * int -> 'a | Get $i$th element of array<br>(index $0 \ldots n-1$)<br>May raise Subscript |
| Array.app | ('a -> unit) -><br>'a array -> unit | Apply function to each<br>element |
| Array.foldl | ('a * 'b -> 'b)<br>-> 'b -><br>'a array -> 'b | Fold function over array<br>from left to right |
| Array.foldr | ('a * 'b -> 'b)<br>-> 'b -><br>'a array -> 'b | Fold function over array<br>from right to left |
| Array.modify | ('a -> 'a) -><br>'a array -> unit | Replace each element by<br>value of function |
| Array.appi | (int * 'a -> unit) -><br>'a array * int * int option<br>-> unit | Replace each element in slice<br>by value of function<br>May raise Subscript |
| Array.foldli | (int * 'a * 'b -> 'b)<br>-> 'b -><br>'a array * int * int option<br>-> 'b | Fold function over slice<br>from left to right<br>using index in<br>function argument |
| Array.foldri | (int * 'a * 'b -> 'b)<br>-> 'b -><br>'a array * int * int option<br>-> 'b | Fold function over slice<br>from right to left<br>using index in<br>function argument |
| Array.modifyi | (int * 'a -> 'a) -><br>'a array * int * int option<br>-> unit | Replace each element in slice<br>by value of function using index<br>May raise Subscript |
| Array.update | 'a array * int * 'a<br>-> unit | Replace the $i$th element in array<br>May raise Subscript |
| Array.extract | 'a array * int * int option<br>-> 'a Vector.vector | Extract slice and copy into<br>vector. May raise Subscript |
| Array.copy | {src: 'a array,<br>si: int, len:  int option,<br>dst: 'a array, di: int}<br>-> unit | Copy slice starting at dest.<br>index di<br>May raise Subscript |
| Array.copyVec | {src: 'a vector,<br>si:  int, len:  int option,<br>dst: 'a array, di: int}<br>-> unit | Copy slice starting at<br>dest. index di<br>May raise Subscript |

## D.7  Timers and time

This section describes functions measuring the time used by the program and functions computing sums and differences of times. The functions use the types in Table D.22.

**Table D.22**   Measuring time.

| Type | Value |
|---|---|
| `Time.time` | An amount of time (a duration). Cannot be negative |
| `Timer.real_timer` | A timer measuring the total time since the start of the timer |
| `Timer.cpu_timer` | A timer measuring the computing time used by the program since the start of the timer |

Timers are handled by the functions given Table D.23.

**Table D.23**   Operations on timers.

| id | Type | Value |
|---|---|---|
| `Timer.startCPUTimer` | `unit -> cpu_timer` | Create and start CPU timer |
| `Timer.totalCPUTimer` | `unit -> cpu_timer` | Get CPU timer started at load time |
| `Timer.checkCPUTimer` | `cpu_timer ->` | CPU time used since start timer: |
|  | `{ usr : time,` | total user CPU time |
|  | `sys : time,` | system CPU time |
|  | `gc  : time}` | used by garbage collection (included in the user CPU time) |
| `Timer.startRealTimer` | `unit -> real_timer` | Create and start timer |
| `Timer.totalRealTimer` | `unit -> real_timer` | Get real timer started at load time |
| `Timer.checkRealTimer` | `real_timer -> time` | Time passed since start of timer |

Table D.24 lists functions on time values. Note that `Time.+`, etc. are *prefix* operators, and that the time values are not included into the overloading of the infix operators +, etc. Nevertheless, one should *not* use open `Time` as this would overwrite the operators on numbers. Conversion functions for time values are found in Section D.9.4.

**Table D.24**   Operations on time.

| id | Type | Value |
|---|---|---|
| `Time.zeroTime` | `time` | A zero time value |
| `Time.now` | `unit -> time` | Current time |
| `Time.+` | `time * time -> time` | Sum of time values. May raise `Overflow` |
| `Time.-` | `time * time -> time` | Difference of time values. May raise `Time` |
| `Time.<` | `time * time -> bool` | Compare time values |
| `Time.<=` | `time * time -> bool` |  |
| `Time.>` | `time * time -> bool` |  |
| `Time.>=` | `time * time -> bool` |  |
| `Time.compare` | `time * time -> order` |  |

## D.8  Date

A date (date-time) is represented by a value of type `Date.date`. One may, for example, get the current date (and time) by evaluating the expression:

```
Date.fromTimeLocal(Time.now())
```

A textual representation can then be obtained from this value by use of the conversion function `Date.toString` (cf. Section D.9.3). Other conversion functions for dates are found in Sections D.9.4 and D.9.5. One may also use some of the functions below to do further computations on the date.

The current time (as obtained by `Time.now()`) is a universal time expressing the number of microseconds elapsed since a fixed starting point. The corresponding date value (containing day, hours, etc.) for a time value will, however, depend on *time zone* and possible *daylight saving time* for the location where the date should apply. The universal date, abbreviated UTC, is the date for Greenwich (time zone 0) with no daylight saving modification.

The functions `Date.weekDay` and `Date.month` in Table D.25 use the following types from the `Date` library:

```
datatype weekday = Mon | Tue | Wed | Thu | Fri | Sat | Sun
datatype month = Jan | Feb | Mar | Apr | May | Jun
               | Jul | Aug | Sep | Oct | Nov | Dec
```

**Table D.25**  Operations on dates.

| id | Type | Value |
|---|---|---|
| `Date.fromTimeLocal` | `time -> date` | Local date for time *t* |
| `Date.fromTimeUniv` | `time -> date` | UTC date for time *t* |
| `Date.toTime` | `date -> time` | Time for date *d*. May raise `Date` or `Time` |
| `Date.year` | `date -> int` | Year of the date |
| `Date.month` | `date -> month` | Month of the date |
| `Date.day` | `date -> int` | Day in month (1..31) |
| `Date.hour` | `date -> int` | Hour of the date (0..23) |
| `Date.minute` | `date -> int` | Minute of the date (0..59) |
| `Date.second` | `date -> int` | Second of the date (0..59) |
| `Date.weekDay` | `date -> weekday` | Weekday of the date |
| `Date.yearDay` | `date -> int` | Day in year (0..365) |
| `Date.isDst` | `date -> bool option` | Daylight saving time? |
| `Date.offset` | `date -> time option` | NONE for a local time, SOME *t* for other time with time zone offset *t* |
| `Date.localOffset` | `unit -> time` | Time zone offset for local time |
| `Date.compare` | `date * date -> order` | Compare dates |

## D.9  Conversions

Conversion functions are used for conversion between different representations of values.

## D.9.1 Number-to-number conversions

**Table D.26** Number-to-number conversions.

| id | Type | Value | Exception |
|---|---|---|---|
| real | int -> real | Real value for integer | |
| round | real -> int | The nearest integer | Overflow |
| floor | real -> int | Smallest integer ≥ number | Overflow |
| ceil | real -> int | Largest integer ≤ number | Overflow |
| trunc | real -> int | Nearest integer between number and zero | Overflow |
| Word.fromInt | int -> word | Bit-mask for integer | Overflow |
| Word.toInt | word -> int | Corresponding integer for word | Overflow |

## D.9.2 Conversions for characters and strings

**Table D.27** Conversions for characters and strings.

| id | Type | Value |
|---|---|---|
| ord | char -> int | ASCII code for char |
| chr | int -> char | Char for ASCII code |
| str | char -> string | One-character string |
| Char.toLower | char -> char | Corresponding lower case letter |
| Char.toUpper | char -> char | Corresponding upper case letter |
| Char.fromString | string -> char option | Char for one-char string or ML escape sequence |
| Char.toString | char -> string | One-char string or ML escape sequence for char |
| Char.fromCString | string -> char option | Char for one-char string or C escape sequence |
| Char.toCString | char -> string | One-char string or C escape sequence for char |
| implode | char list -> string | List of chars to string |
| explode | string -> char list | String to list of chars |
| String.fromString | string -> string option | Converts each ML escape sequence to corresponding char |
| String.toString | string -> string | Converts each non-printable char to ML escape sequence |
| String.fromCString | string -> string option | Converts each C escape sequence to corresponding char |
| String.toCString | string -> string | Converts each non-printable char to C escape sequence |

### D.9.3    Simple conversions to and from strings

Values to strings:

**Table D.28**  Conversions to strings.

| id | Type | Value | Exception |
|---|---|---|---|
| Bool.toString | bool -> string | The string "false" or true | |
| Int.toString | int -> string | Signed decimal representation | |
| Word.toString | word -> string | Hexadecimal representation | |
| Real.toString | real -> string | Fixed-point or scientific | |
| Date.toString | date -> string | Date in 24 character standard format like: Fri Mar 07 15:07:03 1997 | Date |
| Time.toString | time -> string | Fixed-point repr. of seconds (3 decs.) | |

Strings to values:

**Table D.29**  Conversions from strings.

| id | Type | Value |
|---|---|---|
| Bool.fromString | string -> bool option | SOME $b$ if the string has a prefix (after possible initial whitespace) which is either false or true |
| Int.fromString | string -> int option | SOME $i$ if the string has a prefix (after possible initial whitespace) which is a signed decimal integer. May raise Overflow |
| Word.fromString | string -> word option | SOME $w$ if the string has a prefix (after possible initial whitespace) which is an unsigned hexadecimal integer. May raise Overflow |
| Real.fromString | string -> real option | SOME $r$ if the string has a prefix (after possible initial whitespace) which represents a real number. May raise Overflow |
| Date.fromString | string -> date option | SOME $d$ if string (after possible initial whitespace) has a date as a 24 character prefix like: Fri Mar 07 15:07:03 1997 |
| Time.fromString | string -> time option | SOME $t$ if string has a prefix (after possible initial whitespace) which is a decimal integer, possibly with fraction part, representing a number of seconds. May raise Overflow |

An Overflow exception is raised if the conversion generates a number outside the legal range of the target type, e.g. by too many digits for an integer.

## D.9.4    Date and time conversions

**Table D.30**    Date and time conversions.

| id | Type | Value |
|---|---|---|
| Date.fromTimeLocal | time -> date | Local date for time $t$ |
| Date.fromTimeUniv | time -> date | UTC date for time $t$ |
| Date.toTime | date -> Time.time | Time for local date $d$. May raise Date |
| Time.toSeconds | time -> int | Seconds. May raise Overflow |
| Time.toMilliseconds | time -> int | Milliseconds. May raise Overflow |
| Time.toMicroseconds | time -> int | Microseconds. May raise Overflow |
| Time.fromSeconds | int -> time | Time value for $n$ seconds. May raise Time |
| Time.fromMilliseconds | int -> time | Time value for $n$ milliseconds May raise Time |
| Time.fromMicroseconds | int -> time | Time value for $n$ microseconds May raise Time |
| Time.toReal | time -> real | Number of seconds |
| Time.fromReal | real -> time | Time value for $r$ seconds. May raise Time |

## D.9.5    Formatted conversions to strings

The .fmt functions convert values to strings according to format:

**Table D.31**    Formatted conversions.

| id | Type | Value |
|---|---|---|
| Int.fmt | StringCvt.radix -> int -> string | String representation for given radix |
| Word.fmt | StringCvt.radix -> word -> string | String representation for given radix |
| Real.fmt | StringCvt.realfmt -> real -> string | String representation for given real format |
| Time.fmt | int -> time -> string | The number of seconds in $t$ rounded to $n$ digits in fraction |
| Date.fmt | string -> date -> string | String where each format command "%?" in the string is replaced by corresponding part of date |

Examples:

```
Int.fmt StringCvt.HEX 17358;
val it = "43CE" : string


Real.fmt (StringCvt.SCI (SOME 4)) 14357.38;
val it = "1.4357E04" : string


Date.fmt "Today is a %A in %B"
        (Date.fromTimeLocal(Time.now()));
val it = "Today is a Friday in November" : string
```

The formatted conversion of integers or words to strings is controlled by the use of a *radix* which is a value of type `StringCvt.radix`:

| | |
|---|---|
| `StringCvt.BIN` | Binary form (digits 0 and 1) |
| `StringCvt.OCT` | Octal form (digits 0, 1, . . . , 7) |
| `StringCvt.DEC` | Decimal form |
| `StringCvt.HEX` | Hex. form (digits 0, 1, . . . , 9, A, B, . . . F) |

The formatted conversion of real numbers to strings is controlled by the use of a *format* which is a value of type `StringCvt.realfmt`:

| | |
|---|---|
| `StringCvt.SCI(SOME n)` | Scientific notation $n$ decimal digits |
| `StringCvt.SCI NONE` | Scientific notation 6 decimal digits |
| `StringCvt.FIX(SOME n)` | Fixed point notation $n$ decimal digits |
| `StringCvt.FIX NONE` | Fixed point notation 6 decimal digits |
| `StringCvt.GEN(SOME n)` | Automatic choice $n$ significant digits |
| `StringCvt.GEN NONE` | Automatic choice 12 significant digits |

The conversion of dates to strings is controlled by *time format commands* which are two-letter strings (Table D.32).

**Table D.32**    Format commands.

| Cmd | Legend | Cmd | Legend |
|---|---|---|---|
| `%a` | Abbreviated weekday name | `%S` | Seconds (00-59) |
| `%A` | Full weekday name | `%U` | Week-of-year (00-53, |
| `%b` | Abbreviated month name | | week starts on Sunday) |
| `%B` | Full month name | `%w` | Weekday (0-6, Sunday = 0) |
| `%c` | Date and time | `%W` | Week-of-year (00-53, |
| `%d` | Day-of-month (01-31) | | week starts on Monday) |
| `%H` | Hour (00-23) | `%x` | US standard date (mm/dd/yy) |
| `%I` | Hour (01-12) | `%X` | Standard time (hh:mm:ss) |
| `%j` | Day-of-year (001-366) | `%y` | Year in century (00-99) |
| `%m` | Month (01-12) | `%Y` | Full year (yyyy) |
| `%M` | Minute (00-59) | `%Z` | Time zone name |
| `%p` | Local equiv. of AM or PM | `%%` | A percent character |

## D.9.6    Converting strings containing several values

A string containing several values can be split into substrings by using the functions `String.tokens` or `String.fields` – provided that the substrings are separated in a suitable way. The first argument $p$ of type `char->bool` defines the delimiters between substrings, i.e. a character $c$ is considered a delimiter if $p(c)$ is true. A *token* in a string is then a non-empty maximal substring not containing any delimiters, while a *field* is a token or an empty substring between two delimiters.

**Table D.33**   Function to partition a (sub)string.

| id | Type | Value |
|---|---|---|
| String.tokens | (char -> bool) -> string -> string list | List of tokens in string |
| String.fields | (char -> bool) -> string -> string list | List of fields in string |
| Substring.tokens | (char -> bool) -> substring -> substring list | List of tokens in substring |
| Substring.fields | (char -> bool) -> substring -> substring list | List of fields in substring |

Once a string has been split into tokens, one may of course apply a conversion function like Int.fromString to each token. Examples:

```
String.tokens Char.isSpace "43 false  ~37";
val it = ["43", "false", "~37"] : string list

String.fields Char.isSpace "43 false  ~37";
val it = ["43", "false", "", "~37"] : string list

map Int.fromString
    (String.tokens Char.isSpace "43 false  ~37");
val it = [SOME 43, NONE, SOME ~37] : int option list

map Bool.fromString
    (String.tokens Char.isSpace "43 false  ~37");
val it = [NONE, SOME false, NONE] : bool option list
```

## D.10  Text input

Text input is made by using values of type TextIO.instream.  The instream TextIO.stdIn is used for input from the user's console, while other instreams are created by the use of TextIO.openIn. The input from a string goes via a buffer which may contain characters which have not yet been requested by the program.

The function inputNoBlock raises NonblockingNotSupported if EOF cannot be determined without reading from the file.

**Table D.34**  Input operations.

| id | Type | Value |
|---|---|---|
| TextIO.stdIn | instream | Input stream for console |
| TextIO.openIn | string -> instream | Create instream for input from file<br>May raise Io |
| TextIO.closeIn | instream -> unit | Terminate input from file<br>May raise Io |
| TextIO.input | instream -> string | Input next buffer from stream,<br>empty string if EOF |
| TextIO.inputAll | instream -> string | Input rest of file |
| TextIO.inputNoBlock | instream -><br>string option | Rest of current buffer,<br>SOME "" means EOF |
| TextIO.input1 | instream -><br>char option | Input next char,<br>NONE means EOF |
| TextIO.inputN | instream * int<br>-> string | Input next $n$ chars,<br>$< n$ chars mean EOF. |
| TextIO.inputLine | instream -> string | Input a line including "\n",<br>adds "\n" if missing at EOF. |
| TextIO.endOfStream | instream -> bool | True if EOF and false otherwise,<br>may read new buffer |
| TextIO.lookahead | instream -><br>char option | NONE at EOF, SOME $ch$ otherwise,<br>may read new buffer |

## D.11  Text output

Text output is made by using values of type `TextIO.outstream`. Output to the user's console is obtained by the use of the outstream `TextIO.stdOut`, while `TextIO.openOut` or `TextIO.openAppend` are used to create other outstreams. The output from a string goes via a buffer which may contain characters which have not yet been written to the file. The buffer contents are automatically written to the file by `TextIO.closeOut`. The function `TextIO.flushOut` forces writing of the buffer.

**Table D.35**   Output operations.

| id | Type | Value |
|---|---|---|
| TextIO.stdOut | outstream | Output stream for console |
| TextIO.stdErr | outstream | Standard error stream |
| TextIO.openOut | string -> outstream | Create output stream for writing to file. Existing file lost |
| TextIO.openAppend | string -> outstream | Create output stream appending to existing file or writing new file |
| TextIO.closeOut | outstream -> unit | Close output to stream |
| TextIO.output | outstream * string -> unit | Write string to output stream. May raise Io |
| TextIO.outputSubstr | outstream * substring -> unit | Write substring to output stream. May raise Io |
| TextIO.output1 | outstream * char -> unit | Write character to output stream May raise Io |
| TextIO.flushOut | outstream -> unit | Write output buffer to file May raise Io |
| print | string -> unit | Output string to TextIO.stdOut and flush buffer |

# Modules of sets and tables

This appendix describes modules for finite sets and tables as introduced in Chapters 10 and 12. In using the modules the following should be observed:

● The representations use SML equality for comparing set elements and for comparing the values of keys in table entries. This gives the limitations described in Section 10.3.

● The execution time for the functions are proportional with the number of elements in the set or number of entries in the table, and the implementation could hence be too slow for programs using sets with many elements or tables with many entries.

The modules are intended for educational purposes and for implementation of prototype programs where simple and systematic interfaces to the modules are more important than top performance. The reader may look in the used SML system for more sophisticated implementations of sets and tables (hash tables, AVL trees, splay trees, etc.).

## E.1 Sets

The Set module implements the following functions on sets:

**Table E.1**  Functions on sets.

| id | Type | Value |
|---|---|---|
| empty | ''a set | The empty set $\emptyset$ |
| singleton | ''a -> ''a set | $\text{singleton } a = \{a\}$ |
| insert | ''a * ''a set -> ''a set | $\text{insert}(x, s) = \{x\} \cup s$ |
| union | ''a set * ''a set -> ''a set | $\text{union}(s_1, s_2) = s_1 \cup s_2$ |
| inter | ''a set * ''a set -> ''a set | $\text{inter}(s_1, s_2) = s_1 \cap s_2$ |
| delete | ''a set * ''a -> ''a set | $\text{delete}(s, x) = s \setminus \{x\}$ |
| diff | ''a set * ''a set -> ''a set | $\text{diff}(s_1, s_2) = s_1 \setminus s_2$ |
| subset | ''a set * ''a set -> bool | $\text{subset}(s_1, s_2) = s_1 \subseteq s_2$ |
| equal | ''a set * ''a set -> bool | $\text{equal}(s_1, s_2) = (s_1 = s_2)$ |
| fromList | ''a list -> ''a set | $\text{fromList}[a_1, \ldots, a_m]$ $= \{a_1, \ldots, a_m\}$ |
| toList | ''a set -> ''a list | $\text{toList } s = \text{list of elements in } s$ |
| member | ''a * ''a set -> bool | $\text{member}(x, s) = x \in s$ |
| card | ''a set -> int | $\text{card}\{a_1, \ldots, a_n\} = n$ $a_i \neq a_j \text{ for } i \neq j$ |
| filter | (''a -> bool) -> ''a set      -> ''a set | $\text{filter } p\, s = \{x \in s \mid p(x)\}$ |
| exists | (''a -> bool) -> ''a set      -> bool | $\text{exists } p\, s = \exists x \in s : p(x)$ |
| all | (''a -> bool) -> ''a set      -> bool | $\text{all } p\, s = \forall x \in s : p(x)$ |
| find | (''a -> bool) -> ''a set           -> ''a option | $\text{find } p\, s = \text{SOME } x$ with $x \in s$ and $p(x)$ $\text{find } p\, s = \text{NONE if } \forall x \in s : \neg p(x)$ |
| map | (''a -> ''b) -> ''a set           -> ''b set | $\text{map } f\, s = \{f(a) \mid a \in s\}$ |
| fold | (''a * 'b -> 'b) -> 'b            -> ''a set -> 'b | $\text{fold } f\, b\, \{a_1, \ldots, a_n\}$ $= f(a_1, f(a_2, \cdots f(a_n, b) \cdots))$ |
| split | ''a set      -> (''a * ''a set) option | $\text{split } \emptyset = \text{NONE}$ $\text{split } s = \text{SOME}(a, s'),\ s = \{a\} \cup s'$ |

## E.2 Tables

The Table module implements the following functions on tables:

**Table E.2**  Functions on tables.

| id | Type | Value |
|---|---|---|
| empty | `(''a,'b) table` | empty = empty table with no entries. |
| singleton | `''a *'b -> (''a,'b) table` | singleton $(a, b)$ |
| | | = table with single entry $(a, b)$ |
| update | `''a * 'b * (''a,'b) table` | update $(a, b, t)$ = table $t$ with entry |
| | `-> (''a,'b) table` | for key $a$ changed to $(a, b)$ |
| | | - or table $t$ extended by entry $(a, b)$ |
| insert | `''a * 'b * (''a,'b) table` | insert $(a, b, t)$ = NONE if $a$ is key of $t$ |
| | `-> (''a,'b) table option` | insert $(a, b, t)$ = SOME $t'$ |
| | | with $t'$ = update $(a, b, t)$ |
| delete | `''a * (''a,'b) table` | delete$(a, t)$ = the table obtained by |
| | `-> (''a,'b) table` | deleting a possible entry of $t$ for key $a$ |
| remove | `''a * (''a,'b) table` | remove$(a, t)$ = NONE if $a$ is not a key of $t$ |
| | `-> (''a,'b) table option` | remove$(a, t)$ = SOME $t'$ with $t'$ = delete$(a, t)$ |
| fromList | `(''a * 'b) list` | fromList $[(a_1, b_1), \ldots, (a_n, b_n)]$ = |
| | `-> (''a,'b) table` | table with entries $(a_1, b_1), \ldots, (a_n, b_n)$ |
| toList | `(''a,'b) table` | toList $t = [(a_1, b_1), \ldots, (a_n, b_n)]$ where |
| | `-> (''a * 'b) list` | $(a_i, b_i)$ are the entries of $t$ |
| getval | `''a * (''a,'b) table` | getval $(a, t) = b$ if $(a, b)$ is an entry of $t$ |
| | `-> 'b` | raises exception Table if $a$ is not a key of $t$ |
| lookup | `''a * (''a,'b) table` | lookup $(a, t)$ = SOME $b$ |
| | `-> 'b option` | if $(a, b)$ is an entry of $t$ |
| | | lookup $(a, t)$ = NONE if $a$ is not a key of $t$ |
| isKey | `''a * (''a,'b) table` | isKey $(a, t)$ = true if $a$ is a key of $t$ |
| | `-> bool` | isKey $(a, t)$ = false if $a$ is not a key of $t$ |
| map | `(''a * 'b -> 'c)` | map $f$ $t$ = table with entries $(a_i, f(a_i, b_i))$ |
| | `-> (''a,'b) table` | where $(a_i, b_i)$ are the entries of $t$ |
| | `-> (''a,'c) table` | |
| filter | `(''a * 'b -> bool)` | filter $p$ $t = t'$ where $t'$ contains those |
| | `-> (''a,'b) table` | entries $(a, b)$ of $t$ where $p(a, b)$ = true |
| | `-> (''a,'b) table` | |
| exists | `(''a * 'b -> bool)` | exists $p$ $t$ = true if there is an entry |
| | `-> (''a,'b) table` | $(a, b)$ of $t$ with $p(a, b)$ = true |
| | `-> bool` | exists $p$ $t$ = false otherwise |
| all | `(''a * 'b -> bool)` | all $p$ $t$ = true if all entries |
| | `-> (''a,'b) table` | $(a, b)$ of $t$ satisfies $p$ |
| | `-> bool` | all $p$ $t$ = false, otherwise. |
| fold | `(''a * 'b *'c -> 'c)` | fold $f$ $c$ $t$ = |
| | `-> 'c` | $f(a_1, b_1, f(\cdots f(a_{n-1}, b_{n-1}, f(a_n, b_n, c))\cdots))$ |
| | `-> (''a, 'b) table -> 'c` | where $(a_i, b_i)$ are the entries of $t$. |
| split | `(''a,'b) table ->` | split $t$ = SOME $(a, b, t')$ |
| | `(''a * 'b` | where $(a, b)$ is entry for $t$. |
| | `* (''a,'b) table) option` | and $t'$ contains remaining entries of $t$ |
| | | split $t$ = NONE if $t$ is empty |
| find | `(''a * 'b -> bool)` | find $p$ $t$ = SOME $(a, b)$ |
| | `-> (''a,'b) table` | for some entry $(a, b)$ of $t$ |
| | `-> (''a * 'b) option` | with $p(a, b)$ = true |
| | | find $p$ $t$ = NONE if no entry for $t$ satisfies $p$ |

## E.3  Signatures

**Table E.3**   The signature Set.

```
signature Set =
sig
    type 'a set
    val empty     : ''a set
    val singleton : ''a                      -> ''a set
    val insert    : ''a * ''a set     -> ''a set
    val union     : ''a set * ''a set -> ''a set
    val inter     : ''a set * ''a set -> ''a set
    val delete    : ''a set * ''a     -> ''a set
    val diff      : ''a set * ''a set -> ''a set
    val fromList  : ''a list -> ''a set
    val toList    : ''a set -> ''a list
    val member    : ''a * ''a set     -> bool
    val subset    : ''a set * ''a set -> bool
    val equal     : ''a set * ''a set -> bool
    val card      : ''a set -> int
    val filter    : (''a -> bool) -> ''a set -> ''a set
    val exists    : (''a -> bool) -> ''a set -> bool
    val all       : (''a -> bool) -> ''a set -> bool
    val find      : (''a -> bool) -> ''a set -> ''a option
    val map       : (''a -> ''b) -> ''a set -> ''b set
    val fold      : (''a * 'b -> 'b) -> 'b -> ''a set -> 'b
    val split     : ''a set -> (''a * ''a set) option
end;
```

**Table E.4**   The signature Table.

```
signature Table =
sig
    type ('a,'b) table
    exception Table
    val empty    : (''a,'b) table
    val singleton: ''a * 'b -> (''a,'b) table
    val update   : ''a * 'b * (''a,'b) table -> (''a,'b) table
    val insert   : ''a * 'b * (''a,'b) table
                                    -> (''a,'b) table option
    val delete   : ''a * (''a,'b) table -> (''a,'b) table
```

*Continued*

**Table E.4** Continued.

```
    val remove   : ''a * (''a,'b) table -> (''a,'b) table option
    val fromList : (''a * 'b) list -> (''a,'b) table
    val toList   : (''a,'b) table -> (''a * 'b) list
    val getval   : ''a * (''a,'b) table -> 'b
    val lookup   : ''a * (''a,'b) table -> 'b option
    val isKey    : ''a * (''a,'b) table -> bool
    val map      : (''a * 'b -> 'c) -> (''a,'b) table
                                            -> (''a,'c) table
    val filter   : (''a * 'b -> bool) -> (''a,'b) table
                                            -> (''a,'b) table
    val exists   : (''a * 'b -> bool) -> (''a,'b) table -> bool
    val all      : (''a * 'b -> bool) -> (''a,'b) table -> bool
    val fold     : (''a * 'b *'c -> 'c) -> 'c
                                        -> (''a, 'b) table -> 'c
    val split    : (''a,'b) table ->
                   (''a * 'b * (''a,'b) table) option
    val find     : (''a * 'b -> bool) -> (''a,'b) table
                                        -> (''a * 'b) option
end
```

## E.4 Structures

The implementation of sets uses a representation as lists of elements, i.e. the list $[a_1, a_2, \ldots , a_n]$ represents the set $\{a_1, a_2, \ldots , a_n\}$. The representing lists should be without replicated elements.

**Table E.5** The structure Set.

```
structure Set:> Set = struct
    type 'a set = 'a list (* [a1,...,an] with ai <> aj for i <> j *)

    val empty = [];

    fun member(x, ys) = List.exists (fn y => x = y) ys;

    fun insert(x,ys) = if member(x,ys) then ys else x::ys;

    fun union(xs, ys) = List.foldl insert ys xs;

    fun inter(xs, ys) = List.filter (fn x => member(x, ys)) xs;
```
                                                                *Continued*

**Table E.5**   Continued.

```
    fun diff(xs, ys)    = List.filter (fn x => not (member(x, ys))) xs;

    fun delete([], _)     = []
      | delete(x::xs, y) = if x=y then xs else x::delete(xs,y);

    fun subset(xs, ys) = List.all (fn x => member(x, ys)) xs;

    fun equal(xs, ys) = subset(xs, ys) andalso subset(ys, xs);

    fun fromList xs = List.foldl insert empty xs;

    fun toList xs = xs;

    fun card xs = List.length xs;

    fun filter p xs = List.filter p xs;

    fun exists p xs = List.exists p xs;

    fun all p xs = List.all p xs;

    fun find p xs = List.find p xs;

    fun map f s = List.foldl (fn (y,ys) => insert(f y, ys)) empty s;

    fun fold f = List.foldl f;

    fun split [] = NONE | split (x::xs) = SOME(x,xs);

    fun singleton a = [a];
end;
```

The implementation of tables uses a representation of tables as lists of pairs $(key, data)$, i.e. the list $[(a_1, b_1), \ldots, (a_n, b_n)]$ represents the table with entries $(a_1, b_1), \ldots, (a_n, b_n)$. A list representing a table must not contain the same key twice, i.e. for any two list elements $(a_i, b_i)$ and $(a_j, b_j)$ we should have $a_i \neq a_j$.

**Table E.6**   The structure `Table`.

```
structure Table :> Table =
struct
    type ('a,'b) table = ('a * 'b) list
            (* [(a1,b1),...,(an,bn)] with ai <> aj for i <> j *)

    exception Table

    val empty    = []

    fun singleton(a,b) = [(a,b)]

    fun update(a,b,[])         = [(a,b)]
      | update(a,b,(a1,b1)::t) = if a = a1 then (a,b)::t
                                 else (a1,b1)::update(a,b,t)

    fun insert(a,b,[])         = SOME [(a,b)]
      | insert(a,b,(a1,b1)::t) = if a = a1 then NONE
                                 else case insert(a,b,t) of
                                          NONE     => NONE
                                        | SOME t1 => SOME((a1,b1)::t1)

    fun fromList []          = []
      | fromList ((a,b)::abs) = case insert(a,b,fromList(abs)) of
                                    NONE    => raise Table
                                  | SOME t => t

    fun toList t = t

    fun getval(a,[])         = raise Table
      | getval(a,(a1,b1)::t) = if a = a1 then b1 else getval(a,t)

    fun lookup(a,[])         = NONE
      | lookup(a,(a1,b1)::t) = if a = a1 then SOME b1 else lookup(a,t)

    fun isKey(a,t) = List.exists (fn (a1,_) => a1 = a) t

    fun delete(a,[])         = []
      | delete(a,(a1,b1)::t) = if a = a1 then t
                               else (a1,b1)::delete(a,t)

    fun remove(a,[])         = NONE
      | remove(a,(a1,b1)::t) = if a = a1 then SOME t
                               else case remove(a,t) of
                                        NONE    => NONE
                                      | SOME t1 => SOME((a1,b1)::t1)
```

*Continued*

**Table E.6**  Continued.

```
  fun map f t = List.map (fn (a,b) => (a, f(a,b))) t

  fun filter p t = List.filter p t

  fun exists p t = List.exists p t

  fun all p t    = List.all p t

  fun fold f e t = List.foldl (fn ((a,b),c) => f(a,b,c)) e t

  fun split []        = NONE
    | split((a,b)::t) = SOME(a,b,t)

  fun find p []          = NONE
    | find p ((a,b)::t) = if p(a,b) then SOME (a,b) else find p t
end
```

# The ASCII alphabet

**Table F.1**   The ASCII alphabet.

| | | | | | | | |
|---|---|---|---|---|---|---|---|
| 0 | NUL | 32 | SP | 64 | @ | 96 | ` |
| 1 | SOH | 33 | ! | 65 | A | 97 | a |
| 2 | STX | 34 | " | 66 | B | 98 | b |
| 3 | ETX | 35 | # | 67 | C | 99 | c |
| 4 | EOT | 36 | $ | 68 | D | 100 | d |
| 5 | ENQ | 37 | % | 69 | E | 101 | e |
| 6 | ACK | 38 | & | 70 | F | 102 | f |
| 7 | BEL | 39 | ' | 71 | G | 103 | g |
| 8 | BS | 40 | ( | 72 | H | 104 | h |
| 9 | HT | 41 | ) | 73 | I | 105 | i |
| 10 | LF | 42 | * | 74 | J | 106 | j |
| 11 | VT | 43 | + | 75 | K | 107 | k |
| 12 | FF | 44 | , | 76 | L | 108 | l |
| 13 | CR | 45 | – | 77 | M | 109 | m |
| 14 | SO | 46 | . | 78 | N | 110 | n |
| 15 | SI | 47 | / | 79 | O | 111 | o |
| 16 | DLE | 48 | 0 | 80 | P | 112 | p |
| 17 | DC1 | 49 | 1 | 81 | Q | 113 | q |
| 18 | DC2 | 50 | 2 | 82 | R | 114 | r |
| 19 | DC3 | 51 | 3 | 83 | S | 115 | s |
| 20 | DC4 | 52 | 4 | 84 | T | 116 | t |
| 21 | NAK | 53 | 5 | 85 | U | 117 | u |
| 22 | SYN | 54 | 6 | 86 | V | 118 | v |
| 23 | ETB | 55 | 7 | 87 | W | 119 | w |
| 24 | CAN | 56 | 8 | 88 | X | 120 | x |
| 25 | EM | 57 | 9 | 89 | Y | 121 | y |
| 26 | SUB | 58 | : | 90 | Z | 122 | z |
| 27 | ESC | 59 | ; | 91 | [ | 123 | { |
| 28 | FS | 60 | < | 92 | \ | 124 | | |
| 29 | GS | 61 | = | 93 | ] | 125 | } |
| 30 | RS | 62 | > | 94 | ^ | 126 | ~ |
| 31 | US | 63 | ? | 95 | _ | 127 | DEL |

A character is a letter, a digit or a special character. Punctuation symbols such as comma and semicolon are special characters, but other special characters are used for formatting, e.g. spacing, line change and page change, and for controlling the communication over a communication line. Characters are encoded in the computer as integer values from 0 to 127 using the *ASCII alphabet* shown in the Table F.1. The characters with ASCII code between 32 and 127 are *printable characters*, while the characters with ASCII code between 0 and 31 are *control characters*.

There are extensions of the ASCII alphabet using the values from 128 to 255 to encode national characters (such as ç or æ) and special symbols (such as © or ¶), but the use of the values from 128 to 255 depends on the set-up of the operating system and is therefore not given here. The interested reader should consult the manuals of the operating system.

Escape sequences give a textual representation of non-printable characters:

**Table F.2**   Escape sequences

| Escape sequence | Legend |
| --- | --- |
| \a | The alert character (BEL). |
| \b | The backspace character (BS). |
| \f | The formfeed character (FF). |
| \n | A single character interpreted by the system as end-of-line (LF in UNIX systems). |
| \r | The carriage return character (CR). |
| \t | The horizontal tab character (HT). |
| \v | The vertical tab character (VT). |
| \\ | The backslash character (\). |
| \? | The question mark character (?). |
| \' | the apostrophe character ('). |
| \" | The quote character ("). |
| \^c | The control character with ASCII code $\mathrm{ord}(c) - 64$, where $c$ may be any character with ASCII code $\mathrm{ord}(c)$ in 64-95. |
| \ddd | The single character with ASCII code $ddd$ (3 decimal digits denoting an integer 0-255). |
| \f…f\ | This sequence is ignored, where $f \cdots f$ stands for a sequence of one or more formatting characters (SP, HT, CR, LF, FF). |

The last form allows long strings to be written on more than one line or page by writing a backslash (\) at the end of one line and at the start of the next.

The escape sequences for the quote and backslash characters are required as these two characters play a special role in the textual representation of characters and strings: a quote character marks the start or the end of a string, while a backslash character marks the start of an escape sequence.

Examples:

```
"a \n b \n";
val it = "a \n b \n" : string
print it;
a
 b
val it = () : unit


#"\^B";
val it = #"\^B" : char


#"\066";
val it = #"B" : char


"\^J" = "\n";
val it = true : bool
```

## Appendix G

# Further reading

## The SML programming language

The following books are the standard references for the SML language:

[1] R. Milner and M. Tofte. *Commentary on Standard ML*, MIT Press, 1991.

[2] R. Milner, M. Tofte, R. Harper and D. MacQueen. *The Definition of Standard ML* (Revised), MIT Press, 1997.

[3] *Standard ML Basis Library* (to appear from Cambridge University Press). On the WEB: http://www.cs.bell-labs.com/~jhr/sml/basis/index.html

## Programming in SML

There are many books on programming in SML. The following have adapted to the new language definition:

[4] L.C. Paulson. *ML for the Working Programmer*, 2nd ed., Cambridge University Press, 1996.

[5] J.U. Ullman. *Elements of ML Programming, ML97 Edition*, 2nd ed., Prentice-Hall, 1998.

## Functional programming

There are many books on functional programming. The following books are of great interest although they are using other functional languages than SML:

[6] H. Abelson and G.J. Sussman. *Structure and Interpretation of Computer Programs*, MIT Press, 1985.

[7] R. Bird. *Introduction to Functional Programming*, 2nd ed., Prentice-Hall, 1998.

[8] S. Thompson. *HASKELL The Craft of Functional Programming*, Addison-Wesley, 1996.

## Data structures and algorithms

This is a vast subject, and there is a large collection of books. We recommend the following books:

[9] T.H. Cormen, C.E. Leiserson, R.L. Rivest. *Introduction to Algorithms*, MIT Press, 1996.

[10] C. Okasaki. *Purely Functional Data Structures*, Cambridge University Press, 1998.

The first is probably considered the standard reference of the subject. The second addresses the problem of making efficient data structures and algorithms in SML.

## VDM and RAISE

The 'problem solving' chapters in the book are based on a tradition of 'formal methods' in software engineering. The following books represent this tradition:

[11] D. Bjørner, C.B. Jones (Eds.). *The Vienna Development Method: The Meta-Language*, Lecture Notes in Computer Science, Springer-Verlag, 1978.

[12] C.B. Jones. *Systematic Software Development Using VDM*, Prentice-Hall, 1990.

[13] The RAISE Language Group. *The RAISE Specification Language*, Prentice-Hall, 1992.

[14] J. Fitzgerald, P.G. Larsen. *Modelling Systems – Practical Tools and Techniques in Software Development*, Cambridge University Press, 1998.

## Implementation of functional programming languages

Implementation of a functional programming language (e.g. like any of the SML systems) is a interesting and demanding task. This subject is e.g., treated in the following book:

[15] S.L. Peyton Jones. *The Implementation of Functional Programming Languages*, Prentice-Hall, 1987.

# Index